The Nickel Was for the Movies

The Nickel Was for the Movies

Film in the Novel from Pirandello to Puig

Gavriel Moses

University of California Press
Berkeley / Los Angeles / London

University of California Press
Berkeley and Los Angeles, California

University of California Press
London, England

Copyright © 1995 by
The Regents of the University of California

Library of Congress Cataloging-in-Publication Data

Moses, Gavriel.
    The nickel was for the movies: film in the novel from Pirandello to
Puig / Gavriel Moses.
       p.   cm.
    Includes bibliographical references and index.
    ISBN 0–520–07943–4 (cloth: alk. paper).— ISBN 0–520–07944–2
(pbk.: alk. paper)
    1. Fiction—20th century—History and criticism. 2. Motion
pictures in literature. I. Title.
PN3503.M627   1995
809.3′9357—dc20   93–16283
                                                                             CIP

Printed in the United States of America

1 2 3 4 5 6 7 8 9

The paper used in this publication meets the minimum requirements of
American National Standard for Information Sciences—Permanence of
Paper for Printed Library Materials, ANSI Z39.48–1984 ♾

To Yael

... perché tutte le immagini portano scritto:
« piú in là » !

"It was like I was in a movie," I say to them, "and I couldn't stop the movie." "Is that how it came down?" asked Gibbs. "Shit no," said Gilmore. "I walked in on Benny Bushnell and I said to that fat son of a bitch, 'Your money, son, and *your life.'"*
—Norman Mailer, The Executioner's Song

And in the next story, if the moving picture doesn't run so fast that it jumps out of the window and scares our cat, so she falls into the milk bottle, I'll tell you about Uncle Wiggily and the Snow Plow.
—Howard R. Garis,
Uncle Wiggily Learns to Dance

I think [the camera is] a terrible medium, it sees anything.
—Dorothy Parker

To call a movie house a theatre is the same as to call an undertaker a mortician.
—Vladimir Nabokov, Lectures on Literature

Contents

Abbreviations xi
Acknowledgments xiii
Preface xvii

Part One   **Pirandello**

1 Man Makes Movies Make Man   3

2 Icons Unreal Irony   20

Part Two   **Nabokov**

3 Memory Unreals   39

4 Albinus Fakes Movies   62

Part Three   **Film Theory and Literary Genre**

5 Film Theory as Narrative   99

6 The Film Novel as Literary Genre   122

Part Four **The Film Novel**

    7 The Hollywood Novel 163

        Isherwood: "Infernal Machine" 163
        Fitzgerald: "Dream Made Flesh" 174
        West: "The Barber in Purdue" 192

    8 The Eyes Have to Know 207

        Moravia: "Ghost in the Cave" 207
        Percy: "Monkey See, Monkey Do" 217

    9 You Can't Imagine 233

        Puig: "Dark Inside the Movie House" 233
        Puig: "Lots of Lovely, Lovely Films" 247

Part Five **Conclusion**

    10 The Return of Genre 259

    Notes 275
    Bibliography 303
    Index 317

Abbreviations

Bend   Vladimir Nabokov. *Bend Sinister.* New York: Time Incorporated, 1964.

Betr   Manuel Puig. *Betrayed by Rita Hayworth.* New York: Avon Books, 1971.

D   Vladimir Nabokov. *Despair.* New York: Putnam's, 1979.

Disp   Alberto Moravia. *Il disprezzo.* Milan: Bompiani, 1955.

DoL   Nathanael West. *Miss Lonelyhearts* and *The Day of the Locust.* New York: New Directions, 1969.

Eye   Vladimir Nabokov. *The Eye.* New York: Phaedra, 1965.

GaN   Alberto Moravia. *A Ghost at Noon.* Trans. Angus Davidson. New York: Farrar, Strauss and Young, 1955.

Hum   Luigi Pirandello. *On Humor.* Trans. Antonio Illiano and Daniel P. Testa. Chapel Hill: University of North Carolina Press, 1974.

Im/E   Jean-Paul Sartre. *The Psychology of Imagination.* Trans. Bernard Frechtman. Secaucus, N.J.: The Citadel Press, 1972.

Im/F   Jean-Paul Sartre. *L'imaginaire, psychologie phénoménologique de l'imagination.* Paris: Gallimard, 1940.

Ir   Luigi Pirandello. "Ironia." *L'idea nazionale,* 27 February 1920.

Kiss   Manuel Puig. *Kiss of the Spider Woman.* New York: Knopf, 1979.

KQKn   Vladimir Nabokov. *King, Queen, Knave.* New York: McGraw-Hill, 1968.

L	Vladimir Nabokov. *Laughter in the Dark.* New York: New Directions, 1967.
Lanc	Walker Percy. *Lancelot.* New York: Avon Books, 1978.
LaT	F. Scott Fitzgerald. *The Last Tycoon.* New York: Scribner's, 1970.
LoL	Vladimir Nabokov. *Lectures on Literature.* Ed. Fredson Bowers. New York: Harcourt Brace Jovanovich, 1980.
Lum	Luigi Pirandello. *L'umorismo, Saggi, Poesie, Scritti varii.* Ed. Manlio Lo Vecchio Nusti. Milan: Mondadori, 1960.
M	Vladimir Nabokov. *Mary.* Harmondsworth: Penguin, 1973.
Mov	Walker Percy. *The Moviegoer.* New York: Noonday Press, 1977.
NW	*The Nabokov–Wilson Letters: 1940–1971.* Ed. Simon Karlinsky. New York: Harper and Row, 1979.
PrV	Christopher Isherwood. *Prater Violet.* New York: Avon Books, 1978.
Quad	Luigi Pirandello. *Quaderni di Serafino Gubbio operatore.* Milan: Mondadori, 1954.
Sh	Luigi Pirandello. *Shoot! (Si Gira): The Notebooks of Serafino Gubbio Cinematograph Operator.* Trans. C. K. Scott-Moncrieff. New York: Dutton, 1926.
SO	Vladimir Nabokov. *Strong Opinions.* New York: McGraw-Hill, 1973.
SpM	Vladimir Nabokov. *Speak, Memory: An Autobiography Revisited.* New York: Putnam's, 1966.

Acknowledgments

One gathers many debts on a project such as this, over a long stretch of time and across several disciplines. I thus want to thank for their staying power, insight, and patience Robert Alter (ever watchful over "i piaceri della lettura"), Ernest Callenbach (ever helpful about those of the screen), Seymour Chatman (his useful comments even spilled over the outside of the envelope), and Guido Fink (who gives the term *doppelgänger* a new meaning). Also irreplaceable were Remo Ceserani, Sergio Moravia, and Meir Sternberg. Always generous with their help and advice, all of them are responsible for many of the virtues (and none of the shortcomings) of this book which, at crucial moments in its progress, also benefitted from the help, attention, and occasional skepticism of Alfred Appel, Cesare Segre, Carol Cosman, Teresa de Lauretis, Marilyn Fabe, Ezio Raimondi, and Suzanne Fleishman.

They all were important to this project in the recent past, as were, in a more distant one, Arnold Weinstein (who demonstrated that passion and scholarship may coexist), Edwin Honig (who taught me not to drop my tools in the engine), Robert Scholes (ever metamorphic about matters theoretical), and Roman Jakobson, who took it upon himself to convince me that metaphor may be articulated where least we may suspect. This study, among other things, is an interdisciplinary (intradiscursive) example of the phenomenon. Also from that same distant past derives the inspiration provided by teachers who first demonstrated to me the serious study of film, in settings to me then unexpected. I thus owe thanks to Peter Harcourt, who at film school first engaged me in serious discussions (beyond, that is, the nature of sprockets and Kliegs) about helicopters, the cinematic text, and the limits of a naïve diegetic interpretation. Also due thanks is Steven Vinaver, whose range (from study of

Brecht, Pirandello, and Rilke, to work on the set with Fellini, to songs for Dankworth, Martin, and Lane, to the importance of getting our hands—the first this side of the channel—on Coutard's new camera) taught me to aim for the serious with lightness and to address what seems light with respect. I am also grateful to Henri and especially Geneviève Agel who first called to my attention, with lectures that took place in the unlikely setting of the staid Aula Magna at the University of Fribourg, that such a thing as "film studies" existed and that it could be a wonderful way to make a living.

Gian Piero Brunetta and Francesco Casetti, beyond their friendship, hospitality, and professional acumen, provided many a warm and friendly Italian forum in which to test some of my ideas for this book. For this I am grateful, as I am to Gerald Mast, belated as this may be, for his spirited public defense (in colder northern climates) of my right to these same ideas. Among those who would give far more than a nickel for the movies, I also thank Rick Altman, Anton Kaes, Edith Kramer, Marcia Landy, Bruce Kawin, Mirto Stone, Vivian Sobchack, Robert Stam, Yuri Tsivian, and the many film students at Berkeley who for years, upon finding that IT175 was not all that much about films, stayed anyway. They were all, in a variety of ways, helpful with, interested in, and supportive of this project. I also want to acknowledge for similar reasons the wonderful students and faculty at University of Bologna's DAMS and on the editorial board of *Cinema & Cinema*. Among these I owe special thanks to Sandro Bernardi, Antonio Costa, Giovanna Grignaffini, Franco Minganti, and Leonardo Quaresima.

Several public venues were helpful with their spotlight and generous with a hospitality that contributed to the evolution of this book. Among these are the Centro di Ricerca per la Narrativa e il Cinema in Agrigento, for whose invitation I am thankful (as I am for its success in getting me to Sicily in the teeth of the usual air strike); the University of Bologna, which allowed me (and Daffy Duck) to participate (a rare opportunity) in celebrating its nine-hundredth anniversary; the Ente Teatro Romano di Fiesole, which I thank for persisting in the belief that scholarly meetings contribute to the tourist trade; the Centro Internazionale di Semiotica e Linguistica at the University of Urbino, where I learned why one does not trust the only copy of tomorrow's conference paper to the battery of a laptop computer (but where I also learned that anything can be rewritten from scratch by 5 A.M.). Also, the Università degli Studi di Roma "La Sapienza" (and Guido Aristarco) and the Biennale di Venezia, nonchè Fondazione Giorgio Cini, hosted "live" segments of this work, and I thank them for it.

A year at Wesleyan University's Center for the Humanities, which I gratefully owe to the Andrew Mellon Foundation, is responsible for the very inception of this book. To the wonderful and attentive colleagues, fellow Mellons, and guests at Wesleyan's Center I owe special thanks. The captive audience they provided, sharp yet kindly, was crucial in confirming my hunches and disconfirming my delusions. I want to mention especially Josué Harari, Stephen Holmes, Howard Needler, Murray Schwartz, Richard Stamelman, Khachig Tölölyan, and Hayden White. Yet in doing so I am, alas, neglecting many others, to whom I apologize. I also thank for allowing me to reach a wider audience, for putting their ink whence their words, and for permission to reprint, Gian Paolo Biasin, Corrado Catania, Guido Fink, Vita Fortunati, Giorgio Luti, Nicolas Perella, Carlo Ferdinando Russo, Aldo Saccone, and John P. Welle, editors of journals, Festschriften, and conference proceedings in the pages of which earlier versions of some of the following first appeared: *MLN* (ch. 1); *Inventario* (ch. 2); *Belfagor* (ch. 3); *Pirandello 1986: Atti del simposio internazionale* (Roma: Bulzoni, 1988) (ch. 3); *Annali d'Italianistica* (ch. 5); *Pirandello e d'annunzio nel cinema: Atti di un covegno* (Agrigento: Centro di Ricerca Narrativa-Cinema, 1988) (ch. 6); and *Cinema & Cinema* (ch. 7). Help from the National Endowment for the Humanities and continuing support from the University of California Committee on Research were also generously granted (and gratefully received) to aid this project.

Finally, special thanks go to Itamar Moses, a most reliable research assistant and most observant editor; to Edward Dimendberg, Diana Feinberg, Peter Kosenko, and Michelle Nordon, who saw to the details of this book with subtle editorial skill; to Murray Krieger and, again, to Hayden White; to my parents, who at last have concrete proof that film school was not a total waste; to Giampiero, Nuccio, and Graziella, whose prescient gift provided the text for this project long before I knew of it; to Shlomo Engel, who, like Isherwood's Bergmann, read (I am sure) *Die Weltbühne,* and who bought all those books, so long ago, in Vienna. But most of all to Yael and to Ronli and to Itamar, who cared; and to Raskolnikov, who took care of security.

In the end, a thankful tribute must go to Rosalie Colie, whom we continue to miss. She had always known of the resources of kind and, it turns out, had beat us to the stacks even about the resources of the kind that this book aims to define. Her signature on the library slip of a volume that had not been checked out since confirms that she had read long before me the lines by John Hollander that were always meant to conclude these acknowledgments:

> ... think how, at night, the fastest
> Train might stop for water somewhere, waiting, faced
> Westward, in deepening dusk, till ruby illuminations
> Of something different from Everything Here, Now, shine
> Out from the local Bijou, truest gem, the most bright
> Because the most believed in, staving off the night
> Perhaps, for a while longer with its flickering light.
>   ("Movie-Going")

Preface

Summarizing for his readers the outline of Pirandello's 1915 novel *Quaderni di Serafino Gubbio operatore* on the occasion of its 1925 edition, an anonymous reviewer offers the following plot in a pot:

> There is this vamp, a film actress, who has on her conscience a suicide, that of Giorgio Mirelli, as well as the corruption of Aldo Nuti who, for her sake, has abandoned his fiancée Duccella Mirelli. Aldo Nuti who, after many years, is still hopelessly in the throws of passion for this beautiful woman, turns movie actor and in a feature-length film, instead of killing a tiger, kills the terrible woman and lets himself be mangled to death by the tiger. This story is told with ability, perhaps even too much ability, with clever interruptions, with digressions that tickle one's curiosity, with deliberate juxtapositions; and with a spectacular multiplicity of episodes, settings, and characters in generous profusion. But the conclusion, once reached, prompts one to ask: What does it all mean? And all of Serafino Gubbio's philosophy cannot raise the tone of his puny little drama worthy of the tabloids and, if you want, also a little of the fan magazines. (Anon 1925:171)

In a sense the following study can be seen as a response to this kind of glaringly ina-Propp-riate response to a novel that does for cinematography what *Six Characters in Search of an Author* does for the theater: examine, that is, the implications of an open awareness of the "nuts and bolts" of a form of representation; expose the "formative" pressures of the medium of film upon our notions of character and "real" life; question the motives of the artists engaged in articulating the kinds of lives, stories, and feelings that the medium tends to favor; test the effects of the medium upon individual notions of reality; involve the readers (just as the audience in the movie theater) in a challenging interraction with a text that forces participation in the dilemmas of vivid yet opaque unfolding.

My own outline of the "fabula" of Serafino Gubbio (and, by implication, of the works that seem to follow in his generic wake) is of course tendentious, and meant to be so in its polemical opposition to the outline quoted above. From the contrast emerges, however, what I believe to be the unique and seminal role of Pirandello's novel. In its "sujet" is enfolded a new narrative genre permeable to the conventional structures of more established genres (narrative mostly) but also distinctive enough to impose thematic and formal conditions of its own.

Akin at first sight to subsequent and more widely known titles such as Nathanael West's *The Day of the Locust* and F. Scott Fitzgerald's *The Last Tycoon* (so-called Hollywood novels), Pirandello's work is nevertheless more encompassing as a realization of the type. It does not equate cinema as a phenomenon with the locality in which it happens to be practiced, nor does it assume, as do the aforementioned novels, that the personal and philosophical issues that film as a medium tends to raise are reducible to a place for which, moreover, the medium simply provides a metaphor (Hollywood-Babylon). Such novels, when seen in the wider context opened up by Pirandello's novel, turn out to be more than their place-bound designation suggests. West's and Fitzgerald's novels thus represent a subset of a wider genre in which one can include authors such as Vladimir Nabokov, Christopher Isherwood, Alberto Moravia, Walker Percy, Manuel Puig. *Laughter in the Dark, Prater Violet, Il disprezzo, Lancelot,* and most recently Puig's *Betrayed by Rita Hayworth* and *Kiss of the Spider Woman,* represent filmmaking in a variety of locations (Berlin in the twenties, London in the thirties, Rome in the fifties, New Orleans in the sixties), they integrate film in its many guises into the narrative structure of their tales, and they tend to evolve so as to include (Puig is most notable for this) the point of view of spectators as well as filmmakers of all types. They follow, that is, the evolution of film and its theories as they affect the lives of human beings, while encompassing, as a genre, the full range of communicative functions characteristic of the medium. All such film novels, moreover, can be traced back in one way or another to Pirandello's story of a troubled cameraman.

While the strictly literary aspects of a generic definition of this narrative tradition involve a multiplicity of factors and considerations, a common feature of all such novels that goes beyond the strictly "literary" is the presence within their text of film and its theory in one guise or another. A firm notion about the art of cinematography as a whole, intermittent and sometimes extensive attempts at the creation of film-mimetic literary passages, and an exploration through narrative means of the place that this medium has in human experience are all features of the generic definition of this kind of novel. Film thus contributes to the generic distinctiveness of a new and particular type of narrative that in its turn responds to the appearance of a medium endowed with unprecedented power. Never before had human perception been affected in such an all-encompassing way by one art form, nor had the promise of a total involvement of the senses been realized as fully as was to be with film.

I would suggest, then, that because of the emergence of this powerful new art form, and because its technology and problematics correspond to a particular stage in the evolution of culture more closely than had happened before with other media, the novel as genre was stimulated to create a space for it.

Precinematic novels may perhaps, as is sometimes argued, contain anticipations of a so-called cinematic sensibility, but they cannot for obvious historical reasons make the peculiar problematics of this new art form an integral part of their narrative structure. Novels written after the advent of cinematography, on the other hand, stimulate inescapably debatable speculations as to which medium is influencing which, especially since what is usually cited as "cinematic" can be found in earlier precinematic literature as well. In the absence of some kind of evident indication that film references are intended (and the film novel as I define it provides just such an indication), it seems to me that effects of film in literature amount at best to a passing allusion, at worst to a debatable impression.[1] And yet Jean-Louis Baudry (1976) surmises that cinema existed as a "wish" (to see in a certain way, to be allowed a particular kind of consciousness) well before the technology evolved.[2] Does this suggest perhaps why one might find filmlike antecedents in earlier literature in spite of reservations such as mine? Perhaps so, but what Baudry's "wish" seems to confirm with more certainty, I would say, is the possibility that at least as the new medium of cinematography began to emerge, a powerful psychological response to it (an inherent philosophical yearning) was ready to be triggered. It is such a response too that the film novel as genre illustrates.

I have organized my study in the following way. The first two parts explore the highways and byways of narratives (Pirandello's *Quaderni* in Part One, Nabokov's *Laughter in the Dark* in Part Two) that overtly propose to intersect with the peculiarities of film. In the case of Pirandello I also take time to explore whether a specific notion about the nature of film appeals to cultural paradigms that may help to explain its power and fascination. With Nabokov I stop to see how an early and thoughtful sensitivity to the formal and perceptual components of photography and film allowed such media to become central motifs in literature. I thus juxtapose Pirandello's work on film with *L'umorismo,* his important essay on irony, and I explore Nabokov's autobiography *Speak, Memory,* in which film and photography turn out to be key images. The first two parts of my study are followed by a theoretical section that deals with the narrative articulation of film theory and puts forth a model for the narrative genre I call the film novel derived inductively from the previous two parts.

Part Four of my study then proceeds more rapidly, exploring deductively specific examples of the film novel and of novels in which film represents a major narrative strand. I have kept the body of these sections (despite the proleptic promise implied in the shift to poetics found in Part Three) as free as possible of theoretical discourse on film theory and genre so as to make it accessible to a broader spectrum of readers. Part Three in itself provides, I believe, sufficient theoretical grounding to illuminate what follows and is supported by my concluding chapter. In Part Four I first deal with instances of what is usually thought of as the "Hollywood novel" (Isherwood's *Prater Violet*, Fitzgerald's *The Last Tycoon*, and West's *The Day of the Locust*), arguing, among other things, that they really belong within a broader narrative kind that can be traced all the way back to Pirandello. In what follows I look at more recent examples of film in the novel (Alberto Moravia's *Il disprezzo*, Walter Percy's *Lancelot*, Manuel Puig's *Betrayed by Rita Hayworth*, and *Kiss of the Spider Woman*), works in which the focus seems to shift from the productive end of filmmaking to such things as the role of film spectatorship as well as the peripheral, vicarious, and therefore alienating involvement of characters with the medium of film.

In looking at my sample of authors, and in noticing that the theories of film that they reflect tend to be mostly those of theorists from the first ("classical"?) period of speculation about film, one may well ask why there are no female authors writing in the genre, or why so little recent film theory is found implicit in it. To the first question I would answer that the evolution of the genre so far may well reflect and confirm the central critique of cinema found in much feminist film theory that the medium, at least in its early stages, was largely male-centered and controlled. Given the historical development of cinema so far, it is thus not surprising that women writers have not been attracted to the genre. It would be possible to compensate for this only if we posit the film novel as a "theoretical genre,"[3] and then identify areas not yet explored by writers, but that are ready to be filled in the future: say, a novel written from the perspective of Pirandello's Varia Nestoroff or Nathanael West's Fay Greener, or one that would use the literary rather than the film medium to do what Marguerite Duras does in her film *Le camion*. One should note, however, that the novels of Manuel Puig are an indication that a narrative point of view positing "difference" is joining these kinds of narratives. For most of its life so far, however, the genre is yet another example of Foucault's point about a male fellowship of discourse that encourages the circulation of common beliefs. As in the political realm, where this selective focus favors the maintenance of homogeneous communities of power, so in literary ones it encourages "communities of books"—that is, genres. These, it thus turn out, are as much about "gender" as they are about "kind."

As to the matter of film theory, the answer is similar. Considering who it is that mostly does the writing, and taking into account what the world of film has been so far, it is not surprising that recent theoretical perspectives aimed at decentering the dominance of the male gaze are mostly absent. Many of the formative components of such a view, however, are to be found in the film novel, and I do point them out.

Thus the book analyzes a series of novels from Pirandello to Manuel Puig that in some way relate to the medium of film: as metaphor, by imitation of form, or in other ways that are productive from a narrative point of view. Given the multiple approaches that I use in this study (detailed analysis of novels, the explication of film theory implicit in them, the elaboration of genre and narrative theory), I am not able to also offer a fully fleshed out historical contextualization of the novels as they relate to the individual film histories to which they refer and as they represent the individual aesthetic histories of each author. Interesting as this might have been, I had to limit the scope of my study. Let me also point out that if the theory of genre and narrative discourse is invoked, it is to show where the film novel may be placed within current discussions on such issues. My use of the elements of narrative analysis and genre theory is not meant to take sides with one or another theory of narrative or view on genre. I use such categories merely to illustrate my own genre and its narrative functioning.[4]

It seems to me, if I may indulge here in a bit of proleptic wisdom, that these novels are examples of narrative fiction in which a specific number of elements common to all narratives tend, because of genre-related overdetermination, to be stressed more than in other kinds of narratives. Thus the focus on film contributes in more than a random way to such matters as the movement of plots and the dimensions of character. The theoretical outline of this is discussed in chapters 5 and 6, where, devoid as it is of the detailed textual exemplification found in other chapters, the film novel may be encountered in its schematic glory. I don't, on the whole, leave it at that, inspired as I am by the proviso that Nabokov introduces on the first page of *Laughter in the Dark,* where, after a schematic outline of the story to come, he concludes: "This is the whole story and we might have left it at that had there not been profit and pleasure in the telling. . . . detail is always welcome."

Part One

Pirandello

1

Man Makes Movies Make Man

As one reads Pirandello's *Quaderni di Serafino Gubbio operatore,* at first the novel appears (this has been generally noted) as an extensive document on the mimetic context of early Italian cinema.[1] What has not been noted is the extent to which this mimetic aspect of the text is articulated to express with great coherence a variety of meanings to do with cinema and its relation to a wide range of topics typical of modernism. Nor has the precise way in which it is deployed so as to inform the story line with a distinctly cinematic form been explored. All of these mimetic aspects turn out to fulfill symbolic, thematic, and ironic functions rather than to have a purely mimetic justification. Film and its projection are used in three principal manners by Pirandello: images seen on screen (by Gubbio and Aldo Nuti), the nature of the actors' physical appearance as projected (as perceived existentially by actors and symbolically by Gubbio), and finally as projection independent of an actual film image. Related to these are also instances of reality perceived as filmlike in viewfinder vision, scenario outlines, and undeclared but obvious "schemata" of description beholden to the process of camera-eye selection and editorial combination. Many of these are integrated into the narrative and conceptual structure of the novel.

Close to the novel's opening we find a description that calls attention to itself by suggesting a distinctly filmic way of selecting elements from reality and then recombining them into the "scheme" of rapid montage.[2] The ubiquitous presence of the camera, its effortless shift of position, the fluid alternation and quick integration of large scenes, details, objects, and episodes recall what is most typical of the syntagmatic aspect of film. The minimal presence of linguistic means used to blend these elements into a stylistically elaborate texture suggests the bare essentials of a cinematic scenario. Yet, even at a minimum, literature must use language. The result is a heightened parataxis that, directed as it is to the imitation of another art form, becomes in effect a figurative as well as a stylistic device. The section's introductory allusion to the "mechanical" aspect of reality intimates the rapid cutting and jerky motion typical of early cinema: "to-day, such-and-such; this and that to be done hurrying to one place, watch in hand, so as to be in time at another. 'no, my dear fellow, thank you: I can't!' 'no, really? lucky fellow! I must be off. . . .' At eleven, luncheon. The paper, the house, the office, school. . . . 'A fine day, worse luck! but business. . . .' 'What's this? Ah, a funeral.' We lift our hats as we pass to the man who has made his escape. The shop, the works, the law courts" (Sh:4, Quad:9).³

This may well strike us as nothing more than a way to set up a suitable context for a novel that takes place in the film world, yet the existential application of such a film scheme is immediately stressed and the intensity and frenzy that man must escape is epitomized by the buzzing persistence of a hovering, mechanical sound that, drowning out the beat of human hearts, assails man's sensibility in a rising sound-montage: "The hum of the telegraph poles? The endless scream of the trolley along the overhead wire of the electric trams? The urgent throb of all these countless machines, near and far? That of the engine of the motor-car? Of the cinematograph?" (Sh:11, Quad: 13). Gubbio confirms that this is not a general view of reality as much as the cameraman's vision of it (Sh:5, Quad:10) and from the outset underlines the critical dimension of such a professional bias:

> Already my eyes and my ears too, from force of habit, are beginning to see and hear everything in the guise of this rapid, quivering, ticking mechanical reproduction.
> I don't deny it; the outward appearance is light and vivid. We move, we fly. And the breeze stirred by our flight produces an alert, joyous, keen agitation, and sweeps away every thought. On! On, that we may not have time nor power to heed the burden of sorrow, the degradation of shame which remain within us, in our hearts. Outside, there is a continuous glare, an incessant giddiness: everything flickers and disappears.
> "What was that?" Nothing, it has passed! Perhaps it was something sad; but no matter, it has passed now. (Sh:10–11, Quad:13)

Such passages are remarkably accurate in capturing filmic style and, what is more, close to prophetic in anticipating applications of the film medium and technologies not yet available (such as sound) to the significant treatment of reality by cinema. They also are penetrating in their perception of the paradoxes inherent in the simultaneously seductive and heuristic nature of film. The cameraman is unable to see reality in a way other than that dictated by the aesthetic peculiarities of his medium, is drawn to the excitement provided by this, yet is also dimly aware of the superficiality of such a view of life. In the final analysis, however, Gubbio (this particular cameraman in this particular novel) tries to evade the painful intensity that he locates in life itself by using a technique he has acquired from the film medium: "On nothing, on nothing at all now, in this dizzy bustle which sweeps down upon us and overwhelms us, ought we to fix our attention. Take in, rather, moment by moment, this rapid passage of aspects and events, and so on, until we reach the point when for each of us the buzz shall cease" (Sh:11–12, Quad:14). The continuous flow and ceaseless movement of film are seen as a reflection of life in modern times but are also ways of escaping from it.

At times descriptions that try to suggest the impression of film viewing are used to advance the story, as happens when Simone Pau leads Gubbio to the flophouse and we find an objectively described scene ascribed to a specific point of view, with easily recognizable camera setups, camera movements, details, and the final explanatory signpost which functions as a verbal intertitle giving us the first hint of our location, Pau's eccentric "house" (Sh:17–18, Quad:17). This "sequence" moves typically from a large setting to a final close-up. Such progression towards a significant detail, a structuring of materials reminiscent of filmic sequences that open with an establishing long-shot and then move towards the significant center, is typical of these filmlike sections and allows us to see in what way the structuring tendencies of film as a medium lead to the narrative cores of the novel itself. As a cinematic procedure, this one was noted in the history of Italian film theory by Sebastiano Arturo Luciani as early as 1912 (Brunetta 1972:44–51). He described the film process as "a succession of *details* of the same picture enlarged and thusly marked for the attention of the viewer, by that procedure . . . called *close-up*. . . . Through it the film director submits to the viewers' attention . . . that part which he believes literally most illuminating of a certain scene, of a certain action, as if lighting it with a blind lantern." In directing a film, he continues, "it is first of all necessary not to develop a specific situation, but to know how to catch its essential face and to know how to mark its climax through the *close-up*" (Luciani 1928:21–22, 51, my translation).[4]

Pirandello uses such progression towards a telling detail extensively. The most notable examples occur in connection with the "vamp" Varia Nestoroff. For Gubbio—first-person narrator of this story and our constant camera eye—she is indeed the center of all that happened and will happen, and his interaction with Varia is always structured by one or another type of film element. As cameraman and actress confront each other in her apartment we find a sequence of purely mimic reactions easily perceivable as dramatically charged cinematic close-ups (Sh:262–263, Quad:147). This "sequence" plunges us into action already in progress, to a new location, and across a time lapse in the fashion typical of film editing. The shots culminate in a close-up of the six canvases of Varia painted in Capri by her dead lover Giorgio, a peculiarly cinematic climax in its reliance on images and their multiplication. This is a moment of some complexity, foreshadowing as it does a negative critique of the film medium in its blunt juxtaposition to the vital and vibrant essence of the art of painting. Those multiplications are not at all "mechanical," in clear contrast to the way in which film reproduces its own images.[5]

We witness here features basic to silent film aesthetics as well as characteristics typical of film as a medium. The deliberate overacting, as well as the stylized posturing, has a definite period flavor. More generally typical of film is the tendency to build up a context through the accumulation of metonymic details (Metz 1977:220–229, Metz 1982:183–191). Sectioned anatomy of facial and bodily features are found here and elsewhere, as well as the cobbling together of settings and sounds from fragments. Pirandello is thus sensitive both to filmic features typical of primitive film and to film elements universal to the medium. What is more, Pirandello seems to have felt free to extend such filmic features as rapid montage and shifting camera positions to materials that could not actually be shown in film as he knew it in 1915. The generalized essence of rushing about found in the opening quotation ("such-and-such; this and that") appropriates to language a filmic mode but does not depend upon the specificity of subject matter necessary for film. The montage of dialogue snatches is also filmic only in structure, since the actual use of such materials in silent cinema would result in an utterly textual (i.e., noncinematic) sequence of intertitles. Even more ahead of its time is the assumption that sound as an element is available for film montage, resulting in what to us is a veritable *musique concréte crescendo* on the sound track of Gubbio's interior film. It can be asserted on the basis of Gubbio's evidence that we have not merely a film-mimetic scheme inserted intermittently into the verbal narrative, but an attempt to show how the whole of reality may be perceived by a sensibility that has absorbed the schemata of film aesthetics, well beyond the historical limits of what film had achieved at the time. It is because of this that film in the novel becomes a generating principle in the area of ideas and in the actual narrative.

Progression towards a central image is used to lead the reader to the narrative and emotional cores of the story. At Nestoroff's first appearance we are led twice to the image of the actress, first as she emerges out of the general context of the film company and second (for Gubbio is not sure it is she) as she materializes from a veritable accumulation of details:

> Nestoroff? Was it possible? It seemed to be she and yet it seemed not to be. That hair of a strange tawny colour, almost coppery, that style of dress, sober, almost stiff, were not hers. But the slender, exquisite body, with a touch of the feline in the sway of her hips; the head raised high, inclined a little to one side, and that sweet smile on a pair of lips as fresh as a pair of rose-leaves, whenever anyone addressed her; those eyes, unnaturally wide, open, greenish, fixed and at the same time vacant, and cold in the shadow of their long lashes were hers,

entirely hers, with that certainty all her own that everyone, whatever she might say or ask, would answer yes.

Varia Nestoroff? Was it possible? Acting for a cinematograph company? (Sh:32, Quad:25–26)

Despite the emphasis on metonymic details all seemingly present in the denotative context viewed by Gubbio, it is evident that we are facing a complex interplay of features present and absent, an application of filmlike perception to the shifting field of memory and recognition, to an attempt at matching what is and what is not there. Objective details are perceived, analyzed, and collated through the subjective filter of memory and feeling. Yet in attempting to match presence with memory, it is ironically the contiguities of reality which fail, while metaphorical attributes (body like tiger, lips like roses) serve to identify Nestoroff for certain. A filmlike way of perceiving is thus applied to areas beyond the reach of immediate representation itself. What is more, the distorting mediation of this filter triggers in Gubbio's mind another kind of progression, backwards through time now, which results in a sudden and rapid surge of images (Sh:32–33, Quad:26). We recognize immediately the by now commonplace filmic device of flashback-montage, an accumulation of temporally discontinuous but experientially contiguous images, bridging in a few seconds chasms of time and space. In its imagistic objectivity, however, this montage is colored by the feeling emphasis of the narrator ("a house, a dear house") and by his carefully plotted development to the final climax ("confusion and death"). Retrogression is thus being used as more than purely mimetic texture, for it leads us to the narrative kernels of the whole book, and to their subjective significance for the narrator.

The use of narrative flashback is not in itself peculiar to film. More direct and filmically unique is the technique of placing a camera on a moving object and photographing the resulting alteration in one's view of the world. A favorite device of early filmmakers,[6] its use in the novel raises a film scheme to the level of thematic clue, both narrative and philosophical. A dizzying sequence based on this device opens the section in which we are introduced into the hellish bowels of the film-studio laboratories where "the work of the machines is mysteriously completed" (Sh:84, Quad:51). This is the section that deals most thoroughly with the philosophical implications of film as a medium:

A slight swerve. There is a one horse carriage in front. *"Peu, pepeeeu, peeeu."*

What? The horn of the motor-car is pulling it back? Why, yes! It does really seem to be making it run backwards, with the most comic effect.

The three ladies in the motor-car laugh, turn round, wave their arms in greeting with great vivacity, amid a gay, confused flutter of many-coloured veils; and the poor little carriage, hidden in an arid, sickening cloud of smoke and dust, however hard the cadaverous little horse may try to pull it along with his weary trot, continues to fall behind, far behind, with the houses, the trees, the occasional pedestrians, until it vanishes down the long straight vista of the suburban avenue. Vanishes? Not at all! The motor-car has vanished. The carriage, meanwhile, is still here, still slowly advancing, at the weary, level trot of its cadaverous horse. And the whole of the avenue seems to come forward again, slowly with it.

You have invented machines, have you? And now you enjoy these and similar sensations of stylish pace (Sh:77–79, Quad:47–48).

This sequence is so inherently filmic that what would be crystal clear when viewed on the screen (a shot of a horse-drawn carriage seen from behind, photographed from a point of view placed on a fast moving car; *cut to* a view of the carriage receding rapidly seen from the back of the motorcar; *cut to* a shot of motorcar in the distance seen from the slowly advancing horse-drawn carriage) is very awkward and ambiguous when read on the printed page. The verbal text is trying to retain the visual effect of its filmic equivalent, yet we are able to adjust only slowly to the sudden change in perspective and direction of movement caused by the switch in camera position. This film scheme is an attempt to transfer into words film elements more complex than the way film typically selects and combines elements from reality. It speaks of the relativity of judgment inherent in the choice of point of view, of the cultural values attached to speed, direction of movement, and of the lack of a stable narrative point of view. The narrative structuring of what is described is totally controlled by cameralike points of view alternating between two moving objects.[7] The two types of conveyance are related to each other through movement (inherently filmic) to express a philosophical contrast, while the vision of the world around them (a concretized idea) is controlled by the speed at which each of them proceeds. Notably, this "vision" of the world is caused not so much by what is there, as by how it is seen. Gubbio latches onto this, here and in the following paragraph, to illustrate his thoughts about the superficially exciting pace of mechanized modernity; he contrasts this to his own leisurely consideration of the beauty and symbolic significance of the individual trees that open to his inspection one by one thanks to the slow pace of his carriage.

But more than general ethical considerations are carried by these contrasting "vehicles": the issues are central to what unbeknownst to Gubbio, its narrator, is the real story of the novel. It is a "plot" that goes beyond Gubbio's awareness of it. We find a first hint of it if we notice that in "admiring one by one, at my leisure, these great green plane trees by the roadside" Gubbio goes against his own best advice ("On nothing at all now . . . ought we to fix our attention") and rests his attention upon single images, with the dangers that this entails. And the image of Gubbio himself, receding in an old-fashioned horse-buggy, comes to be a pictorial equivalent of his attitude regarding the past and the decay of time; the "cadaverous" aspect of the horse pulling him along foreshadows this. The center of the book is not, as Gubbio would have it, an attempt to tell us about past events and to have us witness their later consequences. It is rather Gubbio's hopeless entanglement with the past and the onrushing present, his inability to cope with, or even gain a clear, unblurred image of the present because he is too involved in a concentrated obsession with a few single, discontinuous images from the past.

The film medium Gubbio daily handles aptly concretizes his personal dilemma. Nuti's gigantic close-up on screen (the single and disconnected image of a man and its relation to time and death) epitomizes this aspect of the human condition and its emblematic presence within the elements of film art (Sh:319, Quad:176). The inherently disconnecting nature of the medium is also emphasized. For the actors, film is a threat in this specific sense: "Their actions, the *live* action of their *live* bodies, there, on the screen of the cinematograph, no longer exists: it is *their image* alone, caught in a moment, in a gesture, an expression, that flickers and disappears. . . . Their bodies are so to speak subtracted, suppressed, deprived of their reality, of breath, of voice, of the sound that they make in moving about" (Sh:106, Quad:63).

Pirandello thus perceives the inherently metonymic structure of film syntax and plumbs it in its existential dimension, well beyond its mere presence as syntactical peculiarity. What the actors find on the screen are "parts" of themselves that do *not* stand for the whole; the image of a "container" that does not represent truthfully the contained. They are faced not merely with the normal "syntactical" subdivision of their persons (eyes, mouth, arms, trunk) to fit into the syntagmatic flow of film denotation, but they face a metaphysical mutilation.[8] Paradoxically, they lose their real contiguity with life and its essence by being fitted into the contiguities inherent in the film medium. Film diegesis[9] thus *denies* reality; and silence, mimetically the most striking peculiarity of early cinema, is taken to represent the loss of life's vital essence, since for these actors (mostly theatrical) it is the loss of speech in performance that is most striking. Thus once more Pirandello extends the use of film-specific features to the area of sound. Sound, in fact, presides over this view of film as a central symbol, a metaphorical usage of the syntagmatic reality of silent cinema for the purpose of its paradigmatic resonance.

Gubbio is particularly sensitive to this aspect of film since he feels it affects himself. Here too, as seems generally true in modern narrative, the symbolic extension emerges from the denotative reality credibly surrounding the cameraman.[10] He perceives himself as "*a hand that turns the handle*" (Sh:7, Quad:11). The awareness of his own metonymic mutilation, derived from the syntactical nature of the film medium, is turned to metaphorical ends and extended to all mankind. In the infernolike bowels of the studio labs Gubbio observes "hands . . . nothing but hands, in these dark rooms; hands busily hovering over the dishes." They belong "to men who are men no longer." Gubbio himself is absorbed obscenely into a hybrid, half man half machine: "I cease to exist. *It* walks, now, upon my legs. From head to foot, I belong to it: I form part of its equipment. My head is here, inside the machine, and I carry it in my hand" (Sh:86, Quad:51–52). The significance of this process is underscored by its multiple appearances at the center of Simone Pau's parables of the violin player assigned to "feed" lead cakes to a monotype printer "quietly chewing away at its long ribbon of perforated paper" (Sh:27, Quad:23) and to play his beloved violin to the music churned out by a mechanical piano: "a violin, in the hands of a man" accompanying "a roll of perforated paper running through the belly of this other machine!" (Sh:28, Quad:23). The ribbon and roll of perforated paper (brilliant synecdochic images) establish a significant symbolic continuum that links monotype printer, pianola, and, of course, camera. The camera's strips of perforated celluloid end up in those red-lit dungeons where we find "the life swallowed by the machines . . . in those tape worms, I mean in the films" (Sh:85, Quad:51). Like the camera-spider to which Gubbio feeds life and people (Sh:106, Quad:63; Sh:141, Quad:81) these animal-like machines metaphorically ingest chunks of humanity (the monotype printer completes the whole cycle from feeding to excrement as a pachyderm "flat, black, squat" which eats lead and shits books). This existential suffering, however, does not remain metaphorical. It comes "unmetaphored" in a shocking figurative reversal at the climax of the novel when Gubbio feeds his spider a real human life.[11] It is thus that the medium's central metonymy (silence) turns into a physical reality for the cameraman who loses his speech. Faced with the unmetaphoring of his philosophical figure, Gubbio suffers upon his own body the unmetaphoring of the film trope central to the medium he has allowed to take possession of him.

The sudden conflation of metaphor and reality, the eruption of a paradigmatic line of associations into the contiguities of Gubbio's life, is "abnormal" and painful. If metaphor and metonymy are indeed representative, as Roman Jakobson argues, of fundamental ways of being in reality, such a disruption of existential assumptions can well account for Gubbio's traumatic reaction. Moreover, this final tropical "malfunction" is a succinct instance of an interference between paradigmatic substitution and syntagmatic contiguity which is constant throughout the novel, specifically at the level of narrative. Gubbio, a narrator who claims the cool and detached stance of a camera eye, is in fact unable to sustain such machinelike objectivity. He is, furthermore, unable to communicate the contents of referential reality and consequently fails to "edit" this story for us in anything that resembles proper narrative continuity.

Gubbio establishes a claim to credibility on the basis of his privileged access to greater objectivity, perceptiveness, reliability through a kind of camera vision. Most of the "facts" he presents are based, on the face of it, upon a process of objective observation of external clues. Nestoroff's inner truth is clear to him, in opposition to everybody else's view of her, while he feels that as cameraman all perceive him as someone in a position to pass judgment. He is consistent in feeling superior when some abstract consideration about life and values is at issue and buttresses his superiority with statements such as "This I know, I who turn a handle" (Sh:16, Quad:16). In the midst of sarcastic remarks about the ridiculous nature of film plots, film characterizations, and the impoverished view of reality that film depicts, Gubbio believes that the medium itself, if used at its best, does indeed reveal the essence of human behavior (Sh:150–151, Quad:86). This is why the *significant* revelations Gubbio achieves through a camera view of reality are not those derived from plotted, finished films. They grow out of pieces of film unusable for showing, disconnected rushes, or even film "sequences" in which no camera was present.

Gubbio's posture of superiority (ethical, philosophical, observational) is largely based on diffused claims of perceptive observation and analysis. He presents himself to us as a student of people, thus implying a more thoughtful and methodical observation of reality than is normal. He stops to look deep into their souls and claims they are disturbed by being faced with a "something more" gleaming in his own eyes. He is acquainted with "the external . . . framework of life" (Sh:4, Quad:9), and he presents himself as looking at and analyzing all of this in great detail. Even his ironic posture of disbelief—"At times it seems to me so impossible to believe in the reality of all that I see and hear" (Sh:5, Quad:10)—is meant to reassure us about his critical perspective, despite the fact that he himself admits to being an observer limited by a kind of professional atrophy of the senses (Sh:10–11, Quad:13). Beside the implicit ambiguity in such contradictory claims, Gubbio, in the midst of his presumably critical self-appraisal as a passive slave to his machine, retains a certain professional pride. He possesses, he tells us, "the chief quality that is required of a man in my profession . . . *impassivity* in the face of the action that is going on in front of the camera" (Sh:7, Quad:11). Polacco and the film company, he reiterates later, should be grateful to him for these abilities (Sh:49, Quad:33).

A measure of perspective distance from the all-encompassing claim of Gubbio's first-person voice is provided us by Simone Pau, a strong character external to the central story line, who confronts Gubbio with parablelike events and stories, not all of the implications of which are fully seized by the cameraman. It is Simone Pau who provokes Gubbio's thoughts about the fundamental potential of film as a medium[12] and who presents the violin player and his grotesque yet exemplary story. Even the introduction of Gubbio to the flophouse where Pau teaches as an act of charity is conducted in an exemplary fashion meant to contain an object lesson for Gubbio. Yet the cameraman goes through the experience, in which Pau pretends to be just another bum subject to the routine of the flophouse, shielding his embarrassment and insecurity behind an air of amused detachment and unmoved coolness. Pau clearly intends the situation as an emblem of the human condition and prods

Gubbio into taking it seriously, yet the cameraman cannot do so, barricades himself behind a front of defensive impassivity (the very same he assumes as he moves behind the camera), and unwittingly reveals that Pau tried to warn him: "He, realizing my intention, looked me in the eyes and, seeing them to be completely impassive, exclaimed with a smile: 'What an idiot you are!'" (Sh:22–23, Quad:20).

Gubbio's claims for his objectivity and analytic perceptiveness are thus of limited value.[13] This is confirmed by the manifold cases in which Gubbio reveals his inability to understand what is there, his tendencies to claim he sees what he cannot, or even his lack of awareness of the implications of what he says. When Ferro surprises Nestoroff and Nuti in intimate conversation on the studio lot, Gubbio describes Varia's masterful behavior in staring down Ferro's fury: "The effect of that look on the savage face, the disordered person, the excited gait of Carlo Ferro was remarkable." Yet in his next breath he tells us, "We did not see his face" (Sh:299, Quad:165). Piqued by Ferro's tendency to ignore him (Sh:103–104, Quad:62) he forces the actor to call out to him, rather than allowing him to catch up and pretend it is a chance meeting (Sh:152, Quad:87). To the actor this looks plainly as if Gubbio is accelerating his pace to get away from him. Gubbio, at this suggestion, bursts out in a "sincere" laugh and explains his true intention: "Not knowing this Signor Nuti, and feeling annoyed at seeing myself looked at askance for the last few days by you, from the suspicion that I had mixed myself up, or wished to mix myself up in this business, I did not wish you, just now, to overtake me, and so increased my pace. That is the explanation of my *running away*" (Sh:155, Quad:89). In other words, he *was* running away. Clearly Gubbio is not being honest, since it is not true that he does not know Nuti or that he does not wish to get involved. His intended involvement is plain to see from the moment he hears of Nuti's impending arrival. He exclaims, "My heart tells me that, as I turn the handle of this photographic machine, I am destined to carry out both your revenge and your poor Giorgio's, dear Duccella, dear Granny Rosa!" (Sh:73, Quad:46). Quite consistently with this momentary slip in his façade, Gubbio will indeed "step into the action," both as our narrator and as a character, and thus abandon his role as objective, uninvolved cameraman.

It is here that Gubbio ceases to be an interesting, if faulty, representative of objective, cameralike point of view and starts to appear as a covert participant in an action that he cannot but regard as one of the cheap melodramas he so often films. Gubbio's pretense to be just a bemused and hapless witness to events beyond his control is shattered. When Ferro points out that negative acts may well be a way of committing a crime, Gubbio admits to us that, indeed, "each of us—however honest and upright he may esteem himself, considering his own actions in the abstract, that is to say apart from the incidents and coincidences that give them their weight and value—may commit a crime *in secret even from himself*" (Sh:163, Quad:93). Ferro detects such a plot in the fact that Polacco casts him as the hunter in charge of shooting the tiger. He thinks Polacco did this knowing full well that Ferro is too hotheaded to shoot the tiger safely, yet too proud to back out, and thus will die, leaving Polacco's friend Nuti a free hand with Nestoroff (Sh:160, Quad:91–92). Ferro points out that even Polacco could deny this to himself. Yet the facts speak for themselves: "You take a man and make him enter a cage, into which a tiger is to be driven, and you say to him: 'Keep calm, now. Take a careful aim, and fire. Oh, and remember to bring it down with your first shot, see that you hit it in the right spot; otherwise, even if you wound it, it will spring upon you and tear you to pieces!' All this, I know, if they choose a calm, cool man, a skilled marksman, is nothing, it is not a crime" (Sh:162, Quad:92). But he is not such a man, Ferro points out, hot-blooded and impetuous as he is, and Polacco's insistence that he is brave is a way of trapping Ferro; his introduction of Nuti into the studio represents an added emotional burden for the actor to bear.

Fortunately for Ferro, Nuti, with impetuous bravado, gets into the cage himself. It is now that Gubbio acts in the spirit of Ferro's lesson.[14] Nuti, on the face of it a skilled marksman, is the epitome of cool as the tiger hunt approaches. Yet Luisetta, loved by Gubbio and in love herself with Nuti, worries that something terrible may happen, and so does her father, Cavalena. Yet Gubbio insists in reassuring them that nothing could possibly go wrong. "But why must you believe that the indifference and mockery of Signora Nestoroff have provoked Signor Nuti to (what shall I say?) anger, scorn, violent plans of revenge? On what do you base your argument? He certainly shows no sign of it! He keeps perfectly calm, he is looking forward with evident pleasure to his part as an English gentleman" (Sh:313, Quad:172–173; see also Sh:309, Quad:170–171). Cavalena rightly points out that this can only be a pose and Gubbio too knows full well that this is so. His words, in fact, are the kind of rationalization that Ferro had attributed to Polacco. The cameraman has revealed several times that he knows that Nuti is likely to do something rash; he in fact had been saying so to Nuti himself. Only Gubbio's own careful separation of relevant facts by elliptical narrative strategies and his deliberate underplaying of emphasis allow us to miss this. Early in the novel, as Nuti tries to interpose himself between Giorgio and Nestoroff, Gubbio seems to speculate when saying that Nuti "wishes to do something other than weep, and we shall have to keep him under observation. Why has he come here? He has no need to be avenged on anyone, if the treachery lay in Giorgio Mirelli's action in killing himself and flinging his dead body between his sister and her lover" (Sh:196, Quad:110). Yet suddenly (and retroactively) he reveals to us that he actually speaks these words to Nuti. Is he not introducing the idea of revenge to the distraught young man; is he not nudging Nuti to act? Nuti finally blurts out his desperation, anticipating the irrational fury and destructive solution he will finally choose and which Gubbio subsequently denies as a possibility to those who fear it (Sh:201–202, Quad:113).

To Nestoroff, who asks Gubbio to let Nuti know that she will never, not even out of pity, allow him close to her, the cameraman puts it quite plainly: "Being, as I have already told you, incapable of doing anything, in the state of mind in which he is at present, he might unfortunately become capable of anything" (Sh:274, Quad:153). If any doubt exists in Gubbio's mind as to Nuti's desperate intentions, such doubts are dispelled by Nuti himself as he talks to Gubbio on the day before the tiger scene is to be filmed and muses about how moving the image is of someone who has died young (Sh:320, Quad:177). Nuti may in fact be thinking, as he hastens to add, of an old photograph of his own father who died young, yet Gubbio does not think so, since he clearly suspects Nuti plans some desperate act. Gubbio tells Nuti that the cage will be surrounded by armed actors and technicians, ready in the event of a mishap. Yet he knows, he says, that Nuti is a crack shot and that such precautions should offend Nuti's pride as marksman. He even makes sure to tell him that in Ferro's case such precautionary measures "perhaps" would not have been taken (unlikely, given Ferro's repeatedly voiced worries and his insistence on a very high insurance policy). The result is Nuti's demand that no one stand by with guns at the ready to cover him.

Gubbio also misleads the reader. Trying to appear unprepared for what was about to happen, he says that "fortunately for the company, I drew a much larger supply of film than would be required" (Sh:328, Quad:181). He then proceeds to ignore the most crucial detail of all. Having been introduced with Nuti into the tiger's cage, Gubbio reports,

> I noticed that Nuti first of all knelt down on the spot marked out for him, then rose and went across to thrust apart the boughs at one side of the cage, as though he were making a loophole there. I alone was in a position to ask him: "Why?" But the state of feeling that had grown up between us did not allow of our exchanging a single word at this stage. His action might therefore have been interpreted by me in several ways, which would have left me uncertain at a moment when the most absolute and precise certainty was essential. And then it was just as though Nuti had not moved at all; not only did I not think any more about his action, it was exactly as though I had not even noticed it. (Sh:330, Quad:182–183)

Gubbio, who never hesitates to interpret and assert on the basis of the scantiest external clues or even on hearsay, claims to have failed to notice that Nuti has cleared his aim toward Nestoroff; Gubbio who has repeatedly asserted that Nuti is capable of any madness and of foolhardy acts. His intervention in the action is thus finally made possible by his worst failure (omission) in the fulfillment of his primary role, that of observant cameraman.

Faced with the results of his own actions, we find Gubbio anxious to reshuffle his own words. He starts rephrasing his previous statements in order to make himself look like a *victim* of circumstances. The vengeance he had announced he sought upon the perpetrators of Giorgio's death now becomes "the vengeance that I sought to accomplish upon the obligation imposed on me, as the slave of a machine, to serve up life to my machine as food," a revenge that "life has chosen to turn back upon me" (Sh:326, Quad:180). About his silence he now says, "*I should like now my silence to close round me altogether*" (Sh:327, Quad:181), maintaining that he is quoting himself. In fact, he had said, "My silence would like to draw ever more closely round about me" (Sh:226, Quad:126), a statement in which he figures less actively. In these shifts from passive to active, in these reversals of subject and object, we recognize the trace of what has occurred.

The last quotation also links two moments in the narrative seemingly unconnected: Nestoroff's death and Gubbio's first meeting with Luisetta. He maintains he loves Luisetta. Now he turns this silence against her too and refuses to acknowledge her advances. It may well be, as he insists, that this refusal, as well as the trauma itself, is caused by the fear he experienced during the tiger scene, or perhaps his current lack of interest in Luisetta is just a consequence of his sense of disgust with the petty passions and cheap melodrama of those around him. Yet there are clues enough to suggest that this silence is pressed upon him by entangled knots of half-conscious motivations and inconsistent attachments: his attachment to Nestoroff for one.

It is in connection with Nestoroff that his claim to dispassionate objectivity and cool uninvolvement is strongest: "I study this woman, then," he tells us, "without passion but intently" (Sh:58, Quad:39). His understanding of what he feels about her image on the screen is correct, he claims, because his view of her is dispassionate, colored by neither love—as he admits those around him would contend, if they could hear what he tells us—nor hatred, which by all rights he should feel in view of her clear guilt in leading his friend Giorgio to suicide and Giorgio's family to despair.[15] He seems well aware that with Nestoroff he may be overwhelmed by feelings, and he states his determination to resist this (Sh:141, Quad:81). Yet he clearly fails, most notably during the filming of Nestoroff's dagger dance. Here we can see to what extent his feelings are involved, belying his claims to cool, distanced objectivity. Seen from his point of view, Nestoroff is performing for him in an exhibitionistic frenzy while he, the cameraman, presides as voyeur and imaginary executioner (Sh:125–126, Quad:72).[16] Gubbio clearly believes that in this instance his view through the camera reveals to him *more* than an existential insight. His description of her dance, highly erotic and charged with personal arousal, clearly states that the actress, practically naked and wet with perspiration, is engaging Gubbio directly with her eyes, intent on involving him personally. What is more, Gubbio sets himself on a par with her current lover Ferro, by reporting that during her dance "softly in a gasping whisper, still with her eyes fixed on mine, [she] asked now and again: 'Bien comme ça? Bien comme ça?'" (Sh:128, Quad:73). She uses French only in one other instance in the narrative, when addressing Ferro, and only, Gubbio tells us, when she is highly excited.

Gubbio's determination to manipulate his very perception in these matters is striking. "I find myself assailed, at times, with such violence by the external aspects of things," he confesses, "that the clear outstanding sharpness of my perceptions almost terrifies me. It becomes so much a part of myself, what I see with so sharp a perception, that I am powerless to conceive how in the world a given object—thing or person—can be other than what I would have it be" (Sh:130, Quad:75). The internal inconsistency in this declaration is quite telling. Gubbio at one and the same time claims an utterly accurate ability to perceive things as they are and yet a total determination to see things as he wants them to be.

As Gubbio, Polacco, Nestoroff, and Ferro sit in uneasy companionship waiting for a tardy starlet to arrive, Gubbio stares relentlessly at the vamp who, he maintains, is trying to pretend to her lover that her discomfort is caused not by these stares but by the brightness of the sun. Her attempt to shield this connection with the cameraman from her notoriously jealous and violent lover would seem to establish a modicum of complicity with Gubbio, yet her discomfort at the sun, Gubbio immediately adds, is genuine. This contradiction leads to an even more revealing inconsistency. He describes the effect of the sunlight on Varia: "A wonderful sight was the play on that face, of the purple shadows, straying and shot with threads of golden sunlight, which lighted up now one of her nostrils and part of her upper lip, now the lobe of her ear and a patch of her throat" (Sh:130, Quad:75). This would seem to be a marvelously precise cameraman's perception of a woman's face, yet it is also the kind of perception of Nestoroff (in terms of light and color) which Gubbio has attributed to his friend Giorgio Mirelli and which he has told us was a perception untrue to the real being of the lady (Sh:67, Quad:43). The artistic results of such a "set" vision are Giorgio's six canvases of Nestoroff. In Gubbio's own words, they "fixed there for all time . . . in that divine light, in that divine fusion of colors" one particular way of looking (Sh:263, Quad:147). This represents on one level an implicit criticism of cinematography, juxtaposed as it is to the transfiguring triumph of the art of painting. Yet, more importantly in the context of Gubbio's own claim of true perceptiveness and in relation to his criticism of Giorgio, it demonstrates that the cameraman is perceiving in an untruthful way at the very moment he claims the opposite. Clearly, if Giorgio's pictorial vision of Nestoroff is a fantasy, so is Gubbio's now. Yet it is a fantasy that allows him to cast himself in the perceptive role of Nestoroff's lover Giorgio and a clear suggestion that Gubbio's way of seeing her is the way of a man who loved her passionately enough to die for this love. Thus the distorted vision of the cameraman allows him to "cast" himself as both of Nestoroff's lovers.

What of his love for Luisetta, then? Less covertly than with Nestoroff, Gubbio sees the young actress as a link to a number of images, situations, and feelings from the past rather than the person he meets in the present and who prompts him to fall in love. From her first appearance in the horse-drawn carriage, her description echoes the rhetoric and aura of feeling associated with the "good old times" and with the house at Sorrento (Sh:37 ff., Quad:27 ff.; Sh:79, Quad:48). Her impersonation of Duccella for the hallucinating Nuti, and her love for him, merely deepens Gubbio's confusion. He is trapped in the web of these images from the past and unable to join the flow of life, unable even to fulfill his chosen role as narrator and keep us abreast of the story as it spans present and past.

This narrative "malfunction" starts early in the novel, as we are jolted into ever new story lines by sudden flashes of past events too rapid and arbitrary actually to explain anything, while these are interrupted by narratively redundant evocations. This dislocation first occurs with the sudden appearance of Varia Nestoroff. She causes a rapid flashback that tantalizes the reader with a shower of past events linking all the characters and promising a great deal of interest. Capri, the Russian Colony, Naples, Bohemian life, Sorrento—all of these parade before us in a rapid montage (Sh:32–33, Quad:26). This narrative flashback leads to the detailed account of at least one of its parts ("a house, a dear house in the country") but does so in such a way that for a long while the reader is frustrated in reconstructing the narrative connections and is forced instead to dwell on the evocation of mood and feeling that the setting revives in Gubbio himself. The house is Giorgio and Duccella's, and it is the house Nestoroff came to when engaged to marry Giorgio, but none of this is made very clear.

It is not just that interrelations of time sequence, events, characters, and setting are obfuscated. Gubbio talks about the house in Sorrento as if it were his own house; he recalls Nonna Rosa as if she were his own grandmother. The house is made to enfold Gubbio himself, and the death of the children's parents is recounted while the identity of the children and their relation to Gubbio is left unclear. He thus boldly inserts himself into these past situations—situations which actually antedate his arrival at the house—and outlines his actions, comments and feelings in the face of those events as if he had been present. Thus the synchronic links created by the paradigmatic break in the flow of narrative continuity do not merely establish a series of symbolic, discontinuous links in the text, but create, further, a "phantom" secondary narrative axis. And the narrator's effort is directed at framing and articulating this retroactive, wishful narrative through the means of filmlike delimitation.

The section thus "frames" Gubbio's view of the past by tone (the charged evocative style is striking) and by strict delimitation of vision. The narrator directs our attention with the controlled deliberation and selectivity that the film medium inherently favors. But he does so for purposes contrary to the narrative clarity of film. Actual framing devices proliferate in the section. The descriptive-emotive paragraphs represent the setting in successive "establishing shots" full of details bathed in the "soft focus" luminescence of evocative flashback sequences. "House" leads to "rooms" and then to one specific "drawing room" with "framed" wall panels. On one of these "screens" ("I had only to turn": the camera pans) a mirror frames and repeats the artificial fruit arrangement and the clock on the sideboard. The whole house, moreover, is described as a series of rooms interconnected by a series of low doorframes. The favorite room is related to the garden just outside through the frames of its windows (also a screen for the outside light), and it is here that Gubbio presents himself as enfolded in the sensual frame of the couch, just as the house itself is "perched in a niche behind the green hill" (Sh:39–40, Quad:28–29).

The main events in this house (Nonna Rosa, the death of her only son, Nonno Carlo's reaction to it, the death of the daughter-in-law, the grandparent's raising of Lidia and Giorgetto, the arrival of Varia Nestoroff, and Giorgio's entrance into life) are also framed, within the previous evocative frame, by the timeless sound of Nonna Rosa's voice calling out for Giorgio. The repetition of her call, framing this section, acts out the tension (one that Gubbio identifies with) between the enfolding frame of the house and the outside world, access to which is gained through the frame of that fateful gate through which death has so many times reached. The physical contiguity of space and story held together by these frames is shattered by Gubbio's willful insertion of himself into the house and its past.

At the center of this existential trap, in the entrance hall to the magical space of the villa at Sorrento, we recognize with a start that very spider which Gubbio now "operates" on others as a cameraman: "This strident machine, which suggests on its knock-kneed tripod a huge spider watching for its prey, a spider that sucks in and absorbs . . . live reality" (Sh:106, Quad:63). We find it in those wall brackets with "spiders' feet" which support the overhanging mirror that holds the image of wax-fruit bowl and clock—an image into which Gubbio physically drags an imaginary Varia Nestoroff cast as "death" and which he insists with hysterical intensity "must be allowed to remain as it is!" (Sh:41, Quad:29). Static mirror images of immutable wax trap Gubbio in the antechamber of his youth at Sorrento, just as actors are trapped by that other spider, the camera—images that cut Gubbio off from the continuing flow of real life as much as they do the actors whom he films. His emotional ambivalence and obsession with his own image of the house are the guiding motives of our narrator; they limit his vision and disrupt his narrative act. His very "style" bears the marks of this distortion quite clearly, encoded in the "text" of his statements, evasions, figures, and ellipses. Gubbio's text is the trace of his motivations rather than the account of his or anyone else's actions. It is his telling of the story that is the story; it is his language which acts, and what he presents as the metonymic contiguities of his experience should be read as metaphors of feeling.[17] If, as in the Lacanian reformulation of Freud, "symptom *is* metaphor," Gubbio's metaphors (house, spider) *are* his symptoms. If "desire *is* a metonymy," Gubbio has treated us to the metonymies of his desire through the stylistic exercise that is his narrative act. His long evocation is indeed "nostalgia . . . in the service of metonymy" (Lacan 1970:137, 125).

These images and structural distortions have all been controlled by Gubbio's idiosyncratic role as a cameraman and have thus allowed the specific framework of film aesthetics to shape narrator and narrative. Pirandello, in setting out to write a "film novel," has succeeded in giving us a text that is shaped by the new art form but which is also intimately affected in its specific narrative by this initial choice. What is more, the generic framework and the story have led to a significant existential vision of man shaped by the emergence of a new art form. The novel thus is a masterful integration of emerging generic specificities with a riveting treatment of a particular historical environment and a particular individual story. The formal infrastructure of a new art form (cinema) is made to capture the idiosyncrasies of human destiny in the modern age, while it also articulates the unique destiny of one character and his particular way through life.

2
Icons Unreal Irony

Serafino Gubbio manifests in his personal history some of the consequences—relevant to us all—that derive from the intense instrumental mediation of reality typical of this century. Contemporary humanity experiences a totally new manner of being aware of the world, at once more immediate, seemingly more objective, and yet far less comprehensible than before and less compatible with our individual subjectivities. Gubbio is a victim of a medium that has taken possession of his life by controlling and distorting his awareness. His plight, exaggerated for narrative effect, contains actual echoes, for those of us who watch (for fun, for instruction, for insight) the work of Gubbio's colleagues: all those men-with-a-movie-camera who have become the most authoritative and subliminally pervasive mediators of reality to modern consciousness. All of us, even the most aware (and this is the problem), tend to absorb their assertive concretizations without questioning. To the emerging modern concern with questions about consciousness and perception, film as an art form—and its immediate and necessary forerunner, photography—lends the artistic means to embody the dilemmas of such typically modern questioning.

A protagonist who perceives as a camera eye, and who connects with the editorial syntax of montage, double exposure, and traveling shots, can dramatize and explore with great effectiveness the puzzles and conflicts of a view of reality which provides for the first time a tangible surface—an image upon a screen—that makes physically real those dimensions of imaginative concretization and those relativities of objective presence which modern consciousness considers of great importance. It is precisely this new availability of a concrete representation of imagined realities that at one and the same time reveals and hides their unreality. It is precisely this visualized revelation of a discontinuity between the claim to a concrete presence of reality and the illusionary and relativistic basis of the same presence that, I would maintain, causes film to be the first medium able to concretize for all to see the mental perspectives of ironic vision previously relegated to the interior life of the few. And it is precisely such a tropological definition that characterizes, as we shall see, the art of cinematography as Pirandello sees it.

But the ironic essence of the film image is alas not easy to perceive, whether it leads the spectator to notice a discrepancy between represented appearances and lived truth, or whether it reveals at its own center a deeper and more serious ironic rupture between presence and absence, between connotative individual meaning and a denotative connection with external reality. Gubbio's own frequent claim to truthful, objective observation confirms the aggressive claim of the medium itself: even at its most evidently fantastic and tricky, the film image intimates objective reality rather than declares its own unreality. The ambiguity of this situation is precisely what Gubbio defines as a "hybrid game" of cinematography: "Hybrid, because in it the stupidity of the fiction is all the more revealed and obvious inasmuch as one sees it to be placed on record by the method that least lends itself to deception: namely, photography" (Sh:87, Quad:53).[1] Gubbio's faith in the fact that photography reveals its trick openly is, of course, misplaced. To the viewers who allow the industry to flourish in the way described by Gubbio himself, the paradox inherent in cinematic fictions is clearly not apparent. On the contrary, it is the very immediacy of photographic reproduction which guarantees the reality-status of the silliest simplifications; the most fanciful flights of the imagination are "made real" by the medium. The basic claim of the photographed elements of life which are made present on the screen is that same "effect of the real" ascribed by Roland Barthes (1968) to naturalist writing.[2] What appears to be the closest possible imprint of reality on the medium is in fact yet another rhetorical strategy. Very much in the limited sense of Pirandello's view of rhetorical irony,[3] then, film *says* something that is untrue but leaves no clue in the text as to this untruth. What is there, seen as part of the text of the image in conventional entertainment films of the kind that in Pirandello's time were already popular, purports to be what it is not: truthful and real. But film over and above its commercial applications is also a concretized mediation of deeper and more philosophical ironic visions. Beyond the rhetorical sleight of hand we will find that it opens up a view upon the true recesses of life not visible to the naked eye. It is also this more complex perspective on film, film in its essence, which Pirandello explores.

At this level of analysis Pirandello approaches film beyond the one-sided support—as some claim—of one specific type of film poetics: that of neorealism.[4] The passage most cited in this regard is the one in which Gubbio observes of his profession that if it were applied to the recording, without any stupid invention or imaginary construction of scenes and actions of life, life as it comes, without selection and without any plan; the actions of life as they are performed without a thought, when people are alive and do not know that a machine is lurking in concealment to surprise them. Who knows how ridiculous they would appear to us! Most of all, ourselves. . . . Ah, if my profession were destined to this end only! If it had the sole object of presenting to men the ridiculous spectacle of their heedless actions, an immediate view of their passions, of their life as it is. Of this life without rest, which never comes to an end. (Sh:150–151, Quad:86)

Whether or not this truly anticipates the aesthetics of neorealism, these words propose the cinematic image as a mediating surface that allows the viewer to penetrate beneath appearances and illusions and to come face to face with the true nature of reality; to provide the viewer with the critical evidence (in the shape of a concrete image) that allows him to survey himself and reality from a distance.[5]

This serious view of film as a positively heuristic medium parallels in important ways Pirandello's notion of ironic distance as he explores it in *L'umorismo*. The very distinction which he makes in this essay between irony and his own notion of true humor helps us to place his treatment of film (mostly implicit in *Quaderni*) within the framework of his discussion. Pirandello distinguishes between a deeply felt human response that participates in the pain others feel when caught in the midst of unbridgeable conflicts and an abstract, impersonal, intellectual appreciation of contradictions. The mechanical and impersonal nature of film mediation lacks precisely the element of empathic feeling which separates a mere *awareness* of contradiction and paradox (*avvertimento del contrario*) from a *feeling* for it and its implications (*sentimento del contrario*) (Hum:131–132, Lum:127).[6] But film puts into a structure— and does so in a summary and visible way—the evidence needed for our awareness to reach such feeling. It provides everyone with an easier access to that "immediate view" of behavior which before the birth of this medium was accessible only to the most perceptive ironist. At its worst, in superficial, conventional, and fake imitations of reality, or at its best, when it presents the essence of life, film makes visible the evidence that will take the willing spectator from awareness to feeling. It draws our attention, for example, to comical views (now framed and inescapable) such as that of the dolled-up old lady cited by Pirandello in *L'umorismo*—a true forerunner of many a "serious" slapstick figure, of all the Vladimirs and Estragons present behind the Laurels and Hardies of our screens—and allows the spectator to "*perceive that she is the opposite* of what a respectable old lady should be" (Hum:113, Lum:127). Pirandello points out that in works of art such critical awareness need not be openly stated in didactic fashion: it emerges spontaneously from the aesthetic structure of the work. Film, by implication, allows this to happen more dramatically still. Like the experience of true humor, film causes in the perceiver the kind of perplexity, mentioned in the essay on humor, which leaves him suspended between two forces. "I feel like laughing," Pirandello states, "and I do laugh, but my laughter is troubled and obstructed by something that stems from the representation itself" (Hum:118, Lum:131–132). This is very much like the perplexity mentioned above which arises in noticing the discrepancy between the silly fictions of film and their photographically transparent nature on a screen. The reality of film art thus revealed by Pirandello already during the early years of this new art form finally turns out to present us with powerful and quite serious images of the modern existential condition. Presented with the perplexing perspectives described in *L'umorismo,* humanity finds itself faced with

> a reality different from the one that we normally perceive, a reality living beyond the reach of human vision, outside the forms of human reason. Very lucidly, then, the texture of daily existence, almost suspended in the void of our inner silence, seems meaningless, devoid of purpose; and that new reality appears to us dreadful in its sternly detached and mysterious crudeness, for all our usual fictitious relationships, both of feelings and images, have separated and disintegrated in it. (Hum:138, Lum:152)

Film images in *Quaderni* repeatedly evoke such perceptions: for Varia Nestoroff as she faces the showing of her daily rushes; for Aldo Nuti as he finds access to insights about the nature of time and space by way of a cinematic image. More than just perplexed, Varia Nestoroff is deeply upset when she faces the images of her actual deep self on screen. It is with shock that she faces the apparition of the "violent expressions which she assumes, involuntarily, unconsciously, in the parts that are assigned to her" (Sh:59, Quad: 39). When viewing this screen-realized image of her own different reality, that "reality living beyond the reach of human vision," her subconscious self, "she herself remains speechless and almost terror-stricken at her own image on the screen, so altered and disordered. She sees there someone who is herself but whom she does not know. She would like not to recognize herself in this person, but at least to know her" (Sh:61, Quad:40). Aldo Nuti too finds the view of his close-up—one of his "pieces," as he puts it—very unsettling indeed and declares that he could not wait for it to disappear from the screen (Sh:319, Quad:176).

These are instances in which viewers perceive via the film image precisely that realm "beyond the reach of human vision" mentioned in the essay on humor. It is *made visible* for them by this unique new artistic medium in a way that goes well beyond the view of reality later envisioned by neorealism. The "texture" of true existence is presented to these characters in the dark and silent setting of viewing rooms which concretize that very same "void of our inner silence" in which such revelations are said to occur in *L'umorismo.*

Furthermore, this particular view of life as mediated by film—so bare and essential in its objectivity—clashes with the more comfortable and "edited" versions of a life led according to the "usual fictitious relationships" of conventional social propriety. And cinema provides us with an even clearer view of this second type of vision (if we are ready for it) than does real-life observation. Conventional film melodramas usually represent this second view of life, since they build up their "fictitious relationships" of "images" precisely in order to provoke those "feelings" which conventional expectations would seek out in cinematic experience. This use of the film medium tries to present the viewer with an image of life that is very different from the one discovered by Nestoroff and Nuti in the film image at its purest. It tries to propose an image of what a hypocritical and domineering society regards as the decorous verisimilitudes of human behavior. This kind of film spins its tales to form the web of a representation of life similar to the web Pirandello says is spun by the "spider of experience." Reflection reveals that this spider "abstracts from social life the silk floss in order to compose in the individual the web of opinions in which the moral sense often lies enveloped." The camera too, we may recall, is seen as a spider that perverts the true essence of life. We may well say that the tales presented through that mechanical spider on screen are just like those webs of ambiguous propriety, like that "hypocrisy behind morality," which it is "the task of humorism" to discover "through a laugh and without indignation" (Hum:132, Lum:146–147). The visible web of such "humorism" exposes, in the words of one critic, "the paradigm of a basic conflict between society, with its rituals of oppression and hypocrisy, and the individual trapped in them to his own detriment and destruction" (della Terza 1972:23).

Quaderni therefore also advances a view of cinema that contradicts the positive essence of the medium. This view reveals the medium's peculiar power in imposing as "real" very limited views of reality. The film image, while on the one hand suggesting that it can intimate the true essence of the "real," on the other mostly participates in that other representation of the real, the mimetic "verisimilitude" which society has always required of traditional art. It presents the kind of narrative discourse described by Gérard Genette "in which actions correspond, as so many applications or particular instances, to a corpus of maxims accepted as true by the public to which it addresses itself"; maxims, continues Genette, which "because they are conceded, remain most often implicit" (Genette 1968:8, my translation).[7]

At the stage of film history during which Pirandello was writing, it could not yet be entirely clear that even the most seemingly real photographic representation of life is a pattern of conventionalized signs connoting "we are reality" rather than denoting the imprint of life upon emulsion. This is why Gubbio's attitude to the medium anticipates André Bazin's suggestive but by now superseded notion of the cinematic image as something akin to an actual imprint (like a death mask) of reality left upon the pliable emulsion of film.

Film, according to this view, is the only medium in which the world can actually ooze onto the mediating materials and is therefore the most highly "motivated" art we have; a discourse, that is, in which the gap between signifiers and signifieds is completely eliminated.[8] Thanks to Bazin we can well understand how such an impression may well survive the better understanding of the most clear-headed critical consciousness. But beyond such insights based upon the priority of experience over reason, it seems that the only relation to "true" reality of the elements captured on film (through the manipulation of technical factors by cameramen and through the staging of actors and scenery by directors) is what Christian Metz has called the "making true" of cinematic verisimilitude. The kind of film which relies on this rhetorical posture, Metz points out, "tries to persuade itself, to persuade the viewers, that the conventions which force it to limit the range of possibilities are not laws of discourse or rules of writing—are not conventions at all—and that their effect, verifiable within the content of the work, is in fact the result of the nature of things and corresponds to the intrinsic characteristics of the subject which is being represented. The verisimilar work wills itself to be, and wants to be believed as directly translatable into the terms of reality" (Metz 1968a:30–31, my translation).[9] The verisimilitudes imposed by commercial considerations and by cultural conformism therefore form an alliance with an inherent illusion of conformity to the true essence of life typical of the film image itself.

The fact that what people find acceptable as "likely" and as "decorous" is sharply bound by idiosyncratic cultural conventions is clear to Pirandello too. Gubbio's art director, Polacco, tailors his company's production to the notions of what is acceptable to his major export market, England. As Gubbio observes, "We must . . . in selecting our plots, adapt ourselves to English taste. And is there any limit to the things that the English will not have in a film, according to Cocò Polacco? 'English prudery, you understand! They have only to say "shocking" and there's an end of the matter!'" (Sh:107, Quad:64). This is why poor Cavalena's view of life, colored as it is by his personal troubles, produces scripts which, to his Italian colleagues, seem perhaps excessively replete with suicides but can be passed. They are utterly unacceptable, however, to British decorum (Sh:134, Quad:77). What was accommodated by the Mediterranean temperament within a melodramatic genre convention strained to its limits is not acceptable even within those limits to Anglo-Saxon sensibilities.

Careful calibration of film codes according to the rules of verisimilitude—style codes, action codes, logical codes, codes of cultural canon—occurs even at this early stage of film history. This is illustrated by the range of specialized film genres found in the early Italian cinema.[10] Some of this range is reflected in *Quaderni*. It seems, however, that such generic works do not represent, as Christian Metz maintains in theory, an alternative to the discourse of verisimilitude in which "the language of the work refuses with an elaborate purpose to give the illusion of being translatable into the terms of reality" and *"renounces verisimilitude,"* renounces the attempt "to *seem real*" (Metz 1968a:30).

What this early shift into limited stylizations indicates, a fact illustrated by several episodes in *Quaderni,* is the powerful imposition of limited perspectives upon life. Genre becomes a model for life. Pirandello shows the extent to which real behavior and true events are seen and experienced as if occurring within the limited bounds of various film genres. Even in 1916, life clearly imitates the movies: "What men, what intrigues, what life, at a time like this? Madness, crime or stupidity. A cinematographic life?" (Sh:266, Quad:149). Gubbio's inner horror at coming face to face with Luisetta's emerging love for Nuti is reduced to a grotesque shadow projected on a wall, clearly echoing the generic peculiarities of horror films (Sh:189, Quad:106), just as the ghost of Giorgio is inserted between Nuti and Varia by Gubbio himself in what the cameraman refers to as "a splendid cinematographic effect" (Sh:122, Quad:70), a special effect, we may note, closely bound with the specific genre conventions which circumscribe tales of passion, melodramas, and the filmic concretizations of the supernatural.

Even didactic film genres that aim at concretizing factual truths in order to enrich the viewer's experience can, in the last analysis, limit this experience. Having viewed *Marvels of the Heavens* by the astronomer-senator Zeme, Gubbio complains that "since that cursed Senator Zeme has been to the Kosmograph, I see even in the sky a *marvel* of cinematography" (Sh:203, Quad:113).

As a consequence of such authoritative generic stylizations of life created by cinema, we find that life itself adopts these stylizations. People either appear to each other or behave like pale reflections of the melodramas they see upon their screens. In such cases it is not an interior truth which is revealed through the perceptual viewfinder of film vision, but it is rather the inner essence of people which is hidden and falsified by a veneer of film *clichés*. Pirandello repeatedly dramatizes this consequence of cinematography.

Actions are thus represented cinematically when observed in life, and life comes to proceed with the shorthand, summary economy, the jerky stops and starts, the sudden lulls and the iconic sketchiness of film. Thus the very real and significant actions of Varia Nestoroff as she decides to seduce Nuti are seen entirely through the stylized filter of a triangular melodrama of passion and betrayal (Sh:291, Quad:161). And through the process that cinematography uses for the generic representation of historical dramas, Gubbio can see his beloved Luisetta, too, through the colors, costumes, and stylistic peculiarities of a Watteau (Sh:249–250, Quad:139). She is a perfect eighteenth-century porcelain doll, wig and all, hastening to arrange an assignation while her first effort in cinematic acting casts her in a scenario which in its essence parodies closely the actual lives of the characters we come to know (Sh:136–

137, Quad:78). This fact, however, may be easily missed under the glittering generic veneer. In such instances, the exchange between life and the movies is close to total, and one is hard put to tell the difference between film parodying the very real dramas of life and life resolving itself into the shallow generic postures of the movies.

Society, on the whole, prefers to cling to conventionalized views of reality such as these. This is understandable when we note that cinematic representations confirm and even dictate the surface of a life that, if breached by a deeper kind of probing, proves to be unsettling. The price of such probing in search of more essential insights into the true nature of such existential realms as those of time and space can be high:

> The inner void expands, surpasses the limits of our body, and becomes a weird emptiness that engulfs us as if time and life had come to a stop, as if our inner silence had plunged into the abyss of mystery. With a supreme effort we then try to recapture the normal consciousness of things, to renew our usual relationships with them, to reassemble our ideas and to feel alive again in the usual way. But we can no longer trust this normal consciousness, these newly recollected ideas, and this habitual sense of living because we now know that they are deceptions which we use in order to survive and that underneath them there is something else which man can face only at the cost of either death or insanity. (Hum:138, Lum:152–153)

It is the view of a cinematic image of himself which prompts Nuti to point out that the image concretizes upon the screen the experience of arrested time. Gubbio expounds on this, maintaining that, paradoxically, the photographic image at one and the same time—right in front of our eyes—concretizes youth and old age. Only through such an image of ourselves (mediated through the process of photographic reproduction) can we ever directly witness the aging of our own young selves: "The time, there, of the picture, does not advance, does not keep moving on, hour by hour, with us, into the future; you expect it to remain fixed at that point, but it is moving too, in the opposite direction; it recedes farther and farther into the past, that time. Consequently the picture itself is a dead thing which as time goes on recedes gradually farther into the past: and the younger it is the older and more remote it becomes" (Sh:320, Quad:177).

But it is Gubbio alone who confronts the kind of insanity described in *L'umorismo*. This is caused by the changes wrought by time in his beloved Sorrento, where even space has been displaced and where he must confront those "deceptions which we use in order to survive." The sight of Duccella (now old, fat, and exiled from that villa which means so much to Gubbio) propels him "towards madness, through the night" (Sh:283, Quad:158), a feeling reinforced by the sight of a man on the train, so conventional as to be a caricature ("oval eyes, like disks of enamel and hair gleamed with oil"). The experience of unavoidable confrontation between the conventional realities of society, of its stereotypes, and the deep existential reality he has to absorb, causes Gubbio to question his own reality. He is then assailed by a rush of images that echo the cinematic montages which usually characterize his vision of the world, images which this time articulate his subjective inner reality. This subjective montage manifests the very same kind of disintegration described in *L'umorismo* where such moments mirror the jerky, mechanical, and headspinning nature of Gubbio's cinematic perception of life: "a sort of dizziness which contrasts with the stability, itself so illusory, of things." Life itself is described, just as Gubbio describes it in *Quaderni*, as unreal, "like a mechanical phantasmagoria" (Hum:138, Lum:153).

The particular series of images that assails Gubbio in the train underlines also the extent to which cinematic images partake of the precarious relation to reality and to certainty of mental images in general. Despite the apparent solidity and reliability of images on the screen, reflection on their true nature makes them a palpable symbol of the kinds of images which have to obliterate true, objective reality in order to affirm their own presence. These images, in which the affirmation of connotative truth requires the elimination of all true connections with their own denotative content, are very much like Gubbio's images on the train:

> Images I carried in me, not my own, of things and people; images, aspects, faces, memories of people and things which had never existed in reality, outside me, in the world which that gentleman saw round him and could touch. I had thought that I saw them, and could touch them also, but no, they were all imagination! I had never found them again, because they had never existed: phantoms, a dream. . . . But how could they have entered my mind? From where? Why? Was I there too, perhaps, then? Was there an I there then that now no longer existed? No; the middle-aged gentleman opposite to me told me, no: that other people existed, each in his own way and with his own space and time: I, no, I was not there; albeit, not being there, I should have found it hard to say where I really was and what I was, being thus without time and space. (Sh: 284–285, Quad:159)[11]

We have already explored Gubbio's stubborn determination to make reality conform to his own will. Here we see again to what lengths he will go, even in the face of a clear realization that his inner reality does not exist anywhere, to hang onto his illusions, to the images in his mind, even if this means with inescapable logic that his own reality in space and time dissolves and that Gubbio himself remains "without time and space." And it is at this point in Gubbio's experience that we find the cameralike imagistic montages of the modern perception of reality paradoxically dissolving into the unreal just as the reality and significance of these montages to the individual are strongest.

The powerful realization of imaginative constructs of reality on the screen or in one's mind—ranging from genre stereotypes and deep essence to memory and wishful thinking—all share in the nature of imaginative consciousness as it is described by Sartre, whose observations dovetail so nicely with Pirandello's as to make them pertinent and useful to our discussion.

Central to Sartre's thinking is the notion that images, while giving the overwhelming impression of existing within one's mind in some sort of physical way (what he terms the "illusion of immanence"), are in fact merely a positional act, "a certain manner in which the object makes its appearance to consciousness, or, if one prefers, a certain way in which consciousness presents an object to itself" (Im/E:5, 8; Im/F:16, 19). This way of presenting an object to itself involves, paradoxically, a negation of the real object in the very act of making it most present to oneself through imaginative concretization, for "the characteristic of the intentional object of the imaginative consciousness is that the object is not present and is posited as such, or that it does not exist and is posited as not existing, or that it is not posited at all" (Im/E:17, Im/F:30–32). An integral, if not always conscious, part of perceiving an image is the awareness that its object is not there. The drama of Gubbio's confrontation with the unreality of his mental images derives precisely from the fact that all along he had been unable to recognize their positional nature. In this sense, Pirandello's narrative articulates in fictional form some of the insights later arrived at by philosophical methods and may be said to use narrative means to explore and to display philosophical subject matter no less than Sartre himself was to do in his works of fiction.

We can go further, however, if we recognize that in the novel, film images are repeatedly presented as involving large doses of misplaced belief in a reality they do not contain, as clues to a wider awareness of a reality hidden below their unreal surface, or—very much like Sartre's mental images—as leading to an awareness of the absence of their content. This occurs despite the fact that film images differ from mental images precisely because they do offer that "solid and opaque residue" which is only an illusion in mental images (Im/E:19, Im/F:35).[12] Film is thus used by Pirandello as a metaphor to illustrate the illusion we get from the vitality and solidity of mental images.

Aldo Nuti faces the experience of what we might term the paradox of the image when confronting his own image on the screen. This experience occurs in two complementary ways: Nuti's awareness of his father's absence from himself when viewing an old photograph (an old family experience now brought back to him by the occasion) and Nuti's own anticipated absence from Gubbio and from those who will view his image on screen. Father and son thus exemplify the same condition as that of Sartre's Peter:

> What my actual intention grasps is the corporeal Peter, the Peter I can see, touch, hear, if I did see him, hear him or touch him. It is a body . . . which nec-

essarily has a certain position in relation to me. But at this moment I know that the Peter whom I could touch is not being touched by me. It is of the very nature of my image of him not to touch him or see him, a way he has *of not being* at such a distance, in such a position. In the image, belief posits the intuition but not Peter. The characteristic of Peter is . . . to be "intuitive-absent," given to intuition as absent. In this sense it can be said that the image involves a certain nothingness. Its object is not a single portrait, it asserts itself: but in doing so it destroys itself. Alive, appealing, and strong as an image is, it presents its object as not being. This does not prevent us from reacting to the image as if its object were before us. (Im/E:17–18, Im/F:32–33)

This powerful suggestion that the image represents something that is real, really there, is common to film also; as film viewers we too react "to the image as if its object were before us." The inescapable sense of absence in the image which is present Nuti also feels as his father "presents himself before me empty, devoid of all the life that for him has not existed; he presents himself before me with his old picture of himself as a young man, which says nothing to me, which cannot say anything to me because he does not even know that I exist" (Sh:321, Quad:177).[13] This same kind of awareness is intensified by a tautological structure for Varia Nestoroff, who finds herself unable to touch, reach, or even recognize the person she watches on screen, that person who in fact is her own self. The paradox cannot be resolved. In Sartre's words, "The object as an image is an unreality. It is no doubt present, but, at the same time, it is out of reach. I cannot touch it" (Im/E:177–178, Im/F:240). Put in terms of a Peter again, the "absence of Peter, that which I see directly, which constitutes the essential structure of my image, is precisely a nuance that colors the image completely, and it is this we call his unreality" (Im/E:180, Im/F:243). One of the consequences of all this, one proposed as a logical corollary by Sartre, is experienced by Gubbio in the train. The only way he can enter entirely and "really" into the realm of his images himself is by dissolving his own reality status. As Sartre points out, "the world of imagery is completely isolated, I can enter it only by unrealizing myself in it" (Im/E:188, Im/F:254).

Pirandello, too, formulated quite explicitly the analogy between the element of unreality present in every artistic endeavor, and the unreal in all common, nonartistic self-representations of the realities of life. Of art he states bluntly that "we must be clear . . . on the fact that in general the author does not believe in the reality of the world which he represents" (Ir:933).[14] This, we find, is also true for life itself, since "not only not for the artist, but for no one does there exist a representation, be it artistic or be it the kind of representation which we all make for ourselves of ourselves, of others, of life, which can be believed as a reality. At bottom it is the same kind of illusion, the one created by art as well as the one that commonly comes to us all from our senses" (Ir:993). This has, of course, consequences for the kind of art one should produce: "Once we understand that every conclusion we might make [about reality] is arbitrary, and every construction we make of reality is, although necessary, inevitably illusory—arbitrariness for arbitrariness and unreal for unreal—by divesting our fables of all fake semblance of truth, we can represent in its essential mechanical nature the arbitrariness of that conclusion, and the illusion in its evident fraud, so that it may appear for what at bottom (alas) it is: a game, but willed and felt and represented as such" (Ir:995).

But most viewers will seek out the illusion for its own sake. When faced with the inescapable delusiveness of images that seem so real, so present, Gubbio and humankind will tend to prefer clinging to the illusion. They will face existential dissolution into "phantoms" and "dream," into those "ghostly beings" that they perceive upon the screens of movie houses and inner imaginative consciousness.[15] As in Pirandello's reading of Ariosto's world, the human drama (be it comical or tragical) emanates from the fact that "everything is fable and everything is true since it is inevitable that we accept as true the empty appearances emanating from our illusions and passions; to have illusions can be beautiful, but the deception of too much fantasizing always results in tears" (Hum:79, Lum:94–95). Just like the ironic artist of German Idealism, Gubbio is aware of the unreality of his own creations,[16] yet like Don Quixote, he will refuse to yield to the artist's corrective self-awareness. He will agree to do so only when "true reality, if for a moment it allows itself to be changed into improbable forms by the fantastic contemplation of a madman, will resist and fight back" and only "if this madman no longer satisfied only to contemplate it from, a distance and in his way, comes close enough to clash against it." Pirandello concludes: "It is one thing to fight against an invented castle, which can suddenly be made to vanish, and another to fight against a real windmill, which does not let itself be struck down like an imaginary giant" (Hum:82, Lum:97).

The film image is therefore unreal in two opposite ways: unreal as it relates to the texture of true existential reality if used to reflect the stereotypical verisimilitudes of social fictions, and also unreal as a naturalistic rendition of surfaces in its ability to prove the invisible depths of existential truth. The rhetorical ironies that derive from the first type of unreality, as well as the self-conscious romantic ironies that derive from the second, are ultimately joined and enriched by a more fundamental kind of irony. This is the "cosmic" irony given to modern man by the technological instrumentation that culminates in the technology of film.

Pirandello is more explicit than most about the direct connection between his fictions and advances in the instrumentation of perceptive awareness. As he points out in the conclusion to *L'umorismo*,

> it was the discovery of the telescope which dealt us the *coup de grâce*: another infernal little mechanism which could pair up with the one nature chose to bestow upon us. But we invented this one so as not to be inferior. While our eye

looks from below through the smaller lens, and sees as big all that nature had providentially wanted us to see small, what does our soul do? It jumps up to look from above through the larger lens, and as a consequence the telescope becomes a terrible instrument, which sinks the earth and man and all our glories and greatness. (Hum:142, Lum:156)

As we well know, this new optical discovery wrought profound changes in man's view of the world and of his own place in it.[17] One such man is represented by the persona speaking in Pirandello's poem "Globo," in which the cardboard globe built for diversion is a mere toy and the builder is a "God" who can see how petty and minute human pretensions are: "Rome is this point, both visible and not." While the speaker seems to concede a human point of view ("Who would say so at first sight? Yet / There are great men, nay immortal ones, / within this little thing and great ills / and great good and great affections and cares"), in the end he turns ironist ("their very large world is from one hundred steps, alas, invisible"), implying that, for the real force holding the real globe and spinning it on his finger, the end of the world would be very easy to cause (Pirandello 1960:769–770, my translation).[18] Zeme, too, we recall, feels that a lesson may be drawn from the juxtaposition of the infinitely great, the "formidable greatness" of his *Marvels of the Heavens*, with his own representative smallness, "insignificant little creature as he is" (Sh:111, Quad:66). Pau, in his usual fashion, punctures the pious propriety of such a modest posture and suggests to us that what Pirandello states more explicitly in *L'umorismo* is meant to be inferred here too: the application of a marvelous optical invention may well be used to belittle mankind instead of plumbing man's true grandeur. Zeme is a prisoner of this new technology, just as Gubbio is of his technical apparatus. Pau asks Zeme,

> What do you do? What do you suppose you are? You see nothing but the object! You have no consciousness of anything but the object! And so, a religion. And your God is your telescope! You imagine that it is your instrument? Not a bit of it! It is your God, and you worship it! You are like Gubbio here, with his machine! The servant. . . . I don't wish to hurt your feelings, let me say the priest, the supreme pontiff (does that satisfy you?) of this God of yours, and you swear by the dogma of its infallibility. (Sh:112, Quad:66)

Being in command of such a revealing and potent technology does not guarantee that what is *seen* is also *perceived* correctly. Zeme's inability to see beyond "the object" parallels the insensitive and nonperceptive fascination with the surface glitter of cinematographic images. It is like seeing Nuti's profile on screen and not perceiving any of the implications outlined above; it is like seeing Nestoroff's exaggerated posturing and not being aware of what she discovers in them. Zeme and Gubbio are not at all in command of their "infernal little mechanisms"; they are slaves to them. Such technologies may improve one's view of the surface of things, of their outside. But this occurs at the expense of inner vision and may in fact strain the human organism beyond its bounds.

At the violinist's deathbed, Cesarino applies this lesson to the rapid evolution of lighting technology:

> So many things I used to see in the dark with those lamps, which you are perhaps unable to see by electric light; but then, on the other hand, you see other things with these lights here which I fail to see; because four generations of lights, four, my dear Professor, oil, paraffin, gas, and electricity, in the course of sixty years, eh . . . eh . . . eh . . . it's too much, you know? and it's bad for our eyesight, and for our heads too; yes, it's bad for the head too, it is. . . . Light, a fine light, I don't say it isn't! . . . I can remember when you went about with a lantern in your hand so as not to break your neck. But light for outside, that's what it is . . . Does it help us to see better indoors [inside ourselves]? No. (Sh:143–144, Quad:82)

Sparked off by a veritable critique of the history of modern lighting technology as experienced in the lifetime of one character (oil to paraffin to gas to electricity), we can see that Cesarino's words raise the very same issues as does film technology.[19] As Arnheim puts it, "the more perfect our means of direct experience, the more easily we are caught by the dangerous illusion that perceiving is tantamount to knowing and understanding" (Arnheim 1969: 195–196).[20] What we really need to see better, Cesarino points out, is our own "indoors," and advances in technology may not necessarily bring this about. A better, clearer view of surfaces may actually be bad both for eyesight and for reason, as indeed we find in the case of Gubbio. If not bad, moreover, such views may be at the very least most painful to bear. The telescope too, while promising greater power to human sight, may give pain with insight and may reduce the human condition to microscopic proportions.

Pirandello's views on the effects of the telescope, film art, and advances in the techniques of "illumination" illustrate and extend the notion of ironic distance proposed by German Idealists years before the invention of cinema. Pirandello himself cites G. P. Richter's definition of "romantic humor" as the kind of humor that is caused by "the serious attitude of the person who compares the small finite world with the infinite idea" (Hum:108, Lum:122).[21] The ironic posture which assumes a serious distance from which to oversee the dilemmas and paradoxes of daily living may ultimately lead, in the wider tradition of irony, to a positive (if painful) insight which towers above the intense pessimism and dizzying voids contemplated at times by Pirandello. While irony (and its optical agents, be they telescope, electric bulb, or camera) can indeed frame humankind in a limiting fashion, it can also filter out the superfluities and pretensions and allow us to penetrate below the surfaces of appearance and illusion. When used in this way, the medium of cinema is the ideal medium to concretize the positive type of irony pointed to by Schlegel and his followers. Pirandello's "mechanical phantasmagoria" of life is then, indeed, *mechanically* mediated, and his "diabolical imp" (now equipped with the ideal technology for his operation) "takes apart the mechanism of each image, of each phantasm produced by the emotions" and does so "in order to see how it is made" (Hum:125, Lum:138–139). Art, Pirandello tells us, fixes life "in one moment or in various given moments—the statue in a gesture, the landscape in a temporary immutable perspective." But, he notes, it does not provide us with a flexible and continuous view of mutability. "What about the perpetual mobility of successive perspectives?" he asks, "What about the constant flow in which souls are?" (Hum:142, Lum:157).

Conventional art cannot transcend, Pirandello insists, the ordering perspectives of each individual artist's view of reality. It is clear from his fictional representation of the drama surrounding cinema that here we finally have one art form which displays the mobility, perspectives, and flow of life consistently and vividly, because of the inherent properties of its apparatus. Cinema thus may well be able to "take into account, as it should, the causes, the *real* causes that often move this poor human soul to the most mindless and totally unpredictable actions." Cinema at its best, moreover, can avoid the kind of representation which "oversimplifies nature and tends to make life too reasonable or at least too coherent" (Hum:142, Lum:157). As an art that "realizes" and gives structure to ironic vision, film thus provides a physical and permanent projection of the grotesque and comical shadows that Pirandello finds in some tragic situations as in those farces which might include "in the same representation of a tragedy also its parody and its caricature, but not as overlayed elements, but as the shadow projection of its own body, clumsy shadows of every tragic gesture" (Ir:995).

When interpreted in this light, Pirandello fully anticipates that later philosophical view of the medium which regards its structural essence as residing in the mechanics of perception and considers its importance as that of providing an analog to the process of human consciousness in the world. Film supports the philosophical view which maintains that

> the joy of art lies in its showing how something takes on meaning—not by referring to already established and acquired ideas but by temporal or spatial arrangements of elements. . . . A movie has meaning in the same way that a thing does: neither of them speaks to an isolated understanding; rather, both appeal to our power tacitly to decipher the world of men and to coexist with them. It is true that in our ordinary lives we lose sight of this aesthetic value of the tiniest perceived thing. It is also true that the perceived form is never perfect in real life, that it always has blurs, smudges, and superfluous matter, as it were. Cinematographic drama is, so to speak, finer-grained than real-life dramas: it takes place in a world that is more exact than the real world. But in the last

analysis perception permits us to understand the meaning of the cinema. A movie is not thought; it is perceived. (Merleau-Ponty 1947:941–942).[22]

The relation of art to understanding and the pursuit of meaning is fundamental to Pirandello's views as well as to Merleau-Ponty's. In both of these thinkers' views, moreover, the apt structuring of temporal and spatial elements overcomes the conventional and stereotypical views of reality and does so by that purer type of perception which is so central to Merleau-Ponty's thinking and which already in Pirandello's earlier formulations was assuming great importance as the critical and self-aware, perceptive stance of ironic distance. For Merleau-Ponty, of course, meaning can be achieved and the world can be deciphered in its relation to humanity. For Pirandello, by contrast, it is only the eternal struggle to pursue such a meaning that characterizes life and is therefore the suitable subject for stories. Such meaning, when achieved, he considers utterly illusory. As Dante della Terza summarizes this aspect of Pirandello's thinking,

> Things do not mean, they are: the meaning we attribute to them is an arbitrary construction, an illusion to be dismantled by the humoristic writer. There are, on the one hand, the subjective illusions and affections which would like to give a direction to the world; on the other there is the world, which stands indifferent and unmodifiable. Nothing is true except the sea, the mountain, the rock, the blade of grass; man cannot be true to himself because he continuously changes, cannot be true to the world because he can neither know nor modify it.
>
> The task of attempting in an ever-renewed act of heroic despair to bridge the gap between the unknown, unpredictable self and the mystery of the universe is entrusted to the character. (della Terza 1972:28)

Pirandello's detailed attention to the peculiarities of perception as made accessible through the new technology of cinema and his interest in the implications of this new form of vision for the psychological and spiritual history of humanity parallels in artistic terms Merleau-Ponty's extensive philosophical critique of modern scientific psychology and his exploration of its philosophical implications. The outcome is hopeless in Pirandello and hopeful in Merleau-Ponty; but the drama is the same: the construction of meaning out of idiosyncratic interaction of the individual with the things of the world.

Film art, as Pirandello depicts it, provides a new "finer-grained" and "more exact" picture of the world. The meaning-laden aspect of objects in reality is set into the frame by cinematic selection. Pirandello's representation of film in this novel assumes that "in immediate reality the availability of the object causes it to lose its implicative value. At the cinema, on the contrary, objects are present in their signifying guise. . . . They are introduced into a reality which is oriented. It is *this* table's 'necessity of being there' which implies the 'necessity of being there' of all possible tables and, through that, the 'idea table.' If you like, that emphasis which escapes us in reality is emphasized by the film image, more so since what is implied in the film is less the object itself than an aspect of that object, an *image*" (Mitry 1963/65:I, 128, my translation). There is no question that the objects and beings isolated on screen, in a photograph, in a mirror by Pirandello are indeed captured in their essence and significance. It is not merely a generalized significance either, but one that through the personal "readings" of Nuti, Nestoroff, and Gubbio is brought to our attention as the individual significance we all tend to feel within film images.

Part Two

Nabokov

3
Memory Unreals

Vladimir Nabokov, as both his fiction and his interviews make clear, was acutely concerned as an artist with issues of epistemology and ontology. His use of film, let me suggest, provides an essential clue to his underlying views of knowing and being. Explaining to an interviewer his notion of the role the poet plays in focusing a sequence of simultaneous, unrelated events into "an instantaneous and transparent organism," Nabokov turns to television as an example of the kind of synthesis which is possible only through cinematic technology. He states that "the simultaneousness of . . . random events, and indeed the fact of their occurring at all as described by the central percipient, would only then conform to 'reality' if he had at his disposal the apparatus to reproduce those events optically within the frame of one screen; but the central figure in the passage you quote," he points out to the interviewer, "is not equipped with any kind of video attached to his lawn chair and must therefore rely on the power of pure imagination" (SO:154).

This direct juxtaposition of elusive inner states of artistic invention with a concretizing technology that one usually regards either as a vehicle for unimaginative formulaic popular entertainment or as best suitable to the reproduction of the factual, objective details of the surfaces of existence is startling in its parallels to what we have found in Pirandello. There too an abstract mental insight (irony) is seen as concretized and made visible through the novel mediation of cinematic technology. Like Pirandello, Nabokov suggests that the structural peculiarities of cinema and its mechanical facilities may provide a surface upon which to project visibly the invisible contents of the mind. In no sense am I suggesting of course that Nabokov saw film as a possible substitute for verbal art forms or for the workings of the imagination. But the process and conditions of writing on the one hand and the contributing factors of memory and imagination on the other are consistently presented by Nabokov as akin to the mechanisms of photography and cinematography. As his son recalls being told in 1975 during their last walk together, "his writing . . . was all there, ready inside his mind, like film waiting to be developed" (D. Nabokov 1979:129). The choice concerning which language to use in concretizing these latent emulsions is embodied for an interviewer by a statement such as this: "Images are mute, yet presently the silent cinema begins to talk and I recognize its language" (Robinson 1979:123).

Nabokov's autobiography *Speak, Memory* provides a wealth of examples to show that if in Pirandello the tight interaction between projected images and personal life is a topic for fiction, in Nabokov's case it is first of all an area of individual experience for the novelist himself. Nabokov thus displays a wider phenomenology of individual interactions with images and reflects a more complex range of attitudes about images than does Pirandello.

In his characterization of the poet's imagination as a split-screen image that might be produced by the far-flung mobile units of a major television network, we find a concentrated example of his tendency to describe images of invention and images of memory in the manner Anthony Manser defines as "the conventional view of the imagination"—that is, in the guise of "'mental pictures' which are in many ways like actual perceptions of external objects." Traceable back to such views as Hume's description of perceptions as actual impressions in the physical sense, such a way of regarding mental images "leads to the belief that images are some sort of mental picture, a kind of internal analogue to a real picture or photograph." Nabokov's image for such processes in imaginative creation and in memory is precisely of the kind described by Manser (1966:20–21).[1]

Nabokov seems to have stored a host of personal memory images on a variety of photographically related surfaces. Such a one is the "wonderland" traversed by Nabokov's imaginative Mademoiselle on the way to the Nabokov country house in *Speak, Memory*. The Russian winter scene, village lights, snow, sleighs, moon, and clouds are presented at first as a beautiful three-dimensional magic-lantern projection and then made to fade into a parallel present reality, as "somehow the two sleighs have slipped away, leaving behind a passportless spy standing on the blue-white road in his New England snowboots and storm-coat." The photographic emulsion retaining the past and the impressions (similar but different) of the present are thus articulated on the basis of images regarded as concrete, repeatable, photolike traces. The "stereoscopic dreamland" becomes the present moment filled with echoes of loss, the elements of which are held in suspension on the photographic emulsion figured further in the surface of a mirror: "The vibration in my ears is no longer their receding bells but only my old blood singing. All is still, spellbound, enthralled by the moon, fancy's rearvision mirror. The snow is real, though, and as I bend to it and scoop a handful, sixty years crumble to glittering frost dust between my fingers" (SpM:99–100). The poignant awareness of time lost and place dissolved is captured here by means of photolike memory images just as the same consciousness is forced upon Pirandello's Nuti by a photograph of his father.

The personal need to hold onto a lost past, and the additional fact that this particular loss entails, through exile, even the loss of access to objects and places from that past, may well explain the intensity in Nabokov's writing of the naïve-realist fallacy described by Manser as the illusion that from the pictures in one's mind, "from these internal snapshots we can obtain information in the same way that we can obtain information from a real snapshot," and that "memory consists partially in looking at our picture collection" (Manser 1966:21). Impressions are deposited in Nabokov's mind in a most photographic way. Of his repeated visits to his parents' rooms he observes that "this accumulation of familiar things in the dark" seemed to be "doing its utmost to form the definite and permanent image that repeated exposure did finally leave in my mind" (SpM:89). The memory *is* as if physically engraved into his mind. Actual family snapshots are even "mounted" by Nabokov into *Speak, Memory* as a veritable parody of family albums, captions included. Even such humble artifacts are shown capable of summarizing a whole life. The caption to one (SpM, opposite p. 256) outlines all the elements in the photograph, from the date, to the title of the novel Nabokov is seen in the process of writing, to the formal echo represented by the checkerboard tablecloth, to his cigarettes, ink bottle, ashtray, photographs, dictionary, penholder, setting boards, all of it in a practical demonstration of the brimming richness of fact and meaning that a photograph may contain within its frame.

Images are there, tantalizing in their presence, suggestive of a reality that was there in the past but is now lost, and open to the paradigmatic interventions of subjectivity precisely because of the syntagmatic gaps they emphasize. Their very inability to represent fully the reality they suggest opens them to the personal truths of the subject. Photographs and optically created images are Nabokov's recurring concretization of these issues because the photograph summarizes them on a surface. "While the scientist sees everything that happens in one point of space," says the anagrammatic Vivian Bloodmark to Vladimir Nabokov, "the poet feels everything that happens in one point of time" (SpM:218). Photographic reproduction and the semblance of life which movement can add to it allow time to be captured in one space and, by being miniaturized upon photographic emulsion, to be transported anywhere else in time and space.

It is the figurative power of this process which strikes Nabokov, who isolates it in a metaphorical snapshot in an account of his memories of first reading *War and Peace*. The place, the setting, and the surroundings of the occasion have all been as if gathered upon the surface of a photograph and are now forever placed between the pages of the novel. The event, Nabokov tells us, took place "in Berlin, on a Turkish sofa, in our somberly rococo Privatstrasse flat giving on a dark, damp back garden with larches and gnomes that have remained in that book, like an old postcard, forever" (SpM:199). The expansive contiguities of setting and occasion are gathered into the frame of a utilitarian photographic artifact. Memory gathers the diverse and far-flung elements onto the small surface of a postcard, just as imagination is said to reach well beyond the capacities of the human organism through an ideal television screen. Family snapshot, postcard, and television are the kinds of visual representation that are usually regarded as more utilitarian than aesthetic in aim. The nonaesthetic choice is deliberate, I believe, for Nabokov delves into the function of such representations at the level of their deep, personal, essential power rather than making them the object of aesthetic considerations.

Even home movies will do for this purpose. We are shown precisely through this humble medium the unsettling power of moving images to manipulate our consciousness of time and space. The anecdote that opens *Speak, Memory* is strikingly reminiscent of the experience ascribed to Aldo Nuti by Pirandello. It illustrates the psychological panic experienced by a young man "when looking for the first time at homemade movies that had been taken a few weeks before his birth" (SpM:19). Like Nuti's meditation about the photograph of his father taken before his own birth, and reversing Nuti's analysis of the effect of his own film image upon spectators after his death, Nabokov's young man "saw a world that was practically unchanged—the same house, the same people—and then realized that he did not exist there at all and that nobody mourned his absence" (SpM:19). An existential insight is thus given concrete form by the film medium yet again: the family snapshot's tendency to confirm the past presence of things is transcended by the moving picture's tendency to emphasize the absence of what it shows in such a lifelike manner.[2] The sense of the absence of what the film shows leads directly to the spectator's self: "He caught a glimpse of his mother waving from an upstairs window, and that unfamiliar gesture disturbed him, as if it were some mysterious farewell. But what particularly frightened him was the sight of a brand-new baby carriage standing there on the porch, with the smug encroaching air of a coffin; even that was empty, as if, in the reverse course of events, his very bones had disintegrated" (SpM:19). Running the film backward will actually produce this effect in a most comical way (a cliché in film slapstick), but the metaphysical *angst* of such comedy (an insight made possible by the technical conditions of the medium) amounts to but a fraction of the chilling effect that this home movie produces. The direct experience of one's own absence from the world is concretely visible in the photographic presence of everything but the subject. Even the space ready to receive the self—the empty perambulator—underlines this, as well as the fact that this prenatal absence is but a prophecy of the more definitive absence after death, an absence that awaits us all.

Nabokov turns the same cluster of elements to fictional use in *Laughter in the Dark,* where Albinus reacts to the news of his daughter's birth by visualizing "a fine dark rain like the flickering of some very old film (1910, a brisk jerky funeral procession with legs moving too fast)" (L:18), while his feelings about the possibility of leaving his mistress and returning to his wife are embodied in a concise image the elements of which we readily recognize: "This future seemed to him like one of those long, dim, dusty passages where one finds a nailed-up box—or an empty perambulator" (L:178–179). The filmlike precision and succinctness of this image, and the fact that its meaning is conveyed to the reader exclusively in the manner of film expression (the image speaks for itself) is not surprising when we find that the image may well derive from dimly remembered home movies. Such a deceptively simple genre does indeed evoke the technical simplicity, the bare-bones directness, the emotional regression, and the thinly disguised view of the cast and materials of one's most intimate psychodramas, which are also characteristic of that other "primitive" film genre, the porn movie—a connection which in recent years has lead a novelist to entitle one of her novels *Kinflicks* (Alther 1976).

In being so thoroughly imbued with subjective selectivity and with significance of a kind that points beyond the actual content of the image, Nabokov's photographic and cinematographic images are therefore very much like the imaginative concretizations discussed by phenomenologists such as Sartre and Bachelard. But his own concretizations and those he provides for his characters are always lent extra presence by the "opaque residue" of photographic emulsions, the residue which is absent, according to Sartre, from mental images. Nabokov's films and photographs capture in a physical sense the impression of vivid presence that mental images give forth. It is an impression that philosophers tell us is only an illusion but which experience teaches us (and languages enshrine this in their colloquial metaphors) is the overwhelming purpose of imaginative concretizations. This may well be the reason why film as an experience exercises upon us a power well beyond its ostensible contents.

It is a power that explains why Nabokov, an author who is usually remembered for the broad satire he aims at the surface contents of popular cinema—"for it is always windy in filmland," remarks a character in *Laughter in the Dark* (L:118)—should suggest that in its essential structures the medium may well be an acceptable analogue to the mechanism of poetic creation. Nabokov's multiple image and its far-flung cameras illustrates what Sigfried Kracauer calls the film medium's "chimerical desire to establish the continuum of physical existence" (Kracauer 1960:63, 64). The integration of poetic consciousness and the geographical freedom of movable cameras allows ultimately for the kind of novel concretization of human consciousness described recently by Jean-Louis Baudry, who points out that the human eye and subjectivity absorb and become conscious of the transcendence suggested by camera situations. "To seize movement is to become movement, to follow a trajectory is to become trajectory, to choose a direction is to have the possibility of choosing one, to determine a meaning is to give oneself a meaning. In this way the eye-subject, the invisible base of artificial perspective (which in fact only represents a larger effort to produce an ordering, regulated transcendence) becomes absorbed in, 'elevated' to a vaster function, proportional to the movement which it can perform." Ultimately, in Baudry's view, "the movability of the camera seems to fulfill the most favorable conditions for the manifestation of the 'transcendent subject'" (Baudry 1974/75:43, 44). Leaving aside the specifics of particular philosophical claims that Nabokov does not make, it appears that implicit in Nabokov's statement is a bold assumption shared with Kracauer and Baudry that the form of the medium points in the direction of meaningful, all-encompassing aims and that as a consequence humankind may absorb a new coherence and sharpness of vision from the syntax of epistemology peculiar to this medium.

Nabokov deploys a wealth of optical media that are capable of providing such deepened experience and a large number of contexts in which one may encounter this kind of concretization. He presents a whole range of technologies and situations which involve photography, magic lanterns, television, as well as scientific instruments related in one way or another to cinematography. He ends up by outlining a veritable anatomy of modern optical technologies and plumbs their fictional, conceptual, and figurative implications. As far as they relate to his own self, this has the effect of punctuating his personal history and inner imaginative anatomy with a parallel exploration of optics and photography that is encyclopedic in its erudition and that covers a wide historical range. The close refraction of personal history through cinema thus produces in Nabokov an effect much like that described by Baudry:

> You see why historians of cinema, in order to unearth its first ancestor, never leave off dredging a pre-history which is becoming increasingly cluttered. From the magic lantern to the praxinoscope and the optical theater up to the *camera obscura*, as the booty piles up, the excavations grow. . . . But if cinema was really the answer to a desire inherent in our psychical structure, how can we date its first beginnings? . . . It is very possible that there was never any first invention of cinema. Before being the outcome of technical considerations and of a certain state of society's development . . . it was primarily the target of a desire which, moreover, its immediate success as well as the interest which its ancestors had aroused has demonstrated clearly enough. A desire, to be sure, a form of lost satisfaction which its apparatus would be aimed at rediscovering in one way or another (even to the point of simulation) and to which the impression of reality would seem the key. (Baudry 1976:113)

The "impression of reality" is indeed one of the keys to the power of this technology, and the importance of resolving the inherent paradox of its images leads to some of Nabokov's most poignant explorations of photography and film. The paradox inherent in such images, a contradiction, which Nabokov feels as keenly as does Pirandello, between their claim to truth and their limited, conventionalized mediation, comes to be a key factor in his use of film, photography, and optical instrumentation.

Perhaps more than many other artists, and certainly in a way that differs radically from most of them, Nabokov knew directly of the problems one encounters in trying to define the status of reality as it appears through optical mediation. From his interest and work in lepidopterology he derived a keen awareness of the variable interaction of subjectivity and specialized knowledge. He knew from his work on butterflies what has been stated by different students of the process of imaging such as Jean-Paul Sartre and Ernst Gombrich: we *see* what we *know*. Lack of knowledge to accompany the act of seeing makes us quite blind, in life as well as when we activate our memories. Ignorance will produce, for example, such "lep-less" memory landscapes as those which Nabokov remembers of Italy before 1906, the year in which he started learning about butterflies (SpM:129–130). A similar kind of knowledge was imparted by his drawing teacher, "the celebrated Dobuzhinski," to the young Nabokov, who thus learned to visualize in the greatest detail objects he had seen and to use an educated memory for his artistic endeavors (SpM:92). In Nabokov's autobiographical discourse, the artistic expertise is combined with his zoological knowledge in a manner that gives equal weight to the scientific and aesthetic elements. Both are combined, moreover, through the unifying link of optical technology during those "seven years at the Harvard Museum of Comparative Zoology" during which Nabokov immersed himself "in the bright wellhole of a microscope to record in india ink this or that new structure." Most typically, then, the scientific interest and its practice of objective observation triggers in Nabokov an aesthetic response which is characterized by interest in the mediating optical apparatus. The realities of knowledge and of imagination are as if poised at the intersection of mechanism and mind. As is made clear by his comparison of poetic imagination with the gathering of dispersed images on a video screen, Nabokov balances in an unusually even-handed way a view of art that considers the poetic image as an "organism" with a view that conceives of it as a projection of a newfangled "apparatus to reproduce [multiple] events optically within the frame of one screen." As he points out in his *Envoi* to his students at Cornell, "the thrill of pure science is just as pleasurable as the pleasure of pure art. The main thing is to experience that tingle in any department of thought or emotion" (LoL:382). He was able, it seems, to perceive the same tingle in both, and the technologies related to cinematography seem to have formed an effective link. Nabokov thus transcends the traditional opposition between seeing with the eyes of a scientist and seeing with the eyes of an artist, an opposition reflected, for instance, in Bachelard's point that the "phenomenology of the man with the magnifying glass" does not include the common kind of scientific worker for it excludes the one who "has a discipline of objectivity that precludes all daydreams of the imagination. He has already seen what he observes in the microscope and, paradoxically, one might say that he never sees anything for the first time" (Bachelard 1969:156).[3]

Nabokov affirms this intimate bond between scientist and artist by referring to a "machine" that demonstrates quite literally his metaphor of the artistic imagination. He points out that his work at Harvard was in fact also useful to his activities as a writer, activities he describes as the "camera-lucida needs of literary composition" (SpM:92). The Latin tag is not merely a reversal of the most commonly known precursor of the modern camera, meant to remind us perhaps that the creations of the imagination are still brighter than those of mechanical mediation. It actually refers to the attachment Nabokov would have found complementing his microscope at Harvard and which allows "the rays of light from an object" to be "reflected by a peculiarly shaped prism" so as to "produce an image on paper placed beneath the instrument whilst the eye at the same time can see directly the pencil with which the image is being traced."[4] While the able hand of the tracing artist present within the design is often quite visible in Nabokov's work (in the form of hints about his craftsmanlike interventions in *Speak, Memory,* in the person of a "sadistic" artist such as Axel Rex in *Laughter in the Dark*), the peculiar mediation of a prism needed to transform the real object into the beautiful projection waiting to be traced is also an integral part of his aesthetic consciousness. Of Proust's peculiar mediation between the facts of the past and the poetic images of its re-creation he has stated: "Proust is a prism. His, or its, sole object is to refract, and by refracting to recreate a world in retrospect." Citing the French critic Arnaud Dandieu, Nabokov defines the evocation of the past performed by Proust in terms that confirm the central role of lighted images: "Evocation of the past . . . is made possible by bringing to light a number of exquisitely chosen moments which are a sequence of illustrations, of images." Nabokov even picks out Dandieu's notion that the literary text is but an extended rhetorical image ("an extended comparison revolving on the words 'As if—'") in a manner that seems to balance the verbal with the visual (LoL:208).

But if we only follow Nabokov's *camera lucida* a little further down the alphabetical columns of one of his favorite haunts (the *Oxford English Dictionary*), we find that the same instrument is also the oldest known type of projector, "a contrivance of Dr. Hook, for making the image of anything appear on a wall in a light room, either by day or night."[5] The bridge between early optical instruments and film projector is thus complete, in the way remarked upon by Baudry and in a context that even echoes Baudry's resonant evocation of the intimate triple link between the essential structure of such technology, the creative will of the imagination, and the desires of past memories recaptured.[6]

A recurring occasion such as the yearly birthdays and namedays which used to take place in the alley of birches, limes, and maples in the garden at Vyra is thus structured in film-mimetic ways (some openly noted by Nabokov). Nabokov recreates the occasion by proceeding from a silent representation of the memory to the moment when "the colors and outlines settle at last to their various duties" (a more generally filmic introductory trope involving fade-in or focus-shift) and then to the instant when "some knob is touched and a torrent of sound comes to life: voices speaking all together, a walnut cracked, the click of a nutcracker carelessly passed, thirty human hearts drowning mine with their regular beats; the sough and sigh of a thousand trees, the local concord of loud summer birds, and, beyond the river, behind the rhythmic trees, the confused and enthusiastic hullabaloo of bathing young villagers, like a background of wild applause" (SpM:171–172). We find in this delayed introduction of a soundtrack conceived of as distinct from the visual track not merely an awareness of the peculiar technical conditions of cinematography. Nabokov here uses sound to shift from detail to detail and to suggest a complex spatial continuity. The whole scene opens up slowly in front of our "hearing" eyes until we are faced with a specific kind of film-stylistic option: the flowing and continuous exploration of a deep and complex space.

But this memory is distinctly cinematic also in purely visual terms. The poet approaches the scene with the smooth and directional deliberation of a camera track, "always . . . from the outside, from the depth of the park—not from the house—as if the mind, in order to go back thither, had to do so with the silent steps of a prodigal, faint with excitement" (SpM:171). The optical peculiarities of the scene are noted, both "the animation of light and shade beneath a moving, a fabulous foliage" and the "tremulous prism" through which he sees "the features of relatives and familiars, mute lips serenely moving in forgotten speech" (SpM:171).

Nabokov also reveals a cinematic reflex when he singles out movement such as "the stream of the chocolate" and "the small samara that gently descends upon the tablecloth." Yet this is not merely movement in general, something that the medium (Arnheim reminds us) always seeks out as what it does best. Nabokov's stream and samara provide the slow and extended movement that (Epstein notes) tends to convey through the means of cinematography the immediate sensation of time.[7]

Finally, his tutors appear through a quite openly named cinematic trick: "In the place where my current tutor sits, there is a changeful image, a succession of fade-ins and fade-outs; the pulsation of my thoughts mingles with that of the leaf shadows and turns Ordo into Max and Max into Lenski and Lenski into the schoolmaster, and the whole array of trembling transformations is repeated" (SpM:171). Cinematic technology is indicated here, as well as a simile between the flickering light and shade of trees and the mechanical innards of the camera.

Photography and its projections are such a strong presence in Nabokov's work because photography, as we saw above, is the model for his acquisition of memory. But it also represents one pole of what he sees as the intersection between knowledge and imagination. "There is," he tells us "in the dimensional scale of the world a kind of delicate meeting place between imagination and knowledge, a point, arrived at by diminishing large things and enlarging small ones, that is intrinsically artistic" (SpM:166–167). This thought is suggested to Nabokov by the intersection of two powerful experiences in his life: the memory of the frequent magic-lantern shows organized by one of those tutors whom we have left fading in and out in the garden, and the much later experience of looking "at the radiant bottom of a microscope's magic shaft" (SpM:166). The microscopic image of "precise and silent beauty" seems to him equivalent to what he saw as a child when, foregoing the view of these primitive screen projections, he would look at the magic-lantern slides in his hand. "How tawdry and tumid they looked," he observes, "those jellylike pictures, projected upon the damp linen screen (moisture was supposed to make them blossom more richly), but, on the other hand, what loveliness the glass slides as such revealed when simply held between finger and thumb and raised to the light—translucent miniatures, pocket wonderlands, neat little worlds of hushed luminous hues!" (SpM:166). In his perception that the reduction of large landscapes intensified the experience of looking at them, Nabokov echoes Ruskin's words about the small plates of Venice which he said appeared "as if a magician had reduced the reality to be carried away into an enchanted land" (cited in Kracauer 1960:4). Bachelard too, despite the distinction which he makes between poet and scientist (a distinction that does not hold for Nabokov), articulates the same feelings and connections expressed by the novelist.

As in Bachelard's programmatic words in the introduction to *The Poetics of Space,* Nabokov's attitude here suggests that "small and large are not to be seized in their objectivity" since they are (metaphorically for Bachelard but quite literally for Nabokov) "the two poles of a projection of images." The ultimate purpose for both is the aim of "participating more intimately in the movement of the image." Bachelard's conclusion "that [in certain poems] the impression of immensity is in us, and not necessarily related to an object" (Bachelard 1969:xxxiv–xxxv) dovetails with Nabokov's perception that the actual miniature slide (be it one for the magic lantern or for the microscope) contains immensities of detail, of beauty, of poetry which belie its minuscule size and which depend as much on the beholder as on the beheld. Such miniature images of reality are for Nabokov the essential kernels of adult imagination, leading as they do in a natural continuum from a child's miniature toys to the adult "daydreams of born dreamers" (Bachelard 1969:149) (the child Nabokov climbs into the picture on the wall just like the Hesse character cited by Bachelard [SpM:86, Bachelard 1969:150]). The adult scientific inquirer (Bachelard's botanist, Nabokov the lepidopterist) finds again through the optical instrument "the enlarging gaze of a child" and for both "the minuscule, a narrow gate, opens up an entire world" (Bachelard 1969:155). The "dream instrument" of such examples extends also in Bachelard to the kind of optical mediation that adds poetry to the real or allows man to seize dimensions of reality not seen before. The "glass cyst" through which, Bachelard tells us, André Pieyre de Mandiarhues is said to "call forth an entire world" is a reducing lens that forms an image as minuscule as Nabokov's slide. "We can read the landscape in the glass nucleus. We no longer look at it while looking through it. This nucleizing nucleus is a world in itself. The miniature deploys to the dimensions of a universe." As is the case with Nabokov's illustration, "large is contained in small" (Bachelard 1969:157).

Like the views through the right and the wrong ends of Pirandello's telescope, such optically reduced immensities suggest metaphysical implications. As Bachelard points out, "miniature is an exercise that has metaphysical freshness; it allows us to be world conscious at slight risk." Bachelard even outlines the philosophical syllogism which is implicit in the closely perceived interaction between small and large: "Sometimes the transactions between small and large multiply, have repercussions. Then, when a familiar image grows to the dimensions of the sky, one is suddenly struck by the impression that, correlatively, familiar objects become the miniatures of a world. Macrocosm and microcosm are correlated" (Bachelard 1969:169–170). Nabokov's own thoughts triggered by seeing the scale of the universe reversed at the bottom of his microscope extend also to fictional exploration in *Laughter in the Dark,* where a bird's-eye view of events on earth does also suggest an insight into the relative minuteness of things which at ground-level appear at full size. In such autobiographical and fictional elaborations we find a poet ready to respond to the implications outlined by Bachelard. Nabokov confirms that, in Bachelard's words, "tiny and immense are compatible" and "a poet is always ready to see large and small" (Bachelard 1969:172). The view through microscope or telescope is the same, and for Nabokov, film, photography, and projections (as he actually holds a sample of their mediating surface in his hand) are viable metaphors; just as they are for Bachelard, who points out that "we have in our memories micro-films that can only be read if they are lighted by the bright light of the imagination" (Bachelard 1969:175).

On a more philosophical level, however, these augmented views of reality focus underlying issues of epistemology, some of which Nabokov addresses directly. Scientific study through optical mediation raises questions, just as does the powerful illusion of presence and reality provided by film images. Knowledge is important, as we saw, but since different people know quite different things, the democratic lily does not, after all, belong equally to all. "Reality is a very subjective affair," Nabokov tells us. He defines it "as a gradual accumulation of information; and as specialization. If we take a lily, for instance, or any other kind of natural object, a lily is more real to a naturalist than it is to an ordinary person: but it is still more real to a botanist. And yet another stage of reality is reached with that botanist who is a specialist in lilies." Specialized knowledge and a professional point of view will reveal successive layers and different cross sections of reality. But such increasingly microscopic looks into the "real," those looks through "the bright wellhole" now widely available to modern man—be s/he botanist, entomologist, or artist—will ultimately present him with a worrisome multiplicity of vistas. Greater and more precise knowledge leads to a paradoxical succession of receding optical illusions. "You can get nearer and nearer, so to speak, to reality; but you never get near enough because reality is an infinite succession of steps, levels of perception, false bottoms, and hence unquenchable, unattainable. You can know more and more about one thing but you can never know everything about one thing: it's hopeless" (SO:10–11). Photography and film have concretized this human dilemma about the nature of reality just as they have the tensions of irony. Nabokov consciously explores the poignancy of this situation, a poignancy made deeper by the tantalizing illusion of control and of permanence suggested by the diaphanous projections of these media.

Cinema has indeed brought us more: the realities invisible to the naked eye that are made visible by Vertov's camera; the views that Jean Epstein thought were destined to open to us a "reality of another dimension." Yet, for all its "startling physics and strange mechanics," this mediated reality is "but a portrait—seen in a certain perspective—of the world in which we live" (Epstein cited in Kracauer 1960:319). It is a profound and alienating perspective, as Kracauer points out in a programmatic epilogue to his *Theory of Film,* which explains his own opposition to anything but a naturalistic use of the medium. In pursuing the optically enhanced visions of the world that provoke unattainable images such as those cited by Nabokov, humanity may lose the directly available and intimate knowledge of earth, the "thingness" of things. For the practicing scientist, the elusive and relative nature of reality presents a problem in observation and description. For the artist the existential yearning for a solid ground and the tantalizing mirror tricks of ambiguous reflective surfaces offer a temptation and a challenge. Nabokov explores both options. Moreover, he follows through the implications of Rudolph Arnheim's objections to Kracauer: "Man's senses are geared to a particular range of magnitude, located between the atomic and the astronomic realm, and in this realm we observe conglomerations of shapes that lack most of the simplicity found at other cosmic levels. This intricate landscape is our reality in the most immediate sense. But it is not the only reality to which the human mind can refer. Whether, in trying to answer the question: what is reality? we look at what is close at hand or what is remote, apparent to the eye or hidden, superficial or essential, shaped or unshaped, is a matter of philosophical outlook or, aesthetically, of style" (Arnheim 1966:183). This state of affairs, emphasized by modern scientific developments and brought to the personal experience of all by the ubiquitous presence of film and television, is a valid dilemma despite Stanley Cavell's remark that "it is a sad use of a few philosophical terms which discovers that pictures were never really objective on the ground that they were never perfect replicas of reality." To this Cavell adds dismissively that "every semester somebody seems to make this discovery" (Cavell 1971:115). But could the philosopher be missing the point here? The discovery is actually made anew every time any of us sits down in a darkened theater to face what must seem as the most perfect replica of reality ever produced, only then to experience by surreptitious accretions that the reality we view is well beyond the means of our all-too-human perceptions. The discovery, in other words, is an integral, recurring part of film experience.

Nabokov's words about the optical foundations of photographs and films (in memories and in fictions they press similar discoveries upon author, upon characters, upon readers) lead to a position that must necessarily "reject the idea that there is some test of realism or faithfulness in addition to the tests of pictorial goodness and descriptive truth." As the philosopher Nelson Goodman, whose words these are, insists in his attempt to define "the way the world is," a separation must be made between the possible truthfulness of any account of the world and the irrelevant relation of such truthfulness to criteria of realism, which are inevitably culture-bound and variable. This applies as much to photographic reproduction (the kind of image, that is, in which according to tradition depiction and denotation are supposed to coalesce) as it does to painting and to verbal expression. "There are very many different equally true descriptions of the world," concludes Goodman, "and their truth is the only standard of their faithfulness. And when we say of them that they all involve conventionalizations, we are saying that no one of these different descriptions is *exclusively* true, since the others are also true. None of them tells us *the* way the world is, but each of them tells us *a* way the world is" (Goodman 1960:55).[8]

Nabokov's view of the way the world is involves an extensive interplay between the objectively observed and the subjectively understood. It is a constant application of the principle of human perception summarized by Goodman in the observation that reception and interpretation are inextricably intertwined, that "what has been received and what has been done to it cannot be distinguished within the finished product. Content cannot be extracted by peeling off layers of comment" (Goodman 1968:8). Nabokov's writings, autobiographical as well as fictional, articulate the problems and delights of the entanglements of perception, awareness, and interpretation often revealed through the mediation of film and photography. What he stresses for himself and for his characters are the pleasures and pains of the arbitrary in construing what life throws at us in its random and sometimes serendipitous way. Is there a pattern in the carpet? Perhaps! But there are challenges to our own receptivity, and we may make our own patterns in folding the carpet over. We may do so ourselves, in fact, for sheer aesthetic pleasure or when life forces us to fold up our carpets quite literally and carry them half way across the world from the Urals to the Rockies. "I confess," Nabokov tells us, "I do not believe in time. I like to fold my magic carpet, after use, in such a way as to superimpose one part of the pattern upon another. Let the visitor trip" (SpM:139).

The "folding" operation, one notes, produces the same results as traditional photographic superimposition and film montage, resulting in "sequences" (see the butterfly expeditions described in *Speak, Memory*) that convene their elements very much within the range of an ideal "screen" of the kind Nabokov refers to in his interview. They also echo the freedom of movement and the capacity to synthesize diverse elements into the illusion of one "world," which film critics such as Pudovkin have often cited as a typical aspect of the medium (Pudovkin 1960:83–89). The formal imitation of film montage and of lap-dissolves, for instance, are used to represent, with a directness greater than traditional verbal descants, experiences of displacement from place and time. Film mimetics is used to integrate the objective precision of scientific description and the dizzying sensation of a large geographical expanse with a direct recreation of the internal psychological syntax of personal exile. A vibrant, dynamic pictorial image is often used as the "cinematic" center of all this. The personal burden is carried upon wings such as those of the Russian swallowtail that once, in 1906,

> made for the open window, and presently was but a golden fleck dipping and dodging and soaring eastward, over timber and tundra, to Vologda, Viatka and Perm and beyond the gaunt Ural range to Yakutsk and Verkhne Kolymsk, and from Verkhne Kolymsk, where it lost a tail, to the fair Island of St. Lawrence, and across Alaska to Dawson, and southward along the Rocky Mountains—to be finally overtaken and captured, after a forty-year race, on an immigrant dandelion under an endemic aspen near Boulder. In a letter from Mr. Brune to Mr. Rawlins, June 14, 1735, in the Bodleian collection, he states that one Mr. Vernon followed a butterfly nine miles before he could catch him (*The Recreative Review or Eccentricities of Literature and Life,* Vol. 1, p. 144, London, 1821). (SpM:120)

The ironic commentary embedded into the scientific reference, cited by Nabokov with ostentatious pedantry, underlines the lesson that one man's recreation may well become another man's need to recreate a whole life and world upon the wayward flight path of a butterfly. It also illustrates the point, made by Jean-Louis Baudry, that the existentially significant and the poetically resonant may well be found in the midst of erudite pursuits and among the paraphernalia of earlier scientific tinkering. How pale Mr. Vernon's "record" appears by comparison to the implications of Nabokov's transcontinental life-consuming hunt.

While ironic commentary and the confusing accumulation of objective details try to evade the expressive poignancy of the poet's experience of loss and exile, such a poetic center is made available by the conditions of filmlike perception. The core of feeling in such passages can sometimes be reached only after the reader has followed Nabokov into the scientifically detailed landscapes and visualized the richness of color and structure hidden behind the nomenclature. Even more, the reader must notice the unheralded and surrealistic lap-dissolve from one habitat to another:

> Over the small shrubs of bog bilberry with fruit of a dim, dreamy blue, over the brown eye of stagnant water, over moss and mire, over the flower spikes of the fragrant bog orchid (the *nochnaya fialka* of Russian poets), a dusky, little Fritillary bearing the name of a Norse goddess passed in low, skimming flight. Pretty Cordigera, a gemlike moth, buzzed all over its uliginose food plant. I pursued rose-margined sulphurs, gray-marbled Satyrs. Unmindful of the mosquitoes that furred my forearms, I stooped with a grunt of delight to snuff out the life of some silver-studded lepidopteran throbbing in the folds of my net. Through the smells of the bog, I caught the subtle perfume which varies with the species—vanilla, or lemon, or musk, or a musty, sweetish odor difficult to define. Still unsated, I pressed forward. At last I saw I had come to the end of the marsh. The rising ground beyond was a paradise of lupines, colombines, and pentstemons. Mariposa lilies bloomed under Ponderosa pines. In the distance, fleeting cloud shadows dappled the dull green of slopes above timber line, and the gray and white of Longs Peak. (SpM:138–139)

The "editing" here is clearly of a kind noted by the first critic to study the structural influence of film style on modern literature, Claude Edmonde Magny, who describes such radical jump-cuts as one of the most dramatic of such techniques (Magny 1948:49 ff., 88 ff.). The "film style" embedded in such verbal texts allows for the anticipated appreciation of retroactive insights, such as the fact that the evocative merging of sound patterns and tropes of repetition expresses the feelings of the hunter rather than the hunted. The visual displacement and the sense of inevitable movement embedded in the film-mimetic text just below the verbal one transfers these feelings to the reader turned spectator. Only when the detailed landscapes have taken us to the unambiguously named American mountain do we fully comprehend the disruption of time and space that has affected the life of the young boy who so eagerly walked into that Russian swamp so many years ago.

"Poetry is positional" this boy tells us once he has grown. His need to hold together a disrupted life has helped to make him aware that "thinking of several things at a time" is a basic requirement of poetic ability as much as it is a desperate individual necessity in cases such as his. The cinematic metaphor, which posits a poet in Ithaca wired to a multiple-image screen containing the disparate and the far-flung (in time as well as in space), is thus a perfectly apt concretization of the idea of poetry as the attempt "to express one's position in regard to the universe embraced by consciousness" (SpM:218). It is also an aesthetic device which may provide a practical means of holding together the only remaining tracings of family history and personal memory.

It is cinema, thus, that often allows Nabokov to think about several things at once, when he is recalling his most cherished memories, and cinematic technology allows him to see the difficulty of keeping it all together. Repeated episodes of sexual individuation, for instance, are played out under the dim flickering lights of early cinemas, linked into a significant continuum by recurring images. One such, a "remembered rock" from Biaritz, actually appears on a screen in St. Petersburg during one of the late afternoons young Nabokov spends with Tamara in the cinematic setting of the young couple's breathless winter courtship (SpM:236). Biaritz (the real place from which the film rock comes) is the scene of Nabokov's earlier "elopement" with Colette, an escapade which ends in a setting quite similar to the one where the rock now appears: a "pitch-dark *cinéma* near the Casino (which, of course, was absolutely out of bounds)" (SpM:151). It is thus an image on a movie screen (an image that is also a personal memory image) that links the two occasions.

The comical and inexperienced Biaritz elopement of the youngsters who find refuge in the taboo darkness of the cinema while "holding hands across the dog which now and then gently jingled in Colette's lap," embodies the ever-present sexual charge of the movies. More overtly still do the gropings of the sexually maturing couple who find refuge in "the last row of seats in one of the two movie theaters . . . on Nevski Avenue," driven there by the frigid rigors of St. Petersburg's winter and by the voyeuristic and repressive interference of that "foul-mouthed veteran of the Turkish campaign" who "threatened to call the police" upon witnessing the couple's activities behind the tall display stands in the Russian Museum of Emperor Alexander III (SpM:151, 236). Yet the implicit eroticism of the film situation is explored well beyond the promises of untrammeled sexual revelations on the screen and the reality of shaded fumblings in the pits. Nabokov, for one thing, rebels openly against the submissive passivity and the voyeurism forced upon any spectator by the apparatus of film (Metz 1976:85–86; Metz 1975:60–61, 64). That this rebellion is fraught with sexual overtones was made clear by Gubbio who, while filming Nestoroff's erotic dance, hoped to transcend his own role as a mere bolt in the mechanical apparatus by pretending to "take part." Nabokov, however, engages a different kind of projection than Gubbio's, one more directly involved with himself. In the process he breaks down the conventions of film-narrative distance and forcibly restructures the genre melodramas seen on those screens (the "worlds" of Bauer, of Protozanov, of Meyerhold) so as to expose their links to himself.[9]

The author's subjective appropriation of the elements seen on screen is made humorously evident by the parallel characterization of two interlopers (one real, one film-imaged) who break into his widely separated romances and who are linked across "realities" by a recurring mimic peculiarity. We find a very real interloper in Biaritz in the person of the tutor who marches away from the cinema with the captive Nabokov, who meanwhile notices with odd (and seemingly irrelevant) selectivity "the muscles of his grimly set jaw working under the tight skin" (SpM:151). On the screens of downtown St. Petersburg, on the other hand, a symbolic rival often appears in the person of the celebrated screen lover Mozhukhin. He always appears, notes Nabokov, while fixing "a steely eye on a light in one window while"—in a way reminiscent of the tutor's tic—"a celebrated little muscle twitched under the tight skin of his jaw" (SpM:237). The screen image thus confirms the similarity in "role" that these two men play in Nabokov's life.

The film novel also uses film to underline the subconscious meanings of others to oneself, over and beyond their "anecdotal" presence in films. As the twitching interlopers illustrate, in fact, such significance often hides a "story" of its own. The symbolic rival on screen in St. Petersburg is, on the face of it, a screen representation that might simply distract Nabokov's girlfriend and draw her attention away from her companion. He may force the real man in the audience, in other words, to metamorphose into a pathetic replica of the screen man, just as happened to the husband of the "Woman Who Married Clark Gable."[10] But as Bazin points out, actual jealousy of the featured performer belongs in a theatrical setting: what the screen tends to favor is an "identification" between actor and spectator.[11] In fact, as it turns out, Nabokov has good reason to identify with the "role" and even with the "setting" in ways that transcend his courtship of Tamara. The actor always arrives, Nabokov tells us (over and over again: a paradigmatic recurrence that breaks down the distinction between films and thus underlines the symbolic role of these actions as well as the essentializing tendency of the screen images) at a stately country mansion which, Nabokov observes, is "not unlike that of my uncle" (SpM:237). One notes that the identification of the screen image with his uncle's house is inserted into the text in what amounts to a disingenuously parenthetical aside, since the facts indicate that the house plays a greater role in the writer's life than the parenthesis would suggest. Nabokov's uncle Ruka died at the end of 1916, leaving the young Nabokov "a couple of million dollars and his country estate, with its white-pillared mansion on a green, escarped hill and its two thousand acres of wildwood and peatbog." Nabokov felt the loss of this in the revolution, he points out, not as a financial loss but as the loss of his childhood and of what, with evocative womblike imagery, he calls his "ecological niche" (SpM:72, 73). His remark, therefore, as in the movie house he watches his "Tara" with Tamara, discreetly displaces his personal connection with the house down the family network.

This strategy keeps at a distance the fact that the "other lover" on screen (the interloping double interfering with the love affair between the youngsters) recurrently invades what was to be the spectator's own house (the interloping double interfering with the love for his "ecological niche"). It is the house that was to belong to the adult Nabokov, a house he fully expected, at that time, to grow into. The image on screen is thus violently wrenched into deeply personal significance and serves to illustrate the notion formulated with effective succinctness by a film theorist who states that "what distinguishes the cinema is an extra reduplication, a supplementary and specific turn to the screw bolting desire to the lack" (Metz 1975:61).[12] The film image on the screen becomes Nabokov's pictorial analogy to his own "mute, shuttered" presence in the past. The image, by its nature, underlines separateness and unattainable wholeness (let us recall the nature of the unreal in the film image) in ways that echo the author's own separateness and unattainable wholeness following his exile.

But, as I said, Nabokov is quite aware that the balance of this technology, as it holds his far-flung memories together, is precarious at best. He seizes perceptively upon the kind of mechanical peculiarities that were first brought to his attention by one of those tutors we have left behind a few pages ago, fading in and out, in and out. It is one Lenski who, to teach his young charges the beauties of lyric poetry, used to provide them with a "montage" of poetry by Lermontov and slide projections of natural beauties meant, one presumes, for primarily didactic or documentary use. Lenski's attempts to recite the poetry in synchronization with a slide show fail. They produce only an awareness of the pedestrian and literal nature of icons that manage at most to illustrate the referential surface of the verse: "conventional peaks instead of Lermontov's romantic mountains," comments Nabokov (SpM:164). Yet he notices that imaginative élan is provided, on the other hand, by the unintended and serendipitous distortions and wipes that the primitive hand-removal of the slides from the magic lantern cause upon the screen. The comment is, in fact, quite remarkable, since it indicates a precocious recognition that the most "creative" results in the projection of images on a screen may often derive from the exploitation of what seem to be the shortcomings of the apparatus.

This is an insight that happens to be the foundation of one of the earliest theories of film as art, as well as a principle which later (Russian) film theory would regard as fundamental to the meaningful use of the medium.[13] The principle is that of multiple and parallel tracks (words, sounds, images, color), and it is upon the awareness of their creative separation that Nabokov bases the recognition of personal emotional associations to be found within images intended by their authors merely as "document" or "story." This happens, for instance, when Nabokov applies the creativity of asynchronous tracks to the films he used to see with Tamara in St. Petersburg. It is the primitive technology of those films, with their hand-applied tints and unsynchronized sound-machines, which helps to underline the personal meaning of a further image of absence and personal loss (it is now the rock from Biaritz) as it appears on the screen, out of "sea waves . . . tinted a sickly blue" (SpM:236). The sound of those waves, Nabokov notes with humor, extends beyond their proper syntagmatic realm in the text of film representation: the "special machine that imitated the sound of the surf, making a kind of washy swish . . . never quite managed to stop short with the scene but for three or four seconds accompanied the next feature" (SpM:236). These waves, with their contextually interfering additions to the diegetic illusion (meant to enhance it but by failing to do so opening the door to extracontextual associations), take Nabokov back to the elements within the illusion which are his own, just as the house did: "They rode in and burst into foam against a black, remembered rock (Rocher de la Vierge, Biaritz—funny, I thought, to see again the beach of my cosmopolitan childhood)" (SpM:236).

Eisenstein many years later was going to argue that precisely such a discrepancy between sound and image would open sound-film to the poetic and inspired exploitation of its means.[14] But in this early example of such an occurrence (although the result is indeed the initiation of expressive, subjective associations), the event is much closer to the kind of breakdown in the illusory apparatus analyzed most recently by Jean-Louis Baudry. Baudry argues that it is such breakdowns which allow the spectator, prisoner of illusion, to regain his freedom—precisely what Nabokov does by "recognizing" the film rock as his own. Just as in the archetypal model of this situation in Plato's cave, Baudry maintains that the "operators" and "machinists" must be kept out of sight "for, undoubtedly, by associating themselves with the objects they are moving back and forth before the fire, they would project a heterogeneous image capable of canceling the real-effect they want to produce: they would awaken the prisoner's suspicions; they would awake the prisoners" (Baudry 1976:109). Nabokov reveals precisely the kind of heightened awareness of the situation caused by "the disturbing effects which result during a projection from breakdowns in the recreation of movement, when the spectator is brought abruptly back to discontinuity—that is, to the body, to the technical apparatus which he had *forgotten*" (Baudry 1974/75:42). The breakdown in the illusion which Nabokov experiences occurs not in the recreation of movement but in that of sound which Baudry, talking again of the model represented by Plato's cave, points out as the most difficult to fake. Just as in Plato's cave, we find that the sound effects meant to fool the spectator are produced in the theater itself (Baudry 1976:110).

Such breakdowns in the diegetic illusion of cinematography, Baudry argues, are just like that aspect of the subconscious which "manifests itself as continuity destroyed, broken, and as the unexpected surging forth of a marked difference" (Baudry 1974/75:42). This difference, the discontinuity between image and image in the film, is very much like the imaged sensation of discrepancy and lack that Nabokov brings to consciousness when viewing these scenes. His own memories do indeed "surge forth" at the instigation of the film experiences he faces. Nabokov understands the images on the screen immediately at the subconscious level at which they appeal to most spectators but which average viewers do not readily perceive. Stanley Cavell has explained this most eloquently:

> The impact of movies is too massive, too out of proportion with the individual worth of ordinary movies, to speak politely of involvement. We involve the movies in us. They become further fragments of what happens to me, further cards in the shuffle of my memory, with no telling what place in the future. Like childhood memories whose treasure no one else appreciates, whose content is nothing compared with their unspeakable importance for me. . . . The movie's power to reach this level must have to do with the giantism of its figures, making me small again. . . . It must also have to do with the world it screens being literally of my world. (Cavell 1971:154–155)

The autobiographical and subconscious elements triggered by the imagery of cinema are easily activated by the double nature of film images, especially those usually dismissed as too stereotypical, as too much the common fare of "ordinary movies." This duality links personal memory images and film images because, as Jean Mitry has put it, "reality, seen through the film image, that is to say through a 're-presentation,' is somehow related to reality as seen through memory. The reality which appears as immediately there is given to us in a way very similar to the reality of dream and memory. It is the remembrance of an act we have not lived and that we know only through that remembrance which is at present unrolling in front of our eyes" (Mitry 1963/65:II, 266–267, my translation). Nabokov is thus the spectator who "recognizes" that the image presented on screen (a wave, a house) resonates well beyond its own syntagmatic context (the story or factual representation in which it occurs) and invades (seems to emerge from) his own personal stock of memories. We all go to the cinema, confirms Jean Louis Baudry, not so much to follow the referential aspects of its fictions as to ask it "about the wish it expresses" (Baudry 1976:112). This may explain why "spectator Nabokov" rarely tells us the plots of films: as he sees them, film images belong to the realm of his wish and desire.

Yet Nabokov's screen also could suddenly come "unmetaphored," somewhat in the way that it does for the fictional Gubbio when the permeable boundaries of paradigm and syntagma allow the metaphorical death bestowed by his camera to become quite real and cause the silence he enforced upon his actors to invade his own body. A few years after St. Petersburg, Nabokov found himself in Berlin, an exile, standing inside a literal screen, side by side with another exile, that very Mozhukhin who had foreshadowed Nabokov's exile from his home. They were both acting in the same film and, according to Andrew Field's report of Nabokov's testimony, Nabokov, being the only émigré with a decent looking dinner jacket, became the focus of the camera. According to Nabokov, "*I remember I was standing in a simulated theater in a box and clapping, and something was going on on an imaginary stage* (a real murder which the audience took to be part of the performance)" (Field 1977:159).

The sudden shift from one side of the screen to the other did not stop here, it seems. Nabokov's job as an extra led to the unsettling experience of recognizing himself unexpectedly on the screen of a cinema that he attended somewhat later with a friend. This must have made quite an impression on him, since the moment finds its way into his first novel, *Mary*. The story of Mary and Ganin, one notes, is closely related to the Tamara episode in *Speak, Memory*. What the novel stresses, even more than the biographical account, is the inherently alienating effect of film representation. This is true, beyond the moment of self-recognition on screen, in those episodes in which the novel, just as we found in Pirandello, captures the impersonal and chaotic nature of a modern city in cinematic terms. Ganin watches from the top deck of a moving bus while "down below the streets poured by, little black figures dashed around on the shiny sunlit asphalt, the bus swayed and thundered—and Ganin felt that this alien city passing before him was nothing but a moving picture" (M:56). The speed and fluidity, as well as the graphic reductionism, typical of movie street scenes is captured here just as it was through the eyes of Gubbio. What is new in Nabokov's treatment of the theme is the implicit metaphor that links the effect produced by film images to the feelings of an exile in whose eyes the city is distant and strange.

Yet the moment at which the disturbing interaction of the protagonist's self and his own image on screen resonates most deeply with the themes and feelings we have previously found in Pirandello is the moment modeled upon Nabokov's own biographical experience in a film with Mozhukhin. The actor (further ironic fold of the carpet) was appearing in Marcel L'Herbier's famous version of Pirandello's *Il fu Mattia Pascal* in the same year (1925) that Nabokov was working on his first novel. Is it merely coincidental that the exiled Ganin finds himself walking the streets of an alien city in which he and all his fellow exiles are living apart from their rightful identity and away from their rightful community in a manner most reminiscent of Mattia Pascal? The uncontrolled effects resulting from the doubling of one's sense of identity, and the feeling of being violated and alienated from oneself by the impersonation on screen, is a most Pirandellian moment of revelation. It is triggered, moreover, by a film image. It is also a narrative elaboration of the feelings intimated by Nabokov in *Speak, Memory* upon watching his interloping double (and future cast companion) playing the lover on screen and using "his own house" to do it in. Such exchanges of personality and such permeability between the separate realms of life and its representations are indeed reminiscent of Pirandello's explorations of the multifaceted permutations of identity and roles in his writings. Ganin often feels precisely as trapped as Mattia Pascal in his new identity and role, just as the pathetic film extras working with him on the film are forced to play parts (in threadbare stage costumes and surrealistic makeup) which are in fact much closer to their rightful roles in life (Russian nobility) than the roles they are allowed to play in real life now (exiles in a foreign land).

Ganin's recognition of himself and his subsequent thoughts develop these and similar topics with eloquence. The process is the kind of perceptive revelation we have seen taking place before: in Nuti's meditation upon his own image; in Nabokov's own analysis of home movies and his sense of time. The film that Ganin watches is in itself a commentary, involving as it does a protagonist (an opera singer) who breaks down because her role on stage forces her to act out a murder that she had committed in real life. But then "suddenly Ganin sensed that he was watching something vaguely yet horribly familiar. He recalled with alarm the roughly carpentered rows of seats, the chairs and parapets of the boxes painted a sinister violet, the lazy workmen walking easily and nonchalantly like blue-clad angels from plank to plank high up above, or aiming the blinding muzzles of klieg lights at a whole army of Russians herded together onto the huge set and acting in total ignorance of what the film was about" (M:30). The sense of ironic insight into a human condition in which the operators controlling the "story" are distant and aggressive, in which the conditions of "performing" are cold and uncomfortable, and in which the actors are ignorant of the "plot" in which they play a part is captured with chilling vividness and economy of means. Even the appearance of the world on screen and the apparent focus of the actors' actions are illusions: "On the screen that cold barn was now transformed into a comfortable auditorium, sacking became velvet, and a mob of paupers a theater audience. Straining his eyes, with a deep shudder of shame he recognized himself among all those people clapping to order, and remembered how they had all had to look ahead at an imaginary stage where instead of a prima donna a fat, red-haired, coatless man was standing on a platform between floodlights and yelling himself to insanity through a megaphone" (M:30).

What we do is not out of free choice at all, it seems, and we act at the orders of a frantic director bellowing orders through a megaphone. But this results in a split from our true selves ("Ganin's doppelgänger also stood and clapped over there") and in a heightened awareness of time and of the human condition in its impotence: "Ganin felt not only shame but also a sense of the fleeting evanescence of human life" while "now the scene showed an aging, world-famous actress giving a very skillful representation of a dead young woman. 'We know not what we do,' Ganin thought with repulsion, unable to watch the film any longer" (M:30–31).

The implications of what he has seen on screen, and its role as an ironic representation of his own condition, does not remain confined to the movie house. It pursues Ganin into the very streets of Berlin:

> As he walked he thought how his shade would wander from city to city, from screen to screen, how he would never know what sort of people would see it or how long it would roam round the world. And when he went to bed and listened to the trains passing through that cheerless house in which lived seven Russian lost shades, the whole of life seemed like a piece of film-making where heedless extras knew nothing of the picture in which they were taking part. (M:31)

In the same way (but with less awareness), Albinus Kretchmar will set out in his fictional adventures after seeing on a screen the crucial points of his life. He too will complain that he could not know what the film was about.

4

Albinus Fakes Movies

I

Nabokov's most consistent reaction to popular films in their public context is his awareness that the film image (just as in the very private realm we examined so far) is overwhelming in its insistent claim to presence and, as a consequence, to truth. But in formula films perceived uncritically or absorbed inertly, film tends to displace (as we saw happen in Gubbio's case) what is really important in life and to impose its own schematic simplifications upon life's teaming and idiosyncratic details. In the aesthetic economy of Nabokov's works, cinema thus stands side by side with all the other kinds of simplifying arts that may perhaps allow for a shorthand stylization of life, but do not ultimately provide enough substance and sustenance. It may well be feasible to say of Albinus Kretschmar: "Once upon a time there lived in Berlin, Germany, a man called Albinus. He was rich, respectable, happy; one day he abandoned his wife for the sake of a youthful mistress; he loved; was not loved; and his life ended in disaster." But as the author hastens to point out, this fairytale abridgment is teasing and insufficient: "Although there is plenty of space on a gravestone to contain, bound in moss, the abridged version of a man's life, detail is always welcome" (L:7).

A sensible attitude as spectators, therefore, demands awareness that this seemingly objective and neutral medium forces upon us the implications of stylization and a directorial point of view. We should question (as Albinus and Margot do not) whether what seems to be there is, in fact, what it seems. An ideal "reading" of the film image as it is presented in Nabokov's fiction requires the reconstructive subtlety that is also the precondition for the reading of what has been defined as stable irony. We have seen before such "reconstruction" at work in the rational discourse of Gubbio, Nuti, and others, all of whom try to cope with the various ironic dimensions of the film image and of cinematic storytelling. It is through such reconstruction that characters (and people too) can step back and work out the implications of deeply unsettling views and of shallow, anemic experiences. Otherwise they fall victim to them. A healthy individual integration of film into personal experience requires, as with irony, that it be regarded as "a world of discourse in which we can say with great security certain things that are violated by the overt words of the discourse" (Booth 1974:6).[1] Nabokov's view of film as a medium, therefore, points to the need for ironic reading, for questioning the claim to total denotation of the image. The film image is like irony in that its elements, like the words in ironic statement, "do not require retranslation," for "it is always something in their surroundings and it is usually something merely implicit in their 'place,' that gives them away" (Booth 1974:39). This is precisely the function of film tropes as they occur in *Laughter in the Dark*. The film and filmlike fantasies of characters such as Albinus and Margot should prompt the viewer to reject the structure of belief which they imply. This is because, as Wayne Booth suggests, irony in general tends to enlarge the group of those who might agree to be critical of something, even if fewer would have tended to criticize the same something if presented as a straight statement (Booth 1974:22–30). For those, therefore, who may enjoy a filmic view of life without critical perspective, Nabokov's irony focuses on the critical distance necessary to see its implications. This is a decidedly ethical attitude in a novelist who is more often considered a playful and disengaged aesthete (but see Pifer 1981).

Nabokov's ethical emphasis leads him to parody and satire about the clichés of recurrent film situations as well as the hackneyed poses of "stars." His sensitivity to the fact that these are demeaning simplifications appears in frequent rib-nudging asides and structural plot parodies. More central to the novel, however, and functionally more integrated than the many witty remarks, we find a cast of characters trapped by the very limits of a perceptual stance which is filmlike in its delimitations. In Nabokov's fictional treatment of film, what is filmlike at the most general level and what is criticized most openly is an emphasis on the entrapments of a limited "viewing situation." As a consequence of this, his narrative space is offered to the reader as a setting that elicits the open-ended and free-flowing exploration typical of a specific camera style, one that retains the integrity and perspective entailed by an active and responsible viewing.

This choice of "camera style" is prevalent whenever the writing becomes clearly film-mimetic. It is a style that favors the sharply etched three-dimensional perspectives of deep-focus and the montage-free and uninterrupted camera "takes" first isolated as an important film technique by André Bazin, who insists that it grants the audience greater freedom. This is better, he holds, than the didactically directive techniques of shallow focusing range (which tend to preselect the area of the picture upon which we are to concentrate and thus "tell" us where meaning resides) and of intellectual montage (which attempts to select and combine the iconic elements of reality into authorially circumscribed "sentences"). As J. Dudley Andrew aptly points out, such an emphasis amounts to a moral disposition: "The spectator *should* be forced to wrestle with the meanings of a filmed event because he *should* wrestle with the meanings of events in empirical reality in his daily life" (Andrew 1976:163).[2]

It is precisely this style that Nabokov employs in his most spectacular film-mimetic sections. Such sections are usually designed to expose the extent to which the characters lack a moral perspective on the total picture of the events in which they participate and to encourage the reader to get actively involved in entering that same total picture. The final section of *Laughter in the Dark* is a case in point:

> Stage-directions for last silent scene: door—wide open. Table—thrust away from it. Carpet—bulging up at table foot in a frozen wave. Chair—lying close by dead body of man in a purplish brown suit and felt slippers. Automatic pistol not visible. It is under him. Cabinet where the miniatures had been—empty. On the other (small) table, on which ages ago a porcelain ballet-dancer stood (later transferred to another room) lies a woman's glove, black outside, white inside. By the striped sofa stands a smart little trunk, with a colored label still adhering to it: "Rouginard, Hotel Britannia."
>
> The door leading from the hall to the landing is wide open, too. (L:291–292)

This form of writing must be visualized by the reader. We are made to realize that "active" viewing and "reconstructive" reading are necessary by noticing the discrepancies between this scene as presented and Albinus's pathetically inadequate "view" of it as he enters: "He could see the room distinctly—almost as if he had the use of his eyes; to the left, the striped sofa, against the right wall, a small table with the porcelain figure of a ballet-dancer; in the corner by the window, the cabinet with the valuable miniatures; in the middle, another large table, very shiny and smooth" (L:289). But alas, the cabinet is empty, the miniatures gone; the porcelain dancer is there no more.

The whole scene, moreover, is presented as if shot by a neutral and objective camera slowly retreating backwards through the entrance door (or, alternatively, as a long static deep-focus shot that invites us to scan the desolate scene) while analysis, collation, and empathy are forced upon the viewer.[3] This scenario openly lists the "ingredients" of such audience collusion: we see an empty cupboard and must remember its contents and draw our conclusions about Margot's and Rex's actions and about their implications for Albinus. We see the suitcase and label and are suddenly absorbed into the rush of associated images just as Albinus would be. These elements function as visual icons that generate acts of retroactive and empathic narrative in the reader's mind. The fate of the porcelain dancer is, in fact, rapidly narrated; the invisible presence of the pistol explained.

Such three-dimensional cinematic space puts the reader at the hub of a camera eye; sometimes, as we shall see, several eyes. This is most reminiscent of the television cameras described by Nabokov to the interviewer from *Vogue* magazine, a statement that thus suggests a writer fully aware that a specific representational technique based on his comparison of the poet to a "cosmic studio" may be applied to narrative fiction too. It is also evident that, when multiple cameras are deployed to the maximum for this kind of writing, Nabokov intends the reader to take an active part.

Take, for instance, the car accident scene in *Laughter in the Dark*. Ironic perspective, multiple points of view and the features of deep-focus continuous representation control what turns out to be the most spectacular instance of a filmlike sequence to be found in Nabokov's fiction. As Albinus drives recklessly along the steep and winding road, the reader's cinematic memory is stimulated to recall a specific shot on a screen witnessed by Albinus earlier in the novel: "a car . . . spinning down a smooth road with hairpin turns between cliffs and abyss" (L:13). The text then reenacts the "anecdotal" visual double take and recapitulation at the level of form by means of a "structural" repetition. The situation is set up: "A sharp bend was approaching and Albinus proposed to take it with special dexterity. High above the road an old woman who was gathering herbs saw to the right of the cliff this little blue car speed toward the bend, behind the corner of which, dashing from the opposite side, toward an unknown meeting, two cyclists crouched over their handlebars" (L:236–237). But the setup occurs at the end of a chapter, allowing the next one to open with a summary. The effect is a lot like the mirroring repetitions of weekly reel-ends in serialized suspense movies as the "next installment" starts: "The old woman gathering herbs on the hillside saw the car and the two cyclists approaching the sharp bend from opposite directions" (L:236–237).

The text then opens up onto a dizzying camera-eye sequence that sets up and executes the mishaps from higher and higher camera angles until the far-reaching interconnections of the event are tied together by the soaring camera of an airborne director:

> From a mail plane flying coastward through the sparkling blue dust of the sky, the pilot could see the loops of the road, the shadow of his wings gliding across the sunlit slopes and two villages twelve miles distant from one another. Perhaps by rising still higher it would be possible to see simultaneously the mountains of Provence, and a distant town in another country—let us say, Berlin—where the weather was hot too; for on this particular day the cheek of the earth from Gibraltar to Stockholm was painted with mellow sunshine.

> In Berlin, on this particular day, a great many ices were sold. Irma had once used to look on with the gravity of greed when the ice-cream man smeared a thin wafer with the thick yellowish substance which, when tasted, made one's tongue dance and one's front teeth ache deliciously. So that, when Elisabeth stepped onto the balcony and noticed one of these ice-cream vendors, it seemed strange to her that he should be dressed all in white and she all in black.
> . . . .
> "What can it be," she wondered. "Why am I all a-tingle?"
> From the balcony she could see the ice-cream vendor with his white cap. The balcony seemed to soar higher, higher. The sun threw a dazzling light on the tiles—in Berlin, in Brussels, in Paris and farther toward the South. The mail plane was flying to St. Cassien. The old woman was gathering herbs on the rocky slope. For a whole year at least she would be telling people how she had seen . . . what she had seen. . . . (L:237–238)

Set in the midst of this large-scale landscape filled with eyes that see but do not understand, Albinus, who had been given to see at the outset and had not understood either, hurtles towards a now quite unmetaphorical blindness. The ironic serendipity of narrative juxtapositions ("let us say, Berlin") is there to underline the fact that only active reconstruction will reveal that Irma—Albinus's daughter, now dead—and Elizabeth—his estranged wife, only now recovering—and the setting of their now shattered family in Berlin can be held together by an imaginative act that requires the soaring technology of an airborne camera ("optical instruments of yet unknown power," is what Hermann, the protagonist of *Despair*, yearns for [D:38]). At this point in the story, of course, Albinus could not see all of this, caught as he is in the unfolding events—caught in fact because he had failed to see the emerging interconnections of the events leading up to this moment. He will be plunged into blindness immediately after the most spectacular instance of extended, omnipotent vision in this novel, as if to underline the poignancy of this event.

What Nabokov uses to make such a point is not explicit statement, or even the kind of parenthetical ironic aside which so often characterizes his texts. Rather, he uses structural representation—the dramatic foregrounding that can be achieved through "formal mimetics"—to convey feeling and idea. The bird's-eye view that holds everything together echoes in method the kind of cinematic synthesis which may hold together the random happenings of life (Berlin, after all, may be a quite arbitrary choice) into the "frame of one screen" as described by Nabokov in the interview cited earlier. The optical apparatus, the "video attached to his lawn chair" which the poet lacks, has been here provided for Albinus's accident by the novelist's "power of pure imagination."

There is no question that Nabokov was thinking of film when writing this passage. He tells us so explicitly: "The scene of the accident I saw vividly as a film" (cited in Appel 1974:259).[4] There seems to be no question also that this narrative instance illustrates precisely the extension of human consciousness that is possible through the optical advances which we saw were so interesting to Nabokov. The ironic commentary implicit in the fact that the optical apparatus is seen to work at its most spectacular at the very moment that the human optical apparatus is about to be destroyed (in itself a thematic and formal juxtaposition of the instrumental and organic extremes contained in Nabokov's remarks to the interviewer) can be shown as firmly based in Nabokov's instinctive understanding of the implications of such soaring camera views. It is such implications and their consequences that make *Laughter in the Dark* the most consistent and extended example of the importance of film form and the thematic exploration of cinema in Nabokov's work.

In examining *Laughter in the Dark* more extensively, we can come to see how the features of a narrative structure thematically and formally related to the art of cinematography have changed and deepened since Pirandello first put them to use. The poetics of this narrative genre is still clearly recognizable (enough so to link the two works without doing either of them violence), but at the same time this poetics is pliable enough to adapt to the changing situation of cinema and to the imaginative characteristics of each author. Above and beyond the continuities of Gubbio's and Albinus's stories, the two novels remain very much the products of a Pirandello and a Nabokov. But to us, of course, it is the generic continuity in its consistency as well as permutations that is important.

First of all, we find a diversified presence of characters in this novel who parallel in their roles (albeit not as relentlessly) Gubbio's filmmaking perspective on the world. They range from directorlike figures to spectator substitutes within the novel and anticipate the film-related narrative focus of many characters in subsequent novels that fall within this mode.

Most extensively complex, however, is the development in this novel of what I have called the formal-mimetic aspect of such film novels. Responding to the evolution in the means and ambitions of cinematography since Pirandello's time, Nabokov displays subtle insight into the idiom of film: from the stylistic imitation of the tone and texture of films current at his time, to the extensive narrative use of elements made prominent by film style, to the metaphysical implications of the qualities inherent in film representation. As we shall see, his sensitivity to the multiple possibilities of film idiom leads to radical effects in the area of plot and interesting parallels to film theory as it has evolved since the time of Pirandello.

It is not so much the extent to which Nabokov parallels film theory that stands out (the only film theorist to which he alludes openly is Arnheim, and that he does in a satirical vein) but rather the fact that imaginative writing about film as a new art form has managed since the earliest days of cinematography to dramatize in vivid detail the interaction between man and film. The conceptual formulations of this interaction by theorists sometimes parallels, sometimes lags behind, and sometimes misses the subtlety and liveliness of these imaginative articulations. Many times, however, film theory can be used to pinpoint what exactly it is in film that the narrative development relates to. Especially in the case of formal mimetics, this will allow us to isolate the extensive way in which Nabokov brings to bear aspects of film upon the experiences of his characters.

Ultimately, the film-formed views of life and the imaginative power of film and its glittering promises affect the life and destiny of Nabokov's characters just as extensively and brutally as they do those of Gubbio and his fellow cast members. To a remarkable extent camera technology, the ranges of screen style current in the thirties, the elements of the cinematic apparatus, and the characteristics of film genres are integrated into the experience of Nabokov's characters.

The use of film-mimetic technology to articulate his story makes of the novelist, fully aware as he is that he is representing things cinematically, a directorlike figure. While the open-ended, deep-focus kind of camera style outlined previously engages the "viewers" in a challenge to see, to integrate, and to take responsibility, it is clear to anyone who has read Nabokov that the kind of filmmakers originally associated by André Bazin with such directorial representations (Renoir, the neorealists) are not at all analogous to the camera-wielding Nabokov soaring over the French *corniche* at the fatal moment. The kind of "director" Nabokov is being at this moment is rather like the ones illustrated by Leo Braudy. They move "between total omniscience and a claustrophobic identification of our point of view with that of one character. When we watch a film and feel somehow that the camera's point of view is the perspective of the Enemy, personal or providential, we are watching a film in the style of Lang and Hitchcock." Clearly while we "watch" the scene of Albinus's accident as Nabokov imagined it, we get the feeling that inimical forces are closing in on the protagonist and that "all the characters and all the objects . . . are controlled by outside forces, ultimately by the director himself" (Braudy 1976:48, 51). This camera view of the accident is indeed a film equivalent of the omniscient narrator who places himself outside and above the action and who ultimately cannot but leave the readers with the lingering feeling that it is he, the ultimate puppet master, who controls events.

Braudy points out that such narrative strategies tend to generate representatives of the extrastructural impresario within the story, representatives who mirror the same overbearing manipulation in which these kinds of directors engage. Such a character is "potentially more equal to the director" and "creates facts more often than he searches for them. He is a kind of impresario of the real. Lang's films, especially the silents, often center on characters like Mabuse . . . Haghi (in *Spies*), and Rotwang (in *Metropolis*) who are controllers of the entire world of things. . . . They create the order of objects; much like the director, they are masters of inner space, Gods within the film. But not Gods outside the film, for in the end . . . all either die or lose their power" (Braudy 1976:86).

Axel Rex is, of course, such a representative within the story and is the "personal" enemy (as opposed to the providential one) who controls much of the way in which things appear to Albinus in the novel. Rex's view of art is quite in keeping with the notions defined by Braudy, and this art is aimed at Albinus precisely as if Rex were directing him in a performance the structure of which is as "closed" as in Braudy's definition. Rex "watched with interest the sufferings of Albinus . . . who thought, poor man, that he had touched the very depths of human distress; whereas Rex reflected—with a sense of pleasant anticipation—that, far from being the limit, it was merely the first item in the program of a roaring comedy at which he, Rex, had been reserved a place in the stage manager's private box" (L:183). The supernatural omnipotence of such a directorial perspective is quite clear to Axel Rex, as well as the moral implications inherent in this power. So he carefully defines for himself the nature of this controlling perspective:

> The stage manager of this performance was neither God nor the devil. The former was far too gray, and venerable, and old-fashioned; and the latter, surfeited with other people's sins, was a bore to himself and to others, as dull as rain . . . in fact, rain at dawn in the prison-court, where some poor imbecile, yawning nervously, is being quietly put to death for the murder of his grandmother. The stage manager whom Rex had in view was an elusive, double, triple, self-reflecting magic Proteus of a phantom, the shadow of many-colored glass balls flying in a curve, the ghost of a juggler on a shimmering curtain. (L:183)

Rex has no use for the benevolent humanism of Renoirian character representatives such as Octave of *The Rules of the Game* (1933), whose role it is "to make connections of feeling between the other characters"—representatives who suggest that the director is indeed like "God as the chief gardener." Nor does he consider himself the great impresario as absolute evil, the kind of director represented by Lang's "God as the head of the spy ring." In an image that captures with filmlike economy and visual precision the drabness of evil (very like the image which opens Dupont's 1926 film *Variety*), Rex rejects the role of director as gangster in favor of what sounds most like Braudy's definition of the early film directors: "Impresarios, simultaneously inventors, artists, and businessmen. Combining the talents of the barker and the magician, they embodied the ambivalence in their films: illusion in the service of a supposedly clear and distinct reality." These, like Fritz Lang, are "somewhere between Mabuse the psychiatrist and Rotwang the magical scientist . . . immersed in the detailed technology that filmmaking demands and yet in touch with the artistic intelligence that controls the hidden and magical connections between the things of the world" (Braudy 1976:94, 49, 93).

But ultimately such authorial representatives are only partly equivalent to the director himself (be it a Lang, a Renoir, or a Nabokov) and, their power neutralized, they leave the final word to the real aesthetic controller of all things. Thus Rex too finally succumbs, but not before his technical brilliance and manipulative sadism lay down a veritable chamber of horrors for the blinded Albinus. For Albinus's mutilated sense perceptions, the protean and scientifically inclined vivisector stages a theater of illusions in which everything (from cast of characters to the colors of the world) is changed to suit his own creative whims. This evil manipulator is finally vanquished by the stolid, overweight, loyal, and simply good Paul, a veritable Octave without the wit.

But it is not only Rex who places Albinus inside an illusory set of situations. Margot does her own share of stage managing, and Albinus himself places his own perceptions within the limiting confines of partial perceptions of reality. These we can readily recognize as Braudy's "claustrophobic identification of our point of view with that of one character" (Braudy 1976:48). Finally the novelist himself, in view of the cinematic source of most of Albinus's delimitation of reality, sets his protagonist in a context that echoes directly the world and the style of the movies at the Argus cinema, suitable locale for Margot's and Albinus's first meeting.

In many instances a cinematic perspective on the world is suggested by repeated "framings" which open up a view of the bustling impersonal activity of street scenes. One such moment (as Albinus leaves after his first night with Margot) stresses that all the things filling the "shot" (street cleaners, sparrows, milk van, sunlight reflections, airborne sounds, blooming lilacs, butterflies) "surround" Albinus as he walks through Berlin-West (L:83). Another case actually shows us a street scene (sharply etched in vivid visual details and serendipitous irrelevance) as Albinus sees it through the frame of a window, a scene the range of which is extended through the optical mediation of yet another windowpane facing him. The visual conceit that summarizes a camera-like reflection in the image of a windowpane aptly, if probably by chance, echoes the same metaphor of cinematic representation of city life found in Vertov's *The Man with a Movie Camera* (1929).

City life in its chancy bustle and kinetic chorality has always been thematically and formally popular with filmmakers. Gubbio, as we saw at the outset of this study, finds himself caught in a most filmlike rendition of the urban machine in ways that foreshadow treatments of the theme in films such as the one by Vertov mentioned above and (much closer to Nabokov's Berlin) by Walter Ruttman in his 1927 production *Berlin, the Symphony of a Great City*. When we find Rex describing to Albinus "certain aspects of Berlin as if it were a distant picturesque city" and doing it "so well that Albinus promised to look up, in his company, that lane, that bridge, that queer-colored wall" (L:133), it might well be that the artist (who at this point of the story is still hoping to collaborate with Albinus on a film project) is raiding Ruttman's film for his own purposes. What is certain, however, is that the bustling, impersonal activity that prevails in all the street scenes in *Laughter in the Dark* is the kind of typically modern material most notably congenial to photography and cinematography. The overwhelming impression of "unstaged reality" captured in such scenes in the novel (full of details such as the fortuitous reflection of sunlight on a window and the asynchronous use of car sounds),[5] as well as the precision and durability with which this way of looking at the world endows its elements, indicates that the text is striving to suggest the ground-level experience of a filmlike perception of the world.

But even more than in the manner that these scenes capture reality and hold it there for our observation, the selection of materials reflects a preference for the kind of aesthetic experience favored by the new medium, characteristically located in crowds, public places, and street scenes.[6] Sometimes this preference even manages to divert the course of the action, as when Margot's attempted suicide is halted when "a red-and-gold fire engine drove up, snorting loudly, and stopped in front of the house opposite. A crowd had collected, clouds of smoke billowed from the top window, and black scraps of charred paper floated in the wind. She was so interested in the fire that she forgot her intention" (L:38). There is no question that we are to identify this type of persistent presence of irrelevant objective details as related to cinema, since Albinus himself, faced with the collapse of his marriage and unable to shake off the awareness of Greta Garbo's photograph inside Margot's book, muses, "How strange. A disaster occurs and still a man notices a picture" (L:79). But mostly such details just seep into the structured and motivated framework of the story, suggesting the "permeability" of real life in the manner that Kracauer (1960: 254–257) suggests is so characteristic of film aesthetics.[7] Such is the case with the report of Irma's encounter with the trunkless baby elephant (L:70); the lorry that passes outside, rattling the windowpanes as Albinus is confronting Paul over Margot (L:88); Irma's rash (L:108); or the "olive-skinned lift-boy" who takes Albinus, Margot, and Axel up to their room in Rouginard and stands "with his handsome profile toward them" (L:203).

A character may seize upon such a detail and try to make it seem relevant (Axel uses the lift boy to extend his pretense to be a homosexual) or the same character may find that what seemed a secondary detail of interest may unexpectedly become of primary significance: "'Did you notice a small man in white with a goldenish beard?' 'I did,' said Rex. 'Sat behind us. What about him?'" (L:211). As for Albinus, such details—"Tennis rackets? Sun on a tennis racket. Why was that so unpleasant?" (L:241)—may in fact block the relevant facts with their merely contiguous presence. In films the foregrounding of such details can only occur through overly powerful means such as extreme close-up, noticeably selective lighting and composition, special filters, and so on, which is why "figure and ground" tend to merge more evenly in film than in literature.

In Nabokov the cinematic call of the outside street and of its promised adventures takes shape in one of those public gathering places (a cinema) that Kracauer mentions as an extension of the street setting, while Albinus's view of the world outside the Argus cinema where "the snow was melting, the night was damp, with the fast colors of street lights all running and dissolving" (L:22) echoes in style precisely the subjective, expressionist point of view with which Karl Grune's protagonist (*Die Strasse*, 1923) looks at the outside world. The film's hero, once he plunges into the "street" with the same resolve to seek sensations as Albinus, encounters a brutal and destructive world "with card sharpers, prostitutes and a murder to boot. Life, an agitated sea, threatens to drown him" (Kracauer 1960:72–73).[8] Characters such as these found in the street are clearly stock figures related to those that surround Albinus: nimble-fingered tricksters close to the "elusive, double, triple, self-reflecting magic Proteus of a phantom," Axel Rex; venial sexual seductresses similar to Margot. Are we too far off in suggesting that this stereotype movie plot (which in its cliché economy echoes the stereotypical nature of the opening paragraph of *Laughter in the Dark*) is but a variation on the story of Albinus Kretchmar? He too is dragged to his doom by the glittering attractions of the "street" and its inhabitants. He actually is "drowned" in the end as he walks "very slowly along that bright sand of pain, toward that blue, blue wave" until he can see that wave "coming, coming, coming to drown me" (L:291–292).

Indeed, the inanimate objective details of reality may become (and this again is essentially cinematic in nature) the very protagonists of the story. Elements initially present because of their being inevitable parts of the continuous context of reality will on occasion take over. Thus street, tennis racket, door, and stairwell do become, as Kracauer puts it, "carrier[s] of action" displaying the filmmaker's "urge to raise hats and chairs to the status of full fledged actors" (Kracauer 1960:45). For the moment that it occupies Albinus's consciousness, Margot's tennis racket does indeed "overshadow the rest of the cast," just as that most cinematic of inanimate protagonists, "the Staircase" ("not as a symbol of glorious ascension, but as a thing to be kept nicely polished," notes Nabokov [L:24–25]), becomes the center of Margot's mother's existence.

Albinus is in fact surrounded by such actively engaged objects, be they the mirrors that "were having plenty of work that day" (L:61) or the doors that, unnoticed by him, were playing a "queer part . . . in his and her life" (L:205). Virtually inanimate repertory companies such as the "furniture in an abandoned apartment" cited by Kracauer do star opposite human protagonists (Kracauer 1960:97). After Albinus sets his mistress up in his own apartment, "the bedroom and the nursery seemed to gaze at Albinus with touching and innocent reproach" (L:120). An even more complex action sequence is "narrated" by the furniture that witnesses the consequences of Margot's letter to

Albinus reaching his wife Elizabeth instead: "The disorder in the bedroom told its tale. His wife's evening gowns lay on the bed. One drawer of the chest was pulled out. The little portrait of his late father-in-law had vanished from the table. The corner of the rug was turned up" (L:86). The upturned corner of the rug, in echoing the carpet "bulging up at the table foot in a frozen wave" (L:292) that is part of the novel's final "shot," demonstrates how these inanimate objects can even foreshadow narrative events such as the blue wave that drowns Albinus in its blissful blueness.

The inanimate cast can undergo the kind of psychological change characteristic of human protagonists as a consequence of the fact that in being made into "actors" they inevitably acquire anthropomorphic attributes.[9] It is peculiar to cinematography that through the articulation of settings by means of camera position and of framing, such an anthropomorphic aura is emphasized. This is precisely the case with Albinus's apartment as it goes from being imbued with the lingering presence of Elizabeth (if not actually the imprint of her "human face") to her replacement by Margot, who even engages in a kind of projective transference with the setting:

> He grew accustomed to Margot's presence in these rooms, once so full of memories. She had only to change the position of some trifling object, and immediately it lost its soul and the memory was extinguished; it was only a matter of how long she would take to touch everything, and, as she had quick fingers, in a couple of months his past life in these twelve rooms was quite dead. Beautiful as the flat was, it no longer had anything in common with that flat in which he had lived with his wife. (L:122)

Whole settings can also become such performers, much like those Kracauer (1960:45, 131) describes (the Coney Island of *Little Fugitive* [1953], the harbor overview of *On the Waterfront* [1954]).[10] The ice-hockey match at the Sport Palace is a notable example, as it absorbs the human figures within it (L:149–154). The interaction of Albinus, Margot, Rex, Paul, and Irma is visibly conditioned by the setting. What is more, the action is almost exclusively articulated by the spatial requirements of the arena along a continuous sequence of limited points of view. These amount to eyeline-shots that range from Albinus's sighting of Paul and Irma all the way to Margot's view of the same pair and the final reverse-angle of Margot and Rex as seen by Paul. It is clear that filmlike syntax is used to stress significant failures to see in the proper way: be it Albinus's self-revealing mimic behavior ("hunching his shoulders, trying to make himself as small as possible") or his failure to notice Margot's "strange glance" and "how her cheeks flushed and her lips quivered" at the prospect of being left alone with Rex (L:149). The narrative articulation is therefore film-mimetic on the one hand, while on the other it turns the peculiar focus of filmlike structure to narrative and thematic use.

The human beings present in this setting are, furthermore, cut up into selective representative parts of themselves (echoing the metonymizing tendencies of filmlike vision caught by Gubbio) and spliced into the arena setting precisely in the cinematic manner described by Kracauer when he says of the actor: "Nor is the whole of his being any longer sacrosanct. Parts of his body may fuse with parts of his environment into a significant configuration which suddenly stands out among the passing images of physical life" (Kracauer 1960:97). Paul is thus reduced to his shoulders and to his horn-rimmed glasses and to plumpness, while Irma is a fair plait to the father and a generic "little girl following the game through a large pair of field glasses" to the mistress (L:149, 153). The indelible stamp upon one's memory of such integrations of the animate and inanimate is nicely indicated by Nabokov when, later in the novel, as Paul rushes to warn Albinus of Irma's illness, he bumps into Rex in the entrance hall. With their mutual physical recognition comes the apparently undetachable Sport Palace with "a great outburst of cheering as the puck was shot into the Swedish goal" (L:170).[11]

Setting and occasion impose their own characteristics by being strongly outlined and organically fused. The physical presence of such details as the "little table with a very white cloth" is echoed by "the vast frozen area" of the ice rink and its own "oily blue gloss" to form an unforgettable moment as individualized as a sharply drawn character. The sudden emergence of such physical elements and objects which acquire a momentary role recalls some of Nabokov's own biographical memories, such as that "small helicopter of a revolving samara that gently descends upon the tablecloth" at Vyra (SpM: 171). The whole setting can emerge with similar presence too, until the main action is overwhelmed and a secondary backdrop claims the full attention of primary perception. The technical execution of such foregrounding in the cinema is performed by taking advantage of the separation between visual and sound tracks. This is a technical peculiarity of film to which Nabokov is sensitive, as we saw in the previous chapter, and to which he repeatedly refers.

The selective amplification of focus and periphery that is part of the technological peculiarities of film is thus applied in a typically cinematic fashion as we observe Margot and Rex's animated discussion until suddenly "their lips continued to move, but the clamor around drowned their swift quarrel" (L:151). Just as with Brando's confession to the girl he loves in *On the Waterfront,* "the salient point" is overwhelmed by the setting: "The piercing sound of a ship's siren drowns both his confession and the girl's answer" (Kracauer 1960:131). While the inability to overhear a conversation because of the sudden amplification of environmental sound may be part of everyone's experience, it seems to me that drawing attention to the peculiar separation of sound from pantomime amounts to a formal-mimetic distortion of the literary text towards the properties of film text, very much like the visual cuts that articulate Gubbio's experience on the horse-drawn carriage. The reader is made to feel the introduction of filmlike perception into the texture of the novel and into the experiences of its characters. This is important because the novel tries to deal with characters who see in a particular way (mostly cinematic), but it also tries to appear to the reader as the experience of film viewing would appear. There is thus a double burden imposed upon the text: on the one hand to make the reader experience the perceptive perplexities of his characters; on the other to present the reader with a "vision" of the world that conforms to cinematic mediation in general as well as to some specific stylistic options of such mediation.

II

The fictional focus thus tends to be on a protagonist entangled in the problems of vision and perception; on characters either willfully manipulated in their own perceptions by outside agents or, if in part manipulated, also manipulating others in their own turn. We have even identified a particular kind of visual style of staging and representation that corresponds in its outlines to one of the primary options of film style. The open-ended, deep-focus camera style that characterizes much of Nabokov's filmlike setups is not in itself a means of freedom. Its effect is that of ironic commentary upon the ultimate helplessness and entrapment of characters (as in the case of Albinus's car accident). This camera style, moreover, captures yet another dimension of world vision closely associated with film, a vision of the world that was at first proposed, as it happens, by modern painting. In 1919 Giorgio de Chirico's brother Andrea (better known as Alberto Savinio) stated that "in painting irony occupies a most important position, once the mind of the artist achieves the maximum degree of clarity. Then he perceives exactly the original precision of Nature. This precision is reflected in man, and is destined, through him, to be externalized in subsequent representation, producing a very subtle but elementary and human reaction, which . . . can be called modesty [reticence]. This is what induces the artist, in spite of himself, to deform in some way as he reproduces them the terribly clear appearances he perceives" (Savinio 1968:162). This is the very same understanding of ironic vision as a vehicle of philosophical insight that we have found in Pirandello, applied here to the visual arts being produced during the early years of film history. These are pictorial analogues to poetic distillation of modern *angst* such as those found in Montale's poems ("Goodness has been to me unknown, aside from / the prodigious which disclosed divine Indifference, / the man of stone amid the somnolence of noon, / the cloud and, high above, the soaring hawk" [Montale 1970:28]) and which Giorgio de Chirico himself tracks back to writers of popular fiction. They (like the pop filmmaker Feuillade, one might add) capture "the metaphysical element of a city like London, with its houses, streets, clubs, squares and open spaces; the ghostliness of a Sunday afternoon in London, the melancholy of a man, a real walking phantom, as Phineas Fogg appears in *Around the World in Eighty Days*" (de Chirico 1968:87).[12]

This "ghostliness" (de Chirico uses the term *spettralità*) is glossed further by Savinio, illustrating the connection between the quality sought by these painters and that which we found in Pirandello: "Spectrality is the true, spiritual and substantial essence of every appearance. To reproduce this essence in its complete genuineness is the highest aim of art" (Savinio 1968:161). This anticipates and provides historical context for the formulations by Merleau-Ponty and Mitry which I have suggested as a possible context for Pirandello's views on the nature and role of the cinematic image.[13] It also seems to describe the one type of modern painting which Nabokov's Albinus is actually able to appreciate (find it as he might in a seventeenth-century item) as well as the subjective "views" of reality he provides that seem to echo such paintings. Of his Baugin ("a mandolin on a chessboard, ruby wine in a glass and a white carnation") Albinus observes, "Doesn't it look modern? Almost surrealistic, in fact?" (L:146).

The world itself provides metaphysical still lifes that in being suddenly seized by the eye offer a distillation of mystery and dread. Such a one is the moment during Irma's last hours, when Albinus notices that "on the table, a glass bowl with oranges gleamed" (L:174). It is noticeable that such views, moreover, are often framed (implicitly or explicitly) by someone's heightened attention (here, Albinus's emotional anguish as his daughter dies) or by the movement into the foreground of the "view" as set piece:[14]

> Berlin-West, a morning in May. Men in white caps cleaning the street. Who are they who leave old patent leather boots in the gutter? Sparrows bustling about in the ivy. An electric milk van on fat tires rolling creamily. The sun dazzling in an attic window on the slope of a green-tiled roof. The young fresh air itself was not yet used to the hooting of the distant traffic; it gently took up the sounds and bore them along like something fragile and precious. In the front gardens the Persian lilac was in bloom. Despite the early coolness white butterflies were already fluttering about as though in a rustic garden. (L:83)

In views like this one a contrast between the haphazard contingencies of chance discussed earlier and their seemingly "chosen" aura (at once suggestive yet stubbornly nonsymbolic) seems to be intentionally maintained. They suggest a kind of "effet de filmique" that parallels Barthes's "effet de réel" cited before.

Such scenes appear cinematic because of the sense of heightened, selected, suggestive but indefinite intention that they convey. In Nabokov's novel these set pieces and individual perceptions are remarkable for their heightened insistence on the visual and aural sensations that they describe or evoke. The hallucinatory quality of these moments is evident even more because they are often isolated into quick, unforgettable notations. One is led to pick out such images as the corridor in which Albinus waits for his daughter's birth—"the long, whitewashed, white-enameled passage with that nightmare palm in a pot at the top of the stairs" (L:17–18)—and which causes so much dread and hate in Albinus. Or one recalls the image of Albinus "as he lay by his wife's side in their bedroom, dimly lit, quietly furnished, with, as usual, part of the central heating apparatus (painted white) reflected in the mirror" (L:46), an image that once again finds Albinus in the grip of conflicting emotions. The choice, number, and treatment of objects in Nabokov's scenes thus nicely reproduces the special status of film images: not too openly symbolic, yet clearly not inertly expository either.

The sense of aesthetics and of plotting one gets from *Laughter in the Dark* leads further into film aesthetics in two complementary ways. One, which we have already analyzed, has to do with the presence of director-representatives of several kinds who "order the world" much in the way film directors do. Were it not however for the fact that Nabokov is explicit about this novel's affinity with film, we could not argue that such manipulators are inherently cinematic. The other "plotters"[15] found in this novel are elements (such as color, sound, patterns, and objects) that, while admittedly shared by writing and cinematography, are nevertheless used in *Laughter in the Dark* in ways that make us think of film and the way we experience it.

One of these visual elements is controlled by synaesthesia. This has the effect of emphasizing the sensory surface of Nabokov's text. It also underlines the gap that exists between this text and what may be actually "seen." Early silent cinema struggled from the outset with the need to suggest specific sensations by synaesthetic means, especially the suggestion of sounds by visual means. For this reason Nabokov shares with Eisenstein (a film theorist he knew and disliked as a filmmaker and whose name he keeps misspelling as Eisenstadt) a keen interest in the phenomenon of *audition colorée*.[16] For this writer, of course, the problem of linking colors with sounds and with letters is not central because of its relevance to film, but his technically self-conscious use of the phenomenon turns out to be very similar to the pragmatic interest in this problem by filmmakers. Nabokov thus often triggers sensory "translations" in the reader in most cinematic fashion. Once he even provides a gloss: "Gay parasols and striped tents seemed to repeat in terms of color what the shouts of bathers were to the ear" (L:113). This kind of thing challenges the reader who must let the heightened perception of sensory data manifest itself in the act of reading. The reader must supply the ingredients missing on the page until what is created in the mind is very much like the film experience Nabokov aims for in this novel. Albinus himself, after his blinding, exemplifies the dilemma of one whose perceptions have been deeply impaired in ways similar to those of the literary audience. The reader cannot see the story s/he is reading and is repeatedly made to be aware of this situation. Albinus thus is the audience's representative within the text, just as Rex is the director's.

This emerges, for example, as we follow Albinus, who upon waking up for the first time after the accident "lay for some time motionless, endeavoring to transform the incoherent sound into corresponding shapes and colors. It was the opposite of trying to image the kind of voices which Botticelli's angels had" (L:241–242). For Albinus such unattainable sensory data end up by constituting themselves into a "world" from which he is now excluded as he listens "to daytime sounds, which seemed to have turned their backs upon him in merry converse with others" (L:245) or as he goes for walks "in the depths of a night which employed the bright small-talk of daylight" (L:249).[17] For the reader, on the other hand, such heightened awareness of the limitations of vision stimulates the imaginative concretization of a "world" that in its details, precisely because of the heightened awareness, corresponds closely to the filmlike appearance intended by the author. But the plotting which occurs through the use of elements that play a primary role in cinematic expression goes even further and relies for its structuring on the composite nature of film.

The synaesthetic and participatory acts triggered by deliberate attention to such things as the roles of sound lead to an unusual use of the separation of sensory tracks (sound, vision, black and white, color). This contributes even more to the type of aesthetic experience favored by film.[18] In film the attempt to suggest "our way of experiencing the 'real' world" is much stronger than in all other arts. This is why the heightened awareness of *separate* tracks can become (needs to become) a ground rule for the creative use of the medium. Eisenstein, more than most other early film theorists, formulated this need in his notion of *vertical montage,* which led him to conclude that in the creative synchronization of all the elements available to the filmmaker (a synchronization which on the analogy with music he subdivides into "natural," metric, rhythmic, melodic, and tonal) "full possibilities exist for the play of both corresponding and noncorresponding 'movements.'" In either case, he adds, "the relationship must be *compositionally controlled.*" He underlines also that "any one of these synchronization approaches may serve as the 'leading,' determining factor in the structure, dependent on the need" (Eisenstein 1943:72).

Nabokov's unusual stress on the separation and exchange of functions between sensory data, as well as his continuous play with the "translation" of signifying elements from the purely linguistic realm to that of "evoked" film experience, provides the key, I believe, to much of the sense of plotting present in the novel and to the reason why such plotting is more filmlike than the formalist patterns of other texts. The plotting is obtained by orchestrating elements of sensory perception rather than just counters of plot, of dialogue, of description, and of action. Nabokov allows the sensory data to "tell the story" just as they are used to tell the story in film. This kind of telling relies on the fact that everything present in the film text is potentially signifying on the primary rather than supportive level.[19]

Just as we found that in filmlike fashion settings and inanimate objects are raised to the status of "protagonists," we now discover that literary discourse, in this film-mimetic novel, allows the inherently filmic elements of its texture to take the leading role. Formal mimetics in Nabokov thus moves well beyond the scope of Pirandello. Formal mimetics still takes in the perception of things as conveyed through the medium of cinema, but that medium is seen as infinitely more supple and complex than in earlier times.

The transition from the party scene to Margot's and Rex's first talk after their unexpected reunion provides an excellent example of the way in which an image (wave), its connection with different moments of the plot (Solfi, Albinus's death), colors (blue, black), a routine action (revolving), or a piece of environmental notation (cold air through a window) convey a network of important story materials and a sense that "the plot is thickening." All of this is "performed" by secondary pictorial means, the kind of visual clues that in a film would tell us something without any referential exposition taking place. As the party draws to an end, for instance, "the guests were caught in that wave which, beginning as a low murmur, swells until, in a whirl of foamy farewells, it has swept them out of the house" (L:133–134). The simile is in itself apt, beautiful, and effectively analyzed in its pictorial as well as dynamic unfolding. But more than that it functions as a pivot that relies on visual and pictorial echoes to recapitulate and anticipate at one and the same time. It creates the same sense of a circular, enclosed-world pattern that we find in certain kinds of film. It recapitulates, on the one hand, the transition from a dream-Margot who "had long been wont to run along the shore of his [Albinus's] dreams" (L:84) to her actualized body stepping into the blue sea at Solfi where "the foam toppled over, ran, slowed down, then receded, leaving a smooth mirror on the wet sand, which the next wave flooded again" (L:113). On the other hand, the simile anticipates the final moment of Albinus's life when he sees himself being caught in the upswell of an oncoming wave and observes, "What a bliss there is in blueness. I never knew how blue blueness could be" (L:291).

The color blue in itself (only implicit in the wave of guests but noted twice otherwise in this transition) also gathers into a visual tone-chord its own various appearances and relational patternings. The range of its possible applications is captured in this transition by the opposition between the simplistically idyllic "wide blue sea" of Rex's riddle for Margot (L:135) and the threatening undertone of the "blue and heavy" air that hovers in Albinus's apartment after the party (L:134). One more color that sets off echoes in this transition is hidden in the "sealskin coat" tightly wrapped around Margot (L:135). The coat, without color here, just like the wave of guests, activates a color memory of a specific place and time (still the beach at Solfi) and of the seal-like black bathing suit Margot wore there.[20] But the use of filmlike devices to suggest a sense of concerted pattern extends beyond color and object.

We find, for instance, a pun hidden behind a standard silent-comedy slapstick routine when the farcical *pas de deux* of Margot (who "revolve[s] on one spot" as she turns away while he persists in trying to reach for her) and Rex actually hides under the verbal denomination of its action the nominal designation of the object that from the outset is Albinus's obsession: the deadly revolver.[21] This intramedial pun, which can function only within the conventions of the verbal text, thus reverses the kind of synaesthetic relationship between sound and vision seen above.

A related effect is produced by Rex's double-edged remark, "I couldn't believe my eyes, as the blind man said" (L:135), which is soon played out in a background exchange between porter and postman (L:185) and ultimately enacted in dead earnest by the principal player Albinus. The same sense is conveyed by such less obvious parallels between the moment in which the windows in Albinus's apartment are opened after the party—"the black clear frosty night streamed in" (L:134)—and the moment in which "a delicious ice-cold gust of air entered the room" when the feverish Irma opens the window to see if the man who whistles the same tune that her father used to whistle is not perhaps, against all hope, her father after all (L:159).

As we are made to stand at Irma's side while she looks down from her window to the man in the street below (it is not her father but a lovelorn man seeking an assignation with the girl upstairs), we as readers find ourselves once again caught within the actual mechanisms of personal interaction with the elements of film. In this instance they are represented by the shorthand iconic summaries characteristic of film posters and publicity stills, for what we "see" is a situational setup that reproduces the very movie poster that enticed Albinus to his first meeting with Margot. Again we find a sense of pattern, this time involving similar visual placements of character and setting. Albinus, who sought the safe limits of filmic seductions, finds that the *same* setup in life may have quite uncontrollable consequences.

We are made to realize that Albinus had actually seen the very moment that leads to his daughter's death, the moment at which a common flu turns into deadly pneumonia. Is this perhaps the connection that Albinus tries to make in his mind to save Irma's life? The impression Nabokov conveys here by the structuring of his materials is that if only Albinus had seen the film images in the proper way he could have changed his own future. But the proper way turns out to be the solipsistic kind of reading we have seen take place in *Speak, Memory*. The films Albinus watches are meant to be used quite differently, and Albinus himself is very much the average moviegoer, the typical prisoner in Plato's cave. His own vision of the truth, his memory of what he had in fact seen, is just as dim as that of Platonic man.

As he waits in the dining room while his daughter dies, Albinus sees sitting "on the divan in the corner two ladies, whose names he could not remember" and has "a queer feeling that if he remembered everything would be right again" (L:174). We the readers, of course, are the only ones who could actually remember the film image that (if interpreted correctly as a foreshadowing of real events rather than an emblematically enticing promise of assignation) could have saved Irma's life. Albinus, in fact, could at most only "foresee," and even that foresight (since he cannot stand beside us to watch his daughter open the window) could have merely absorbed some of the separate elements that contribute to "put together" the fatal image. Yet some of these elements are perversely present (and elusively displaced) as he tries to remember the names whose only relevance rests in their coded symbolizing of parts of the answer. One lady's name (Blanche von Nacht) is a displacement of the snow falling outside which caused the cold gust of air that chilled Irma too quickly. Next to her, the other lady's name, Rosa, echoes in a synaesthetic and punning relationship the "muffled noises" that "rose from the street," bringing up the sound of "someone" who "whistled four notes (Siegfried)." This pun, stretched across discontinuous sensory realms, parallels the elusive relationship between the missing "sight" of the truth by Albinus and the sound of those same four notes that brought Irma to the window (L:175).[22]

The elements Albinus sees, as they conspire to create a particular kind of meaning, reenact within the text of the novel the "parallel tracks" of cinematic expression and the kind of "democracy of signifiers" we have seen defined most eloquently by Eisenstein.

Awareness of the creative potential available in separating "tracks" was part of Nabokov's early film experiences. This awareness was especially pronounced with sound (we may recall the unsynchronized roar of the Sport Palace bursting forth in Albinus's stairwell), and not surprisingly in view of his interest in *audition colorée,* it is even more striking in his treatment of color. In a novel that Nabokov regarded as a failure in film-mimetic terms because of his inability to limit it to the blacks and whites of film as he knew it, the use of color is in retrospect actually prophetic in the way it prevents mindless polychromies from overwhelming everything in sight. For instance, the color blue sets off in itself a pattern of echoes, a veritable visual montage that fulfills as a color leitmotif the same function we saw fulfilled in Pirandello's novel by the image of Varia Nestoroff. The blue leads us into a dense narrative network of objects and actions.[23]

This network of separate images linked by "tonal" concurrence ties into a "plot" such disparate elements as the final blue wave that engulfs Albinus (L:291), a perfume called *l'heure bleue* (sensual color-coded index of Margot's presence to the blind Albinus [L:289]), the "glossy blue road" that remains in Albinus's memory as the center of his recollection of the car accident (L:240), the "sparkling blue dust of the sky" from which pilot and omniscient narrator and camera view see the total setting of the accident (L:237), the color of the car in which the accident occurs (L:236), the irrelevant secondary detail of that "bluish shade on" Margot's "neck where the hair had been shaved" that conspires to stop Albinus from leaving his mistress while there is still time (L:225), and the blue of the French colonel's eye that sees Margot's compromising embraces (L:219). The latter also reflect in their bloodshot veins the glimmer of the intersecting color motif of red (from Margot's "old red frock" to her bloodsoaked tennis sock [L:32, 225]), quite apt, given what it is the colonel sees. And then there is the atmospheric blue of the Sport Palace ice with its "oily blue gloss" (L:150) which echoes the "blue and heavy" air after the party (L:134) and which, with the implied echoes of blue cited above, brings us back to that morning at Solfi when Margot "drew herself up, clasped her arms round her knees and remained sitting motionless" only to remark eventually, "Heavens . . . how blue the sea is today" (L:112–113).

Just as in the most controlled and creative use of color in film, Nabokov's color notations are scattered over a wide area of the text rather than reiterated as a constant droning presence. They tend to impose themselves quite suddenly and with just the purpose Alexander Dovzhenko (cited in Viazzi 1949) recommends when he claims that color is to be brought to the foreground only at salient points, and only to irradiate the rest of the film. Eisenstein similarly stresses the importance of sparing use of suddenly emerging color notations: "So long as the situation does not require the color element to give a dramaturgic expression to action and no bright blue or gold diverts our attention from the whispered words . . . color veils its self-asserting power and acts as a frame." But this is merely a "color pause," an "accumulation by the color element of force in order to overwhelm the spectator with the bluish-black indigo of waves edged by white foam." Just like an actor, "the 'color line' weaves its way through the plot as one more independent part in the dramaturgic counterpoint of the film's expressive means" (Eisenstein 1970:123–124). Unquestionably it is this use of color that we encounter in the series of blues outlined above.[24]

But it is possible to be even more specific in defining what is cinematic in Nabokov's use of color: the representation of colors as perceived by a subject in the way a movie camera would record them. The sea at Solfi, for instance, reveals a startling articulation of shades: "purple-blue in the distance, peacock-blue coming nearer, diamond-blue where the wave caught the light" (L:113).[25] Albinus experiences in detail a sunset in which the change of light itself plays a role in affecting the protagonist: "Lights were being put on, and their soft orange glow looked very lovely in the pale dusk. The sky was still quite blue, with a single salmon-colored cloud in the distance, and all this unsteady balance between light and dusk made Albinus feel giddy" (L:77). Albinus also finds himself the only one awake after his first night with Margot and thus can become the perceptual protagonist as "the electric light was already turning a death-cell yellow and the window a ghostly blue" (L:84). Shifts such as these are of course the stuff of cinematic depiction, what sets it apart from still photography, just as are such ephemeral effects as "the air above sand on a very hot day by the sea" (L:289) or the "silver-blue blaze" that forces one to blink (L:112). These are precisely the cinematic uses of color in film cited by Béla Balázs, who notes that

> the movement of colour is sometimes so delicate as to be imperceptible but nevertheless effect a change in atmosphere. A landscape shown at noon in summer, although it appears motionless, yet makes quite a different impression in a colour film than on the best painting. For however skilfully a good painter can convey the effect of vibrating hot air, he can never match the effect of the colour film in which the dark-blue sky really vibrates, and thereby, however imperceptibly, changes the impression made on us by the landscape. (Balázs 1952:243)[26]

If one single episode can be found in the novel which epitomizes many of the obvious and less obvious cinematic qualities of the text discussed so far, it is undoubtedly the beach episode at Solfi. In it we find an interrelated use of what one may term movie-poster vision and filmlike editing. We find also the kind of extreme close-up made most common by cinematography. All these features are mediated by the willful and limited perceptions of Albinus, who thus comes to echo the cinematic limitations of Serafino Gubbio. Also, the formal-mimetic aspects of film syntax (such as metonymy) and filmic ways of isolating action and motion can be found as constants in this scene. In one continuous and extended episode we can see how these elements, discussed so far in separate examples, are orchestrated into a complex unit.

The scene opens with a setup that places Margot on the beach in a stereotyped composition recalling in its simple strong colors and its enticing staging the poster that attracts Albinus to the Argus cinema. As the chapter opens she is nothing but a "perfect seaside poster" exhibited "with nothing but deep blue above" lying "spread eagled on the platinum sand, her limbs a rich honey-brown, and a thin white rubber belt relieving the black of her bathing-suit." We are therefore not surprised to find that in a balanced manner the paragraph ends with Margot still enticingly displayed in the shape of a generic pinup in her "close-fitting seal-like black thing" that is "much too short to be true." Albinus is quite consciously creating these posterlike frames by isolating Margot from the total context of reality, a private fetish to suit his purpose. At one point he actually uses what is very much the selective visual style of a shallow-focus lens setting. He concentrates on entirely visual sensations and "freeze-frames" her into an "exquisitely colored vignette," making of that image "frozen" out of the moving context of the beach the chapter-head graphic device illustrating the willed change in his life: "Slim, sunburned, with her dark head of hair and one arm with the gleam of a bracelet still outstretched after her throw" (L:112). The technique was used in fact in 1929 precisely in a German beach film in which "snapshots of the bathers, taken by a photographer on the spot, are inserted in different places; and the snapshots snatch from the flow of movement precisely such bodily postures as are bizarre and in a sense unnatural" (Kracauer 1960:44–45).[27] The technique, which anticipates actual freeze-frame filming and which parallels a similar sequence in Vertov's *The Man with a Movie Camera,* is used by Albinus without, of course, the satirical aim.

The flow of events in this scene continues to stress Albinus's filmlike perceptions (as if having brought Margot out of a cinema, he now tries to force the world surrounding her back into it). From her opening "poster," the scene cuts to a low-level, extreme close-up in which Albinus "propped up his cheek and looked [vertical tilt] with endless delight at the oily gloss of her closed eyelids and at her freshly made-up mouth" (L:112). Most of the details being observed constitute a series of different and clearly defined "framings" (dark wet hair as it appears on Margot's head, grains of sand glittering inside her ears, iridescent sheen in the "pits" of her shoulders) conditioned by close, sequential observation clearly noted in the text ("if you looked very close"). Notable too is that the contents of these framings appeal specifically to the kind of visual experience which cannot be captured by traditional visual arts techniques or by still photography. The gloss of oil, the fresh luster of lipstick, the dark wetness of hair, the glitter of sand, the iridescent sheen of crystal refraction—all of these visual peculiarities belong to the cinematic visual motility mentioned by Balázs.

Visual points of view clearly delimited in range, direction, and choice of information continue throughout the whole scene, as well as the typically filmic tendency to metonymic subdivision of limbs and settings and the visual experiences of shifting colors and vibrating light. Thus close-ups of Margot (alternatively metonymized and assembled into generic stereotypes) continue to be noted (first he sees "her back . . . with the glitter of sand grains along the curve of her spine" [L:113], then "the movements of her little feet" [L:114]) in conjunction with long-shots of the beach and inserts detailing its activities through vivid human vignettes (man at edge of water wiping glasses, boy building sand castles). Finally, beach and vignettes are etched into our visual sensibility by stressing movement. The boy, thus, "shrieked with glee as the foam gushed into the walled city he had built" while a "large bright ball" (size and color saturation noted) appears from off frame with dynamic abruptness and bounces on the sand next to Margot, who grabs it and gets up to fling it back (L:113). Descriptive details of movement are thus also used to articulate events and to integrate one part of the sequence (Margot in her fragmented and iconic isolation) into the other (the large, colorful, and busy beach).[28]

III

Just as in *Quaderni di Serafino Gubbio operatore,* the ways of looking at reality that were either newly introduced or given renewed focus by the advent of cinematography affect the personal perceptions of Nabokov's characters. Camera views ultimately imply that the human eyes behind them and problems in the coherent understanding and continuous flow of filmlike perception reflect similar difficulties in the conduct of life. The human eye is the ultimate locus of all the "ways of seeing" made available by cinematography. Just as with the points of view on the beach at Solfi, distinctly cameralike perspectives imply a subjectivity that is paying attention.

Nabokov channels the personal dilemmas and narrative vicissitudes of his characters through the alternating facets of watching subjectivity and subjective watching, the very same poles (deceptively symmetrical) we found at the origin of his autobiographical writings. He does so in concrete and detailed ways by exploring the narrative possibilities of many of the topics we have found in his writings before. But in *Laughter in the Dark* themes such as the metaphorical subjectivity of soaring cameras, the ways the world appears to laymen as opposed to professional watchers, the nature of public and private images, the role of spectatorship in life and in the movie theater, and cinematic representation as it ranges from generic simplifications to unexpected revelation are integrated into an extended and tightly woven human story. Ultimately it is from the various aspects of images (and film images in particular) that Albinus's destiny unwinds. Film-mimetic bravura passages relate directly to the character's human destiny, while his professional expertise as an art critic qualifies his everyday manner of dealing with reality. In an even more specific way, his role as a film watcher makes of him an early representative of the movie-going generation that may find it important to perceive, from a clearer vantage point than Albinus's, how wide the gap between real and reel is.

The free-soaring camera that renders the accident episode in *Laughter in the Dark* manages to suggest, more than in the case of the many film tropes encountered so far, that the structural properties and formal manifestations of cinematography can come to stand for certain aspects of the human mind. The camera views presented by the novelist possess a generalized subjectivity which puzzles the reader by its disembodied presence and which is akin to that of a conscious human eye.[29] This floating consciousness seems to affect a transcendental synthesis out of the elements of the story, out of seemingly acausal events. Presented as part of a narrative unmarked by cinematic form, this kind of treatment would suggest at most an ironic use of omnipotent authorial control and omniscience. As part of a section admittedly cinematic in its conception, however, the treatment of materials illustrates Baudry's contention that seen through the camera, "the world is no longer only an 'open and unbounded horizon.' Limited by the framing, lined up, put at the proper distance, the world offers up an object endowed with meaning, an intentional object, implied by and implying the action of the 'subject' which sights it" (Baudry 1974/75:43).

I have discussed how film-mediated views of life can present themselves as projected concretizations of subjective consciousness (Nuti's inner experience of time and space, Nabokov's own projection of his exiled self).[30] The authorial representation of the best and most far-seeing that a camera view can offer (a representation that parallels Pirandello's presentation of the ironic film images that could potentially enlighten) contrasts with the character's self-imposed lack of vision. This lack of vision continues throughout the novel to be related to camera views of reality that Albinus does see and to the more general topic of a reality seen exclusively through the limiting mediation of artistic styles. This is why one can ultimately state that the failure to notice the interconnected network of events that affect him is the crux of Albinus's dilemma. His inability, unavoidable in this instance, to be both inside and above the events in which he is involved, his failure to "become absorbed in, 'elevated' to a vaster function, proportional to the movement which it [the camera] can perform" repeats his more avoidable inability to see before this moment (Baudry 1974/75:43).

Albinus's limits as a film theorist (we actually find him writing on the subject and quoting Arnheim's theory of sound in film) are indicated by Nabokov and only surpassed by his limits as art critic. Artistically mediated ways of looking at reality have always been formed by the way human consciousness saw reality in the first place. Even the most seemingly unformed products of illusionist perspective follow this rule. A critical view of painting therefore requires a modicum of awareness as to the implications of such formative background, just as an individual application of these formative distortions to an aesthetic view of reality demands measure and a sensible limitation of such projections. But Albinus as art critic is notable for his way of looking at reality through the "auteurial" and cultural idiosyncrasies of classical painters to such an extent that his access to reality is blocked by a double barrier: the submerged presuppositions that must have preceded the formation of those ways of rendering reality by the painters and Albinus's own overwhelming and inappropriate application of their pictorial means to his own surroundings.

The implicit relationship that may have existed between Rembrandt's pictorial means and his subject matter is shattered and trivialized when it is Margot whose "melting outline of a cheek" appears as if "painted by a great artist against a rich dark background" (L:20). What is more, Albinus's very ability to identify correctly those essential features of a painter's style which control so much of his view of reality is put into question when we learn that he cannot tell the fake from the real among his own paintings (L:145–146). Both selective projection and carelessness about the authenticity of this process (added to the ignorance about the authenticity of individual styles) combine to characterize the Albinus who extends the painterly filter he uses for Margot to the whole world: "As an art critic and picture expert he often amused himself by having this or that Old Master sign landscapes and faces which he, Albinus, came across in real life: it turned his existence into a fine picture gallery—delightful fakes, all of them" (L:8). In the end, however, only Margot will remain, turning the collector's art gallery into a pinup calendar: "Remembered scenes peopled the picture gallery of his mind: Margot in a figured apron drawing aside a purple curtain . . . Margot under the shining umbrella tripping through crimson puddles; Margot naked in front of the wardrobe mirror gnawing at a yellow roll; Margot in her glistening bathing suit throwing a ball; Margot in a silvery evening gown, with her sunburned shoulders" (L:256).

Knowledge of objective, factual details is clearly a necessary component of aesthetics for Nabokov, who as a young student had been taught by Dobuzhinsk that the artist should use an educated memory to visualize in his mind the objects of painting in their greatest detail. Thus Albinus's tendency to reduce aesthetics and beauty to the generalized and unspecified outline of "a distant lone tree against a golden heavens" and the diffused "ripples of light on the inner curve of a bridge" is an implicit indictment of the art critic, just as is his conventional reaction to sunsets such as the one at Rouginard where "Albinus was going into ecstasies over the outlines of the purpling hills" (L:201–202). Detailed knowledge and observation, features that the film medium inherently emphasizes, are crucial to the salvation of Albinus.[31]

Misjudging the visual clues of Margot's true emotions turns out to be fatal to him as, from the first moments of Margot's reunion with Rex, he misses the fact that Rex is the focus of her violent blushing and subsequent lack of self-control (L:127 ff.). Albinus does not see all of this correctly, just as he admits to Rex that he had "pictured" him in his mind quite differently from his true appearance—"short, fat, with horn-rimmed glasses" (L:128). There is a teasing complicity with the reader at this point, since we too are taken through the motions of an act of recognition. We too must identify Rex (whose name we have not encountered before and whose connection with Margot's emotions we too may miss at this point) from a clue that is evident only to a precise visual observer of gesture and attitude: qualities inevitably emphasized by film more than by literature. Rex "was rubbing his hands as though he were soaping them" (L:37), just as Margot's lover Miller had done on the morning he had left her. But then, of course, also Margot's first thought upon meeting Miller at Frau Levandovsky's had been that she "had pictured him quite differently" (L:33). Albinus's observation that his own mental picture of Rex did not correspond to his name, which "always remind me of an axe" (L:128), does parallel Margot's introduction to Miller at that time through the man's jocular "And I'm little Axel" (L:33). Seeing correctly is important to such an extent in the total economy of this novel that the reader must be made to feel the brunt of missing such clues (whether by being surprised when realizing later that Rex *is* Miller or by feeling pleased at noticing all of this now). The reader must share the limits of Albinus's vision because the plot is consistently structured around the ramifications of these limits.

Conclusive evidence that Albinus is caught between the clear and detailed seeing that goes with self-awareness and the blurred and silly stereotypes that more commonly characterize his lack of critical self-reflection (evidence that points to the fact that Albinus's shortcomings as art critic affect the total range of his life) can be found at those moments in which his usual veneer of helplessness is pierced by glimmers of awareness. Such a moment first occurs as he leaves Margot's apartment after their first full night together—"this had been the night of which he had dreamed for years" (L:84)—and walks back to his own home to see what he would find as a consequence of Margot's "careless" letter to him. The clearness of vision is here noticeably juxtaposed to a stress on Albinus's willful concretization of imaginary wishes. The evening before, having rushed home to try to intercept the letter before Elizabeth read it or to see if at least he could explain it away with the kind of invention that naïve Elizabeth might well believe, Albinus seemed to decide not to forestall discovery (L:80). This act allows him almost immediately to return to Margot's "nudity . . . as natural as though she had long been wont to run along the shores of his dreams" (L:84). In other words, his strategic withdrawal from specific and effective action in the real world of his family life allows him the momentary concretization of inner fantasies and wishes, of those "dreams" which formed the content of "his most reckless visions" (L:84).[32]

Next morning, however, as he leaves Margot's apartment, he walks in a world full of newly objective details. They are dramatically richer and are registered with a keenness that comments upon Albinus's previous tendency to see himself in the midst of settings which were perceived solipsistically and in which all elements merged into a synaesthetic soup. The opposition in the two styles of vision parallels closely, it so happens, two of the alternative cinematic styles of representation current at the time on German screens: the gritty and sharply etched details of the urban-realist dramas associated with "new objectivity" and the fluid, subjectively focused plastic emotionalism of expressionist films. Both may well be found at times in the same film, as both styles of vision alternate in Albinus's consciousness. His earlier views produce the kind of world which meets him as he leaves the cinema in which he first meets Margot. On that occasion, he "stepped into a blood-red puddle; the snow was melting, the night was damp, with the fast colors of street lights all running and dissolving" (L:21–22). Like the expressionist Berlin that appears to the defective vision of Franz in *King, Queen, Knave,* here too we find the "Stimmung" and visual aids (soft-focus, watery distortions, fluid boundaries of objects) that are typical of such a film style. Upon leaving Margot after the first night, on the other hand, we find Albinus walking out into the clearly etched Berlin-West street cited above as an example of "metaphysical" objectivity (L:83).

But for Albinus even the kind of setting that used to melt into an undifferentiated flow of liquids and color can, under the stress of deep and painful emotion, emerge into increasingly greater distinctiveness. Following his daughter's death we find that Albinus perceives the sidewalk (one much like the sidewalk outside the Argus cinema) with new sharpness, while distinct and detailed memories float through his consciousness:

> He walked along the white, soft, crunching pavement, and still could not quite believe what had happened. In his mind's eye he pictured Irma with surprising vividness, scrambling onto Paul's knees or patting a light ball against the wall with her hands; but the taxis hooted as if nothing had happened, the snow glittered Christmas-like under the lamps, the sky was black, and only in the distance, beyond the dark mass of roofs, in the direction of the Gedächtniskirche, where the great picture-palaces were, did the blackness melt to a warm brownish blush. (L:176)

Gone are the puddles, snow, night, street lights all running into each other in the kind of fuzzy overall haze that Albinus admires so much in sunsets and in "the early Italians" (L:19, 45). The elements of the scene retain their distinct and individual integrity now, while their properties and qualities stay with them rather than becoming internalized and being appropriated as the wallpaper of Albinus's own sensations. Specific and recognizable styles of film representation come to stand for quite specific levels of perception, of human awareness.

In similar fashion we also can see that the film-inspired conflict between the concreteness of filmlike images and the potent persistence of personal memory informs this moment of Albinus's experiences. His inner eye too is capable now of projecting clear and significant visualizations of his daughter *in vita.* Again, these particular inner visions do not overwhelm or replace the objective reality surrounding him, as his inner visions of passionate erotic escape had done when, deciding not to return to his family, he had started the course of events that leads to this sad moment. Yet looming over this sudden and uncharacteristic clearness is the ever-present threat of confusing imaginative escape: those "picture-palaces" that manage still to wash the blackness of night into their melting patches and which stand significantly beyond the church named Gedächtniskirche, the holy temple of remembrance.

Memory images of real moments and imaginative concretizations placed in filmlike fashion in his fantasy by an artful stage manager of desire jostle in Albinus's mind as he tries to decide whether to return now to "his pale, faded wife" (L:178, 256–257) or to stay with Margot, around whose naked body striped with sunshine Albinus flutters helplessly like that "clumsy moth . . . round a rose-shaded lamp" (L:116). Recollections (concrete, distinct, and significant) continue to pursue him as he realizes that Paul indicated to him with his "moist imploring look" that things could be repaired now that his daughter is dead and concludes that Elizabeth's glance to him through the mirror confirms this.

But Albinus's imagination has been effectively manipulated by a willful stage manager, the directive usherette whom he brought into his own home plucked out of the darkness of the Argus picture-palace, the concrete representative of those luminescent screen projections. She too, by now, has placed memories in Albinus's mind. One of them—"a graceful, lively, wanton girl, laughing, leaning over the table, one heel raised, as she thrust out her ping-pong bat" (L:178)—now displaces Irma from her own nursery and leads Albinus to conceive of a possible future back with his wife as the grim, foreboding corridor we have seen before (L:178–179). So he remains with Margot, fully aware "of the thin, slimy layer of turpitude which had settled on his life" (L:177). He rejects the urgings which fate presents to him "with dazzling distinctness" and looks outside (there is no doubt this time that we are seeing through Albinus's eyes) at a world as clear and sharply focused as the one that greeted him after his first night with Margot:

> It was thawing. Bright motorcars were splashing their way through the puddles; at the corner a ragged rapscallion was selling violets; an adventurous Alsatian was insistently following a tiny Pekinese, which snarled, turned and slithered at the end of its leash; a great brilliant slice of the rapid blue sky was mirrored in a glass pane which a bare-armed servant girl was washing vigorously. (L:179)

Rather than exhibiting a simple opposition between clear and unclear vision (the kind of contrast that we found characteristic of Serafino Gubbio as he claims that he sees clearly when seeing not at all), Albinus displays a complex and modulated relationship to images and imaginative concretizations. Things and people around him are part of a rich and varying range of possible ways of appearing and being perceived which recall the complexity and range of optical instrumentations used as theme and metaphor in Nabokov's other writings. The complexity in the treatment of these matters in *Laughter in the Dark* separates Nabokov's work from Pirandello's.

As we have seen, the images provided by the optical instrumentations of cinematography are mostly those that control Albinus's imagination. It is befitting, therefore, that the alternative styles of filmmaking current in German cinema in the twenties and thirties and which we originally saw as formal-mimetic devices, should ultimately come to stand for the conflicting views of reality that control Albinus's life. That the problematic relationship of images such as those provided by film to reality and to life is indeed the ultimate issue is given narrative body by wondering whether Albinus fully comprehends the compromise he is making in accepting as fully "real" the posterlike presence of Margot on the beach. He is at least somewhat aware, we find, that in a summary and iconic way his manipulated vision of her starts a new phase of his life. But he sees this life as a "chapter" in a book and Margot as a decorative editorial device.

And once we move beyond the "posters" at the gate of the Argus cinema, once we enter with Albinus into the dark hall of the theater, the images we find continue to be isolated from their natural context, so much so that Albinus is moved to complain that they don't make any sense. Though now "in motion," these images are like the posters in being emblematic reductions of certain kinds of situations. They lose their individuality by being disconnected from the specific story in which they occur, and thus gain a generic applicability that Albinus, in whose mind they reappear obsessively and ubiquitously, readily absorbs. But here, too, their relevance and suitability to individual experience is questioned.

It is as if Albinus chooses to limit his human reactions in a variety of real situations to a generic film loop that gets switched on over and over since this "moviegoer" has a vested emotional interest in its repetition. It is thus that the image of "a girl . . . receding among tumbled furniture before a masked man with a gun" (L:20) which Albinus first sees on the screen of the Argus theater generates moments such as one that occurs earlier in the novel (but is actually subsequent in the course of the *fabula*) when Albinus exclaims, "No, you can't take a pistol and plug a girl you don't even know, simply because she attracts you" (L:13). Like the use of film materials shot for a previous film in a subsequent one, this "editorial" intrusion from another context is slightly incongruous, as are its subsequent appearances. The irrelevance of the response is pointed out when Albinus, not anticipating the correct content of Margot's "confession" (which has to do with the truth about her background), activates the film loop:

> "Now you'll leave me," groaned Margot. He gulped and immediately leaped to the worst conclusion: she had been unfaithful to him. "Good. Then I'll kill her," he thought swiftly. But aloud he repeated quite calmly: "What's the matter, Margot?" "I have deceived you," she whimpered. "She must die," thought Albinus. (L:99)

The impossibility of acting in appropriate ways by enacting such simplified film-derived clichés, which fail to take into account the full range of variables and of interferences present in real life, Albinus actually experiences when Margot's "deception" turns out in the end to be of the kind feared by him all along. Predictably enough, he reaches "into the pocket of his yellow camel's-hair overcoat" and grabs hold and examines "the thing he had got out to see if it was loaded" (L:224). He then proceeds to ambush Margot in a scene that stresses in its development the filmlike imagination of Albinus as he projects his mind out of the room, going "out to track her." Yet this very moment contains its own critique, which Albinus himself might notice (but does not!), since it also points to the conflict between the imaginary framing of someone's actions and the unpredictable events of real life.

His plan of action is simple enough in its motivation and generic melodrama:

> As soon as she opened it [the door] he would shoot her down. He would not bother to ask her any questions. It was all as plain as death and, with a kind of hideous smoothness, fitted into the logical scheme of things. They had been deceiving him steadily, astutely, artistically. She must be killed at once. (L:224)

No human interaction is left in this scenario. It is locked in with the inevitability of ritual formulaic drama. But this all breaks down in the face of real events. First of all, Albinus's mental "track" fails pathetically: "Now she would have entered the hotel; now she would be coming up in the lift. He listened for the click of her heels along the corridor. But his imagination had outstripped her. Everything was silent" (L:224). And when finally she does catch up with him, his "continuity"[33] proves faulty as a bit player not part of the original scenario interferes:

> He almost fired at the white closed door when he heard the light patter of her rubber soles—yes, of course: she was wearing tennis shoes, there were no heels to click. Now! But at that moment he heard other steps. "Will Madame permit me to fetch the tray?" asked a French voice outside the door. Margot came in at the same time as the chambermaid. (L:224–225)

Margot can thus start a conversation that he cannot interrupt with a fatal, wordless shot because of the presence of a third party, and when the chambermaid leaves, Margot finally "with a shiver of pain" drops "on a chair by the bed" not because of a violent attack by Albinus but because of a blister on her heel.

The blister in fact occupies her so much that at no point does she find herself in the position of receding before Albinus's brandished pistol. When she finally does notice it, she doesn't even realize he is not just playing with it. And when he directs her to stand in the posture appropriate to her execution, she just flatly refuses to be cast in this manner. After this, Albinus's insistence on setting up the situation just in the fashion in which he is used to seeing it done in the movies conspires with Margot in offering her the way out of her dilemma. When he describes the basis of his suspicions, it turns out to be based on the kind of filmlike point of view in which we all derive a story content from what it appears to us viewers that the actors do: "I know all. He sat behind you in that bus, and you behaved like lovers." "Oh, of course, I shall shoot you," he says, and proceeds to try and behave like the betrayed lover in movies (L:227). Margot points out that people who behave *like* lovers may, of course, not necessarily *be* lovers (she certainly knows about this even without having acted in films). And Albinus seems to accept this explanation, the kind which he had earlier planned to foist on Elizabeth to account for Margot's letter: "a young artist in need . . . not quite right in head, writes love letters to strangers" (L:80). These are, after all, the kinds of predictable, repetitive genre formulas that are just as recurrent as the gun-toting melodrama Albinus has allowed to displace his perceptions of a subtle and lifelike unfolding of his relationship with Margot. He is locked into the inevitable cycle of such a plot and will almost manage in the end (almost despite his by then all too real blind groping) to consummate the stereotype as he tries to kill Margot in the final "sequence" of the novel. But even that will be foiled by Margot, who, with all her screen-dreams, retains a better hold on reality.

Margot can use the simple structure of film clichés on Albinus because he himself tries to live by them. Even the kind of experience that allows Pirandello's Varia Nestoroff to see well below the surface of her own stereotypical melodramas and to meet her true inner self escapes Albinus's attention. It does not strike him at all as ironic that in the film production that he finances, his home-breaking mistress is cast as the innocent girl. In the film her fiancé is stolen by a ravenous vamp, but she, having given birth to his child, awaits patiently his return at his mother's farm. Nabokov, no less than Pirandello, allows actual film settings and the implications of film genre to represent the intimate perceptions of its characters. The scene of the film premiere in which Albinus, Margot, and Rex go to see the film in which Margot stars reads like a choral narrative expansion of the separate experiences of Nestoroff, Gubbio, and Nuti.[34]

The confrontation between conflicting kinds of images paradoxically occurs in the very same setting in which Albinus's delusion takes hold of him: with Margot available for appraisal on that very screen on which she had longed to appear when she met Albinus in the darkness of the little cinema. But if the projections of that screen distort Albinus's reality (as they do Gubbio's and Nuti's), we find also that Albinus refuses to recognize those screen images for what they are when they happen to reveal that reality for what it is. Margot's pathetic self-exposure on the screen, her appearance as a "ghastly creature . . . awkward and ugly, with swollen, strangely altered, leech-black mouth, misplaced brows and unexpected creases in her dress" (L:187) strikes Albinus as "sweet, marvelous" (L:188). He is truly "enchanted" and "touched . . . that Margot could act so atrociously—and yet with such a delightful childish zeal, like a schoolgirl reciting a birthday poem" (L:188). He is not aware that his paternalistic suspension of aesthetic criteria is inconsistent with the real performance taking place.

Margot, as we said, is quicker to regain contact with reality and recognizes well enough all the implications of what she sees up on the screen. And she knows what Albinus *should* be seeing. As she puts it to him, "I'm afraid you'll leave me, now that you've seen me in that disgusting film" (L:194). As we have seen, however, she need not worry. More importantly for herself, however, Margot undergoes an experience very similar to that of Varia Nestoroff and, for that matter, of Nabokov's own Ganin. She feels, first of all, totally alienated from her appearance on the screen: "The girl on the screen stared wildly in front of her and then broke in two with her stomach on the window sill and her buttocks to the spectators" (L:187). She does not recognize herself in that image at all: "That monster on the screen had nothing in common with her—she was awful, awful! She was in fact like her mother, the porter's wife, in her wedding photograph" (L:187). Her reaction is just as profound as Nestoroff's and Ganin's. It is not merely a realization that her dreams of film stardom have been dashed for good. What she is faced with is an ironic revelation of her true, inner self, a glaring recognition that she cannot escape her true nature: "She felt like a soul in Hell to whom the demons are displaying the unsuspected lining of its earthly transgressions" (L:189). Margot thus perceives the film image of herself in its deep significance as well as in its surface unsuitability to the occasion; Albinus, on the other hand, dismisses it in its actual significance and embraces it for its irrelevant generic charm.

The only one who sees the film for what it is, and calmly measures its meaning in the real world of everyday interaction, is Rex. He has the pragmatic way with images (even, as we see now, film images) of a film director who is used to shuffling them around on the editing bench to suit his own needs. He is delighted by what he sees on the screen: "He had never doubted that Margot would be a failure on the screen, and he knew that she would revenge herself on Albinus for this failure. Tomorrow, by way of reaction, she would come. At five punctually. It was all very pleasant" (L:188).

So finally we can see that it is quite befitting that Albinus, in picking a film project for himself, should choose one that involves the animation and cinematic expansion of famous paintings. This peripheral and specialized film genre epitomizes the full range of his attitudes from his limited way with art to his attraction for circular, repetitive, and controlled plotting.[35] The fact that Albinus sees nothing wrong in such an exercise is a further confirmation of his limited professional capacities. The choice seems befitting, however, in a more profound way, since it has to do with Albinus personally and with one of the aesthetic consequences of the turning of cinematic means towards the articulation of pictorial worlds.

The application to paintings of cinematic fragmentation and of the kind of continuity which is specific to film emphasizes what is most essential to cinematography precisely because these cinematic qualities are imposed upon artifacts that exist in a state of acausal simultaneity. Film by its nature "stages" cause and effect, "articulates" continuities. Painting, on the other hand, suspends chains of events and synthesizes time. Albinus is fascinated with the possibility of opening up a sequence of actions and reactions by applying cinematic rules to static paintings, by "continuing" with movement and with lateral expansion the actions and worlds implicit in the frozen moment of the painting:

> How fascinating it would be, he thought, if one could use this method [colored animated drawings, which had just begun to appear at the time] for having some well-known picture, preferably of the Dutch School, perfectly reproduced on the screen in vivid colors and then brought to life, movement and gesture graphically developed in complete harmony with their static state in the picture; say, a pot-house with little people drinking lustily at wooden tables and a sunny glimpse of a courtyard with saddled horses—all suddenly coming to life with that little man in red putting down his tankard, this girl with the tray wrenching herself free, and a hen beginning to peck on the threshold. (L:8)[36]

Albinus, as we have seen, is implicated in the constant attempt to control the causalities of his life in a fashion that only the limitations of genre films can allow. Ultimately his need for control is so great that only a cinematic genre in which the filmmaker draws every line will do for him. And it is his overwhelming aspiration to control, so finely rendered by the novelist through this network of film analogies, that leads to Albinus's final downfall.[37]

Part Three

Film Theory and Literary Genre

5

Film Theory as Narrative

Pirandello

Pirandello's *Quaderni di Serafino Gubbio operatore,* as I stated at the outset, is not just a novel that happens to choose a new and original mimetic context (the world of filmmaking) for the unfolding of its plot. Nor is it enough to consider the presence in its structure of what has come to be called the cinematic apparatus a mere metonymy for the emerging industrial complex. The novel is, rather, the prototype of a narrative subgenre one might call the film novel, in which film is at the center and in which the epistemological and existential repercussions of this new twentieth-century medium are explored through the means of narrative. It is a narrative type that displays distinct thematic, formal, and mimetic features peculiar to itself.[1]

What is more, Pirandello's notions of cinema as an art form are an integral part not only of the narrative texture but also of the literary genre characteristics of the film novel.[2] Studies that have looked at film theory in Pirandello's work tend to abstract film theory and other conceptual areas from *Quaderni* or to assume that its representation of film, rather than a central element of its meaning, simply stands for something else (usually machines or progress). This approach tends to sift out the elements of film theory from the full range of narrative functions within which they exist and encourages one to "read" this theory according to the external sequence of its history or to internal hierarchies of theoretical coherence. What gets lost, in this way, is attention to the stress such topics receive within the narrative structure itself, attention, that is, to their full meaning. Yet what Pirandello says specifically about the film medium, and what he does with it, is given context and perspective by such elements as what may be happening in the narrative, who may be present in the scene, or in what way metaphoric extensions sparked off by the film medium extend to the literary context.

Pirandello and Film Theory

Take for instance the meeting between Gubbio and Pirandello's transparent self-portrait. To this curious and questioning gentleman (his face, like indeed Pirandello's, is "delicate, pale, with thin, fair hair; keen, blue eyes; a pointed yellowish beard, behind which there lurked a faint smile"), Gubbio talks about the necessity of retaining absolute "impassivity" and of the operator as a mere reductive "hand that turns the handle." Yet he takes pride in being a necessary appendage to a machine that cannot "regulate its [own] movements according to the action that is going on in front of the camera." He says, "I, my dear Sir, do not always turn the handle at the same speed, but faster or slower as may be required" (Sh:8, Quad:11–12). What we have here is a very specific technical peculiarity of silent film (the variable cranking of the camera in accordance with the feeling one wants to give to the scene). This feature of film technique, moreover, turns out to be functional to our understanding of the character. It is this delicate balance between a specific character and notions of film theory that provides the reader with an early hint that Gubbio, despite claims to the contrary, seeks involvement with the action in front of the camera and even lays claim to a measure of creative control. In other words, film theory and the technological reality of the medium are an integral part of the narrative texture in which who is present, their narrative interaction, and the place an episode has in the interpretation of the action as a whole are important factors.[3]

I would also give greater weight than is usual to Gubbio's famous (and single) positive statement about the medium of film in which he yearns for a cinematography that is truthful and instructive (Sh:151, Quad:86). By separating film theory from the narrative context, one may arrive at a skewed evaluation of what he says. When seen in context, however, it is clear that we have here an encapsulated summa about what the medium could be in its essence: its ability to concretize for the first time in the history of culture (into a concrete image, onto a visible screen) notions of ironic perspective such as the ones outlined in Pirandello's *L'umorismo*. These, as I have argued, in the absence of cinema, had previously been dependent on inner vision and thus inaccessible to most. But whether Gubbio's outburst is an anticipation, as some have argued, of the principles of neorealism[4] or, as I maintain, the attribution of "visible" ironic insight to the cinematic image, the full narrative context of the novel lends this statement greater weight than its isolated status in the text might suggest. For it is spoken by the very character who more than most goes on to betray these positive possibilities of the medium by ignoring the evidence of a crime despite his claim to special insight.

Even Pirandello's use of film-mimetic style takes us beyond a merely chronological reading of film theory. This is so, for one thing, with his precocious extension of the principle of "montage" from image to sound. He seems able to catch the synaesthetic reflex often triggered by silent film much as we find it later, for instance, in the "musical" sequence of Dziga Vertov's 1929 *The Man with a Movie Camera*. He is also able to anticipate the place of sound as a coequal partner with the other codes of cinematography, much as Walter Ruttman did (also in 1929) in his film *Melodie der Welt*. The significance of Pirandello's "narrative" anticipation of film theory becomes evident when we remember that in 1929 Pirandello coined the term "cinemelografia" for the ideal kind of film he planned to make. The project came into being in 1933 with the film *Acciaio*, filmed with none other than the same Ruttman.[5]

Pirandello's views of Marcel L'Herbier's 1925 filming of his novel *Il fu Mattia Pascal* are also prescient. In L'Herbier's work the writer discovered "a cinema [no longer] just mimetic, but fantastic" which created a "linguistically autonomous [space] . . . independent of the necessary link with the reproduction of objects" (Puppa 1978:228). This kind of cinematic effect is also anticipated by the film-mimetic texture of *Quaderni,* especially in the projections of horrifically expressionist shadows that appear on the wall when Nuti hallucinates or in the rush of cinematically rapid images and memories that are triggered by Gubbio's slide towards insanity in the train that returns him from his visit to Sorrento. These film-mimetic passages illustrate well what Pirandello was to describe in 1924: films able to represent "dream, memory, hallucination, madness, and the splitting of personality" (Puppa 1978:227).

Pirandello's film theory, thus, must be seen as part of the narrative texture of his novel. It moves the story forward, conditions the experiences and evolution of the characters, and defines the mimetic context. It also provides a clue to the film-mimetic distortions that occur from time to time in the normal progression of the literary style. Finally, a theoretical perspective on film is also, on a narrative level, integral to the way in which the text involves the reader.

There is a theoretical coherence to what the novel has to say about film, therefore, not so much because it conforms more or less to the state of the art in film theory at the time, nor necessarily because it anticipates one or other subsequent theory. *Quaderni* has such coherence because Pirandello turns into narrative the full range of what might be called the "functions" of this new art form. This translation of film into narrative goes beyond the mere coverage of all the aspects of cinematography as it existed in 1916. It involves a full consideration of the interrelatedness of aspects of production (cameraman, director, scriptwriter, producer, and actors with all their intentions, experiences, and techniques, but also the filmmaking apparatus), aspects of reception (audiences "professional" and otherwise, but also the structure of the viewing situation itself), and all the elements in between (the world that is represented, the nature of the representation, the means of representation, the linguistic codes peculiar to the medium, the text-embedded elements that provide information, contact, context, and other forms of "guidance"). The novel also goes beyond the mere use of technical film terminology and talk about film.

Discourse on Film

Most prominent at first in *Quaderni* is the presence of a coherent discourse about film as a medium. This discourse involves considerations of the nature of the medium as such, as well as awareness of the aesthetic, ethical, psychological, philosophical, and other issues raised by it, and can be recognized at different levels of the narrative such as Gubbio's inner monologue and discussions among some of the characters. It is also implicit (another kind of discourse, this one) in the actions and reactions of characters. What such discourse first engages, as it winds its way through the narrative, are the two poles of human interaction with artifacts that have always defined the aesthetic horizon: those of production and reception.

Issues of initiative and control appear to be especially vivid at the intersection of the cinematic text with the human agencies that generate it (production). Take, for instance, Gubbio's director Cocò Polacco in the context of a "utopian" theory of film. In general, because of who s/he is, or thanks to an allegiance to the "correct" kind of aesthetics, the director is the individual who may control all dimensions of vision; the agent whose initiative brings distance, time, memory, and cause and effect under control. Yet these initiatives and this control are not without their shades, and *Quaderni* qualifies artistic creation in film with a subtlety that anticipates later film theory. Pirandello's specific director bullies and cajoles crew and actors to come up with what he wants, yet his mastery is hemmed in on all sides by limitations he can't ignore. Actors "act out" rather than act; personal currents interfere with the fictional interaction he tries to stage; the viewing public (or the studio) decides what stories he may or may not film; and finally his own cameraman "stages" by default his own ending of the film.

Gubbio for his part yearns for the ideal director, one who would use the medium for the truth it can show, yet does not recognize the one character who is clearly such a guide (even if strictly speaking not a "film" director): the philosophical Simone Pau who stages and retells parables full of truth drawn directly from the visible and commonplace reality that surrounds us (the flophouse that some have recognized as a perfect setting for realist sociopolitical film discourse). The other major technicians of the creative act of film (Gubbio as cameraman and Cavalena as scriptwriter) illustrate how little the two texts of film (the verbal foreshadowing outlined in the written scenario and the filmed images that implement it) have to do with anything other than the artist's personal obsessions.

Rather than extolling the creative omnipotence that the medium allows, then, this novel stresses the obstacles that film production places in the way of creative freedom and the personal limitations to which it lends brilliant technological support. It also starts to hint at the extent to which the director's freedom depends on the spectator's acquiescence as well as upon the spectator's active contribution.

When it comes to reception, *Quaderni* is notable for its extensive narrative development of theoretical issues that concern the spectator. The narrative instances involved are especially cogent, since the same characters who produce the work stand by to view the result. This allows for a subtle exploration of the diaphanous membrane that separates the two sides of the screen. Aldo Nuti, Varia Nestoroff, and even Gubbio find themselves at one and the same time actors and spectators. While the novel does not yet deal (as subsequent ones will) with the phenomenology of sheer spectatorship, its characters already experience the opposing tugs of "production" and "reception" that characterize this art form more intensely than most because the productive aspect of spectatorship in film is so vivid.

One distinctive motif, then, of the film novel is the narrative exploration of the area of awareness that recent film theory has insisted must be fostered in film viewers, lest the overwhelming illusion of the medium rob them of critical distance. In this particular novel such moments are always used to define in a succinct and thematically focused way topics (human perception, narrative reliability, reality, illusion, human and instrumental mediation, subjectivity) that take us beyond the trivial level of moviemaking. It is at moments such as the one that finds Nuti simultaneously aware of the two sides of his presence on film (as actor he *is* image, as audience he *perceives* it) that the significance of the image to the actor and to the audience starts to transcend the individual narrative instance. This doubled awareness leads, as we saw, to considerations that embrace an individual's sense of time on earth, relationship to family, and awareness of death. Nestoroff too reaches a painful and special insight into her own nature when she finds herself in the double role of performer and spectator and may well represent the first example in contemporary narrative of a woman rebelling against the way in which film turns her body into a fetish.[6] Similar moments will become central in novels such as these, and one of their distinguishing characteristics. In situations such as these a genre-specific type of human experience is staged—one that involves a clearly defined range of issues all of which derive from the special kind of awareness that "critical" film viewing fosters.

The compulsive thrust of personal obsessions such as those exemplified by the scriptwriter Cavalena and the overwhelming control of memory over images such as that experienced by Gubbio, but also the exploitative opportunism of directors such as Polacco, raise further issues that link the two ends of this communicative tension: the power that film puts in the hands of those who control it, the transgressions that film can perpetrate upon the privacies and sensibilities of those it "captures" in its net, and the vicarious thrills (free of all responsibility) it can provide to its audiences.

People will apparently submit to almost any indignity, suffering, and even danger in order to be included in a director's project. This places at least some responsibility on the filmmaker, for, as Pirandello emphasizes, participation in the "fictional" reality of the movies compromises and alters actuality to a point where actors and technicians find themselves diminished as total human beings. Some of them (Ferro, Nuti) even put themselves in actual physical danger. Tacit exploitation of such interaction between two very different kinds of reality raises a moral question in the case of film more than in any other kind of art because film draws its fascination from an ambiguous claim to realism. As Gubbio himself points out, the medium lends itself to a "hybrid game" in which the greatest unrealities are presented through most real-seeming means. Pirandello finds narrative strategies to take such a dilemma (a major point of theoretical discussion in later film theory) to its extreme. His cameraman (despite his claim to be sensitive to such issues) ultimately compromises himself by committing the most severe moral transgression in the trade: the deliberate filming of what amounts to a "snuff" movie.[7] Gubbio is actually proud of this and feels that the film company can thank him if the film is guaranteed to attract droves of spectators who know that *this* fiction *is* reality.

The medium of film at its broadest, then, is seen to illustrate a specific instance of the illusion of technological control, of the double-edged sword that such control represents, and of the human shortcomings that undermine it. In the world of filmmaking such shortcomings happen to be the shortcomings of producers, the expectations of viewers, and the struggle between both camps (filmmakers and spectators) over what is to be controlled. That these issues are of wider import than the isolated case of filmmaking is clear from Pirandello's allusion to such other (but related) areas of modern technological progress as electric lighting and the telescope. All of these technologies of vision provide an illusion of greater clarity that in the end turns against their users. This kind of extrapolation from cinematography tends to be typical in subsequent film novels too.

Discourse of Film

If anything in Pirandello's novel underlines the dilemmas of technological control with immediacy, it is what might be called the "discourse of film." In his mimesis of it (in his textual attempts to render the flow of film upon a screen), Pirandello makes it clear that, whatever the source (who produces, how, and why) or whoever the recipient (spectators variously disposed to subjection or rebellion, or just out to have a jolly good time), the discourse of film tends to escape people's control and interpretation.

Central to the discourse of film is the image itself, and much that happens in *Quaderni* has to do with the status of the image and its relation to the perceiving subject. But here lies a difficulty noted by film theorists, whose later theoretical "dialogue" is foreshadowed in the pages of *Quaderni*. Does reality actually imprint itself upon the emulsion and do filmmakers therefore owe the audience a special responsibility (Bazin and Kracauer)? Or is the "impression" of imprint merely another level of what remains in essence a rhetorical apparatus (Metz)? Practitioners of the film novel have no stake in adjudicating the puzzles of subsequent film theory, and indeed Pirandello's narrative explores the tension between these two views without trying to resolve it. He displays for all to see with the utmost concreteness the point where film images intersect with human imagination, memory, and desire and thus give rise to an intricate narrative interplay that demonstrates sensitivity (long before the formulations of film theory) to the paradox of this art form in which the most concrete and the most general dissolve into the most abstract and personal.

As much recent film theory has stressed, what viewers see through the medium of film may mislead them as to its sufficient "fit" with reality. Yet it is not just that realistic verisimilitude (so overwhelming in much film) tends to mislead viewers into taking images at face value. Even the most stylized stereotypes tend to have such an effect, connecting as they do with generalized stereotypes that lie well below the surface of individual critical self-examination. Again, long before its explicit appearance in theoretical discourse about film, this theoretical subtlety occurs to Pirandello. He makes it into an important element in the psychological motivation of his characters and the evolution of his plot in such instances as the reductive scenarios that transform Gubbio's world into a veritable gallery of film cutouts (the reliance on filmlike stereotyping of people is positively dehumanizing) or Nuti's way of conducting himself. Even the movie clichés that are used as mechanisms of narrative resolution owe their power to the collective recognition by spectators of their subliminal power.

Awareness of these aspects of cinematography culminates, of course, in Pirandello's stress on the reduction by film technology of even the most individualized of human beings into a mechanical stop-motion shadow, a mechanical hybrid of camera and person. Such a "robot" as Gubbio becomes at one point (or the stylized one that Nuti is throughout) produces a mere illusion of real life and is in itself a brilliant metaphor for film's own mechanical reproduction of life. These dehumanizing transformations, as is well known, are at the core of Pirandello's critique of the mechanical nature of the film medium, suggesting as they do the futility of any attempt either to control reality or to affect it through the technology of this new medium. All of this happens, one must note as Pirandello does too, despite the fact that the medium itself labors to suggest otherwise.

Since questions about the reality-status of the image are so central in this novel, the parsing out of the different levels of interaction between the image and the individual leads Pirandello to a more philosophical plane than one encounters in anecdotal accounts of the fascinating world of movies. Film images come to be treated as analogous to images in the mind and acquire some of the same attributes assigned to mental images by philosophers such as Sartre. Here Pirandello touches upon some of the most evocative and unsettling topics of contemporary thought and manages again to flesh out in brilliant and concrete detail abstract ideas such as the paradoxical impression of presence triggered by an experience of absence. He gives them human life through the multiplicity and idiosyncrasy of individual experience. It is through concrete human experience, thus, that Pirandello defines the essence of the film image, a central task of much subsequent film theory. In linking this notion of image with the resonances of irony (be it in its rhetorical manifestation, be it in the more telling guise of a special kind of insight), he contributes to this discussion early and with originality. Just as he does with his anticipations of such topics as the heuristic power of film, its truth-value well beyond the rhetorical sleights of hand of hacks, and especially with questions about the extent to which what the image represents is actually there.

These are topics broached much later by film theory, where their specific details turn out to be as contradictory as the broader opposition between a formative and a realist view of the medium that underlies much of Pirandello's novel. In Gubbio's claim for the cinema one may hear anticipations of Bazin's view that the image on the emulsion is, as I hinted above, a veritable "imprint" made by the world upon the medium, a presence within the medium of the actuality of the world which cancels the mediation that is inevitable in all other art forms (Bazin 1967:9–16). One may also hear in it Kracauer's realist claim, in fact just as immanentist as Bazin's, as well as his views on the limits of this presence. One may find implicit in Gubbio as well as in Kracauer, moreover, such recent views as that of film as pure mediation; as "sign," even if this sign is admittedly the most "motivated" sign we have—a veritable multisensory onomatopoeia. "Cinematic films," says Kracauer, "evoke a reality more inclusive than the one they actually picture." Since images "evoke a reality which may fittingly be called 'life,'" he continues, "they fail to give us the fullness of life, while teasing us with the illusion that they do." Kracauer feels, as other theorists indeed do too, that such a dilemma is central to a typically modern malaise, but so did Serafino Gubbio before him.

Gubbio's denunciation of the cheating "reality effect" of film fantasies is only one example of the narrative exploration of film theory that characterizes Pirandello's novel. No less evocative of its dilemmas is, for instance, the cameraman's intense involvement with the production of Nestoroff's dancing image, utterly deluded as he is about being the real focus of her intense erotic excitement. His cinematic preview leaves him with the heightened sense of desire and of loss quite typical of that produced (recent film theory assures us) by the film-viewing situation as a whole. Similar, if more explicit, is Nuti's prediction of a false experience of presence that will assail the viewers of his own screen image. But the most complex variation on this theme is found in the novel's grand finale, in which the genre "contract" agreed upon by all (filmmakers and audience alike) about a specific fictional reality suitable to the film representation of a tiger hunt flips over to reveal itself a sham—a void—for all to see.

It is because he explores the cinematic effect of reality and the inevitable existential void which it elicits that Pirandello manages to anticipate and surpass in subtlety some recent theoretical developments. Jean-Louis Baudry may be right in theory when he states that "almost exclusively, it is the technique and content of film which have retained attention . . . in complete ignorance of the fact that the impression of reality is dependent first of all on a subject-effect, and that it might be necessary to examine the position of the subject facing the image in order to determine the need for cinema-effect" (Baudry 1976:118–119). Yet Pirandello's narrative exploration of the experience of several film spectators demonstrates in practice a subtle awareness precisely of the dimension that Baudry maintains is neglected. We read in this novel about real and convincing experiences of the "subject-effect."

Questions at the core of film theory are extensively explored in Pirandello's novel, and their "narrative" unwinding stresses the fact that the distinction between theoretical treatment and fictional elaboration amounts to an opposition between lived experience and abstraction. The answers don't always come out the same in fiction and out of the mouths of theorists (this will tend to be true of the genre as a whole), but, if one may say so, those derived from the narrative exploration of characters actually "living the question through" are often more credible and alive than those obtained in the absence of such imaginative existential testing.

This is so, for instance, with the similarity between film viewing and the experience of dreaming (another area of interest to recent film theory). For Mitry the similarity exists since the flow of cinematic images approximates easily (like a memory of an act we have not lived) the immediacy of dreaming and parallels its absence of reality. For Bazin it is the very situation in the movie house that appears as "the night of our waking dreams." More recently, Baudry encapsulates the effects of such a situation where "no exchange, no circulation, no communication with the outside" occurs so that "projection and reflection take place in a closed space and those who remain there . . .

find themselves chained, captured, or captivated" (Baudry 1974/75:44). But most detailed of all on this subject is Metz. In his view it is in their "flux," as Metz calls it, that film and dream resemble each other most; in the way, that is, that "signifiers" in both situations (in both cases images accompanied by sound and movement) have an affinity. "'Imaged' expression"—pictorial means that carry within themselves the meaning—are at the core of both experiences, according to Metz (1976:90).

The elements of this theoretical dialogue are anticipated with great, almost tactile, immediacy in the "syntax" of dreaming that renders the hallucinations and nightmares of Pirandello's characters. Such moments as Nuti's illness or Gubbio's train ride, moreover, are the very occasions when the text indulges in sudden displays of cinematic formal mimetics. *Quaderni,* furthermore, offers narrative versions of the differing and idiosyncratic ways in which spectators do or do not acquiesce to oneiric subjection. Such episodes as Nestoroff's rebellious reaction to her image on screen and Gubbio's ready submission to the filmlike images that assail him in the train intimate some of the most recent developments in film theory. The range of attitudes explored by Pirandello thus starts to sketch the outline of the very "socioanalytic typology" of spectatorship proposed by Metz, inaugurating what will become a major strand in subsequent novels in this tradition (Metz 1976:77).

More extensively and in greater detail than with other theoretical issues, the film-mimetic passages in *Quaderni* anticipate recent thinking on the syntax of film. It is at points where the texture of Pirandello's writing tries to capture the stylistics of film that vision is transformed to suggest a new view of the world, that matters of existential and philosophical import come to the fore, and that key points in the narrative are advanced. While some of the devices that I and others have pointed out are relatively obvious, some of the more sophisticated film tropes used by Pirandello (cinematic progressions from long-shot to detail; retrogression mediated by flashback montage; tracking shots combined with alternating points of view oriented in opposite directions) are surprising in their complexity and in the extent to which they are functionally integrated into several levels of the narrative. It is thus again that Pirandello equals (and at times refines) our contemporary insight into this medium. At times he can be as technically astute as Vertov, Jakobson, and Metz about the process of selection from reality and combination into an invented one; about organization of materials by syntagmatic continuity and paradigmatic similarity; about the interaction of metaphor and metonymy; about the paradoxes of losing reality in the very act of creating its closest possible approximation. In all these passages one is made aware of the strict interrelatedness of the texturally minute and the experientially universal.

Vivid passages in Pirandello's novel also tend to confirm, just as Kracauer suggests, that the attempt to "be cinematic" leads to the settings (city, streets, public places) that attract the medium and to situations (the filmically realized car ride) that favor the dynamic essence of film. The very same passages, on the other hand, also illustrate a view of cinema antithetical to Kracauer's notion of film as mere mirror. Through the eyes of Gubbio and his colleagues we are treated to the kind of "Kino-Eye" that tends to distort raw, vivid realism, be it in the ideologically tinged constructivism of Vertov (whose term I am using to describe the horrid merging of organism with machine), be it in the more theoretical application of Arnheim. In other words, both a realist and a formative emphasis is accommodated at the textual level just as we saw that it is at the conceptual one. The flow of city life, the glitter and excitement of the streets (in Kracauer's view a "natural center for a cinematic perspective on the world") figure prominently and in fact become occasions for the display of film-mimetic writing.

Pirandello also imaginatively plumbs film-specific devices for their meaningful application to plot, to narrative progression, to ideas, and to feelings in ways that anticipate and "confirm" the insights of filmmakers and theoreticians. Furthermore, as my pages on the novel clearly show, creative applications of such devices and topoi allow them to "say things" (from expressive effects to philosophical insights) that in later years will become part of film repertory. They mirror, in fact, the characteristics (formal and thematic) of a sister art very much like the polemical use of the "paragone" topos did in the late Renaissance.[8] This is the kind of awareness of the guts of the film medium that, as is well known, recent film theory puts at the center of the creative potential of film.

Discourse on Film Theory

Beyond what we can extrapolate from *Quaderni* in the realms of a discourse on film and of a discourse of film (and precisely because so often what Pirandello enacts speaks in detail to the later concerns of film theory), a third area emerges from the novel: what one might well term "discourse on film theory." At the level of this type of discourse *Quaderni* also manages to be quite sophisticated.[9] We don't find, of course, a consistent and thorough "theory" of film in the novel (theoreticians such as the ones mentioned above develop these later). But often enough, implicitly or explicitly, Pirandello anticipates points and distinctions. The stringent qualifications attributed to the power of film by opponents such as Arnheim and Kracauer, for instance, can be seen in the attitudes of the novel's characters. Kracauer can be glimpsed especially in Serafino Gubbio, a cameraman drawn to the surface excitement and vitality of reality so readily captured by the film image. He is, in fact, a cameraman-philosopher whose fascination with the medium leads to an apocalyptic synthesis quite similar to Kracauer's pessimistic conclusion to his book, or Benjamin's to his essay. But Gubbio also anticipates Arnheim's observation that the director in silent movies is able to correct even "the shape of motion" in his boast that he can "regulate ... movements" according to the speed at which he turns the handle. In fact, Gubbio's inability to perceive reality in any way other than that dictated by the aesthetic peculiarities of a medium that takes over his sensibility amounts to a grotesque "personification" of what was to become Arnheim's fundamental assumption about the formative nature of film.

Gubbio echoes most closely Kracauer, on the other hand, about the formative power of film settings that cut up and absorb human protagonists who lend their bodies to cinematic enactments. It is Kracauer also who, like Gubbio, insists on the estrangements produced by cinematic distancing: his example of Proust's photographer echoes Pirandello's fictional cameraman in his plea that cinema be carefully controlled in what it is "allowed" to show. Pirandello, it turns out, anticipates fundamental points of film theory in such a way as to underline inherent agreements between views that later will tend to be seen as opposites.[10] Where film theorists and characters differ, however, is in drawing some of the consequences: Kracauer, very much like Gubbio, recognizes the formative potential of film as a threat to one's peace of mind and recommends tight control; Arnheim, as would any aesthetic opponent of Gubbio (one such, as we saw, is the figure of Nabokov's Axel Rex), is interested in understanding and exploring the aesthetic foundation of the medium, without the imposition of a priori strictures.

Pirandello also anticipates Kracauer's view that the peculiar syntax of meaning allowed by the new technologies (optical, photographic, cinematographic) amounts to a philosophical topos that characterizes the first half of the twentieth century. Kracauer calls it a "period topic" that addresses itself to the relativity of viewpoint and the instability of moving perspectives (Kracauer 1960:8–9). The "moving camera" view that Gubbio provides in order to cope with the fast moving car that overtakes him, therefore, is destined to become a new cultural archetype. In the literature of cinematic perspective it represents one of the most important devices, be it (as we have seen happens in the car accident that is the turning point of Albinus's story in *Laughter in the Dark*) as a way of articulating the narrative, or be it (as it is used elsewhere by Nabokov, but also, we shall see, by Isherwood, Percy, or Puig) to capture the metaphysical suggestiveness of the medium.

In all such instances (literary as well as cinematic) a tension is found in the "problematic" implications of the scenes, despite the almost pure cinematic surface of the device. Such form-specific topoi (it is these, after all, that Kracauer regards as "inherent affinities" of medium and situations and that Arnheim considers the elements in reality that the medium is best at foregrounding) turn out to be only apparently devoid of "content." Even such an abstract element as "movement" soon becomes (we have seen the passage in Nabokov's autobiographical *Speak, Memory* in which an openly cinematic evocation of childhood birthday parties culminates in the slow helical descent of a floating samara) a way to intimate the concretized sensation of time in a way that is typical of film technique. These formal topoi often become meaningful in a conceptual way just as the film-specific topoi in Pirandello (progression from long-shot to close-up for instance) are functionally intertwined with the narrative progression of the story.

The role of film theory within Pirandello's novel thus indicates an attempt to depict the spectator's experience in the movie-house seat (a fundamental feature of this genre and interesting in and of itself) through the technical means of literature, yet the attempt leads to more ambitious ends. This "more" has a great deal to do with what Baudry describes as a cinematic instinct that precedes the mechanical means of its fulfillment. It is the instinct to take a wider look at things from the perceptually self-conscious stance provided by rhetorical and philosophical irony, the very stance (and definition of film image) we have found in Pirandello. He is the first to suggest implicitly (and to dramatize quite explicitly) that a link exists between a particular kind of "epistemological lust" and the emerging technologies of perception, film among them. In this, as we have seen, he anticipates theorists of this new art form who similarly claim for it synoptic insights, revelatory of "a boundless, indeterminate, unfathomable world," a world that captures the romantic image through the means of photographic realism (Arnheim 1966:183). He also anticipates those who attribute to the medium (the phenomenologist Merleau-Ponty and film theorists heavily indebted to him do this) a view of the world as "an object endowed with meaning" (Merleau-Ponty 1964:57–58, Baudry 1974/75:43) and a presentation of "objects . . . in their signifying guise" (Mitry 1963/65:I, 128).

It is because of the impact produced by the fact that the film experience tends, as Kracauer puts it, to "evoke a reality which may fittingly be called 'life'" but in the end fails to deliver it (Kracauer 1960:70) that what Pirandello was moved to write has become the prototype of a narrative genre in which the conflict remains central. For the contemporary descendants of Gubbio (the characters of Manuel Puig are the most recent), film may indeed be the only available locus for passionate involvement. The film theory implicit in what Pirandello produced generates a "kind" of novel especially suited to explore the individual existential repercussions of the central art form of our time.

Nabokov

Nabokov and Film Theory

Since Nabokov's attitude to theories of any kind (literary, psychoanalytic, as well as cinematic) is testy at best, it is unlikely that we may find him as explicit as Pirandello on what film is, what it could be, and how it may be used. Yet in ways that may well be more fundamental (for they go to the roots of film aesthetics), much of what Nabokov has to say is quite insightful from a theoretical point of view. What is more, in his case the relationship of film to experience is explored in modes that reach beyond fiction since, as we have seen, distinctive genre elements (stylistic, thematic, philosophical) appear in Nabokov as part of autobiographical discourse.

The autobiographical element in Nabokov is the most dramatic departure from the strictly fictional realm of Pirandello. It does matter, for instance, in ways that are fundamental in real life to us all, that the imprints of celluloid which allow time past to be made present include humble "home movies" and that these turn out to be about mortality and offer the shudder of existential serendipity in the privacy of bourgeois parlors. It matters because the direct existential applicability to the individual goes here hand in hand with the "domestication" of a medium that in its public forum may seem too grand, too complex, and too distant to speak to us directly one on one. Having this described as vividly as does Nabokov makes a deeper awareness of the modalities of human existence accessible to many more of us than ever before (and with more immediacy than the average undergraduate curriculum on the philosophy of existentialism). Reading about the experience in the context of an autobiography removes even the remaining element of distance that fiction may provoke.[11]

Film theory becomes an integral part of the narrative texture of Nabokov's work as much as, if not more than, we find in Pirandello. Our extensive discussion of *Laughter in the Dark* has provided ample illustrations of the fact that film perception, film syntax, and the cultural ramifications of the medium are integral to the story of Albinus, Margot, and Rex. The fact that the medium reveals the true nature of Margot, for instance, rather than endowing her, as she wishes, with an aura of glamor (this is an issue that in film theory appears readily in debates about film and reality) matters in ways that are integral to the devolution of destiny for Nabokov's characters.

Discourse on Film

Consider, on the one hand, the Arnheim that we find "voiced" in the view that Axel Rex holds about cinema and that thus provides a focused view on the medium. Cinematic reality is there, they both believe, to be manipulated and recreated by exploiting the peculiarities of film. This, moreover, becomes "art" thanks to the limitations of the optical apparatus which, for "director" Rex, is a blind Albinus functioning just like a limited camera. On the other hand, the flow of city life and the glitter and excitement of the streets, central to the motivation of Albinus as it is to the formal mimesis of the novel, echoes Kracauer's views about what is the natural center for a cinematic perspective on the world. Nabokov, expanding Pirandello's thematic focus, also provides a narrative exploration of views that regard film as the "chimerical desire to establish the continuum of physical existence" (Kracauer 1960:63); that notice the ability of the camera to concretize such abstract categories as "the manifestation of the 'transcendent subject'"; and that stress the kind of subjectivity which, through the faculty of vision, considers itself the origin of all meaning (Baudry 1974/75:43–44). This dizzying view of the world is given by Nabokov great narrative variety: whether it be seen through the well of a microscope, on the confined emulsion of a lantern slide, or through the airborne freedom of television and film cameras. Similarly, in his use of what might be termed a "metaphysical" film-mimetic style, Nabokov imbues his narrative with that other quality captured by the camera: the serendipitous atmosphere of a world that is caught unawares, laden with an undefinable but quite definite sense of mystery and dread.

But the infinite potential of the medium is, alas, limited by human agency. Albinus Kretchmar, for one, demonstrates this in his multiple roles as film producer, as originator of artsy animated cartoons, and as fascinated spectator. He personifies with great economy the two opposing facets (production and reception) of man's interaction with the film medium. As the novel's representative of "production," he illustrates some of the problems inherent in the creative and financial impetus that stands behind the production of most film. He displays very well the nonprofessional and often whimsical motives of many film promoters. This is of course one of the weaknesses of a medium that, because of its enormous expense, is always dependent on such as Albinus (who bankrolls a film to star his untalented mistress) or beholden to agencies who similarly act out of anything but artistic motivation (be it financial, be it political, be it "scientific" purpose).

Nabokov's narrative exploration of the productive end of filmmaking also addresses the issue of control. We do find an Axel Rex (talented, cool, manipulative, driven) who, as we saw, functions in the mold of a Langian "character as director." But on the whole Nabokov's representation of directors does not suggest such freedom. We can see this most clearly if we look to some of his other novels. A typical director is the one we find in *Mary*: a "fat, red-haired, coatless man . . . standing on a platform between floodlights and yelling himself to insanity through a megaphone" (M:30). When Nabokov's characters, moreover, assume the actual role of a film director (Hermann does so in *Despair* to plot his escape, Smurov in *The Eye* to tell us how he feels about those around him), this happens at moments when they actually *lose* control altogether.[12] Albinus himself, moreover, reveals how much his film ventures owe to lack of control. It is his aesthetic limitations and his psychological quirks, as we saw, that lead him to propose an elaborate project for animated paintings. It is, moreover, his trivial "mental framings" of Margot (circumscribed as they are by a sexual obsession that reduces this educated art historian to the level of a voyeuristic paparazzo) that account for his funding of her film career.

It is interesting to note that for Nabokov, as opposed to Pirandello, despite such limitations, film allows for a positive creative role of directors, metaphorical as may be. This is so most extensively, of course, with the directorial formal mimetics that characterizes *Laughter in the Dark* as a whole. Yet even the very same obsessions that interfere with Albinus become (*vide* Vladimir and Tamara at the movies) the creative rockbed from which meaningful images can emerge. These are meanings, as we saw, open to an audience attuned to the archetypal aura of film images. In the name of such personal focus, Nabokov is led to challenge the directorial privilege of those bona fide directors who present him with their own spectacles; indeed to take over from them. We saw him do this as a teenager, but such skepticism may indeed go back to an interesting childhood experience he recounts in *Speak, Memory*.

Finding himself one day suddenly facing a blank screen during a slide show mounted by a tutor ("the flustered operator could not find the fourth slide, having got it mixed up with the used ones" [SpM:165]), Nabokov notes the reactions of his young contemporaries: a livelier commotion to this deprivation than to the show itself. Their behavior (riotous and bordering on the obscene) reveals an instinctive reaction to the passive yet expectant situation of watching a magically nurturing screen. Protected by the darkness of the womblike auditorium (and given access by the sudden failure of the apparatus) the children feel free to act out the wish to place oneself (one's self) upon that screen. "Some of the spectators," Nabokov tells us, "started to project the black shadows of their raised hands upon the frightened white screen, and presently, one ribald and agile boy (could it be I after all—the Hyde of my Jekyll?) managed to silhouette his foot, which, of course, started some boisterous competition" (SpM:165).

This episode, centered upon the failure of a hapless "director," turns out to be a vivid narrative realization of the basic situation of movie watching as we have come to know it from recent film theory. The breakdown of the apparatus (a framework in which "film" includes the conditions of its performance) exposes the conflict between magical nurturing stimulation (the screen provides our passive and receptive self with fulfilling excitement) and the aggressive projection of one's own individual shadow upon that screen. As spectators we hover between regression and aggression; between the decorum of the safe social conditions of an incoherently voyeuristic activity and the latent sexual energies that are repressed by displacing fantasies onto a safely "removed" screen. The aggression of these Russian children against the "frightened" screen (controlled by a tutor in a distinctly authoritarian role) betrays their inchoate instinctive awareness that the "removed" is indeed an outer manifestation of their own alienated selves; the screen which may display their own "ribald" lower limbs; the stage upon which "the Hyde of" their "Jekyll" might suddenly appear. It may well have been this early experience that led Nabokov to continue to rebel against the inherently passive and voyeuristic situation of the film spectator as he grew older, that may have led him to the narrative exploration of these issues. Just as Gubbio, if with more success, Nabokov transcends his role as a mere bolt in the mechanical apparatus. His characters, on the other hand, have less success.

Albinus too epitomizes the complicated interaction of the audience with film images: their "reception." In this role he does not (as did his creator) move to control the images on screen. For him, as for most film audiences, the fascination of the image entails a condition of passive and helpless thralldom. Yet Albinus too lends the tissue of his memory and the syntax of his subconscious to the screen. He is just not as successful as Nabokov in keeping his distance. The films he seeks out dovetail nicely with his fantasies of escape, while his notions of passionate human interaction conform to the stereotypes of screen melodramas. He even tries in his own clumsy way to cross the barrier between the two realities and discovers only too late that his passive acceptance of screen models does not conform to the complexities of real life.

In Nabokov, just as in Pirandello, this theoretical issue is a constant thematic center. He relates the application of stereotypical and subjective constraints upon individual understanding and feeling to the field of art history, to the issue of individual choice, and to the very stylistic texture of his novel. Albinus's screen-mediated foreshadowings, Nestoroff's and Margot's confrontations with themselves on the screen, Nabokov's attempt to wrench the actor Mozzhuhin out of the context of his screen fiction and to place him within the writer's own life history—all of these cases remind us that the images that get to the screen (generically trivial or subjectively resonant as may be) tend to be refunneled into the idiosyncratic perspective of individual spectators. In fact, Nabokov's use of cinematic means in a literary context to create the intricate drama of memory, loss, and desire brings him closest (in spirit if not always in detail) to the work of Hugo Münsterberg, for whom the mind molds the world with acts of "attention" quite similar to those prompted by the focus lengths and angles of cinema's lenses (Münsterberg 1970:38, 46); not to speak of the most recent theories by Metz and others that compare the nature of film to that of the human mind (Metz 1982). One may also see in his writing a foreshadowing of the current theoretical focus on the fact that the screen inherently brackets the subject (positions the subject) in forceful and limiting ways. Could the rebellious reactions of these characters (not to speak of Nabokov himself) indicate awareness of this? While the field of film theory is only recently coming to recognize that the situation is relevant to male as well as to female spectators, young Nabokov is in fact trapped (as he is forced to watch side by side with his girl friend an ideal representation of the screen lover). He thus cannot be free to develop into this role by himself and in the way he may wish.

It is because of the assertiveness of this medium that directorial moral responsibility is an issue for Nabokov as much, if not more, than it is for Pirandello. Cinematography used without such accountability can cause real pain, especially in the hands of sadistic directors such as Axel Rex. Nabokov, in a novel written after the ones examined here but relevant in this instance nonetheless, catches this dark corner of cinematography with chilling directness. *Bend Sinister* describes the cold, sadistic alienation with which the Ekwilist doctors make their films of deranged, murderous youth gangs torturing helpless victims. This is ostensibly filmmaking in the name of scientific pursuit, yet these films are eventually used in a manner that clearly belies their search for the truth and exposes their true pornographic aim. The film "versions" projected for the assembled researchers intersperse the obscene cruelty of the action with subtitles such as "A Night Lawn Party," "No Whistling, Please!" and "Bad Luck, Fatso!" Nabokov drives home the perverted horror of such film spectacle by placing in the audience the father of the "little human creature of no value" who is the chosen victim. Here is the one member of the audience who cannot watch with the suspended moral engagement that characterizes most viewers caught in the cinematic situation. It is thus that the horror we all should feel (a horror that the situation of film watching often helps to anesthetize) is stressed. Nabokov manages to suggest the helpless lack of control that an audience may feel when faced with such materials. It is a lack of control that thus mirrors the paradoxical helplessness of filmmakers (Bend:195–196).[13]

Discourse of Film

By "staging" for his readers episodes in clearly cinematic ways, Nabokov explores far more extensively than Pirandello the special kinds of creative vision that cinematography allows. This "effect of film," moreover, does extensive duty in carrying forward what he has to tell about his characters or himself. Albinus's contrasting visions of Berlin, for instance, convey important story materials through the stylistic alternatives open to a cinematic control of imagery. In instances such as this, control through the camera (position, movement, continuity, focus, composition, light refraction) is used by Nabokov with remarkable inventiveness. He takes charge of the ubiquitous camera he wishes upon his ideal poet and structures his materials in directorlike fashion at times broadly reminiscent of the style of real directors (Fellini, Vertov, and Lang) and at times narrowly akin to specific technical effects ("superimpositions," "jump-cuts").[14] Such techniques drive home to us the fate of Albinus as well as the impact of personal images such as the "carpet" of Nabokov's life. Willfully folded ("let the visitor trip"), the superimposition of pattern exposes the continuities of time and space by its filmlike juxtaposition, just as the "cinematic" sequence that follows a butterfly in ways that only the most advanced film techniques can do crosses two continents to reveal the human pain of exile.

As we saw with Pirandello, formal mimetics are most effective in capturing some of the special features of the modern condition. We have found this to be so, for instance, in the "sequence" at the Sport Palace in which Albinus and mistress are seen by his brother-in-law. Here, it is the formative distortion of the medium that modulates reality in meaningful ways as it parses out setting and characters into cinematic units and reconnects them according to its own medium-logic. In the process, medium-specific formativism blends protagonists with setting until the physical integrity of human beings is compromised for the sake of a kind of vision best epitomized by cinema. But Nabokov takes the professional deformation of formative vision beyond syntax into the substance of what life is about. It is in this context that the whimsical notion that film images may function as actual foreshadowings of things to come (a central conceit in *Laughter in the Dark*) seems less than an eccentricity. For Albinus, images on screen that are defined by "genre" (images that respond to their own medium-logic more than to life) become "real" because it is under their influence that he chooses his actions. His behavior thus turns out to be as "flat" and "shallow" as the screen upon which such cinematic stereotypes appear. If in the novel such merging of film and reality (the very notion that movie reality may foreshadow real reality) seems at first to be a mere rhetorical sleight of hand, in his autobiographical mode Nabokov demonstrates that the conceit draws blood.

He describes, as we saw, the effect of his own "real" absence from the "generic" image of his family home with great poignancy. That the actor Mozzhuhine actually turned out to link "film" and "reality" may well account for the fact that autobiography generates fiction with such force. This fold in the carpet leads to the existential double-take that Nabokov shares with Ganin, the protagonist of his first novel, as much as to Albinus Kretchmar setting out on his adventures after seeing on a screen the crucial points of his life and complaining that he could not know what the film was about. This "fictional" experience of a confrontation with images that "seem" to belong to one's own story is not unlike the situation of Nabokov himself in 1916: watching the country mansion so similar to the one he should have inherited and unable to know how his own story would end. Thus the subtle thematic and fictional exploration of personal interaction with cinematic fiction in *Speak, Memory* and *Mary* provides the background for the impact of a figural crossing of life and fiction in *Laughter in the Dark*.[15]

The interaction of medium-specific form and human consciousness is also confirmed by Nabokov's awareness and clever use of a very elementary feature of the cinematic apparatus: asynchronous sound. The clumsy and mechanical sound effect that he notes as a young spectator, with its referentially irrelevant gushing forth of waves beyond the picture (its proper diegetic context), leads Nabokov to note the manner in which images (even those that seem to be controlled by others) are subject to free association and subjectivity. The careful formal elaboration apparent in the way Nabokov treats the episode stands in telling contrast to the primitive formal means (and implicit triviality) of the cinematography he describes. It serves to underline the fundamental resonance and personal meaning that such images have. Paradoxically, the clumsy interference of cinematic technology at its most primitive allows the elemental significance of these images to come through the veneer of the genre plots in which they occur. It also breaks down the superficial claim to referential "presence" made by the illusion-laden medium in which they are couched. Pirandello had anticipated this aspect of film in his transposition of the visual montage of city streets to the area of sound. He had expanded further on this register in the way Nonna Rosa's voice is made to bracket, we may remember, Gubbio's haunting memory of Sorrento. Yet it is Nabokov who applies this formative aspect of film aesthetics most inventively is such instances as the outburst of sportive cheering in the stairwell in *Laughter in the Dark*.

Nabokov thus makes use of a wide range of cinematic features noted by early filmmakers as well as by later theory. Moreover, be it Kracauer's mention of the use of peripheral sound overwhelming the central action (the sport palace), or be it Arnheim's notion of visual transposition of sound (Albinus's blindness), such features are thoroughly integrated into his narrative texture. Even when it comes to features that at first sight may not seem cinematic, it turns out that in their deployment Nabokov echoes the recommendations of filmmakers and approaches their nature with the medium-specific focus of cinematography. In his specific use of color Nabokov reveals, as we saw, an awareness of color in movement, of color synaesthetically conceived within a culture that has been touched by the instrumentation of optics, of projection, and of kinetic modulation.

Discourse on Film Theory

Yet when it comes to open discussions about the nature of film, Nabokov is less explicit, as I said, than Pirandello. His approach is more broadly philosophical, addressing topics that go to the root of the apparatus considered in its broadest sense. He engages such fundamental topics as the mechanics of mediation in a wide range of technologies and questions the distinctions between information and invention; between the richness of detail and the poverty of mental images. Best glossed, as we saw, through the voice of philosophical thinkers such as Sartre and Goodman, it is in narrative development that qualifications emerge to the naïve-realist understanding of images which Nabokov rightly imputes (*pace* Cavell) to the everyday experience of us all. Just as I argue to be the case with Pirandello, Nabokov's theory is intimately linked to the narrative flow of his novel. The narrative elaboration allows Nabokov to go further than Pirandello ever did in exploring topics that are by now central in the discussions of film theory, such as the sense of absence produced by images mechanically reproduced. At the same time, it is philosophical insight that strengthens evocative episodes such as the memory of his mother's photographs or that of his friend's home movies. It is such insight that marks the implications of the selective deletions, the subjective distortions in which his characters indulge, and that explains the force of narrative instances that bring to life the significance of details that human memory retains: the negative personal consequences of incomplete observation or the cultural ones of stereotypical filtering.

The screen becomes with Nabokov (more extensively and literally than is the case with Pirandello) the surface upon which the inner self is revealed. We have seen the screen as occasion for personal insight first with the discrepancy that Pirandello's Nuti and Nestoroff felt when confronted with their images on screen and with Serafino Gubbio's reactions to this. Insights such as these occur in Nabokov, as we saw, in ways that Pirandello never explored primarily because Nabokov describes his own personal experience. He thus knows firsthand about the way film allows the individual access to time before one's own, how camera and cameraman record consciousness that precedes that of the author, and how the apparatus challenges the subject's sense of time as coterminous with self. In the fictional mode, moreover, Nabokov confirms the importance of this generic nexus and extends it well beyond Pirandello. Being on both sides of the screen more extensively than before (as performers as well as spectators) allows Nabokov's characters an awareness of the medium (the kind of awareness characteristic of discussions on film theory) that opens access to an ever-increasing variety of specific human experiences.

As the narrative exploration of film and its implications evolves from Pirandello to Nabokov, one notices a growing narrative articulation of the philosophical meaning generated by a focus on the new technologies of perception and presentation. If Pirandello explores in general terms the status of the image in relation to the reality it tries to represent, Nabokov analyzes it with great specificity in a variety of contexts. If Pirandello measures the merits of cinematic images against those of painting alone, Nabokov takes us beyond such a simple dichotomy and allows the wealth of properties found in all kinds of imagery to inform his writing. Pirandello gives fictional space to the role that cinematic images play in affecting the perceptions of time and of experience for several characters, yet if truth be told these often fail to strike us as credible. Far more convincing is Nabokov's grounding of these effects in the immediacy of personal observation. This is due, of course, to his use of autobiographical discourse, but also to his experience as scientist, balanced as this may have been by the temper and training of an artist.

Because of this combination of qualities, in fact, Nabokov turns out to be "Motopictum Vir" in a deeper and more personal sense than Pirandello ever was, incorporating as he does in his very experience the peculiar combination of technological competence and emotional posture characteristic of individuals in the twentieth century.

Thus it is that Nabokov can define so well the relationship of the film image to the "images" (tropes, schemes) of verbal expression. He does so especially, as we saw, with the role that the trope of irony plays as a focal point in the culture of optical mediation, tugging the trope further along than Pirandello. The same is true of his exposition of the effect of film images on human creativity and of the extent to which the representation of life (its surface as well as its depths, its essence as well as its self-representations) may be true or false depending on how its images are offered to the eye. Nabokov displays a wider phenomenology of individual interactions with images (with what we might call the "epistemological apparatus") than does Pirandello. He also provides a far more complex range of attitudes about images as such than does his predecessor. This amounts to more than a simple juxtaposition between the idiosyncratic preferences of one author or another, however: Nabokov's contribution is to a generic whole that he both confirms and expands. What thus becomes more firmly part of the genre is an incorporation of the "technical" and the "scientific" into the "imaginative." This peculiar balancing of knowledge and imagination at the intersection of mechanism and mind is the result of the addition to the repertory of narrative fiction of a wide variety of similar (but subtly differing) optical artifacts.

It is thus ultimately not surprising that Nabokov offers one of the most powerful imaginative concretizations of the new medium found in the repertoire of film-formed literature. This is his suggestion that the very mechanism of poetic creation may be compared to the deployment of multiple imagery best produced by far-flung cameras. We might term this "poetry as cinematic apparatus." Far from being an incidental remark, such a simile captures some of the speculative attempts by film theorists to account for the power of film as a medium. Be it Arnheim's idea of "a particular range of magnitude, located between the atomic and the astronomic realm," Kracauer's positing of a "chimerical desire to establish the continuum of physical existence," or Baudry's notion that "to seize movement is to become movement," Nabokov stages such abstractions on a lawn, with people, and with a specifically characterized technical apparatus. Implicit in Nabokov's description of poetic consciousness is a bold assumption shared with Kracauer and Baudry that the form of the medium points in the direction of meaningful, all-encompassing aims. What our detailed exploration of the narrative permutations of such a view in Nabokov confirms is that, as a consequence, humankind absorbs a new kind of coherence, a revealing sharpness of vision from the infrastructure of a medium that has come to permeate our lives. If Gubbio's film-structured philosophical ride along the tree-lined avenue may have foreshadowed all of this, Nabokov's exploration of the interplay of human consciousness with photographic technology takes us much further.

6

The Film Novel as Literary Genre

Play of Genres and Discursive Systems

In the formation of new genres, we are told, one can usually detect a line of descent unfolding within the canon of literary discourse.[1] The FILM NOVEL is thus unusual since no such derivation can be established. The central role played in these novels by film and its discourses illustrates a phenomenon noted by the Russian formalists, namely, the renewal of the literary canon through the integration of materials and forms deriving from popular, non-canonical or even extraliterary art forms. Shklovskij calls it "canonizing a minor branch" and points out that it tends to occur at times that art finds itself wandering down a blind alley. It is then that "the tension of the artistic atmosphere falls, and one finds that elements of uncanonized art start infiltrating, having had the time to develop new artistic procedures" (Shklovskij 1979: 121, my translation). As Victor Erlich elaborates, the context and fictionality of such elements is thus reaffirmed, and "inferior" genres may provide a matrix for works of serious philosophical import (Erlich 1955:227–228).

The kind of generic grafting referred to by the Russian formalists applies to *Quaderni* and to *Laughter in the Dark* even from a stylistic perspective. Michael Głowinski has described as "formal-mimetic" works that display a "certain kind of tension or play between different types of expression, such as that between a novel and an intimate diary to whose rules the novel refers" (Głowinski 1977:106). These film novels, as we saw, are indeed based on the imitation of a specific form of extraliterary discourse, that of film.

We would be witnessing here, in other words, what Alastair Fowler in his study on literary genre calls "assemblage of the repertory." In the film novel, however, this building up of a genre takes place at a level of complexity higher than the one contemplated by Fowler, who discusses the simple addition of new themes and forms to a literary genre (Fowler 1982:156–159). Usually, according to this model, a generic evolution takes place when a new emphasis is given to thematic or formal elements already in existence (or at least implicit) in a preceding genre (see for instance the war eclogue studied by Tom Rosenmeyer and the factory novel described by Fowler himself). In the case of the narrative genre inaugurated by Pirandello, the complexity is greater since the thematic materials are completely new, as opposed to older examples such as the piscatory eclogue in which the initial stages of the genre allowed a variety of themes (including that of fishing) before an eventual subdivision into subtypes occurred (Rosenmeyer 1969:6). It would seem clear, at least on historical grounds, that the thematic materials of "cinema" were not even a possibility before a certain date. We have here, moreover, a genre that demands (at least in part) the search for a particular kind of style, marked as it is by an expressive system that has no precedents. Nabokov's *Laughter in the Dark* tends to confirm that FORMAL MIMETICS is indeed integral to the "film novel," given the author's statement that the stylistic texture of the whole novel was an attempt to write an "entire book as if it were a film" (Appel 1974:258).[2]

Beyond the thematic and formal elements typical of a new generic "repertory," therefore, we have thematic and formal elements that could not be foreseen and that derive from noncanonical sources. But even this is exacerbated further: what could be less elevated artistically, in fact, than the cinema of the early years (fairground attraction more than art form); and what more questionable, from the point of view of traditional poetics, than the generic eclecticism that we find here? The noncanonical element in the film novel, therefore, beyond being a matter of sources, becomes a question of aesthetic criteria and of the psychological (even philosophical) relevance of artistic experience.

This mixture of genres and of discursive systems turns out to be a constant in this genre. Be it as a play between different literary genres or between literary elements and the emerging range of film genres, it seems that one of the fixed agendas of the film novel is the horizon of expectations provided by rigid and well-known genres, not to speak of the play of "differences" made possible by their tensions. In the particular case of *Quaderni,* for instance, the interaction between confessional tone and filmic discourse fulfills special functions. Both call into play right away the opposition between the "subjective" reality of Gubbio's behavior and his "objective" pretense. This opposition (the narrative center of the novel) is also the theme of various kinds of cinema (both neorealist and postmodern cinema derive energy from the opposition) and thus involves directly the generic identity of this type of novel. The opening of Nabokov's *Laughter in the Dark* uses one generic style (that of a fairy tale) to offer an implicit comment (structural as well as generic) on the impoverished sensibility of the protagonist, an art historian who readily abandons himself to the clichés current in the so-called street films of the German cinema of those years. The fairy-tale discourse thus comes to stand in contrast to that of *neue Sachlichkeit* both in its literary form and in the cinematic version offered by the UFA studios of those years.

The play between genres and forms extends the intertextual to include the intramedial. To the power of a particular way of seeing the world that belongs to all genres (individual particularities that separate them), the incorporation of the discourse of extraliterary media adds the ability to question the very status of that "way of seeing" (its *truth*, its *validity*) from within the structure of the individual text. The initial temporal priority of one work over another, the eventual mutual interdependence of the two, and their ultimate assimilation into a new composite (the traditional sequence in matters of intertextuality) is in the case of the film novel transposed to the level of intramedial discourse. It is thus one kind of discourse (film) that becomes the starting point and in the end must be incorporated into another: the discourse of literature.

The use by Pirandello and Nabokov of popular art, mixed genre, and extraliterary discourse takes us back to some of the fundamental human reasons for the existence of genre in the first place. Throughout the ages genres have been created as attempts to capture significant cross sections of human experience. The elements of this experience that come to the foreground in different genres are usually chosen for their significance, their truth, and their universality. It is, moreover, only in works that mix the genres (*pace* neo-Aristotelian pedants) that literature manages to approximate the functioning of individual consciousness when it attempts to assemble a sense of our true and essential self from the morass of facts, styles, impressions, memories, lies, truths, ideals, fantasies, wishes, and hopes that characterize experience. It is thus mixed genre that offers the best format for the task of finding out who we really are. The combination of "limited" conventions, their juxtaposition, their clash, and their "bleeding" into each other provide a roundness and complexity missing from the limited range of its individual components.

The film-derived elements of this particular genre (inherently mixed to begin with) emphasize components of human experience specific to the twentieth century. As a separate element, the "cinematic" provides a specialized cross section of experience analogous to those of earlier genres, experience that may not have been part of earlier times. What is more, the cinematic in itself is already a "mixed" art form and thus possesses at the outset (before it "joins" literary discourse, that is) the advantages of mixed genre mentioned above. These advantages then acquire even more power when the cinematic becomes part of a new literary genre.

Genres of Discourse

As we have seen, Pirandello's and Nabokov's novels reveal a consistent number of film-generated discursive elements (functionally integrated into the novels) that contribute their voice to the multiplicity of overlapping utterances, those "genres of discourse" that in Bakhtin's formulations characterize the dialogic presence within narrative texts of the different manifestations of cultural codes.

Extraliterary discourse, Todorov has suggested, can be said to provoke the creation of generic literary manifestations that codify within the literary system specialized verbal gestures common on the outside. Frequency of occurrence and complexity may differ (the "naming" and "inviting" that stand behind the African genres Todorov mentions as examples are more common than the "hesitation" behind the fantastic that is the focus of his attention), but as long as the cultural discourse is codified and distinctive, the potential exists.[3]

I would propose that just as the simple verbal gestures described by Todorov, broader discursive situations may function in the same way. Such a one, I would add, is the discourse surrounding film. New as it may have been at the time *Quaderni* was published, it soon came to be intimately connected with the culture of this century; so much so, in fact, that by now we possess a wide range of discourses "on" and "of" film: the peculiar kind of "interior monologue" that accompanies the viewing of film, the aesthetic generalizations that underlie film from its production to its reception, not to speak of the ideological ventriloquism of the film text, the subject positions it articulates, and so on. These discourses have acquired such consistency within the culture that it is not surprising to find them recodified in terms of literary genre as well. This seems to be confirmed by Todorov, who points out that societies will encourage such codification by favoring the verbal gestures that reflect the most powerful current ideologies. Film as an art form has indeed come to be (and Pirandello was among the first to recognize this) just such a "mirror" of the way our culture thinks of itself.

Quaderni and *Laughter* push beyond the particular narrative instance into the area of genre precisely in the sense meant by Todorov. We have, first of all, the full display of the cinematic apparatus in its mechanical, technical, stylistic, historical, aesthetic, and philosophical guises. These in themselves, I would argue, are genre-specific rather than being merely a mimetic texture dictated by a particular and unique narrative instance. While they seem at first merely a matter of milieu, they slowly rise to the level of metanarrative extrapolations that could not be made in other kinds of setting and with other kinds of characters. They hark back, as illustrated above, to a recognizable DISCOURSE ON CINEMA in the frequent passages that anticipate themes from the subsequent tradition of film theory. They present also, together with the simple data of the apparatus, a DISCOURSE OF CINEMA integrated with the more normal "discourse of literature" we expect to find in a novel: the openly film-mimetic passages merely take this tendency to its extreme and sometimes, as we have seen, to the breaking point. All of this implies, in other words, a generalized (genre-lized) kind of narrative above and beyond the particular plot of such novels. All kinds of motifs that derive from attention to the apparatus of filmmaking function naturally as a nexus between the narrative and metanarrative levels of plot and even lend themselves to "enacting" broad cultural topoi: mimetic verisimilitude, for example, in realist and fantastic discourse (see Gubbio who, furious about the silliness produced by Kosmograph, the company for which he works, denounces the paradox of an art form in its essence verisimilar but used to produce lies); the nature of images in their existential and philosophical implications (see Nuti and Nestoroff and the considerations deriving from their clash with their own images on screen); and the relativity of viewpoints and instability of moving perspectives (think of Gubbio in the carriage meditating about the trees and how the data contradict "his" version of the facts). All of these are instances of story materials that point beyond the particular plot in which they occur to the realm of genre materials.

If we follow the thread of differing "versions" of film theory given narrative context by Pirandello and Nabokov, we discover that their unfolding generates the "ideological" cores of these novels. Such exploration of film theory turns out (in subsequent examples of the genre) to be an important characteristic of the film novel. Defining the essence of film as an art form and exploring its meaning to human experience are in fact pivotal in all the novelists we are examining. Novelists in the genre strive to expose the human weakness for illusions in general and to foster an awareness derived from lessons the cinematic apparatus may provide. To be more specific, film novels do more than explore the "desire to be fooled" (this, after all, occurs even in chivalric romances and epic poems). They exhibit a strictly modern fascination with the apparatus that seduces us: a new urgency (specific to our century) to discover such seduction where it may not be visible. By the time movies come along, the enlightenment magic glasses of E. T. A. Hoffman have moved from the spectator's nosebridge to become the lenses of camera and projector. The mechanical magic contained in the doll that seduces the poet ("she," after all, stands right there before him) would thus by now be hidden behind his back.[4]

But let me try to be even more specific about the applicability of Todorov's poetics of genre to the film novel. "Making movies," "going to the movies," and so on, acquire (having become, as we said, a cultural paradigm) a codifiable textuality. To follow the schema proposed by Todorov for the fantastic (but in the case of our novels one could go further), the film novel would be characterized first of all by the "narratization" of situations behind which one finds the above mentioned discourses. It would then display a "proliferation of typical themes" (in our case the world of cinema from the point of view of those who produce it and those who go to the movies), and finally it would attempt a "verbal representation" of the film experience.

Narrative moments in which film mimesis (as well as film as mimesis) is most intense tend indeed to display the apparatus of cinematography in its total range. To us, jaded by the wealth of detail available today about the procedure of filmmaking, the exploration of this apparatus may seem uninteresting. But in the context of the film novel it represents the center of a special world from which a particular view of life can be derived. The actual mechanics of filmmaking (camera, film, darkrooms, viewing room) and the finer details of technique (the speed at which the camera is cranked, the red light necessary to develop the emulsions) are used first of all to signify the nature, constraints, and possibilities of a new art form. But they also allow, as we have seen, the metaphorical application of this medium to life as a whole.

Significance is also found in the historical evolution and in the inherent medium-specific features of this apparatus as it appears on screen: for example the particular kinds of stylization of the world that film employs through its changing genres or the specific stylizations typically produced by the distorting eye of this technology. The presence in the novel of the first of these (genre) suggests that Pirandello already had a historical perspective on the medium, while the second (what Arnheim was to refer to as the technically possible) indicates that, well before the history and the theory of the medium would make it self-evident, Pirandello was aware of the inherent formative thrust of the camera, of editing, of the whole apparatus. In Pirandello's mimesis of silent cinema (and in the way he proposes it as a metaphor of "modernity"), we thus have consistent attempts to render the "textual" nature of film at various moments in its early evolution as well as "critical" observations about differing styles of filming as they allow us to reflect upon issues of wider cultural import.

What cannot be said about *Quaderni,* however, is that its critical mimesis of film is sustained throughout. One may speculate that such an attempt, if not impossible in theory, would have to forego the advantages of what literary discourse as such has to offer, in the name of the dubious advantages of a brand new art form. Even Nabokov, having set himself the challenge of composing the whole of *Laughter in the Dark* so that the reading of it would give the impression of watching a film, abandoned the attempt. He found that the state of the art in cinema was not up to that of literature (Appel 1974:258–259). Yet, rather than being a failure, this points to one of the defining characteristics of the film novel: the synaesthetic tension that arises from the juxtaposition of two discourses such as literature and film.

One could thus add an additional genre-distinctive element (but this would already take us beyond Todorov): the veritable SYNAESTHETIC SHUDDER ("frisson synesthétique") that derives from the clash of two narrative systems not always compatible (one based on words, one on the complex of cinematic codes). The "reading" difficulties that such a clash creates would thus be an element of the genre. Let me just recall, under this new perspective, the page of *Quaderni* in which the points of view described by Gubbio seated in his carriage are incomprehensible if read upon the written page unless we "view" them during our reading upon an ideal screen. This is also the case, as we saw, in the enigmatic finale of Nabokov's *Laughter in the Dark* (enigmatic unless we interpret it as one does a movie).

The narrative concretization of the abstract cultural thematics mentioned so far allows for an extremely vivid exploration of the existential dimension. From this derive narrative moments that address strictly modern experiences, experiences that by their nature and lacking such concretizations would remain fleeting, relegated at best to essays on existential philosophy and treatises on the phenomenology of perception. It is precisely the film novel's exploration of analogous but not identical ways of perceiving that allows the clarification of such experiences. Upon this follows, as I have said, a new "stylistics." It too reminds us of certain past literary antecedents that engaged extraverbal discourses with the instruments of verbal expression—*ekphrasis*, for example.[5] Yet passages such as the one in which Gubbio describes the coming and going of urban life in strictly cinematic terms, or the above mentioned view from his carriage, imply, I would say, something no less new than the conceptual materials that characterize this new literary genre: a new "syntax" created to correspond to a new way of perceiving things. As Kracauer will point out years later, the type of syntax and the thematics typical to cinema (the elements of reality for which it has an inherent affinity) become an identifyable *topos* of modernity. What other medium than cinema, with its chaotic and rapid succession of framings, could become the expression of the typical experience of being alive in our century. Cinematic representation "not only considerably enlarged our vision," says Kracauer, but "adjusted it to man's situation in a technological age." As a result, he continues, "viewpoints and perspectives that framed our images of nature for long stretches of the past have become relative. In a crudely physical sense we are moving about with the greatest of ease and incomparable speed so that stable impressions yield to ever-changing ones: bird's-eye views of terrestrial landscapes have become quite common; not one single object has retained a fixed, definitely recognizable appearance" (Kracauer 1960:8–9). Pirandello anticipates Kracauer in this vision of modern experience and thus introduces elements of a generic nature (general applicability) rather than merely stylistic procedures unique and limited to his particular novel.

Narrative Condensations of the Apparatus

Kracauer chooses cinema as the concrete manifestation of the modern sensibility. But the fact is, as Nabokov illustrates with his interest in a broad range of mediating technologies (and as Pirandello anticipates with lamps and telescopes), that what the film theorist says applies to an "apparatus" that is more encompassing and more diffused than that of the movies. It is thus necessary to add to the narrative articulation of discourses on film, of film, and on film theory, a broader category of discourses relevant to this genre: those that articulate elements of culture and of experience which are either subsumed in or emblematized by film. We might call this DISCOURSE OF and ON THE APPARATUS (where "apparatus" stands also for all the components of cinema, even if they are not yet—or don't quite come to be—cinema in the full sense of the word). I am thinking of all those passages that, while not being quite about film, nevertheless are related to it either because they depict recognizable components of the film apparatus (the genre clichés mentioned above are such components, but we shall see many more) or because they find in film their most evolved and extensive manifestation (such is the case with the specular intentionality of the busy mirrors cited above).

Young Nabokov's visits to his parents' room work in this way. While not an explicit "discourse on film," the sequential repetition of the same action is said to build up to a permanent impression (static, durable, objectified) that can be carried away from its point of origin but retain its image. This anticipates the imaginative use that Nabokov makes of the celluloid strips of cinema (SpM:236); and so does the ghost of a postcard said to be lodged permanently as a bookmark within the pages of *War and Peace* (SpM:199). Notice that the way in which the elements of town, apartment, and sofa are said to flow onto the surface of an ideal postcard is most reminiscent of the way in which the film apparatus performs the optical conversion of the elements of a composite image through a lens and onto a screen. Note, moreover, that a "postcard" is by definition a noncanonical, "popular" form (even within the poetics of photography). The typical tendency of the film novel to rely on such forms is therefore anticipated even here. The "insertion" of the postcard into a "great work of literature" is significant too, juxtaposing as it does high and low, the inextricable connection of context (as random as may be) and content. All of these are characteristics that film as a form tends to foreground more than other art forms do. Should we have any doubts, let us look forward down the line of generic evolution and recall Margot's appearance as seaside poster at the head of the Solfi episode in *Laughter in the Dark* or the allusion, in the same episode, to the still photographs (freeze-frames) on the beach reminiscent of the "anatomical" slowing down of the apparatus in the film *People on Sunday* (1929).

The display of the parts of the apparatus goes hand in hand with an awareness that they need to be synchronized to "tell a story," primitive as this coordination may be at first. We shall see more about this display later when we discuss discourse of film more specifically, but its implications in terms of thinking about film ("discourse on and about the apparatus") are found in the camera lucida referred to in the Harvard recollection of *Speak, Memory*, in the slides that young Nabokov extracts from the projector and holds up in his hand (SpM:92, 166), and even in the transformation of Proust into Prism as part of a didactic exercise at Cornell (LoL:347). All of these are instances of the foregrounding of the apparatus. One may wonder about the purpose of such a consistent type of intramedial allusion in the midst of literary discourse. Do these instances of discursive break create an "effect of the new" (a reclaimed freshness for materials that might seem scientific, trite, canonical); do they stimulate paradigmatic extrapolation (poetic cymbals that jolt taxonomic listing, slide show, lecture off their prosaic track)? It seems to me that attention to the apparatus is used in all such instances to modify for the better the possibility of a "clumsy" slide show, a "cold" scientific observation, a "sophomoric" reading of Proust.

Even the explicitly poetic moment when the Swiss Mademoiselle is poised in the Russian landscape on her way to the Nabokov estate, with its subsequent "cross-fade" of nanny into author, of Russia into New England, of ideal "wonderland" into present day exile (SpM:99–100), articulates a complex series of elements that are clearly discourse of the apparatus in the sense defined above. In simple narrative terms, the text produces in quick succession an expressionist projection ("for one moment, thanks to the sudden radiance of a lone lamp . . . a grossly exaggerated shadow . . . races beside the sleigh"), a stereoscopic view, the aforementioned cross-fade, and "fancy's rear-vision mirror." One may note that in this case such precinematic elements of the apparatus do more than in the examples given above. They participate in the actual articulation of a story and do so, moreover, in a specific film-mimetic fashion. This is true especially in the case of the cross-fade (a most unliterary trope) which is used to describe a connection across distances in time and in space.

Narrative Productivity of the Apparatus

Such simple PRECINEMATIC INTIMATIONS OF THE APPARATUS find more elaborate narrative development (and become a part that cannot be eliminated from a specific narrative) in Nabokov's *Mary*. In the novel Nabokov stresses the loss of control over the kind of images which in *Speak, Memory* function as the photographic and cinematographic repositories of the writer's past. Ganin, who has discovered that his beloved and lost Mary is actually married to the awkward and ridiculous old man living in the room next to his in the Berlin boarding house, feels the loss most intensely by thinking of her photographs resting in her husband's desk:

> In the hall mirror he saw the reflection of the inside of Alfyorov's room, the door of which was wide open. Inside that sunny room—the weather that day was heavenly—a slanting cone of radiant dust passed across the corner of the desk, and with agonizing clarity he imagined the photographs which had first been shown to him by Alfyorov and which later he had been examining alone with such excitement when Klara had disturbed him. In those photos Mary had been exactly as he remembered her, and now it was terrible to think that his past was lying in someone else's desk. (M:54)

The protagonist is here recreating with these elements (his imagination, the mirror, the cone of sunlight ending in the place where the photographs are) the "situation" of a perceiving subject seeing, through a frame, images which appear at the end of a projected cone of light; the situation, that is, of being a spectator at the movies. The photographs at the bottom of a desk drawer are thus arranged as part of a spatial parody of projection, and the discovery of, access to, and resonance of the content of those photographs is the spring of the action itself.

The photograph as object suggests the possibility of capturing reality in a way that narrative cannot, and from within that very same narrative discourse. Setting it within the narrative provides a different kind of "illusion of reality" from the conventional literary one of realist prose, short-circuiting some of its shortcomings. By taking advantage, for instance, of the "apparent" completeness of mental images we discussed before, images (and herein resides a generic advantage of mixed media) are endowed with completeness in more than mere appearance by the discursively mixed narrative elaboration.

Photographic reproduction and the semblance of life which movement can add to it allow time to be captured in one space and, by being miniaturized upon photographic emulsion, to be transported anywhere else in time and space. In the light of the systematic treatment I have been giving here to narrative matters, one may add that the importance of this insight of Nabokov's is confirmed by the "narrative situations" that he invents to illustrate it. The richness of narrative detail that he contributes tends to underline the productivity of these artifacts. Even the apparent idiosyncrasy of the situations underlines it: a boy who subverts the appropriate arrangement of the elements of the "apparatus" of a slide show by holding the slides up to view in his hands rather than letting them be projected; an ideal "postcard" redolent with time and place that rests forever like a bookmark in a specific book and lends it an aura made up of very specific and concrete details.

This is a narrative productivity (a productivity stimulated by some of the characteristics of this genre) that is evident beyond examples such as the ones mentioned above, most of which derive from an autobiographical text. It can be found too in novels such as *Mary* and, of course, *Laughter in the Dark*. In the case of *Mary,* photographs (the ones at the bottom of the drawer) as well as images on the cinematic screen (Ganin's own image in the film in which he appears) fulfill their narrative function precisely because they "move" in more than kinetic ways. Be it the moment that confirms significant identity, be it the unexpected confrontation with a particular kind of image of the self, significant moments of crisis hang on such photographic reproductions. The Garbo photograph in *Laughter in the Dark,* we may recall, underlines the extent to which such a seemingly peripheral and frivolous object can affect a radical turn in the narrative, "preventing" Albinus from returning home, as it does, to save his marriage and possibly to avert his own tragedy.

The Genres of Experience

Film-formed ways of looking at the world—professional deformations that influence one's sense of time—and similar features are articulated into discourse and then formed into narrative because to begin with they are distinct and meaningful "kinds" of experience. In other words, generically speaking, the repertory of elements that are grouped together by culture as part of such experiences precede narrative. They derive from a situation in which the individual and his culture may recognize what might be termed GENRES OF EXPERIENCE.

This growth of awareness is most clearly illustrated by the way that Nabokov moves such materials from personal experience to narrative fiction in *Speak, Memory*. We find a veritable "narrative evolution" as we go from Nabokov as a student of drawing to Nabokov as a lepidopterist at Harvard, where he handles a genre-significant apparatus (the camera lucida) and derives from it a discursive excursion into the repertory of knowledge and lore (the encyclopedia of culture) that leads us through history to the modern-day movie projector. Note that the final prop in this "narrative" that produces character roles, *bildung* (if not quite *roman*), tools, time, and travel from tundra to tea party (as in "Boston") is a dictionary: repository of the erudition (the culture) that allows Nabokov to organize the narrative paradigm of such a journey. This "story" concludes only as he, now himself the "Professor," lectures his own students about the "artist as prism." The crucial lesson that young Nabokov learned from his art teacher (the lesson that turned, we may remember, "lepless" Italian landscapes into a lepidopterist's delight) also stands behind the narrative instance of Albinus's empty memories in *Laughter in the Dark*.

What Nabokov's education exhibits is the evolution that goes into the making of the "genre-specific protagonist" of the film novel. This figure, of which Gubbio was the first, always exhibits some functional relationship to the filmic apparatus. Even if less "integrated" into the apparatus than Gubbio's (who at a certain point describes himself as half-man, half-machine), the professional deformation of Nabokov's characters, as well as those of Isherwood and others that we shall encounter in Part Four of this study, is always a part of the story and extends from those who produce films (Isherwood's director, Nabokov's producer, Moravia's scriptwriter) to those who go to see them (the spectators of Walker Percy and Puig).

What film novels often stress about such characters (and this is precisely because of their involvement with the world of cinema) is the limits of their field of action, even of their ability to act. This happens in such a way as to remind us of generic features belonging to more famous protagonists. Classical genre-specific characters such as Ulysses (about him Moravia's film director will be most explicit) and the raving Orlando often have to confront the ambiguities of perception, the potential destructiveness of beauty, and the limits of their own control over the world and others. According to Northrop Frye, it is such limits that allow us to characterize the most ancient of literary genres. In the film novel, I would say, we find them surfacing again, this time in strictly modernist guise.

Genre-Specific Modality of Character

Mode is the literary manifestation of what writer and reader alike consider the nature and situation of humankind in the world.[6] Modal considerations, therefore, pose the question: what notions of power, possibilities, dilemmas typical to humankind are foregrounded by the emphasis, by the tropes, by the organization, by the pleasures of this or that text? Mode, that is, addresses how much and in what manner the character may or may not control the world; how much and in what way her or his actions reveal specific powers and limits. Paul Alpers points out that generic classifications inherently imply such a notion of mode.[7] He asks whether Adam's actions in *Paradise Lost* are comprehensible within the generic framework of theatrical tragedy. It is, he proposes, the precise identification of the GENRE-SPECIFIC MODALITY OF CHARACTER thus understood to give us an answer. As with Adam, so with Gubbio, Rex, and Albinus.

It seems that a totally new "modality" typical of the experience of the modern individual is produced by the type of character created by Pirandello and adopted by his successors. Their characters, after all, despite protestations about seeing things as they are, about being in perfect control of what they think, feel, and do, reveal the limits and illusions of modern individuals in the context of technologies and aesthetic principles that emblematize the modern condition. While the authors of the novels with which we are dealing most often view such limitations with great pessimism, Nabokov's interest in the mode of Bachelard's "man with a magnifying glass" indicates that the typical character may also transcend the limits. The scientist at Harvard (who has to balance the inherent conflicts of a symbolic code that is in tension with the technical and the aesthetic) and the "professor of literature" at Cornell (who passes on the cultural code and its repercussions in a situation that invokes code transmission in a didactic context) indicate that such transcendence is indeed possible.

Generic specificity, thus, is closely bound with typical characters embodying particular qualities. Bakhtin talks about genre as "a classification according to the principle of construction of the image of the main character: the travel novel; the novel of the hero's trials [*Prüfungsroman*]; the biographical (autobiographical) novel; the novel of learning [*Bildungsroman*]." Such classification is notably similar to Frye's, who lists characters according to the hero's "power of action."[8] Its use by Nabokov indicates that what is at stake is indeed a notion of personal empowerment through knowledge, its acquisition, and its transmission. The "typical character" of the film novel, thus, is not necessarily limited to the more negative manifestation of this mode as found in *Quaderni* and *Laughter in the Dark,* in which the character-based definition of mode suggests only powerlessness of action.

Genre-Specific Cultural Code

The cultural code learned, pursued, and passed down the generations by the epistemologically aware character that Nabokov personifies resides in the "erudition" required to operate instruments and evaluate the "meaning" of what they produce. As such, it pushes beyond the conventional limits of this narrative code. Rather than resting upon cultural materials known to all, Nabokov's erudition presupposes a knowledge "greater" than the commonplace. He raises epistemological questions about what it is that we take for granted. Yet he remains well within the acceptable conventionality of the cultural code as well, since it is indeed part of this culture (even in the realm of popular discourse) to display a fascination with the cutting edge of technological erudition: How and for what does the "protagonist" use instrumentation? What is the formative role and authority of "teachers" (how indeed *should* one look at slides)? Do the setting of a museum and the role of a scientist indeed preclude aesthetic initiative by a protagonist who finds that s/he is culturally circumscribed? Can s/he (should s/he) indeed take initiative to be consonant with the full extent of his or her knowledge?

Cultural questions such as these (articulated through "narrative" situations) have to do with the kind of control that individuals gain from competence: "knowledge-based" competence as well as "use" competence. The situations Nabokov chooses illustrate the fact that, even from within a biographical context, the narrative elaboration of apparatus extends to the narrative elaborations of its cultural repertory. That the biographical representation is colored at times by the histrionics of a storyteller helps to underline the point by "staging" (narratizing) the epistemological dilemma and by lending it great emotional resonance. Let me recall Nabokov's discussion of a lilly in *Strong Opinions* (the context is an interview), which concludes most "dramatically" with the exclamation "It's hopeless" (SO:10–11). The startling expressive tone of the passage is only out of character with the occasion if we ignore the full context of factors I have been discussing so far.

We thus find what might be termed "genre kernels" even in autobiography and interview contexts, kernels that become fully fledged narrative springs in the novels. It is, for instance, in the contrast between Albinus's loss of erudition and Rex's gathering of it that this element is given narrative articulation in *Laughter in the Dark*. For the former what is at issue concerns what he "knows" about art and representation thanks to his education, but also what he "unlearns" as he watches Margot on the movie screen. For Rex the focus is "education" on film as an art form. He may display this education to impress his rival Albinus, but the most important application of Rex's own "literacy" is to the accurate reading of the net of evolving personal relations that he observes as he too watches Margot on screen.

If we extend "erudition" about the medium to include the more general "conditions of production" that, as I pointed out before, form a major thematic thread of the film novel, episodes such as the one that describes Ganin and Nabokov involved in the making of a film reveal their importance. Quite a lot of detailed contextual and critical texture is given to the filmmaking situation that "contains" the two (four?) alter egos of Nabokov, Mozzhuhin, Mozzhukhin, and Ganin. From klieg lights to megaphoned director, these counters of "cinema" (genre-specific codes that speak to us of a specific thematic overdetermination) help to stimulate the philosophical and existential extrapolations typical of the genre.

From Erudition to Epistemology

But, as we saw, the narratives carry us from "what we know" to "how we know what we know." In general, as Arnheim has pointed out, this is an advantage derived from the nature of film. From the narrative point of view (and specific to the film novel), it is the kind of thing that generates narrative momentum from the paradox of (exposure of) the limits of what is possible in the filmic representation of appearance (a process always at pains to cover up the traces of its conventionality).[9] The film novel thus offers a genre-specific way to expose the dilemma of narrative itself, in the very act of creating it.

Arnheim's epistemological advantage can be recognized, for instance, in the narrative proliferation that we encounter in Nabokov. The limits of what can be shown of what is "potentially" there (the baby in the mother's womb cannot be seen in the home movie) are balanced out by the limits of mental images that suffer as much from human incompetence as from the inherent limits of their nature (Albinus's memories of his former life after the accident as compared to the slide-sharp memory of the car accident itself). Even the inherent shortcomings of actual slides and photographs (the former must be removed from the projector to yield their essence; the latter may need elaborate narrative captions) lead to the desire to transcend such limits (the multiple cameras suggested to the interviewer from *Vogue*; the execution of the car accident). The Harvard episode underlines the fact that the most important "limit" may ultimately be our own: the either/or attitude that divides the ways in which we see.[10]

The limits of the referential uses of projected images, as well as of the temptation to seek paradigmatic resonance within them, are illustrated by the Lermontov experiment of Nabokov's tutor Lenski. His attempt to present to his young charges the inherently paradigmatic and subjective beauties of lyric poetry in "montage" with images of natural beauties is meant, as we said, for primarily didactic or documentary use. Yet Lenski's experiment can be seen as an attempt to break the limits of single-minded vision. Even if this was the tutor's intention, Nabokov's account stresses that the show isolated for him two elements of narrative by transposition to another medium. The mixed representation, as clumsy as it may be, allows a fresh view of the relationship between image and word, between alternative discursive renditions and the reality they address, and stimulates a questioning about how images exist in literature and what it is that they are. Even if awareness about the breaking of limits is achieved by a sardonic exposure of the pedestrian "illustration" approach to literary recitation, the episode is productive, since it leads Nabokov to notice similar limits when confronted with the primitive synchronization of sound, color, and image in early silent movies. Primed by such insights, it is not surprising that the sudden mirroring of self back to subject for the adolescent Nabokov as well as for Ganin leads to insights about the antecedent knowledge of a full context, the discrepancy between "framed" and "fragmentary" representation of the self (representations delayed or in discontinuous contexts) and considerations about an originating situation.

This narrative concretization of the cultural code also incorporates into the narrative materials the cultural competence required of the reader and usually left more implicit (Cremonini asks, "What is the knowledge that he [the narrator] stages?" [Cremonini 1988:11, my translation]). In these types of stories—in this genre—the protagonists are stand-ins for reader competence. We have seen this happen in *Laughter in the Dark,* where the themes are central to the narrative, even if their valence is reversed. The story, as I pointed out, is about the "perversion" of the epistemological process by Rex and the cultural and epistemological "incompetence" of Albinus.

Genre—Story—Discourse

The questioning stimulated by the context of biography ultimately leads Nabokov to question the possible manifestations of a story as it is articulated by discourse. As I stated before, Nabokov stresses for himself and for his characters the pleasures and pains of the arbitrary in construing what life throws at us in its random and sometimes serendipitous way. In terms of storytelling this sets up a distinction between the necessary parts of a story and the peripheral ones; it asks what it is that constitutes a story anyway. We have seen to what elaborate extent seemingly peripheral elements in the story of Albinus (from mirrors to doors, from fire engines to elevator boys and tennis rackets) turn out to be central and unexcisable elements of the narrative. Yet Nabokov seems to be always asking whether there actually is a "story" out there in the seeming randomness of the carpet's pattern; whether he may pursue it on the butterfly wings of its magic flight. Strictly from the point of view of a syntax of narrative, the double metaphor (Nabokov alludes in rapid succession to the pattern in the carpet and to the folding of it so as to create superimpositions) outlines Nabokov's poetics. Yet he also involves in this syntax the visitor-reader, who may stumble over the fold in the carpet as s/he enters the writer's study. Is in fact the reading situation (a visit to the author's study with its uneven floor) a flight on this magic carpet?

Narrative theory differs on the subject of discourse and story interaction (or even status); and this is hardly the context in which to try and adjudicate the question. What is clear, however, is that the film novel tends to raise the issue in its own specific way as part of the narrative. Already in Pirandello's *Quaderni* we find that a distinction is drawn (a distinction that gives rise to a polemical note) between what the scriptwriter Cavalena suggests and what amounts to the discursive elaboration that producers, director, audiences (different ones in different countries at that) will allow. In other words, Cavalena's "story" is never allowed to be set to a discourse that he would find congruent to it. Pirandello's explicit emphasis is on the distance between the two as a consequence of the rules of filmmaking.

With Nabokov we find a broader emphasized awareness of the differential discursive possibilities available for the same story. The repeated use of the same materials in autobiographical and fictional discourse and the encapsulated fairy-tale version of Albinus's story, offered as an alternative to the "novel version," are good examples. But Nabokov too addresses the topic within the genre-specific context of the film-formed narrative. Albinus's proposal for the discursive "translation" of great paintings from canvas to film sets the tone from the opening pages. We actually get to "watch" the elements of discourse on cinema turn into narrative and sometimes even *be* narrative in a particularly resonant way. Thus, for instance, fundamental philosophical considerations made possible by the cinematic medium (one such is the intensified concretization of an experience of our own mortality) are given extra power by appearing in *Speak, Memory* as part of a real individual's experience, or at least the "story" of a "real individual."[11]

Even a particular reaction to the image of an empty perambulator in a home movie (to give another example) bears witness to an early formative experience. The link to Nabokov's narrative fiction is direct, as we have seen, since the very same image is elaborated (a corridor, a nailed-up box, an empty perambulator) into the elements of Albinus's own story in *Laughter in the Dark*. Nabokov does not merely reuse a cluster of elements across texts. It is their film-formed existential charge that moves from text to text. The very "nature" of the images in home movies is shown to generate the particular quality of the later literary rendition: the experience that one cannot "be there" before being alive, other than through the mimetic-affective sleight of hand of cinematography. Further yet, it is the intertextual (and intrageneric) nature of the relationship between these "events" that increases the power of the fictional representation. The movement is not merely from book to book. The circle that holds together film, biography, and the film novel is as tight as the one that links (another example) those evocative houses in *Speak, Memory* that crumble "as soundlessly as they did in the mute films of yore" (SpM:95) with the houses in *Laughter in the Dark* that provide genre gloss to films "with wars and buildings crumbling up" (L:11). The elements often move from "kind" of book to "kind" of book.

Let me stay for a moment longer with that home movie. The episode illustrates quite clearly the pressure to let a story develop and emphasizes what might be termed the PROAIRETIC PARADOX. The contradiction derives from the fact that the medium-specific illusion of certainty about narrative coherence (time and space, continuity, connection) is put into question by the little boy watching that movie. The author's intense personal experience of this tension is perhaps why the "continuity" and "connectedness" embodied in the biographical rendition finds its way into narrative craft, as this very experience resurfaces so unambiguously so much later in life, and at such a "generic" remove. Culler points out, one may recall, that, as opposed to the hermeneutic code which works prospectively, that of actions is only recognized after the fact, retrospectively (Culler 1975:210). The evocative power of this episode in Nabokov is thus redoubled, since it derives from the tension that occurs when looking forward to solving a mystery (that of "life" itself, perhaps?) as well as backward to reconstruct a "plot" (a "meaning," perhaps?). The prospective and retrospective looks intersect with each other, thanks to the unique properties of movies.

Strongest also in this episode is the symbolic opposition between life and death, between presence and absence. Here again, the elements that culturally "must be kept separate" are brought together thanks not so much to the ability of the medium to "invent" reality but to rupture it. This may well be an original treatment (*avant la lettre théorique*) of the notion of "suture" and of its existential impact. Nabokov's "cinematic reader" (in this case reading the subtext of the apparatus) gets an education about the direct (one might say brutal) link of cinema and existence: a formative "genre of experience" that may well account for Nabokov's fascination with the medium of film. The subject of this experience is *in nuce* one of the genre-specific characters of the film novel.

From the point of view of genre-specific elements and their effect on narrative structure, the movement of the elements of this film-specific insight from biography to fiction is of particular interest. I have commented before about the film-related nature of such images (both as subject matter and quality of image). Let me just add that it is those "filmic" qualities that seem to provide the connective tissue in moving from text to text. In other words, the narrative impetus and linkage owes a lot to the cinematic context (the film discourse) from which the images and the experiences derive.

Genre-Specific Effect of Reality

One might of course argue (some do) that experience is only such once it is given shape through discourse. But without stepping here into a thorny philosophical question, it is clear from what we have seen in the work of both Pirandello and Nabokov that the film novel tends to articulate, if not resolve, precisely such a question in finding distinctive narrative manifestations for the tension between discourses and between discourses and imagery that is inherently preverbal and extraverbal. Formal mimetic discourse, especially, tends to underline the nonverbal elements that "cinematic" discourse can provide and language cannot. Preverbal experience finds words in these novels to depict regressive hallucinations such as those of a Gubbio or a Nuti in *Quaderni* or psychotic ones such as Smurin's or Hermann's in *The Eye* and *Despair*. Much more of this kind of genre-specific discursive rendition of experience will be found in West and Puig, but one may conclude already that extraverbal passages tend to expose a gap that reveals that the literary text is but a clumsy substitute for the cinematic one.

One kind of discourse (film) is the initial narrative stimulus, yet in the end it is incorporated into another: the discourse of literature. Such a dynamic amounts to more than a discursive curiosity, however, since even conventional kinds of intertextuality use juxtapositions of genre conventions to question the inherent lack of conformity to "nature" inherent in each. So much more, I would say, in the case of intramedial juxtaposition. While traditional views on poetics suggest that the intertextual variety of conflict is used to create a mere illusion of critical skepticism ("the improbable is labelled and objections thereby disarmed" [Culler 1975:149]), the fact is that intertextual and interdiscursive juxtaposition in the film novel is often performed in better faith. The revelation of inherent artificiality in the devices of differing genres of narrative (and the exposition of this all the way to the foundation of discourse) allows the film novel to advance as part of its typical narratives the open questioning of what it is we know, how it is that we know it, and how we communicate it to each other. This constitutes its own GENRE-SPECIFIC EFFECT OF REALITY.

Nabokov, as we saw, does not only juxtapose literary convention to literary convention. He brings into play cinematic conventions which he questions in and of themselves: on the basis of their own plausibility (is it indeed always windy in filmland?), on the basis of their psychological and historical truthfulness (is that country estate truly Mozzhuhine's and is he truly the ideal lover?), and even on the basis of their discursive competence (should the sound of that water extend beyond the visual evidence of the waves?). Only then does he involve such cinematic conventions in an interdiscursive dialogue with literature. A powerful, complex, and most amusing example is the case of the hero in *Despair,* who plans his escape by trying to slip through the fissures that he hopes to open, by his "narrative" intervention, between conflicting kinds of naturalization: the real (but is that reality not actually just literary?) and the cinematic. This forces even the bystanders within the story to act as we might do; as "readers," that is, who are challenged to make up their minds by the openness of a writerly text and who need to face the arbitrariness of internal conventions necessary to any "narrator."

We shall return to such "kinds" of readers and texts in a minute, but first let us dwell a little longer on the significance of such discursive disjunction for the film novel. Such disjunction is indeed, I would say, another of its defining characteristics.

Discursive Disjunction and Closure

Discursive disjunctions such as the one illustrated above amount to a plurilingual relation to the representation of reality. The disjunctions, in other words, have to do with the very process of representation and, as we have seen above, lend a special kind of credibility to this particular genre because it is "honest" about the discursive gaps it exposes. It is thus evident that gains in credibility that are existentially fundamental (rather than just ideologically manipulative as claimed by such as Culler) are made possible by the film novel.

But discursive disjunction does not affect merely the film novel's effect of reality: it is often part of the stories that the genre tells. In this it is much like the kinds of genre in which discursive disjunctions are as important as (at times more than) the differing cultural ways in which human beings and society are encoded. Film musicals are an obvious example, since in these it is so evident that the discourses of music and of dance are as responsible for the narrative process and for generic distinctiveness as are the cultural discourses triggered by conventional narrative crisis.[12] But even in literature it is often through discursive disjunction that components of narrative structure (crisis and resolution, dramatic conflict, dramatic process, position and closure) are resolved. To give just one example from the main canon of West European narrative literature, Don Quixote's solution to his failure in the discursive mode of chivalric romance is to shift his hopes and aspirations into the discourse of the pastoral. It could be argued that it is the discursive disjunctions between these and between these and the discourse of "reality" that ultimately kills him.

The death of Albinus, similarly, is brought on by his failure to recognize disjunction between the discourse of film genre ("a girl was receding among tumbled furniture before a masked man with a gun" [L:20]) and that of reality ("Albinus stretched out his fist and moved the gun slowly to and fro, trying to induce some sound which would betray her exact position" [L:289]). The sad fact is that Albinus (if not Don Quixote) should know better, since he has already almost shot the chamber maid in his eagerness to "read" the evidence of reality through the discursive filter of genre melodrama. But the principle holds well beyond Albinus individually to embrace much else in *Laughter in the Dark*. We have seen how the whole novel is articulated across the disjunctions of fable and film: the contradictions between the patina of painting and panting in the penny arcade (the primitive setting in which film did indeed exist as repetitive loops of short actions, often pornographic, disconnected from any plot).

In such cases it is the intramedial tension between disjunctive discourses that provokes crisis, narrative development, and ultimate resolution. Rather than the ostensible story materials that empirical extrapolation may reveal, it is the way in which the story "comes into being," the way in which it is "understood" by its protagonists, that determines the plot.[13] Isn't, after all, Serafino Gubbio's decision to stay within his discursive role of uninvolved cameraman (his refusal to "recognize" the discourse of melodrama chosen by Nuti) responsible for allowing two preventable deaths to occur? The film novel seems to rely on plots with conventional, even trite, kinds of crisis elements ("sexual desire," "violence") and thus, at first sight, is difficult to set apart on the basis of the stories it tells.

Noticing the genre-specific function that discursive disjunction plays in the economy of the film novel, however, allows us to see that it shifts the focus of these components so as to lend them freshness and originality of a new kind. The cinematic frame of reference makes it clear that the plot elements, rather than deriving from contextual reality, come into being because they are mistakenly perceived as real, mistakenly interpreted, even actively concocted, by protagonists immersed in the flickering afterglow of movies. Even if the crisis (diegetically speaking) remains one of violence and sexual desire, the way it functions within the film novel is different from other genres in which it occurs. Characters may still lust and still die. Yet the way in which they come to do so, the meaning and devolution of their desire and demise, is quite different in these film novels than it is in stories of detection or in plots about the settling of the Wild West.

Yet even as plot elements taken at face value, the situations that occur, develop, and resolve in the film novel owe as much to the discursive tensions that underlie the genre-specific "stories" typical in this genre as they do to events and actions free of any such generic constraints. The most striking example in *Laughter in the Dark* is that of violence: the twice repeated "shooting" of Margot by Albinus. This action, to begin with, comes into being from the movie fragment that Albinus sees at the cinema. The "crisis" also derives (apart from the not unimportant discursive discontinuity of the two realms of "screen" and "life") from the discursive incongruity embodied in Albinus's words that end chapter one: "No, you can't take a pistol and plug a girl you don't even know, simply because she attracts you." Since this comment occurs in the story progression *before* our encounter with the film fragment that generates it, we have no idea, at that point in the story, why he should be making it. This reversal tends to confirm, it seems to me, the primacy of discursive elaboration over plot element. The central crisis of the novel, in other words, the one encapsulated in the opening "fairy-tale" rendition, flows from Albinus's reaction to (and not from the existence of) the sequence in that film.

The productive primacy of discursive discrepancy goes even further in these novels. The very creation of the conventional elements of plot in any story can be seen as a response (if not quite a "cover-up" as theorists of the poetics of paranoia suggest) to what Neale would think of as the lack of coherence between the discourses involved (Neale 1983:20–30). In other words, the tensions and inconsistencies of a culture tend to be submerged within (translated into) the reassuring familiarity of conventional situations and familiar strife. This masking tends to divert the reader's attention from inconsistencies that truly matter (the contradictions of culture that touch us as individuals) to conflicts that at best echo them from a safe distance (fiction) and displace them onto a plane that appears to be "about something else." While I don't want to plunge too deeply into the rifts opened up by the adversary reading of this situation, it is worth keeping in mind that specific elements of plot, setting, and character are indeed generated by the nature of the discourses that are chosen (or in the case of fixed genres "imposed") for the process of storytelling, rather than vice versa. In other words, the disequilibrium of the empirical data of plots helps us to overlook the ultimate impossibility of reconciling their inherent discursive discrepancies.

Some of the dynamics outlined above may be seen in action most distinctly, as it turns out, in the way that the reconciliation of these discursive discrepancies occurs in Nabokov. In the case of film novels, as we have seen, the discourses at issue are cultural and thematic as well as intramedial. Since the possibility of a positive ideological closure is more important to us in "real life" than it is in fiction (where, after all, the death of a protagonist is quite bearable, if not thrilling), one notes that Nabokov's narratization of the discrepancy between the discourse of science and that of aesthetics is resolved quite differently in autobiography and in fiction. In *Speak, Memory,* the resolution is quite harmonious, going as Nabokov does from pupil to researcher to professor of literature. The discursive disjunctions relevant to Albinus, on the other hand, are not resolved as painlessly. Yet fictional displacement turns out to be more instructive about the process than biography. Narrative compensation is most active in the fictional realm of this genre because at its very origin we find a genre-specific discursive discontinuity: the disequilibrium between the discourse of film representation and those of "life," "culture," "philosophical perspective," and "civilized feeling." Albinus's "narrative" solutions to his problems illustrate vividly that narrative of a conventional kind is indeed used to cover up the discrepancies between various discursive practices.

Thus, while finding examples of dramatic conflict in the film novel is easy enough (since more than most kinds of stories they thrive on the basis of popular narrative tropes), it is important to keep in mind that in these novels the "kind" of disruption that tends to generate narrative (its genre-specific "genre" of experience) is "cinematic" well beyond the thematic level. Yet the film novel, as I mentioned, is quite open about what Neale finds surreptitious in genre narratives. Serafino Gubbio openly questions the very confidence trick mentioned above when he denounces the insincerity of film plots. Nabokov's various protagonists (as well as his autobiographical persona) explore the various rifts opened up by the desperate "plotting" of film and filmlike fictions. Within the film novel, the combination of traditional genres and the discourse of film allows these novels to go beyond what is typical of mainstream narratives in which the plotted cover-up mentioned above ultimately (paradoxically) also draws attention to what Neale terms the "disphasure in the relations between a plurality of positions inscribed in a plurality of discourses." The coherence of such narratives depends, in this theoretical perspective, on the fact that they "never exceed the limits of 'dramatic conflict' (. . . never, therefore, exceed the limits of the possibility of resolution)" (Neale 1983:25).

In the film novel, on the other hand, while the traditional generic elements (melodrama, crime, mystery, what have you) conform to the "safe" oscillations of such a range, the genre-specific focus on discourse of film and discourse on film (even the focus on film theory and on the less medium-specific discourse on and of the apparatus) takes the novel into the realm of modernist excess. Take Serafino Gubbio, for instance. The melodrama of envy, jealousy, and confessional downfall in *Quaderni* unwinds within the conventional extremes allowed by such forms. But, and here is the point, the ultimate closure of the novel is no such thing. It is an unusual and unsettling situation left open-ended. Its lack of closure is particularly extreme inasmuch as the protagonist, who bears some responsibility for the "crime" that has taken place, shuts himself up in a traumatic silence. If closure there is at this level, it has to do with that of psychoanalysis rather than conventional narrative closure derived from the plot materials that the story offers. It is, in other words, a closure that occurs in the realm of symbolic rather than empirical extrapolation. But then *this* kind of discourse (the discourse of psychoanalysis) would regard Gubbio's silence merely as the "symptom" that is to lead to a new beginning, and thus not an "ending" at all.

Closure, of course, is not merely "the way the story ends." It is found in all those elements in the story (even while it proceeds) that pull towards stasis, position, repetition, fixity, or just lack of process in whatever form it might be. Such is "the Law" in the gangster story. Neale's definition of genres as mechanisms that "guarantee coherence by institutionalizing conventions," implicates the very process of narrative progress: the balance between process and position or time-flow and closure. While it is of course easier to see how this applies to such a genre as the detective story, the story of Serafino Gubbio shows that the introduction of film discourse into the narrative produces a distinctive kind of "stressed" process, as in the distinctive kind of closure illustrated in Gubbio's final silence, in which a film trope takes over life. Thus, as in the closure typical of the horror story in which the final moment makes us aware that the supposedly vanquished monster is still among us, film novels provide their own typical forms of closure well before and apart from the way in which they end. Such closure may have negative implications (Pirandello, Nabokov, Moravia) or more positive (if sad) ones, as in Puig's *Kiss of the Spider Woman*, where (to anticipate) the closure of recounted film is the only "opening" or "escape" from the grim reality of prison.

The film novel is thus a genre in which discursive disjunction is as important "thematically" as the culturally bound representations of humanity more common in other genres. Yet even when such conventional representation is the primary focus (since everything in the film novel cannot be totally film-mimetic), the "codes" that the film novel uses to delimit characters and their context are derived from film-related ways of looking at things. At the center of the film novel we thus find that the discourse of and on film determines the importance, positioning and interaction of all other discourses. This very discourse is also often the diegetic element that initiates the narrative disjunction. Some of the defining characteristics of this genre derive from the distinctive way in which it handles the register of narrative disruption. Others derive from the characteristic nature of its diegetic specification, the genre-specific modes in which equilibrium and disruption are articulated, and finally the ways in which the film novel specifies disruption and equilibrium differently and differentially from other genres by its distinctive means of representation (its diegesis).

Genre-Specific Reader

The French "bystanders" in *Despair,* as I hinted before, are forced by Hermann to accept his "cinematic" direction of what they are seeing:

"Frenchmen! This is a rehearsal. Hold those policemen. A famous film actor will presently come running out of this house. He is an arch-criminal but he must escape. You are asked to prevent them from grabbing him. This is part of the plot. French crowd! I want you to make a free passage for him from door to car. Remove its driver! Start the motor! Hold those policemen, knock them down, sit on them—we pay them for it. This is a German company, so excuse my French. *Les preneurs de vues,* my technicians and armed advisers are already among you. *Attention!* I want a clean getaway. That's all. Thank you. I'm coming out now." (D:222)

They are invited to become, in other words, a certain "kind" of GENRE-SPECIFIC READER. It seems clear that this kind of novel activates with special intensity a mechanism that recent readers of response have come to emphasize in the act of reading: the need to become part of the act, the expectation discursively embedded into certain kinds of text that the reader assume part of the creative burden. Because of the heightened "credibility" obtained by the discursive juxtapositions discussed above, but also because these are "narratives of spectatorship" that transpose the axis linking text to consumer to a narratized context of film viewing, the film novel "opens up" for all to "see" the given (but usually implicit) presence of this need and this expectation.

AS NARRATIVES OF SPECTATORSHIP, much narrative elaboration is given in these novels to the situation, setting, and characters involved with watching the screen. We shall see more about this further on when I will argue that as a consequence of this the film novel develops a distinctive kind of setting, but for now let me recall the numerous examples that have been cited in previous chapters of the testy relationship that exists between spectator and screen; between spectator and "apparatus."

Some of them function, as we saw, to confirm the link between spectator and screen actor discussed by André Bazin and other film theorists and to articulate it in narrative terms. That Nabokov's narrative elaboration takes such theoretical insights into new territory is indicated by the apparent conceptual neatness with which his scheme is soon complicated (one may recall the author's biographical involvement with Mozzhuhine and its subsequent fictional elaboration in *Mary*) when "actor" ceases to be just that and appears as part of the "spectator's" life (now in fact sharing the same historical present), not to mention how even this transposition of roles (and "realities") is further redoubled when both Nabokov/Ganin and Mozzhuhine end up side by side on a new screen. The varied articulation of such narrative situations illustrates the complexity with which storytelling can carry the conceptual implications of film, of its viewing, and of the implications of being a spectator. Some of these situations may amount to a philosophical metaphor of life perceived in the mold of Plato's cave. Some may describe fundamental formative moments of individuality that address a full range of personal characteristics to do with human perception, personal control, and individual initiative. Such situations may even raise the specter of "mirror image" alienation from self, the multiple refractions of the other, double, or interloper, not to speak of the intricate interaction between the burden of authority and outbursts of creativity, rebellion, or sexual affirmation.

One may adduce and characterize many more examples, but what is important to reiterate here is that the effect of such narrative instances does not stop at the level of discourse on film. The episodes trigger a mimetic "writerly" response in readers too, the payoff of which is the engagement of the "actual" reader in the experience of a writerly text.[14] The reader of such novels is "inspired" by the dramatic rebellions against passive spectatorship that the texts contain and actually "instructed" in the modalities that such a rebellion may take. Thus Nabokov's resentment of the cinematic interloper who butts into his emotional and economic life starts by breaking down the conventions of film-narrative distance and by forcibly restructuring the genre melodramas seen on those screens. But we can see now that this "creative" rebellion against the enclosedness of the text goes on to influence the nature of the reader's response that this kind of text (the new discursive "genre" in which Nabokov writes) elicits. All those elements of the film novel that question or emphasize the contradiction inherent in the claim of the film image to be the signified (something that, by the way, is easier to see in film than in literature, where the pretense to the reality-effect is not made as explicitly) help to undermine a passive "readerly" response.

The peculiar contradiction between the way in which film functions and the way in which literature does allows for this play to happen most vividly and with the benefit of most untheoretical narrative detail, given the specific context (story, situations, characters, problems) provided by the film novel. What is thus turned into extensive narrative treatment is the very conflict between a readerly and a writerly text, as it occurs between narrative and narrative, between medium and medium. It is a narrative exploration of discursive issues that, before the advent of a critical awareness of film and before the incorporation of such awareness into literature, occurred only occasionally.

Such awareness may indeed be very instinctive and elemental (the rebellious children invading the blank screen at Nabokov's birthday with their own shadows can hardly be assumed to have a clear theoretical awareness of what it is they are responding to), but it is fundamental. Just how fundamental we can see from the directness with which the formative experiences of teens and young lovers (fictional and not) engage the structures of cinema. Episodes such as those in *Mary* and with Tamara suggest that the writerly challenge is inherent in the medium of film itself (and thus an inevitable thematic element in its literary representations).

This challenge exists because the grammar of the medium recapitulates the grammar of a mechanism (that of our subconscious) that is most directly involved in the process of human individuation. Indeed, it is some of the most deeply rending paradoxes of personal growth that trigger the writerly rebellion of *Speak, Memory*'s Nabokov and *Mary*'s Ganin. Both (but are they not one?) are shocked and disgusted to be split in the very instant of self-recognition: between a point in space to which the lines of a mirror reflection converge (is this really me?) and a point behind a screen to which their perception seems to project the same converging lines (how dare Mozzhuhine use my own mansion!). Yet neither point exists in "reality," neither of them "points" to us, even if both are the only viable anchors for our sense (our understanding) of selfhood. Props and settings such as mansions, movie houses, and screen are deployed for the benefit of individuating youngsters to such effect by Nabokov that one might be forgiven the temptation to suggest that it is "kino-genesis" that "recapitulates ontogenesis."

A reader challenged to such awareness by the stability of a genre that provides a consistent reading world will tend to undergo a subtle form of readerly individuation, so much so that to some of what by now are the traditional subdivisions of types of reader one may find embedded within the text, I think we can add the film novel's CINEMATIC READER. We may say of film novels and their implied readers that the *hypothesis* of a "cinematic" reader that they seem to contain, explicitly or implicitly, changes our apprehension of a given text and awakens us to the significance of its filmic codes.[15] Such awareness has extensive narratological effects. From the point of view of the inferential and speculative activity that normally occurs in the act of reading, the film novel gives matters hermeneutic and synaesthetic a special twist, since the limits of what is stated by the words printed on the page lead to inferences highly colored by the way in which another kind of text, that of film, tends to present things.

The film novel thus engages the reading subject differently from other kinds of narrative which tend to tie reader and text in such a way as to cover up the very discursive disjunctions that the film novel reveals.[16] We have seen how often this genre places the subject at the intersection of literary and filmic discourse in such a way as to emphasize lack of coherence, disorientation, and the epistemological topos that is at the center of this genre. In fact, the film novel exposes (nay redoubles) the central failure of film to deliver what it promises. This is because its intensified synaesthesia imitates the tendency of film itself to trigger a crescendo of scopophiliac desire by its inherent "absence." Film as such is ultimately absent from the film novel, while in cinema it is "merely" reality that is absent. In the film novel, thus, the "lack" is redoubled, and in a manner particular to this genre only: the effect of the real that in film watching leads to an experience of lack becomes in the film novel a narratization of film's effect of the real, of its existential experience of lack, and ultimately leads to an awareness of the absence of film itself from the text of the novel. This experience of a double deprivation[17] happens inevitably, despite all of the genre's formal mimetic efforts.

Margot embodies this very mechanism for Albinus as he progresses from film spectator to blind dupe. As I pointed out, Margot manages to replace her own body for the images of unattainable desire that entice Albinus and comes to play the role of a "director" to her lover. Once he is literally blinded, however, she conspires with that other director figure Rex to deprive Albinus of the very substance of reality: falsifying colors, rearranging space, and ultimately deserting him altogether. The subject of desire is thus twice subtracted in the novel's plot, just as it is in the structure of the genre to which this story belongs. As for the aforementioned crescendo of scopophiliac desire (a desire to see that which is forbidden, a position of seeing without being seen) Albinus's story stages yet another cruel split. It is he who ends up with a frustrated desire to see the forbidden object of his desires ("but at night he dreamed of coming across a young girl lying asprawl on a hot lonely beach and in that dream a sudden fear would seize him of being caught by his wife" [L:17]).[18] It is Margot and Rex, on the other hand, who sadistically exploit their ability to see Albinus when he cannot see them. I think it is significant, also, that this story happens to situate both losses in the act of seeing. For it is the virtual (and inevitably frustrated) gaze of the film novel's reader that is set in motion by the genre's formal-mimetic attempt to be "read" as cinema.

Frustrated scopophilia is of course also echoed at the level of plot in the novels themselves. Albinus is somewhat aware of his disadvantage in this respect since his very meeting with Margot is characterized by a rebellion on his part similar to that of Nabokov and his young friends when faced with the screen. With Albinus, however, it is not so much a film-scopic interaction that defines individuality or circumscribes sexuality (while paradoxically undermining the first and promising free reign to the second). Albinus (an adult) seems to react to the fundamental process by which film watching engages the creation and control of desire. Albinus objects to the fragments of films he watches at the Argus because ostensibly "there was no interest whatever in watching happenings which he could not understand since he had not yet seen their beginning" (L:20).

Yet there is more to it, since it is these events' coherence as discourse that he cannot control, unless he is there to engage the narrative flow from the start. These bits and pieces of story don't make sense unless he participates in their continuity so as to give him a safe watching position and the reassurance of smooth, continuous "flow." Only thus could the spectator tolerate the hurtful crisis these moments depict, and only if the spectator's identification is allowed to stay conditional so that any closure, tragic as may be, can be felt to reestablish convenient order. The way in which Albinus, on the other hand, is set adrift among these narrative fragments retains all the danger without the safety net of the classical narrative apparatus. It is thus because the film fragments don't allow Albinus to enter into a "controlling" position with a dominant point of view that he rejects them. The first fragment, we may recall, reveals a figure that foreshadows Albinus's death. It suggests the eventual deprivation of Albinus's present ocular supremacy by being masked. The second fragment is, of course, a foreshadowing of the car accident that blinds Albinus literally.[19]

Look and Point of View

Spectators have an investment in the carefully balanced alternation between the inherent discursive disjunction of film ("delimited" views of "fragments" of "mediated" reality) and its carefully staged illusion of wholeness and of seamless flow. Part of what keeps the Albini of this world in their seats is a kind of "contract" that ensures, after much mediated mayhem, a final identification between the spectator and those aspects of film discourse that confirm security and convention. MacCabe describes this ambivalent (but demanding) spectator thus: "the distinction between the spectator as viewer, the comforting 'I', the fixed point, and the spectator as he or she is caught up in the play of events on the screen, as he or she 'utters', 'enounces' the film" (MacCabe 1985:68). Neale (1983:26) takes this further and points out that the spectator's pleasure is based on the danger of loss of meaning and control (the process towards, not just the closure of specular stasis). But the ultimate assurance of scopic control is essential; otherwise the ideal world of the movie, rather than displaying an ideal closure that echoes subliminal memories of a mothering womb, will reveal the discursive disjunctions of a culture cobbled together with ever inconsistent terms jousting for supremacy. This contrast may well be embodied by the contrast between the generically circumscribed scenario favored by Albinus ("masked man confronting a woman") and the refractory reality that prevents him from shooting Margot once and then twice, because the woman heard (and not heard) walking down the corridor is not inevitably the one to be shot but may be or may not be Margot, and because a masked man is and is not blindfolded—is and is not "blind."

Such oppositions are so resonant because their significance reaches beyond the narrative displacements of cultural alternatives. The example from *Laughter in the Dark* implicates the opposition between what we have come to understand as "the imaginary" and "the symbolic." In objecting to the film fragments Albinus is resisting the irruption of the symbolic (the structure and language of culture independent of a subject's wish and control) into the field of the imaginary (the subjective and wish-driven establishment of identification with the image of another who is, yet is not, me). A most unwelcome (if inevitable) experience for most of us, for Albinus the occasion is particularly troubling because, to quote from MacCabe's summary of Lacan, "entry into the symbolic can be most simply described as the recognition of the world independently of my consciousness—as the recognition, that is, of the possibility of my own death" (MacCabe 1985:66). It is not often, in human experience, that confrontation with the manifestations of a world impenetrable to our desire occurs in the context of an explicit representation of its deadly implications.

In cinematic terms, what Albinus wishes for is the controlling freedom of POINT OF VIEW, which "preserves the primacy of vision" and does so most effectively in cinematic discourse because "what is left out of one point-of-view shot can always be supplied by another." He wishes for this, rather than the delimited and limiting subject position forced upon spectators as the LOOK: "radically defective" and "related to other looks," its "field is not defined by a science of optics in which the eye features as a geometrical point, but by the fact that the object we are looking at offers a position from which we can be looked at" (MacCabe 1985:67).[20]

Nabokov's wish for a floating camera is the expression of such a wish too, but the narrative displacements of this desire in his novels (the murder scene in *King, Queen, Knave*, the car accident in *Laughter in the Dark*) reveal that point-of-view attempts are always interfered with by the look of another. Martha's reverse angle (reverse-look) from the boat in the former novel may in fact (given the nature of her relationship with Franz) transpose the breaking of the magic circle of imaginary identification of the child and his mirror image (of character and his environment, of narrator and his world)[21] to the adult world, by interrupting Franz's point-of-view rendition of his walk. And so does the old woman's look (twice stressed) in the accident scene in *Laughter*, where other looks as well (the pilot's from the plane, Elizabeth's from the balcony) interrupt the univocal potency of bare narrative point of view. Nor should one forget the "clinical" rendition of this process in the bedroom scene in *Despair*: "I sat in an armchair half a dozen paces away from the bed upon which Lydia had been properly placed and distributed. From my magical point of vantage I watched the ripples running and plunging along my muscular back, in the laboratorial light of a strong bedlamp that picked out a mother-of-pearl glint in the pink of her knees and a bronze gleam in her hair spread on the pillow—which were about the only bits of her I could see while that big back of mine had not yet slid off to prop up again its panting front half in the audience" (D:37–38).

Hermann's self-styled "dissociation" while making love to his wife ("that imp Split") is described as a sequence of receding camera setups subject to the physical laws of perspective and distance. This omnipotent staging, carefully analyzed in terms of what would be visible to an objective camera eye, is extended by Hermann's increasing obsession into a repetitive sequence characterized by an ever-growing distance of viewer (voyeur) from scene: "I used to sit every night a few inches farther from the bed" until "eventually I found myself sitting in the parlor—while making love in the bedroom." Hermann's theatrical simile soon gives way to the need for a plethora of longer and more potent optical instruments to refract, mediate, and transmit his alienated split from self and other, as he wishes "to watch a small but distinct and very active couple through opera glasses, field glasses, a tremendous telescope, or optical instruments of yet unknown power that would grow larger in proportion to my increasing rapture." Further and more overt screenlike mediation is finally achieved when, finding his "view of the bed cut off by the doorjamb," Hermann opens "the wardrobe in the bedroom to have the bed reflected in the oblique speculum or *Spiegel*" (D:37–38).

The self-deluding spectacle that holds Hermann in its thrall through the optical mediation of instrumental agency and through the syntax of receding setups is dispelled only by the voice of his wife "saying that if I were not yet coming to bed, I might bring her the red book she had left in the parlor" (D:38). Hermann is here quite like a film viewer confronted suddenly with the illusory nature of the ghosts s/he had been watching on a sheet (Godard's Brechtian ironies, Bergman's melting celluloid personas). Sharing this sudden "alienation effect" with the reader, he finds that it was not himself that he was seeing performing on that bed. It was quite literally, in this case, a ghost on a sheet.

The regressive nature of Hermann's hallucination allows for his wife to interrupt with her very voice the specular projection of potency he has arranged for himself. Hermann's elaborate and most cinematic construction of specular point of view is thus shattered by the female look. But Hermann is, of course, the most vulnerable of Nabokov's characters to this kind of experience ("those constitutive moments at which we experience ourselves in the very moment of separation" [MacCabe 1985:67]) since his central delusion that he is the twin of another man may well rest upon the remembered power of a child's discovery of a replica of himself in his reflection and the characteristic wish that it be not *just* an image.

It is notable that in *Laughter* Margot and Albinus are in fact linked (among other things) by their "look" at the same film. For Margot too has seen the masked man in the movies. We even find her later in the novel recoiling "before the barrel of an imaginary revolver" while making "wonderful faces for the benefit of her dressing-chest mirror" (L:69). Her version of "masked man shooting receding girl" is far more pragmatic than Albinus's (it is part of the "symbolic" inasmuch as it has to do with Margot being and not being a good actress, being and not being suitable material for the cinematic look of others). Yet this is not where the distinction ends. Things turn deadly in the final reenactment of the cliché not least because now Albinus has not merely lost point of view, he has even lost the possibility of the look. Margot, on the other hand, is in a position where her look at this situation (in the movies, in her looking glass) has become omnipotent: no one is looking at her (much as blinded Albinus would wish to)! It is she who now has point of view. So it is that Albinus dies.

Discourse and the "Effect of Film"

That a particular kind of reader is posited by the film novel is also confirmed by the formal-mimetic experiments found in Pirandello and Nabokov. The latter's attempt in *Laughter in the Dark* to produce a film experience in the reader confirms that the discourse itself is called upon to trigger a cinematic response in the reader's consciousness. The stakes are high, since it is only thus, only by creating the synaesthetic shudder discussed above as one of the defining characteristics of the film novel, that the narratized unfolding can occur of such issues as the potent (if not infinite) semiosis of film images, their peculiar modernist version of signs that aspire to the symbolic, or the double jeopardy of lack and desire. It is because such situations are centered on film that their meaning emerges with power. In the case of the last (double jeopardy), the film situation allows for a doubling of the experience we have discussed before: the tension caused by what we "see" as vividly as we would by possessing it at the very time that we "experience" its physical absence.

The genre-specific triggering of an EFFECT OF FILM by filmic discourse in the film novel is made possible, of course, by the fact that its subject matter (the film image) functions by triggering an analogous effect in the spectator. It too, within its proper medium, functions discursively by exploiting an ability to trigger the experience of a reality that is not there (not part of the "rules" of its world). While other kinds of image may trigger resonances and illusions just as effectively (the kind of memory experience described by Nabokov may, after all, be caused by objects other than those that are film-formed) the peculiar nature of film images does provide a difference: other triggering objects (Proustian madeleines and such) don't appear visually to "contain" or even to "be" that other reality.

It is thus that the triggering nature of the film image has, in the film novel, repercussions both formal and thematic. This is because what in film constitutes a solely discursive characteristic becomes thematic as well when found within the film novel. This is probably why these kinds of novel display such an extraordinary proliferation of thematic materials derived from the world of film. Apart from the expected repertory of situations, characters, and settings that the context allows, film as a "form" and as a "problem" can be richly thematized as well.

Thematic Proliferation and Generic Extrapolation

It should be clear by now that the film novel gives rise to a remarkable variety of thematic materials (what Todorov refers to as THEMATIC PROLIFERATION) that are consistent in their focus. As we saw in previous chapters, and will see further in what follows, a veritable flurry of narrative situations is generated by thoughts about film and related technologies, while the situations themselves tend to stimulate additional thought ("narratives of the mind") about what turns out to be a new topical repertory for the age of cinematic reproduction.

Yet thematic proliferation in the film novel turns out to mean much more than the mere "privileging" of a cluster of themes suggested by Todorov.[22] The generative energy of film as theme points to a coherent and complex codex, one we notice because fundamental extra-empirical extrapolations that the reader performs during any act of reading look to "genre" and "ideology." Since thematic proliferation in general, because of the varieties of its manifestations, provides textual activity that differs in some way from the normal run of narrative functions to which theme as such belongs, theme in these novels, rather than simply indicating what the film novel "is about," generates action, dialogue, images, and ideas that explore what "it means to be about this," what "it is like." In a genre such as the detective novel, the point of thematization—the activity that occurs through the so-called semic code—is to mark the situation as a mystery to be resolved or to define a character as the one who has the competence to find the answer. In the film novel, by contrast, the marking of discourse (the definition of character, object, or place in ways which signify "film novel") opens up a creative path that is used to explore the repercussions of the theme itself.[23] Albinus's problem with the narrative fragments he watches at the movies, we have seen, is largely a "plotted" rendition of the relationship between narrative modalities in film (and in this literary genre) and the critical, philosophical, technical, and metaphorical aspects of discourse.

But the specificity of this genre extends well beyond semic thematization.

It embraces a consistent series of symbolic oppositions. While story-specific thematization may contain such oppositions just as any story strongly marked by genre, it is only with generic thematization that one starts to recognize the landscape as consistent. The symbolic code articulates the inherent ideological opposites implicit in culture (the ones that usually demand to be kept clearly distinct) and through it the film novel thematizes opposites that have to do with culture (high vs. low), with perception (natural vs. instrumental), with mediation (verbal vs. visual), and so on. The clash of such differing discourses of cultural delimitation tends to be, as Neale points out about the social movie comedy, a matter of "mapping the field of socio-discursive order." While in the case of the genre that Neale has in mind this involves "a field whose nodal points tend constantly to be those of class and sexuality" (Neale 1983:24–25), in the film novel the field is characterized, at its broadest, by the shifting grasp of human perception as it is given concrete graspable form in the manifestations of photography and cinematography. Also, while in social comedy "the order is disturbed in order for its hierarchy to be rearranged," in such novels as Pirandello's and Nabokov's the disruption in the diegetic order is caused by misapprehensions at the level of the discourse of perception. Finally, while in social comedy "the establishment of a new, 'better' hierarchy is the condition of narrative closure," in the film novel narrative closure occurs along the lines of possible adjustment between the discourse of existential resolution and that of perceptual dilemma. Notably, in the film novel it is the bearers of film discourse who tend to be the disrupters and challengers of the various other discourses of existence that they encounter. Far from providing a discourse that causes an ethically necessary reordering (as happens in the examples of film comedy proposed by Neale) the discourse of film in the film novel usually reveals itself to be ethically suspect or reprehensible. Even in *Kiss of the Spider Woman,* film discourse (healing and necessary as it might be) is the ultimate escape from reality.

While these kinds of ideological antitheses depart from traditional narrative subject matter (language/kinship, sex/money) as defined by anthropologists and rhetoricians of the novel, this is precisely where the film novel is most original.[24] It takes as its subject matter the articulation of the disequilibrium between the ideologically charged values mentioned above, values that have come to be central in modern culture. It is this very disequilibrium that starts the narrative and keeps it going: be it the "details" that befall Albinus, honored representative of High German Culture, when he embraces the low cultural milieu of a working-class mistress and popular movies; be it the multiple narrative repercussions that befall protagonist and antagonists helplessly bent upon "seeing" reality through the mediation of movies; be it the ultimate total dependence of a blind art historian on the "verbal" rendition of the world provided (and abused) by his mistress and her lover.

The Death of Albinus (Take Two)

It might in fact be illuminating to stay for a moment longer with Albinus and to contemplate his death one more time. It illustrates the intricacy with which the novel brings to its climax the mechanism of symbolic disequilibrium, narrative continuity, and ultimate closure. Lesage describes the opening move of any story as caused by a "transgressor that impels the narrative toward its climax or catastrophe" (Lesage 1985:494–495). Albinus indeed thusly transgresses on two levels: against the genre-specific equilibrium peculiar to the film novel that I just described and against the more traditional cultural codes (the contracts, sexual roles, property arrangements) of society. Albinus's death occurs, among other things, because he is unable to reconcile both orders of code. But in the final moments it is the symbolic codes specific to the film novel that trip him up.[25] Indices of this are, for instance, the "cultural" objects he had placed in the apartment and that have been sold off by an uneducated mistress and a venal forger with total disregard for their cultural value. Yet Albinus cannot "see" this as he tries to orient himself in the room by their location. He fails, ultimately, in "reading" this space, in which he is trying to reenact the very story fragment (blind[folded] man aiming a pistol at terrified girl) that he had refused to acknowledge as relevant to himself at a time he "could" still see. He fails also because of his refusal after the accident to acquire a new sensory literacy. In the end it is the details of the plot that conspire in his death. This narrative resolution marks indeed "the end of the symbolic search," what Barthes describes as "symbolic closure" or "return to order." The verbal and the visual finally coalesce; the instrumental mediation conforms to the natural, and the wronged wife finally becomes the dignified widow.

Hermeneutic Code and "Autism as Code"

But does the film novel also telegraph its inherent mystery, the central questions it raises, at the level of capillary narrative? Are the kinds of enigmas and mysteries (or just the questions) that are specific to the film novel to be found only at the generic level, or do they stand out as central and distinctive among all the other story-specific "MacGuffins." While the individual stories in these novels may offer individual puzzles of their own to resolve, it seems that film novels are also linked by typical ones that they share. We have seen many of these in examples that precede *Laughter in the Dark*: Bachelard's man with magnifying glass was engaged in a hermeneutic search, as were the "characters" consonant with his views. Both Nabokov's lily and his carpet in their own ways constitute the subject matter and mechanics of hermeneutic desire (lily) and search (what the carpet "puts together" while we stumble over it). Yet it is the home movie, as we saw, that suggests the deepest mystery of all—that of one's life. The anecdote "stages" a very personal (yet universal) hermeneutic lust (the ultimate enigma of one's own birth and death). At the same time, it articulates the common human effort to seek for clues in the very text of representation, very much like Jonathan Culler's reader, who is led to "look for features which he can organize as partial answers to the questions he had asked" (Culler 1975:210). This hermeneutic focus culminates with the ending of *Laughter* when, as we have seen, Albinus fails to solve the presences within and layout of a room that is a mystery to him (but here the story-specific and the genre-specific mingle).

All through the novel, in fact, Albinus is a kind of proxy for the reader in looking for the "clues" that will yield the truth about Margot and Rex. This is certainly also true in the case of Gubbio, and is, as will be seen, often the case in subsequent film novels such as *Lancelot* (where the "lust" to see forbidden and censored clues is the central spring of the protagonist's character and of the narrative climax) and *Kiss of the Spider Woman* (in which it is the reader, as well as one of the two protagonists, who must make the effort to "visualize" whole films on the basis of selective verbal summaries). The recurrent theme of seeing (or failing to see) what is really there suggests that there is a genre-specific kind of hermeneutic code at work in all these novels. Often, the typical "puzzle" and "mystery" of the film novel is the one that has been staring at us all along, the one that is not hidden at all. Its discovery merely depends on our powers of everyday observation and comprehension.

The narrative tension in the film novel thus arises from what we might call the narrative representation of AUTISM AS CODE. Characteristic in media such as photography and cinematography, it is a code that points to the tendency to see everything while being inherently unable to select what is significant, what is of value. Dorothy Parker is said to have described this as the terribleness of a medium that "sees anything." The codex to which this code would then refer is one that lacks any semblance of coherent organization. Its danger is seeing too much to identify any meaning (is this what happens to Gubbio in the tiger's cage?) or nothing at all (the "lepless" landscapes of Italy before Nabokov was instructed by his art teacher). This tendency to the representation of chaos and to the uncritical selection of "anything" is expressed quite clearly in examples such as the one given by Nabokov to the interviewer from *Vogue* and in formal-mimetic strategies such as the ones deployed by him in *Laughter in the Dark*. It is the desire to bring this code under control that explains the opposite gestures of a desire to transcend (see the putative multiple cameras evoked in the same interview and the implicit cinematic apparatus that articulates Albinus's car crash) and a compulsion to be in charge of the look.

This compulsion to control manifests itself often in the narrative elaboration of focalization which, in novels influenced by film, acquires particular resonance. Take, for example, the murder scene in *King, Queen, Knave*, where focalization provides the foundation for a "classic" genre situation (in the cinema we need only think of Hitchcock, who was a master of this trope). The discourse on film involved in such examples underlines the central difficulty of writing as it tries to transcend the boundedness of time and space characteristic of our everyday reality, sometimes with results that are quite at odds with each other. In *King, Queen, Knave* focalization links the poet to the criminal who tries to be like a god in controlling a totality of events to do with life and death. The same trope in *Laughter* offers a view of a man buffeted by fate and by events out of his reach (in time and in space).

This would perhaps seem fanciful interpretation, or the discovery of an inert generic trope, were it not that a recent example tends to confirm its continuing status and importance. We find it as the central image in Friedrich Dürrenmatt's recent novel *The Assignment: or on the Observing of the Observer of the Observers,* where it is used (albeit in a quite negative way) to express human fate in the grip of a transcendental focalization: "Now everything he observed was observed from above, and not only what he observed, he himself was being observed as he observed, he knew the resolving power of satellite pictures, a god who was observed was no longer a god, God was not subject to observation, God's freedom consisted of being a concealed, hidden god, while man's bondage consisted of being observed" (Dürrenmatt 1989:109).[26]

These kinds of passages, as I discussed earlier, raise related issues to do with narrative omniscience and point of view and often resolve them, as in the case with Albinus, in a genre-specific way. The simile between poet and cameras outlined to the interviewer from *Vogue* (as well as the narratized formal-mimetic versions of this insight) puts forth a specific notion of temporal and spatial simultaneity: possibly a "cinematic" rather than a strictly "literary" one. Since the overarching analogy seems to be between the "poet" and the "apparatus," this trope finds Nabokov in unison with filmmakers such as Maya Deren in assuming that the "natural" state of cinematic language is lyric rather than narrative. He thus keeps activating in narrative contexts the kind of interaction between syntagmatic and paradigmatic construction peculiar to film language that we have seen to be important in Pirandello as well.

Apparatus as Setting

The remark about multiple cameras wired to a central perceiving subject is also an explicit representation of the apparatus as something more than just a machine. It seems to me that it is being conceived as a veritable space for action and experience. In this case the cinematic apparatus becomes setting as the hypothetical individual and his lawn chair are transformed into a kind of open air "studio." Such an interpretation may seem far-fetched if we limit ourselves to this instance only. But consider the way in which a room and a desk and its drawer are transformed into a displaced yet recognizable "apparatus" in *Mary*.

Or look at the train ride in *King, Queen, Knave*. The optical illusions inherent in Franz's view of the train ride (movements are magically reversed as the world parades across the window as if on a screen) are here dependent upon the cinematic limits of the train's window frames. After a while, the windowpane itself is transformed into a perceptible surface by the darkening light outside the train, allowing Martha's swallow-fastener to appear upon it. All of this is described as if seen by a static spectator inside a darkened cinema. The optical illusions in this case, one might object, are not coded as cinematic, yet the text does guide our thoughts to that area of formal mimetics by isolating the alternating flicker of light and dark produced by the trees outside the railway carriage: "a wall of beech trees was flickering by the window in a speckled sequence of sun and shade" (KQKn:5). Moreover, the implicit formal simile is clinched when, as "the flicker of woods in the window became irksome" to Martha, a clearly photographic alchemy occurs: she shuts her eyes and "the sun penetrated her eyelids with solid scarlet, across which luminous stripes moved in succession (the ghostly negative of the passing forest), and a replica of her husband's cheerful face, as if slowly rotating toward her, got mixed up in this barred redness, and she opened her eyes with a start" (KQKn:9). Through the phenomenon of retinal afterimages which is basic to cinema, and by the use of the projector's alternating flicker of light and shade as iconic materials, Martha's eyelids become "screens" for a German expressionist film montage in which the primary materials of story and setting and their paradigmatic associations merge: the stylized bars of what she will eventually come to feel as her prisonlike marriage to Dreyer; the red coloring of the bloody solutions she will explore as her way out; and, floating as a disembodied icon towards her, the face of Dreyer himself. With its veritable "anatomy" of framing, screen, fragmentation of movement (the shutter effect), and film-specific special effects, the train carriage has become a vivid example of what I mean by the notion of APPARATUS AS SETTING.

The cinematic machine is about organizing a space found or created at a point of origin and about providing its reconstructed illusion within a second, highly controlled space. It should not be surprising, therefore, that the apparatus often controls the effect of space of the film novel. This space subdivides into an extensive set of possibilities having to do with focalization and the articulation "in space," as it were, of the cinematic ways in which roles and syntax may unwind. Let me recall, on this subject, the ways in which *Laughter in the Dark* displays setting as protagonist or the components of a setting (and the inanimate objects that inhabit it) in actantial roles. Let me recall the way in which the metonymic syntax of film causes individuals to merge with setting. It is because the film novel is so deeply tied to the essential aspects of film as a medium that it uses spatial setting in such an extensive and disparate manner. The culmination of this tendency, it seems to me, is the transformation of setting into the apparatus itself, most intensely so when (as with Gubbio behind the camera, as with Albinus at the movies) the "space" of the apparatus generates the story with the variety of generic manifestation we have discussed to this point.

Albinus Goes to the Movies

The episode that describes the meeting between Albinus and Margot (L:19–20) is of course an explicit representation of the apparatus from the perspective of the bound spectator, and as such it may well be useful in concluding this long excursus on genre. Semic thematization that carries the meaning "cinema" is quite evident. Such incidental remarks as "the oval beam of an electric torch glided toward him (as usually happens)" indicate that even at the level of individual narrative statements we are witnessing a narrative rendition of a typical situation endowed with the genre-specific features we may expect (discourse on film apparatus, in this case).[27]

We have discussed under several headings what Albinus makes of the film fragments that he watches at the movies. From the simple perspective of their nature as elements in a story, however, they illustrate how entering a setting leads to an implicit narrative momentum: a proairetic wish. These fragments of action entice us to string them into a "story." In this case, the way in which Nabokov applies the tension between film and narrative undermines the impression of syntagmatic inevitability that the code tends to create (not to speak of its need for predictability). Yet in the end Nabokov seems to return us to a confirmation of the "proairetic imperative," one that contains also its own genre, given the reader's tendency to "label" what happens in the sequence. Specifically, we as well as Albinus are confronted with an overlap of several possible stories, several possible ways of putting them together. The fragments could stand simply as parts of their own film story (in which case they presumably occur at the "correct" moment), or they are part of Albinus's main story (in which case they work proleptically), or, finally, they represent an intriguing combination of two intersecting proairetic flows. The merging superimposes the function of these fragments as part of their own story, a tale which, as they appear at this point to Albinus, comes to be also part of his. This is more than the simple combination of the two previous options, since it acknowledges the narrative function within the novel of a narrative structure from outside literature.

What Albinus sees on screen goes from being nonnecessary to the story (presumably it could be any old film) to being nonoptional elements of his own story (car ride, death scene) as they must happen if this story is to go as it does. As such, the intersection illustrates the distinction that Culler makes between proairetic and hermeneutic codes: "Though the action itself may be presented with all the clarity he [the reader, but in *Laughter* "he" is also Albinus] could wish, he does not yet know its function in the plot structure. And it is only when the enigma or problem is resolved that he moves from an understanding of action to an understanding or representation of plot" (Culler 1975:211). In fact, hermeneutically speaking, the film elements stimulate a questioning that is intense and that remains open all the way to the last page of the novel. The images in the movie house are for Albinus the kind of condition towards which the hermeneutic code is aiming. They are, that is, "signifieds that refuse to connote." As the story proceeds, moreover, other aspects of the code are also activated as Albinus needs to request an explanation, formulate possible answers, propose possible solutions as soon as possible. Nor does Nabokov refrain from using these film-marked narrative fragments (and one should not forget the poster outside the cinema) to equivocate with reader and protagonist, even to mislead, as we have seen.

Thus, apparatus as setting initiates, nurtures, and articulates the initial hermeneutic deception and all subsequent interferences. Albinus and Margot from their first meeting are "in the dark" of the apparatus, through which Margot leads Albinus to his assigned seat with her narrow beam of light. They enact from the start, in other words, a charade of hermeneutic snaring marked by the discourse of film. Moreover, the wish to see, know, and understand is frustrated throughout and to the end (a continuous jamming and breakdown of the hermeneutic activity) as Albinus goes from figurative to literal blindness to that most cinematically realized final scene. From the entry level of the story, indeed from the lobby of the movie theater, the novel establishes its cinematic correlation and does so by displaying within the setting of its apparatus its very particular language: what we might call the "effet de filmique."

The power of all this comes from the fact that both at the level of the broad apparatus and at that of minimal discursive units that constitute its stories, film engages the subject position of the film novel's genre-specific kind of reader. We saw this realized with Serafino Gubbio, and now we find it with Albinus, who from the outset is actually enfolded by the darkness of the movie theater. Both the central discursive peculiarity of the genre and the spatial control that implicates the subject, involve it directly in the central experience that the genre sets out to enact. Because the constitution of the subject is a constant and discontinuous process dependent upon the very discourse it is exposed to (according to Benveniste the subject has no existence outside of the specific discursive moments in which it emerges),[28] Gubbio, Albinus, and a host of characters to follow struggle to put themselves together in a situation that is not conducive to such an aim. The typical character of the film novel is alas totally dependent for its own coherence on the coherence of the apparatus as time, as space, and as discourse. We need only to think back to Albinus at the movies to feel the poignancy of this dependence.

Part Four

The Film Novel

7

The Hollywood Novel

Isherwood: "Infernal Machine"

Christopher Isherwood's *Prater Violet,* published in the United States in 1945, is usually regarded as part of a narrative subgenre known as the "Hollywood novel,"[1] the most famous representatives of which are Nathanael West's *The Day of the Locust* (1939) and F. Scott Fitzgerald's unfinished *The Last Tycoon* (1941). Despite its later publication date, it will be useful to consider this novel first since, dealing as it does with filmmaking in England in the thirties (filmmaking by an urbane and colorful German film director at that), it stands in more direct correlation with the thematic and formal texture of Pirandello and Nabokov than with the Hollywood focus of West and Fitzgerald.

More than Pirandello's novel, and far more than Nabokov's, *Prater Violet* concentrates on the process and industry of film production in all its details. Like its predecessors, the novel also emphasizes the metaphorical relationship of film to life and society. Isherwood outlines the process of filmmaking so faithfully that the novel, despite its veneer of parody and sarcasm, has considerable value as a document in film history. It thus offers narrative condensations of the apparatus and thematic proliferation beyond what we have seen before in the film novel. At the same time it extends the emphasis on the conflict between high and popular culture that was implicit in much of Nabokov's subtext (a genre-specific opposition within the symbolic code) by making it part of the explicit narrative level. Most of all, Isherwood's novel turns its attention to areas of filmmaking and to problems in film theory that are more specifically "political" than did either of its predecessors in our discussion. This new dimension in the narrative exploration of film poetics addresses film as a mechanism of power, as a medium that bears responsibility in what it chooses to represent from the surrounding context of history. This is partly due, no doubt, to the fact that by the mid-thirties film had become firmly established as artifact and as sociocultural presence. During the period, historical circumstances tended to underline the importance of a moral perspective on art and to expose the ease with which this particular art form could be hijacked. The social implications of the practice of filmmaking were thus more urgent at the time Isherwood first encountered cinema than at the time Pirandello and Nabokov were first exposed to it.

Prater Violet also represents an ideal "transition" between the European novels we have examined and the Hollywood novels we will look at presently. It reflects a climate of war and ideological strife that cuts deeper and demands specific answers in ways that the historical context of its American counterparts does not. Yet, even if in muted form, the new political focus introduced by Isherwood into the film novel is found in these too. The stakes of ideology thus join firmly the themes typical of the film novel. The actors in Fitzgerald's *The Last Tycoon* (who develop plans to save themselves in the face of the oncoming class revolution) and the film fans in West's *The Day of the Locust* (who act out a rage that can be read in a political framework) are just as touched by ideological factors as are Isherwood's film director Bergmann, Imperial Bulldog's chief editor Lawrence Dwight, and Isherwood himself, who figures in the novel as scriptwriter, interpreter, and companion to the charismatic director. All of them are aware (some more explicitly than others) that beneath the surface of this popular art form lurk issues of aesthetic and human import that in the end have a political dimension.

In the novel Isherwood describes his own participation (at first reluctant, then fascinated) in the making of a Viennese-style musical film produced by a British studio under the direction of a famous German director on the eve of World War II. His novel is thus founded upon a merging of the biographical and the fictional that takes the relationship of the two beyond what we have found in Nabokov. In this case the author himself becomes a version of the "typical character" of the film novel. The director Bergmann too would seem to have been based upon a real artist: the figure of Berthold Viertel, founder, in the twenties, of the German theater company "die Truppe" (Friedrich 1972:125–126). But as we shall see, his figure encapsulates a whole world of cultural attitudes that reflect upon the art of filmmaking as variously as does Pirandello through the figure of Gubbio.

As a director, Bergmann is the spokesman of a cultural code quite specific in its historical contextualization. For one thing, he manifests the broad qualitative spectrum of film work: productions well worth the deepest admiration (both Isherwood and Lawrence know and value his work from the past) and hack work that prompts Bergmann to compare Isherwood and himself to "two married men who meet in a whorehouse" (PrV:32). This variety of film work brings into play (turning it into narrative development of a genre-specific kind) the definition of film as an art form. What it may aspire to, what it may represent, and similar questions are integral parts of the narrative, as is, by extension, a genre-specific kind of representation in the novel itself. Bergmann also illustrates the cultural breadth (literature, theater, philosophy, music, political awareness) that many European directors brought to their work. He personifies the polyphonic discursive components we have defined as typical of the film novel and stimulates (on the formal-mimetic as well as thematic plane) a pluridiscursive representation of reality. This film director writes poetry, quotes widely from the "serious" canon of European texts, and is ultimately able to turn out an interpretation of his student-prince variation that is fully cognizant of the mechanics of empirical and symbolic extrapolation, and that is deeply imbued with the kind of sophisticated political strabismus that opens a host of uneasy questions.

He is also, on the other hand, the histrionic, manipulative, and eerily insightful kind of director we have encountered before in Nabokov and Braudy. In this incarnation he reveals a sadistic streak. He delights in probing his hapless secretary till her most private sorrows and confusions are suitably brought to light in a melodramatic outburst. He intrudes as voyeur upon the privacy of a pair of lovers on the bus and broadcasts his reading of their restrained body language, embroidering with embarrassing detail upon their quiet reticence for the purposes of his own extroverted staging of the world. He generally appropriates for his own idiosyncratic use a panoply of items: British history, animals at the zoo, strangers in the street, artifacts in the museum. All of these are swallowed up into a phantasmagoric production controlled by Bergmann's "theory of camera angles and the lighting of close-ups" (PrV:68). The novel thus displays with remarkable productivity the kind of medium-specific elaboration of details we have described before as characteristics of the film novel, as well as its peculiar way of interpreting the semic code. It also provides delightful examples of the film-mimetic representation of reality through literature.

Isherwood too, as author of the novel, places himself in the role of a directorlike figure, doing often to Bergmann what the German director does to others. We have encountered before the absorption of a cinematic perspective into the texture of the novel. In his version of this genre-specific trope Isherwood differs from Pirandello (who mediates the cinematic texture through the subjectivity of his protagonist) as well as from Nabokov (who makes a separation between his own directorlike interventions and those of his characters). Isherwood introduces the perspective of film into the novel by "merging" with the real director. He absorbs, in other words, Bergmann's mannerisms, words, and anxieties in a cinematic version of the Oedipal struggle between father and son, between creative mentor and artistic apprentice. Confronted with Bergmann's charismatic persona, Isherwood drifts between envious admiration of the master's creative power and resentful awareness of his own creative impotence. The link is cinematically mediated in several ways. Thematically, Isherwood parodies his own tendency to lift Bergmann's ideas about film theory and to repeat them pontifically as his own; then he presents them through formal means. As the identification between Isherwood and Bergmann progresses from physical mimesis ("I had caught myself in the middle of one of Bergmann's most characteristic gestures" [PrV:43]) to the invasion of Isherwood's dream life by the images of Bergmann's fears about the oncoming European apocalypse ("I had a curious suspicion that he had put the whole thing . . . into my head" [PrV:73]), we witness the director's veritable physiopsychological possession of Isherwood.

Bergmann essentially reduces Isherwood to a mere projection of himself (the same power that the images of directors had upon Pirandello's Gubbio and Nabokov's Martha in *King, Queen, Knave*, to name only two) and superimposes upon Isherwood's subconscious patrimony his own heightened cinematic imagination. This provides a narrative context for experiences we have found before to be narrative grist of the film novel: the fact that film provides a perfect mimesis that nevertheless encapsulates a lack of true existence (its reality-effect) and that it forces an imposition of dreamlike images upon spectators plunged into passive receptivity (the analogy in film theory between cinematic discourse and the subconscious). Beyond this, Isherwood's interaction with Bergmann manages to personify the process of mimetic individuation that we have seen fostered by the movie screen. Here the mechanics of the subject position become part of story, setting, characters as the director is said to "take over" his assistant, somewhat in the way that the cinematic apparatus is said to take over the spectator captive in his or her position.

Just as Nabokov before him, Isherwood is restive under this spell. He tries to reclaim the process of representation; he speaks explicitly of the Oedipal mold that threatens his own creativity; he even refuses to provide Bergmann with details of his own love life, lest that too be turned into a set piece not his own. This particular narrative manifestation of the rebellious spectator typical of the film novel is quite specific about the kind of things that are being protected. The potential "possession" is described, as I said, in almost physiological ways, and the personified apparatus is shown as he tries to circumscribe a sexual identity that is particularly sensitive and closeted.[2] Also, just as Nabokov, Isherwood rebels further by arrogating to himself directorial privileges that have direct effects on the structure and texture of the novel. He turns these at the true narrative director Bergmann and provides him with a series of emblematic appearances, all of them extremely formal-mimetic: pointedly iconic in some places and cinematically slapstick in others.

The literary discourse in these sections strives to represent an intramedial directorial control that acts to establish a specific kind of film-effect. As Isherwood, for instance, chases after him through London (from hotel to tobacconist to newsstand to bookstall), Bergmann emerges for the first time in the novel through the quick impressions of several "spectators," all of whom pick out selective and exaggerated details just like those found in comic film characterization. That we are meant here to think of the mutual contamination of world and spectacle is stressed by the little misunderstanding between Bergmann and the newsboy who mistakes *The New World-Stage*—the German newspaper Bergmann is trying to buy—for a theatrical magazine.[3] The spectatorial nature of genre-specific protagonists in the film novel thus penetrates to the cast of secondary characters as well, even if in a comical vein at first. But the economical iconography of type is also used more seriously to allow us to "see" Bergmann in his emblematic dimensions. He sits, for instance, opposite Chatsworth the producer in a vignette that embodies the essentials of a cinematic point-of-view shot: "A gray bushy head, with its back to me, confronted a big pink moon-face, thin, sleek fair hair, heavy tortoise-shell glasses. The gray head was thrust forward intently. The pink face lolled back, wide open to all the world." As he gets up abruptly to greet Isherwood, Bergmann gestures mechanically: "He jerked to his feet with startling suddenness, like Punch in a show. 'A tragic Punch,' I said to myself." Finally, he faces his new assistant, who promptly robs him of much individuality in order to stress the culturally emblematic role that Bergmann is meant to play: "The name, the voice, the features were inessential. I knew that face. It was the face of a political situation, an epoch. The face of Central Europe" (PrV:23–24). These techniques emphasize several of the film-specific features we have encountered before, from the reduction of individuality to type to the manner in which the medium tends to turn what is human into a mechanical travesty.

Such typecasting continues as Bergmann comes to emblematize the contradictory roles of "director" in a notable narrative proliferation of genre-specific character types. He has the face of an emperor, Isherwood notes, and the eyes of a slave: "the slave who ironically obeyed, watched, humored and judged the master who could never understand him; the slave upon whom the master depended utterly for his amusement, for his instruction, for the sanction of his power; the slave who wrote the fables of beasts and men" (PrV: 25–26). As these examples make clear, meaning and interpretation are conveyed by physique, physiognomy, posture, and gesture, precisely in the way that film tends to do. And precisely as happens with film (illustrating the genre-specific way in which the semic code tends to be "read out" in such novels), interpretation of exterior signs is not always foolproof: Chatsworth, for one, is able to read Isherwood's nervous smile merely to suit his own bias.

While Bergmann at times even turns into an object (a marionette, as we have seen above) and is often seen in terms of selective "parts" that are said to capture his essence, other characters illustrate more extensively the effect that a cinematic kind of metonymic selection (a typical feature of the style of film novels) can have. They even "merge" with objects that come to stand for them in a way that extends a genre-specific feature we have encountered before: the tendency of objects to claim cinematic space with the aggressiveness of actors. Such is Chatsworth's cigar and Ashmeade's umbrella, both used as the utmost encapsulation of typecasting. But such objects are not alone in carrying the burden of film-mimetic style. Isherwood repeatedly uses a fully cinematic orchestration of elements (iconic character types, objects, settings, and mood) to convey the texture of cinematic experience in ways clearly reminiscent of Pirandello and Nabokov.

The episode that describes the exit of producer, director, and assistants from the restaurant is such a case. Similarly, the meals with the production staff of the studio, the carefully "staged" confrontation between Chatworth and Bergmann, and the description of the workers' riots in Austria all strive to engrave themselves upon our cinematic memory. In the final "set piece" at night in Knightsbridge, Isherwood—the film over—seems to be competing with Bergmann in the evocative representation of *Stimmung*-filled moments: "I was aware of Bergmann, my fellow-traveler, pacing beside me: a separate, secret consciousness, locked away within itself, distant as Betelgeuse, yet for a short while, sharing my wanderings. Head thrust forward, hat perched on the thick bush of hair, muffler huddled around the throat under the gray stubble, hands clasped behind the back. Like me, he had his journey to go" (PrV: 153). Much in these pages (PrV:153–154) is an attempt to render a literary equivalent of subjective camerawork in which the concreteness of things is suffused with the inner coloring of individual feeling: "How did it feel to be inside that stocky body, to look out of those dark, ancient eyes?" (PrV:154). The narrator seems to be straining to achieve, by means of a culture-specific film style, a representation of the opacity of exterior appearances and of the impulse to break through this barrier. He is trying to find images that convey a view of things as seen through the subjectivity of the film director who is walking next to him. This is an instance yet again of the psycho-epistemological yearning that the special kind of vision promised by film tends to generate.

The opaqueness of a vivid but superficial rendition of things typical of film is but a facet of the rendition Isherwood gives (explicit as well as implicit) of the medium and world of filmmaking. Most vividly of all, he manages to render the superficiality, invasiveness, and fragmentariness of the medium. From the very outset of the novel he uses the abrupt and opaque telephone communications that he receives concerning his possible participation in the filming of *Prater Violet* to display the same qualities of the medium he is to work in. In an instance of precinematic condensation of the apparatus as inventive as those we have encountered in Nabokov, the telephone itself—an instrument of technologically mediated communication—is made to parallel the fragmentation of film syntax. The "continuity" of a film-job offer emerges from several discontinuous and aggressive telephone conversations in which different voices talk to Isherwood as if the context is perfectly understood and as if the recipient's agreement is taken for granted. This dialogue is quite accurate in capturing the structural nature of film communication, in which materials from disparate temporal and geographical locations are forcibly blended into a continuous story while the spectator is subjected to this illusion in a condition of diminished resistance.

The conversations also echo the cultural approximation often encountered as "content" in the products of film technology: "'Your agent says you know all about Vienna.' . . . 'He must have meant Berlin.' 'Oh, Berlin? Well, that's pretty much the same kind of set-up, isn't it?'" (PrV:8). This crassly cobbled and instrumental way of proceeding ultimately materializes concretely at "Imperial Bulldog" when the now literal apparatus of filmmaking finally interrupts Bergmann's and Isherwood's period of isolated preparation and plunges them into the abrupt and disjointed world of the studio. The demands of sound-recording are especially disruptive, but all the procedures (illustrated, as I said, in great detail by the novel) display the impersonal and mechanized fate of human artistic communication in the age of mechanical reproduction.

Isherwood translates a keen awareness of the nature of the film medium into a range of theoretical views variously voiced by Bergmann and the film editor Lawrence. These are often juxtaposed to Isherwood's naïve and condescending views of the medium, generating an internal "debate" between the common uninformed view of the medium ("Really, the films nowadays seem to get stupider and stupider," says Isherwood's mother to humor his snobbish aloofness about the film offer [PrV:11]) and the emerging aesthetic appreciation of it. At one level these appreciations help to gloss and modify Isherwood's frustrations with the difficulty of a medium that is "after all . . . movie work, hack work. It was something essentially false, cheap, vulgar. It was beneath me" (PrV:45). Bergmann's and Lawrence's views confirm Isherwood's emerging realization that such attitudes belie the fact that there is nothing intrinsically inferior in filmmaking, an art form which the likes of Shakespeare and Tolstoy would have known how to handle. Even his solution to the lack of cinematic inspiration (falling back upon the imitation of genre stereotypes) illuminates the fallaciousness of a common assumption about the medium: that it favors such clichés as part of its intrinsic nature. Nothing of the sort, protests Bergmann: "The film is a symphony. Each movement is written in a certain key. There is a note which has to be chosen and struck immediately. It is characteristic of the whole. It commands the attention" (PrV:47). The musical analogy, we may recall, was also at the back of Pirandello's mind as he worked on the film *Acciaio,* directed by Walter Ruttman in 1933. The director, if not the film, may well constitute the link between Bergmann and

Pirandello, since it was that same Ruttman who was responsible for the "symphonic" filming of *Berlin, the Symphony of a Great City* (1927), a work well known, no doubt, to European directors.

But the theoretical issue that is most central to *Prater Violet* involves the responsibility of the artist and the capacity of film as a medium to live up to such a responsibility. Enunciations of film theory in the novel often carry political overtones. Bergmann's stress on "Stimmung" and on musical structure, for instance, is not all he has to say. His central statement defines film as a rhetorical process with powerful political charge: a veritable mechanism aimed at directing the viewer. Film should startle the audience with the violence of an anarchist's bomb. Echoing Gubbio's stress on the inhuman, mechanical dimension of the medium, Bergmann defines film as "an infernal machine" and stresses that, "once it is ignited and set in motion, it revolves with an enormous dynamism. It cannot pause. It cannot apologize. It cannot retract anything. It cannot wait for you to understand it. It cannot explain itself. It simply ripens to its inevitable explosion." The filmmaker guides this aesthetic juggernaut with the fiendish mastery of the Mabuse-like directors described by Braudy or the manipulative sadism of Nabokov's Axel Rex: "This explosion we have to prepare, like anarchists, with the utmost ingenuity and malice" (PrV:41). The threatening and antisocial potential inherent in the very structure of this art form is caught quite well by the German director and is glossed perceptively by his British assistant, who adds to it a description of the captive and dependent condition of the audience. "There's the film," says Isherwood to *his* captive audience (his relatives at home), "and you have to look at it as the director wants you to look at it. He makes his points, one after another, and he allows you a certain number of seconds or minutes to grasp each one" (PrV:43).

Implicit in these views expressed by a newly "educated" Isherwood is the kind of film theory that leads to such notions as "ideological montage" and the argument that the rhetorical structure of film allows the artist greater control over the reception of the work than do those of painting or narrative. These are film theories current in the Russian cinema of the twenties and thirties and which are thus absorbed into the texture of this novel. The same views, albeit given a more formalist stress, are also behind the other eloquent theoretical statement in the novel. Lawrence the film editor (yet another genre-specific character type) thinks that the medium is better off under the tutelage of a "technician" like himself. It is only dispassionate artists such as he who can put film together with cool formal detachment, without outdated romantic notions about art. He does not regard film, he says, "as if it were a bit of my intestine," echoing thus the physiological metaphors that the same medium had suggested to Pirandello (PrV:85). In this view of the medium, the hybridization of mankind effected by the medium (Gubbio's metamorphosis into a monstrous half man/half machine) is transcended into a total control of the medium by the machine. Very much like Dziga Vertov's camera that, animated and alone, takes over in the middle of *The Man with a Movie Camera,* Lawrence would reduce what the "camera eye" allows us to see to an extreme formal abstraction. That the camera's "escape" from the tutelage of the cameraman may produce garbled incoherencies incompatible with human perception (as it does in Vertov's film) is something Lawrence does not seem to know. But Isherwood does, and he underlines the danger, especially in the political dimension.

Lawrence considers film as an effective and impersonal machine, efficient and capable of "reclaiming life from its natural muddle," of making "patterns" that add up to "meaning." He believes that by following the rules of order intrinsic to the medium, the artist can ultimately impose these values upon the viewing public. But, points out Isherwood, his formalist and aesthetically elitist views are dangerously devoid of standards about content. They can open the way to political abuse, even if only through their lack of passion and engagement. "What about the things that won't fit into your patterns?" he challenges Lawrence, who replies, "Discard them." Isherwood is quick to counter, "You mean, kill Jews?" (PrV:89). He has identified the weak spot in all formalist theories: a vulnerability of such aesthetic practices even in situations where no malice is intended. Lawrence, on the other hand, voices the formalist's last-ditch position. Aesthetic structure, he contends, can be compared to society only through "bloody sentimental false analogies" (PrV:89). Yet the truth is that political abuse does occur very easily. This is so especially since the viewers themselves easily become passive accomplices (they prefer on the whole to avoid confrontation with "patterns" that may be meaningful and important but that tend to disturb their peace and illusions) and since politicians (far from passive) take advantage of projective illusion so as to affix in the public's eye the image that they want to be there.

As can be seen, film theory in this film novel is given narrative development well beyond what we have seen so far. Nothing like it, moreover, will occur in the genre again until the publication of Puig's *Kiss of the Spider Woman*. In many sections of *Prater Violet,* in fact, the "story" is "about" such discussions. Isherwood thus turns to narrative use a specific genre of experience that happened to be part of his personal biography, and takes it well beyond the anecdotal level. Genre-specific erudition of the kind we have discussed before is here deployed in dramatic ways, pitting the ideological questioning of the film editor we have just discussed against the epistemological questioning that, as we shall soon see, is reserved for the director. Isherwood enucleates the ideological significance of points of film theory that were voiced before in much more general terms by a character like Gubbio and by figures (real as well as fictional) like those of Nabokov, vulnerable all to the power of escapist images.

Both aspects of the problem (film theory and vulnerability) are deftly related to the actual film being made in the novel. This happens primarily through the person of Bergmann, who finds himself caught (for personal reasons that transcend the immediate needs of his profession) between the need to feel that his work has political relevance and the difficulty of regarding *Prater Violet* as anything more than a formal exercise in the production of genre films. The ultimate fate of the film (the test of Bergmann's dilemma in the praxis of real movie consumption) is reported from Paris by Lawrence, who uses the opportunity to redefine the issues of his debate with Isherwood. He describes the favorable reception of the film by an audience of working-class viewers who "should" actually resent its sham bourgeois sentimentality. He contrasts this ideologically incongruous reaction to the indifference felt by the same audience for the "Russian masterpiece . . . playing to empty seats" in a movie house around the corner (PrV:160). *La Violette du Prater,* Lawrence points out, is "a horrible British picture which, besides being an insult to the intelligence of a five-year-old child, is definitely counterrevolutionary and ought to be banned." None of this seems apparent, however, to "the political consciousness of the French workers" who flock to see it with relish. But Lawrence's own formalist disengagement may be even worse, one must note, given his highly developed "political consciousness." His evaluation of the Russian movie, as it turns out, prizes "form" and discounts "content" with facile irony, while his elitism condescends to the audience: "The Russian film . . . is the usual triangle between a girl with thick legs, a boy, and a tractor. As a matter of fact, it's technically superior to anything Bulldog could produce in a hundred years. But you can't expect the poor fools to know that" (PrV:160).

Lawrence represents in the realm of aesthetics what we are told is the general English disregard for the urgent significance of the moral and ideological content of forms. Bergmann, by contrast, clashes with this indifference, knowing full well that in those "patterns" there is far more than mere aesthetic meaning. He deftly stages, for instance, the grotesque and clownish behavior of contemporary protagonists of European political events such as Buenger, van der Lubbe, Torgler, Goering, Goebbels, Popov, and Dimitrov (a satirical performance much applauded by Isherwood who, here again, functions as a parody of an uncritical audience) only to turn around and insist that these appearances are to be understood as diversionary projections foisted upon the gullible public to distract it from the true puny stature of these political figures. The narrative thus merges the genre-specific impulse to be formal-mimetic with the exposition of one of its genre-specific ideological codes: it openly suggests that it is crucial to be able to recognize formal masquerades of political power and to see through them while proceeding to offer a detailed analysis of the manipulative and controlling structure of the medium. The text argues that the English public should be able to read between the lines, to decipher the "subtext" of the image presented in the media, just as much as the working-class audience in Paris should be able to recognize the political implications of "good" and "bad" movies. Bergmann's intensity and passion about these issues, juxtaposed to the unfolding events in the Europe of 1933 and 1934, dramatizes that missing the ability to distinguish may have grave consequences indeed.

Bergmann is in this a true representative of the German cultural climate that surrounded Bertolt Brecht, whose notions about double-text reading he exemplifies quite well. Like Brecht's Soho scoundrels, the operetta figures of *Prater Violet* can be seen, Bergmann insists, as "of the greatest interest," and the film as a "highly contemporary" work fraught with "enormous psychological and political significance" (PrV:63). From the ups and downs of Bergmann's feelings about his film, it is not clear how seriously he regards this double-text reading of the work: it may well be that subtle ideological education through popular culture becomes irrelevant and insufficient in the face of war and destruction. But in its method his interpretation parallels the Brechtian aesthetic of the period and anticipates the Brecht-derived film theories that regard popular genre films as political wolves in sheep's clothing. As brought to Hollywood by, for instance, that other German refugee Douglas Sirk, this view of film stresses "the interplay of implicit meanings, either subtly different from or actually clashing with the conventional self-gratification." As Jean-Loup Bourget, whose words these are, puts it, the Hollywood director can thus "make valid comments about contemporary American society in an indirect way, by 'bending' the explicit meaning (Sirk's phrase). Genre conventions can be either used as an alibi (the implicit meaning is to be found elsewhere in the film) or turned upside down (irony underlines the conventionality of convention)" (Bourget 1977:70). Just as for his Hollywood successors, Bergmann's interest in *Prater Violet* may indeed be the fact that genre films allow for a subtext that poses political questions about the society in which it is produced and about the industry that produces it.[4]

A musical film like Vincent Minelli's *The Pirate* thus may become a "lesson . . . that piracy can be identified with respectable bourgeois society" (Bourget 1977:70), just as Bergmann's Viennese protagonist Rudolf enacts "the dilemma of the would-be revolutionary writer or artist, all over Europe" (PrV:64). Bergmann spins out with undiminishing ideological momentum the implications of the plot: Rudolf, the protagonist of *Prater Violet,* is a far cry from the true Russian revolutionary writer. He sallies forth from a comfortable bourgeois milieu to dabble in a "romantic interest in the proletariat." He is a phony and takes advantage of his low-born friends until "suddenly [his] home collapses, security collapses. The investments which built his comfortable life are made worthless by inflation. His mother has to scrub doorsteps. The young artist-prince, with all his fine ideas, has to face grim reality." As a declassed intellectual, the student-prince must now choose between "the great liberal-revolutionary traditions of the nineteenth century" and "the bourgeois dream of the Mother, that fatal and comforting dream." But *this* student-prince does not embrace an ideologically correct love for Toni; instead, "he wants to crawl back into the economic safety of the womb. He hates paternal, revolutionary tradition, which reminds him of his duty as its son. His pretended love for the masses was only a flirtation, after all. He now prefers to join the ranks of the dilettante nihilists, the bohemian outlaws, who believe in nothing, except their own ego, who exist only to kill, to torture, to destroy, to make everyone as miserable as themselves" (PrV:64–66).

One gets the distinct impression that the subtext in this case cannot be sustained by the flimsy structure of an operetta. After all, the primary text of this work does not get beyond such thoughts as "Flowers must fade, and yet / One I can't forget: / Prater Vi-o-let" (PrV:110). It is also doubtful that the average audience at which *Prater Violet* is aimed can come close to fathoming depths that articulate the interaction of psychoanalytic, economic, and ideological factors whipped into the froth of a lilting waltz. As a matter of fact, the audience representative who happens to be present at Bergmann's exposition—it is the naïve and sentimental secretary Dorothy—cannot understand a word of it. True, this is mainly because Bergmann's elucidation is "performed" in German. Yet even this turns out to be an apt metaphor, since interpretations such as Bergmann's are very much like complicated "translations" from another language. They require a knowledge of the "syntax," "lexicon," and "context" of ideological presuppositions that is well beyond the reach of most naïve spectators. Bergmann's own disillusionment with the film may be an indication that he harbors such doubts himself. This is certainly the weak point of a theory that is, as we shall see, discussed frequently in subsequent examples of the film novel.

Fitzgerald: "Dream Made Flesh"

F. Scott Fitzgerald's *The Last Tycoon* was published posthumously in 1941 in an edition by Edmund Wilson, who organized the unfinished episodes left by the author into six chapters and provided extensive materials about the unwritten parts.[5] Even in this shape it is clear that the novel would have been an impressive effort on Fitzgerald's part, and from the manuscript as it stands we have sufficient evidence that the novel fits squarely within the thematic framework of the film novel as it has emerged so far.

Set as it is in Hollywood, and since it is considered often side by side with the Pat Hobby stories, it is easy to regard the novel as part of a native genre also represented by Nathanael West's *The Day of the Locust* (of which Fitzgerald wrote eloquently) and by Budd Schulberg's *What Makes Sammy Run?* (on behalf of which Fitzgerald also moved).[6] Such closeness between the writing of Fitzgerald's novel and two other works dealing with the same topic would suggest the danger of derivativeness or at very least the confines of generic stereotypes. It is due to Fitzgerald's own strong ideas about the meaning of Hollywood and, I venture to add, to the inherent dynamics and range of the film novel as a genre that *The Last Tycoon* is broader in its implications than Schulberg's tale of Sammy Glick and quite different in tone from West's apocalypse at Kahn's Persian Palace. Neither the vision of Hollywood as a tacky arena for crass and brutal commercial pursuit (Schulberg's version) nor the use of Hollywood as a metaphor for wide cultural malaise (West's slant) were sufficient for Fitzgerald. If anything, the Pat Hobby stories fit more easily within the narrower limits of narratives that conform to the model of the Hollywood novel. Fitzgerald differentiated as much as possible between these and *The Last Tycoon* (Bruccoli 1977:32–33).

It is quite clear from the outset of the novel that we are within the specific genre of the film novel as outlined so far rather than the narrower field of the Hollywood novel. Right away, in fact, Fitzgerald establishes a point of view that, as in the case of narrators previously encountered, locks us within a perspective that is peculiar to cinematography. Fitzgerald was planning an alternation between omniscient narrator and (more relevant to us) the personal perspective of Cecilia who, as daughter of Brady the producer, is of the movies but is also a relatively uninvolved observer. As it stands now, it is not clear whether Fitzgerald's choice of narrative perspectives would have worked for the whole novel. There are episodes that Cecilia could not possibly have witnessed, and in the novel as we have it one finds awkward phrases that yank the reader abruptly back and forth between Cecilia's point of view and someone else's. In one of the notes published by Wilson with the finished episodes Fitzgerald speaks intriguingly of a narrative technique that mixes subjectivity and objectivity in a way unusual in fiction but (we may note) typical of subjective uses of camera vision: "I hope to get the verisimilitude of a first person narrative, combined with a Godlike knowledge of all events that happen to my characters" (LaT:140). But none of this was consistently implemented in the early version that we have. There are indications, however, that Fitzgerald meant to try for a more film-mimetic style, aware as he was that "pictures have a private grammar, like politics or automobile production or society" (LaT:159), and determined as he seemed to use some of this grammar in structuring his story. At one point in the notes published by Wilson, for instance, one finds: "In a very short transition or montage, I bring the whole party West on the Chief" (LaT:153).

While very little of this prospected semiotic awareness found its way into the early version, Fitzgerald did write most sections so that we see things through Cecilia's eyes. Since she is both on the inside and on the outside, the narrative voice enacts a nonjudgmental acceptance of the film world reminiscent of uncritical filmgoers ("I knew what you were supposed to think about it but I was obstinately unhorrified"). As she puts it, in a phrase that captures in metaphor the darkness of movie houses and a light pulsating at twenty-four frames per second, "the whole equation of pictures" can at best be understood "dimly and in flashes." The peculiar nature of her own involvement with the medium intimates an analogy to the contract of total immersion and of rational regression that the medium imposes on its audience: she had been watching "the wheels go round," she says, since "before the age of reason" (LaT:3).

While she points this out as proof that she is above being taken in by the fascination that Hollywood may have for others (others to whose fifth birthday Rudolph Valentino may not have come), she ends up by admitting that when confronted with the need to express her love to Monroe Stahr, the resources of her imagination cannot come up with anything the producer may not have put there in the first place through his films: "I had nothing to offer that he didn't have; some of my more romantic ideas actually stemmed from pictures. . . . It's more than possible that some of the pictures which Stahr himself conceived had shaped me into what I was" (LaT:18). Cecilia is thus trapped (just as Gubbio, just as Albinus) within the range of stories, situations, and feelings dictated by this art form—a repertory of topoi that limits rather than enriches. She knows enough to be sarcastic about a film director who is caught repeating ad infinitum a film topos meant to signify "glamour" ("A bunch of large dogs entered the room and jumped around the girl. Later the girl went to a stable and slapped a horse on the rump" [LaT:37]), but she cannot stop herself from trying to appeal to Stahr through similar clichés: "Fresh as the morning, I went to see him a week later. . . . I had gotten into riding clothes to give the impression I'd been out in the dew since early morning" (LaT:68). And as she drives towards the meeting in Wylie White's car, she anticipates, only half jokingly, in terms of stilted scenarios: "He's going to look at me and think, 'I've never really seen her before.'" "We don't use that line this year," responds the scriptwriter at the wheel (LaT:69).

Cecilia is a character, then, who presents us with a new twist in the generic balance between "mode" as we have defined it (her ability to act in the world in an effective way) and what may be seen as a particular "genre of experience" found at the root of the film novel. In a sense, what *The Last Tycoon* is illustrating is a human experience that from the outset (since the formative years of a character) is circumscribed by those elements that in the novels we have studied so far come to influence the protagonists only later. This is an intensification of the film-formed individuation of people that goes well beyond Cecilia (as we shall see in a moment, the children who witness the plane crash suffer a similar fate). It also goes well beyond the confines of Fitzgerald's novel, culminating in the experiences of the characters in the novels of Manuel Puig.

Cecilia's point of view, in recompense, is more complex than that of some of her predecessors in the film novels we have examined before. She is aware that what she sees or finds out depends on the limited access offered by mediation. In fact, throughout the novel we find Cecilia in a position of vicarious participation reminiscent of film viewers. She watches as the man she loves falls in love with someone else, most of the time removed from real contact with the events. When present, as she happens to be when Stahr meets Kathleen at the dance, the whole action is punctuated by distant and objective points of view: "I noticed the girl," "I noticed her," "From our angle," "I saw Stahr." The paragraphs that are opened by each one of these "point of view" indications suggest separate shots. Also, the evolution of the action is structured so that we (and Cecilia) discover things as we are led by a cameralike point of view from the man with the funny sign dancing on the floor, to the wandering stare of the faded actress looking over the shoulder of her partner, and finally to the casual "pan" with this secondary character who leads us to a sudden discovery: "I followed her with my eyes when she went back to her table . . . and there, to my surprise, was Stahr talking to the other girl. They were smiling at each other as if this was the beginning of the world" (LaT:72–73). But mostly the events have to be derived from informers whom Cecilia canvasses for the facts. Her story thus emerges from a "corporate" effort similar to the industrial conditions of filmmaking that surround her: "It was Robby who later told me how Stahr found his love that night" (LaT:25); "I know he fainted a couple of times that month because father told me. Prince Agge is my authority for the luncheon. . . . And Wylie White told me a lot" (LaT:67).

It is as if the constitution of the story of this instance of the film novel (as well as the hermeneutic impulse in its genre-specific manifestation) is presented quite openly as an analogy to the progress from discourse to story that characterizes narrative constitution within the Hollywood studio apparatus. Fitzgerald also provides us with an interesting variation of another feature of the film novel that we have discussed before. Cecilia, in fact, displays a genre-specific "erudition" at both the conceptual level (her awareness of mediation and limited access, her proficient use of the corporate method of story editing) and at the formal level as well (her film-formed narrative method). The fact that the two combine so tightly to define her experience (the fact that knowledge and literacy do not help to liberate Cecilia) adds poignancy to the situation and illustrates to what extent the genre-specific features of the film novel participate in the idiosyncracies of individual stories.

Despite the frequent mediation to which Cecilia has to resort, the action is reconstructed for us as fully realized. It thus contains the same paradoxical contradiction we have found in film images as discussed from Pirandello onwards: an illusion of reality intertwined with the absence of real presence. In this case, however, the paradox takes a step further into reality by being provided with a cast of characters who "perform" it. Thus, rather than just a vague "effect" we may attribute to the style of Cecilia's narration (a metaphorical use of stylistics to suggest the film world), it is at times clearly thematized. Cecilia herself admits to looking at reality through the kind of imaginary filter we have encountered before in Pirandello and Nabokov. As she is standing in front of Stahr, for instance, she knows that "what I was looking at wasn't Stahr but a picture of him I cut out over and over. . . . He was my picture, as sure as if he had been pasted on the inside of my old locker in school" (LaT:71–72).

Monroe Stahr—professional practitioner in such images himself and thus presumably more competent than Cecilia—finds himself consciously caught by the same dilemma, one we have seen linking Pirandello's Gubbio with Sartre's Peter. He is struck by the appearance of Kathleen's face, which, despite her real presence in front of him, appears to emerge from his memory like an image fixed on an old celluloid reel: "Smiling faintly at him from not four feet away was the face of his dead wife, identical even to the expression. Across the four feet of moonlight, the eyes he knew looked back at him, a curl blew a little on a familiar forehead; the smile lingered, changed a little according to pattern; the lips parted—the same" (LaT:26). Later, while he muses about the uncanny resemblance between Kathleen and his dead wife Minna, he makes careful distinctions between the screen image of his actress wife and this new apparition. What emerges, as he does so, is a formulation of the imaginary image quite analogous to Sartre's and to Pirandello's view of film images: "Not Minna and yet Minna." Stahr's reaction at that moment to the rest of reality seems as startled as that of a man still imbued with the overwhelming illusion of cinematic projection: "His heart cringed faintly at the intense reality of the day outside his window" (LaT:59).

For Stahr, as opposed to Gubbio, the evocative power of mental and film images does not lead to the disintegration of reality. Yet such images do reveal their pull by heightening that reality to the point of discomfort. They also send the protagonist on a hopeless chase to recapture the lost image, a chase that leaves Kathleen skeptical and bemused by all this attention. Yet, bemused as she is, it is she who is able to put into words the nature of Stahr's infatuation and its relation to the screen images he deals with. Just as those "dreams" hanging on the screen of Stahr's viewing room, her image, she says, is in his dreams even if his head has forgotten her (LaT:75). It is a testament to the evolution of cinematic awareness, I would say, that a character in a novel is able to put this into words. It is the continuity of such evolution, of course, that explains the vitality of the film novel as genre.

That Stahr is trying to reconstruct a fully integrated image from disconnected fragments of feeling and reality (a process that parallels aptly the way films are made) is revealed by the curious misunderstanding that occurs when he tries to track down the two girls that materialize on the head of a floating prop (a gigantic head of Siva) during the flood that follows the earthquake at the studio. The only concrete element he has to go on is the memory of a belt—"a silver belt . . . with stars cut out of it" (LaT:44)—worn by the girl who looks like his dead wife Minna. But when he finds her, it turns out that the face did not belong with the belt. It was the other girl whose "face and form and smile against the light from inside . . . was Minna's face—the skin with its peculiar radiance as if phosphorus had touched it, the mouth with its warm line that never counted costs—and over all the haunting jollity that had fascinated a generation" (LaT:64). The mistake is explained, I believe, by Stahr's "childish association of Minna with the material heavens" (LaT:62), an association that leads him to conflate the memory of the star-studded silver belt with the face that in his feelings belongs with it. This way of performing association through feelings (and the attribute "childish" that floats along with it) also defines aptly Stahr's creative method as a filmmaker. After first seeing Kathleen and, while watching on the screen in the viewing room "the head of Siva, immense and imperturbable, oblivious to the fact that in a few hours it was to be washed away in a flood," Stahr instructs his assistants, "When you take that scene again . . . put a couple of little kids up on top." It is almost as if the "childish" component of his memory of Minna were seeking a filmic concretization in the very location where he finds her double (LaT:54).

One could simply see this as an example that, even in the midst of deeply moving personal experiences, Stahr never ceases to be a filmmaker. Yet there is more, I think. Stahr in this instance seems to be trying to produce existential closure by manipulating the intersection of divergent discursive levels and realities. The imperfections and confusions of referential reality caused by the impulses of wish, memory, and imagination are pulled into Stahr's film-formed sensibility. The discursive disjunctions characteristic of his existential reality and of this narrative genre are used to articulate and control these elements. In other words, the "story" is "told" (advanced) by reliance on the discontinuities characteristic of the medium in which Stahr works, but it is also "reality" that reveals itself thus. Stahr, moreover, can actually use these very disjunctions to "see" more than one who may not own a studio, and to "control" the events of his life.

Most of all, despite brief moments of clarity, Stahr displays in his attitude to Kathleen the metonymizing habits that he derives from film work. In this he turns out to be a genre-specific typical character well beyond the fact that he happens to be a producer. Although he can see that Kathleen resembles Minna as she was in person much more than as she appeared on screen (LaT:89), and despite the fact that he voices relief that hers was "beauty . . . that would not be weighed in the scales of the casting department" (LaT:66), nevertheless his professional deformation prevails. Although he does so in a positive manner (without, that is, the reductionism displayed by a Gubbio or by an Albinus), he judges Kathleen "as he would a shot in a picture" (LaT:80). He appreciates her graceful strength by comparing her to "women in screen tests" whose beauty vanishes as the cameras roll (LaT:89). Just as he appreciates Hollywood because it is "a good illusion" (LaT:62), his memory of Kathleen after their first meeting is strung along a decidedly syntagmatic composite (filmlike in its syntax) that he can test, as he meets her again, by a kind of metonymic reconstitution (filmlike inasmuch as it echoes the process of film editing): "He was the first to be sure it was the same person as before: the upper half of the face that was Minna's, luminous, with creamy temples and opalescent brow—the cocoa-colored curly hair . . . the down on her neck, the very set of her backbone, the corners of her eyes, and how she breathed" (LaT:78). Much more surefooted than Serafino Gubbio, whose filmlike representations (his first view of Varia Nestoroff, for instance) are marred by the interference of emotive materials, and whose "objective" representations are anything but objective, Stahr seems just as caught within the limiting procedures of film vision. He retains his whole interaction with Kathleen, even once she manages to detach herself from the imprint of Minna, with a mental technique reminiscent of film. This applies to her general memory ("the different aspects of her telescoped into the memory of a single thrilling stranger" [LaT:97]) and to the stubborn objectivity of all the details connected with their day together. This day, in the end, collapses into a decidedly cinematic montage:

> The car, the hill, the hat, the music, the letter itself, blew off like the scraps of tar paper from the rubble of his house. And Kathleen departed, packing up her remembered gestures, her softly moving head, her sturdy eager body, her bare feet in the wet swirling sand. The skies paled and faded—the wind and rain turned dreary, washing the silver fish back to sea. It was only one more day, and nothing was left except the pile of scripts upon the table. (LaT:98)

All these details are essential to his way of thinking, and in their absence he feels quite frustrated (aware all the time that this is a need he has acquired from filmmaking). Earlier in his relationship with Kathleen he resented her reluctance to provide him with facts about herself, leaving him with only that first image of her perched on top of the floating head. When he finally gets something out of her, he feels relief: "All right, he knew something of her. It would not be like last night when something kept saying, as in a story conference: 'We know nothing about the girl. We don't have to know much—but we have to know something.' A vague background spread behind her, something more tangible than the head of Siva in the moonlight" (LaT:81).

Given his strong mental reliance on working with the reconstitution of fragments into a coherent whole, it is natural for Stahr to think of his work as the conscious unifying of efforts and contributions that he gathers for his films. As he explains it to Prince Agge, writers can work in separate, parallel teams because there is Stahr to ensure the "unity" of such committee work. The novel devotes long sections to the detailed illustration of this way of making movies. Stahr does not limit this view of "unity" to the writing process. It applies to all other areas of filmmaking, as we see when he reviews the day's work in the screening room. In terms of a theoretical view of the medium, Stahr, in these scenes, emerges as the personification of the studio style attributed to many Hollywood film factories. Beyond that, since his criteria reach further than the mere notion of house style, he appears as a veritable "auteur."

Stahr's kind of auteur does not emerge, however, in tension with the layers of impersonal studio requirements (genre, casting, ideology, censorship, convention) in the way typical of one version of directorial theory. Nor is he the kind of free-wheeling and independent European auteur who flaunts his disorganized creativity in the face of anxious producers. Stahr's auteurship, rather, combines a bit of both. While the impersonal studio machine stimulates Stahr's theory of authorship in the first place, he nevertheless provides decisive leadership.[7] In Stahr's case at least, authorship involves an element of entrepreneurial pride: a vestige of the time when "controllers" and "employees" shared in a creative enterprise, a time when Stahr could thus feel truly responsible for everyone involved in making his films (LaT:131). It also involves an element of industrialist possessiveness with decidedly creative overtones: "He's not interested in it because he owns it. He's interested in it as an artist because he has made it" (LaT:135). And finally, it requires a clear awareness that the producer's unifying touch does not replace the director, although it does replace him as the "King Pin" of film production (LaT: 147–148).

Stahr is quite clear about the focus and import of what he does. He considers it a work of cultural "translation" and "interpretation" no less important than Bergmann's strained ideological translation of his own work from silly musical to political allegory in Isherwood's novel. Stahr, however, operates with a different cultural code: his stress is less on ideology and more on the mythical resonance of what he produces. Films, after all, by being first and foremost a popular art, represent the modern-day equivalent of oral storytelling, of folkloristic formulas, and of mythic accounts that hide within their "stories" the meanings of culture, the purposes of nations, and the recurring rhythms of life.

At the level of the common dreams of mankind, images on the screen speak to all of us in a common and subconscious language. Hence the film novel stresses the importance of personal subtexts and the value of cultural ones, as we have seen before, in its scheme of things. We shall see further how significant in an intensely "private" way are Faye Greener's film-genre daydreams in *The Day of the Locust,* and we see here that the cultural expectations inherent in what Stahr calls "quality pictures" are equally important to him. He feels he must make more of them, in fact, to answer the accusations of people like the black man on the beach who finds more profit in reading Emerson than in going to the movies: "He said that he did not allow his children to listen to Stahr's story. He was prejudiced and wrong, and he must be shown somehow, some way. A picture, many pictures, a decade of pictures, must be made to show him he was wrong" (LaT:95). Stahr thus articulates the opposition between high and low art that in Pirandello and Nabokov was part of a cultural code that separated film from more "respectable" art. He does so in such a way, moreover, that the opposition is transferred into the "body" of cinema as a whole. What Stahr makes is not a movie, nor "stories." He creates a single "story," a continuous, unified myth. Stahr, like Bergmann (if less consciously and less relentlessly) feels the need to tell stories the deep value of which will fit in acceptable and culturally respectable ways ("quality pictures") into the subtext of society.

Stahr thus emerges as the typical provider of the Hollywood subtext which will eventually be recognized for what it is and "bent" by self-conscious genre directors such as Douglas Sirk. Stahr has the perfect background and talent for this. He has, we are told, the "feel of America," the instinctive understanding of the essence of his culture that his associate Brady lacks. It is this that allows Stahr to lead "pictures way up past the range and power of the theater, reaching a sort of golden age" (LaT:28). As auteur of what his studio produces, as "the unity" at the center of all his productions, he sifts and passes judgment over every shot, sequence, and film; he exercises a kind of "grammatological" awareness (instinctively as may be) that assumes each element in the apparatus to be an active counter of meaning. He is present at the conception when, for instance, he inspires Broaca to plan a riveting crane-shot that turns a humdrum piece of business in the script into a memorable scene (LaT:42). He is still present well before the convention-bound scissors of editors can do damage to the simple and poetic beauty of two children together: "A little girl read underneath a tree with a boy reading on a limb of the tree above. The little girl was bored and wanted to talk to the boy. He would pay no attention. The core of the apple he was eating fell on the little girl's head" (LaT:56). He instructs to cut nothing of this scene, explaining that "sometimes ten feet can be too long—sometimes a scene, two hundred feet long can be too short. . . . this is something that'll be remembered in the picture." It is clear that Stahr articulates quite openly what we found only implicit in some of his predecessors: the omnipotent point of view of floating cameras and the manipulation of time-flow through editing are at the service of specific cultural codes.

Stahr is the ultimate controller of the psychic subtexts of America. As he puts it himself, he is in charge of an art in which "we have to take people's own favorite folklore and dress it up and give it back to them" (LaT:105). He sees himself in charge, that is, of the cultural archetypes of his society, but seems also vaguely aware that "the text" is "a *center of reference for multiple acts of sense 'constitution,'* among which the author's 'creative act' [does] not necessarily preserve a position of priority" (Gumbrecht 1992:4). Much as this seems to be an indication that Stahr possesses a "primitive" instinct about the fact that readers and spectators are in charge of creating meaning as much as authors, and that this should lead to a give-and-take in the realm of ideological codes, there are no "explicit" ideological "lessons" in his films as there are in those discussed by Isherwood's Bergmann and Lawrence. Stahr feels that what he does is to activate the process of "recognition" and "self-confirmation" that I described in the case of Nabokov's spectators. But in this case the process embraces a broader anthropological range: we move from individual individuation through movies to individuation that is communal, even national. Stahr is an example of someone who, able to sense the cultural and anthropological importance of this popular art form, seeks the high ground in an industry often bound to the lowest common denominator. He is interested in evoking the valuable and resonant common archetypes of society.

Aided particularly by the dreamlike quality of the film-viewing situation that I discussed before, images such as the ones Stahr seeks can indeed become "well determined centers of reverie." Through the cultural commonality of film viewing they can aspire to become a newly concretized "means of communication between men" (Bachelard 1969:39). We saw the image of the "house" and its multiple meanings for Nabokov; we discussed how such images echo the projections we all share of houses meaningful to us. Paradoxically, it is the very imperfections of technique and the generic simplifications of popular entertainment that allow such images to be general enough and sufficiently undefined to open up spaces for our own interaction with them. But if such single images speak to us beyond their immediate function of reference and escape, so do certain generically stereotypical formulas of action (film is movement) and commonplaces of film-genre situations. Such film-specific encapsulations of meaning-laden movement as Gubbio's dizzying ride on the motorcar, or such visions of life as those represented by the clichés of film melodrama that he notes, illustrate the fact that the archetypal can indeed be found at higher levels of discursive complexity than that of single, isolated images. It is thus a small step from the crashing waves, the cars speeding along winding roads, the wind-swept tree tops, and the Valentino-like lover at Nabokov's country villa to the formative strips of celluloid that Stahr examines as he supervises the daily rushes. These are described, one notes, as "dreams" hanging "in fragments at the far end of the room." Under Stahr's supervision they suffer critical analysis and, in the end, they pass "to be dreamed in crowds, or else discarded" (LaT:56). The powerful cultural centrality that these fragments of sequence contain is captured well in the reaction of the visiting Knights of Columbus upon meeting Stahr's star on the set: "They had seen the host carried in procession, but this was the dream made flesh" (LaT:50).

Such images, when detached from their unimaginative syntagmatic confections (be it by assertive spectators who, as Nabokov does, make a point of detaching them; be it by controlling producers like Stahr who examine them before they are attached), speak to a deeper level of understanding than the one required by their contingent filmic context. What is often merely trivial within single movies turns out to be the stuff of deep and meaningful communication when seen as part of a broader intertextual context that Bachelard terms the "complex of culture," a complex made up of favored images that are at once the stencils of reality and the root images of our subconscious. These are the icons "which one thinks of as fountainheads within the spectacles of the world but which are nothing but projections of a dark, mysterious soul" (Bachelard 1942:25–26, my translation). Bachelard explains far better than Stahr could that such commonly held subconscious and preconscious cultural stereotypes ultimately fulfill positive, creative functions. In other words, negative opinions about genre films and popular melodrama such as those expressed by the man that Stahr meets on the beach need to take into account that the reanimation of such cultural deadwood allows the stereotype to resonate with renewed vigor. "In its best form," states Bachelard, "the complex of culture revives and rejuvenates a tradition" (Bachelard 1942:26, my translation). As he goes on to point out, these societal networks clearly interconnect with the individual webs in which are caught the elements of subconscious desire.[8]

This is why Cecilia can attribute to Stahr a kind of vision that we have encountered before: the enhanced bird's-eye view that was also present in *Laughter in the Dark* (a view that connects enhanced instrumental vision and philosophical insight). With a metaphor appropriate to Stahr the producer, this view is compared to a camera view as airbound and flexible as the one he suggests to Broaca. It is, as Cecilia defines it, a "long-shot" of the human landscape which he took in when "he had flown up very high to see, on strong wings." And what he saw ("all the kingdoms," "how things were") gives him insights reminiscent of what Pirandello's Gubbio attributes to camera vision: "A new way of measuring our jerky hopes and graceful rogueries and awkward sorrows" (LaT:20). Juxtaposed to Gubbio's claim for what the camera can reveal ("your haste, your wish to do this or that, your impatience, your frenzy, your anger, your joy, your grief" [Sh:151, Quad:86]), Stahr's vision is in keeping with the enhanced insight of cinematic point of view. It is also reminiscent of the authorial assumption of such insight by Nabokov, attached as it is to the flight of an airplane: indifferent and serendipitous as it hovers over Albinus's car accident; much more purposeful and filled with intimations of willed predestination as it images Stahr's landing in California. Almost like a supernatural visitation, Stahr is said to have come "from choice to be with us to the end" (LaT:20).

As he comes down "like the plane coming down into the Glendale airport, into the warm darkness," he is much like the airliner Heidegger mentions in his seminal 1949 essay on the modern economy of technology, knowledge, and humankind. Just as that airplane standing on the tarmac "ready for takeoff . . . stands . . . as standing-reserve, inasmuch as it is ordered to ensure the possibility of transportation," Monroe Stahr is here to ensure the possibility of his vision that, like Heidegger's airliner, "must be in its whole structure and in . . . its constituent parts, on call for duty" (Heidegger 1977:17).

Except for his meeting with Kathleen (where Stahr is as limited in his vision of Kathleen as Cecilia is in hers of Stahr) and his confrontation with the labor leader Brimmer (opposite whom Stahr is hopelessly stuck in his socioeconomic role), the insight acquired from that "long-shot" allows Stahr to function better than others both personally and professionally. He is "a man who sees below the surface into reality" (LaT:154). On the personal level he can reconstruct malevolent plots from the outer manifestations of human behavior, as when, for instance, he puzzles out with caring stubbornness and then rectifies the rumors that led to Pete Zavras's attempted suicide.

As a professional, Stahr is able to identify the essence of cinematic expression better than the more educated and pretentious writers who work for him. His professional erudition allows him, in other words, to see beyond the old-fashioned dichotomies of high and low culture most of them still hold to. His strength as studio auteur depends clearly on his ability to see what materials the camera will make its own and what makes effective and riveting drama over and above the cultural prejudices of people like his scriptwriter George Boxley. This capability is most dramatically illustrated in the famous episode in which Stahr transcends the overwrought action (duelling opponents) and stilted funny business (dueller falling down a well, dueller hauled out in a bucket) that his scriptwriter produces and offers a master class during which Boxley (uninvolved, still, and invisible just like a real movie audience) watches with increasing fascination while an imaginary studio stenographer goes through a sequence of mysterious actions quite devoid of contrived melodrama. As Stahr improvises the action, the two dimes the stenographer takes out of her purse and then returns there, the nickel she leaves on the table, the matchbox, the black gloves she burns in the stove, her denial of their existence on the phone, the wind blowing outside, the man hidden in the office— all of these details slowly draw the writer into an emerging movie drama. Stahr's abrupt interruption stimulates Boxley to the point where he is driven to ask about the purpose of the peripheral detail left dangling by Stahr: that nickel which did not make it back, with the dimes, into the stenographer's purse. Boxley's slow seduction is a clear instance of the process of spectator involvement in cinematic discourse that we have discussed before. It represents a new turn in this case only inasmuch as the episode amounts to an open narrative articulation of issues normally voiced in more conceptual terms.

Boxley's ready involvement is, for Stahr, a clue that the writer has it in him to join the producer in the practice of an art form that depends on seeing things unfold: "The nickel," he explains, "was for the movies" (LaT:32–33).[9] Fitzgerald here picks out the importance of foregrounding peripheral details in cinematography and outlines the special nature of such filmlike narration just as Nabokov does in *Laughter in the Dark*. There a photograph of Greta Garbo stands out while greater drama is occurring elsewhere in the scene, or a sudden fire in the neighborhood distracts a character from suicide. In that novel much of the action had to be watched and interpreted (by the characters as well as by us readers) with the kind of attention that Stahr's little demonstration requires. Stahr states explicitly a principle of narration that is central to Nabokov's effect of filmlike narration: "If you were in a chemist's . . . and you were getting a prescription for some member of your family who was very sick . . . *then* whatever caught your attention through the window, whatever distracted you and held you would probably be material for pictures" (LaT:105). And it might well be something as simple as a spider working on a window pane. But in Nabokov's novel such elements remain part of the stylistic texture: no character has the privileged eyesight that would allow him to be in control of things the way Stahr is here.

The issue is not merely a filmmaker's ability to see things differently. The episode in which the director Ridingwood is abruptly taken off the picture by Stahr illustrates that the point is to see things better. Ridingwood attributes to himself a film-honed ability to see through Stahr's behavior and to anticipate what is going to happen: "There was no stop Stahr could pull that would surprise him. His task was the delivery of situations, and Stahr by effective business could not outplay him on his own grounds" (LaT:50). Yet beyond his awareness that Stahr is deliberate in walking just fast enough to prevent Ridingwood from catching up with him, he misses all the subsequent clues of the "situation" in an embarrassing crescendo culminating with the coat that Ridingwood thinks he has left on the set from which he has been banished and which Stahr had been carrying all along in his hand. If nothing else, that detail should have tipped Ridingwood off: he was not expected to return to that set. Clearly it is not just anybody's film vision that is the issue, but Stahr's superior one.

Stahr's work in the viewing theater reveals that "situations" come in a broad range, from good to bad, from acceptable versions of cinematic moments to versions that will never be "dreamed in crowds." And it is Stahr who can tell the difference. Without his ability to select, film is reduced to an infinite serial repetition of frozen moments in which "men fought over and over. Always the same fight. Always at the end they faced each other smiling." It pictures a world in which "men met endlessly in a door, recognized each other and went on. They met, they started, they went on" (LaT:56). We have seen the deadly effects of such generic "loops" in *Laughter in the Dark*. Real life endows such repetitions with change and growth: "Now they were different people as they started back. Four times they had driven along the shore road today, each time a different pair" (LaT:94). But on film they need to be imbued with meaning by someone's creative insight. Stahr's role is sketched in to suggest an almost demiurgic power to create "life on screen" from the subservient fragments of real life used for this purpose with single-mindedness instrumentality.

The superhuman aura that the novel attributes to him contributes to this. His eyes are "the kind . . . that can stare straight into the sun" (LaT:20), and like Isherwood's Bergmann he is compared to an emperor—"the last of the princes" (LaT:27). As such, he is in line with the kind of directors who, like Fritz Lang in Leo Braudy's study, control the world of their films forcefully and in limiting ways:

> Pacing the floor swiftly, Stahr began. In the first place he wanted to tell them what kind of a girl she was—what kind of a girl he approved of here. She was a perfect girl with a few small faults as in the play, but a perfect girl not because the public wanted her that way but because it was the kind of girl that he, Stahr, liked to see in this sort of picture. Was that clear? It was no character role. She stood for health, vitality, ambition and love. What gave the play its importance was entirely a situation in which she found herself. She became possessed of a secret that affected a great many lives. There was a right thing and a wrong thing to do—at first it was not plain which was which, but when it was, she went right away and did it. That was the kind of story this was—thin, clean and shining. No doubts. (LaT:41)

And so, as the scriptwriters and director take notes, Stahr outlines action, camera details, or a moment of high drama, all the while leaving no doubt as to who is in command. He actually seems to know how to carry off the delicate balance that allows a story that is clearly genre-bound to retain some of the vital idiosyncrasy of one that is not. His knowledge affects everyone and everything around him, making him, as I said, the creative center of the studio. "Here was Stahr to care, for all of them," remarks Wylie White. "The effect would not wear off when he left the office—not anywhere within the walls of the lot. He felt a great purposefulness." The control of the studio auteur is clear to Wylie, down to its homogenizing quality and psychological conformism: "The mixture of common sense, wise sensibility, theatrical ingenuity, and a certain half-naïve conception of the common weal which Stahr had just stated aloud, inspired him to do his part, to get his block of stone in place, even if the effort were foredoomed, the result as dull as a pyramid" (LaT:42–43). Stahr as eagle, as emperor, as prince . . . and now as pharaoh too!

To Boxley, presumably a better writer of literature than Wylie White (Boxley seems to have been modeled on Aldous Huxley),[10] Stahr appears no less exalted in stature. He seems like a "helmsman . . . in the always creaking rigging of a ship sailing in the great awkward tacks along an open sea" or a Michelangelo mastering the choice of "newly cut marble" which bears "the tracery of old pediments, half-obliterated inscriptions of the past." Or he appears as Lincoln, "a leader carrying on a long war on many fronts." Boxley has his view, as we said, about the artistic level of Stahr's picture: movies are not "high art." Even Stahr himself in this episode compares movies to public art done on commission. Yet even the likes of Rubens worked at this level, he notes. Then he talks of film as folklore. Within these limits, Stahr is given a great deal of credit: "Almost single-handed he had moved pictures sharply forward through a decade, to a point where the content of the 'A productions' was wider and richer than that of the stage." If his limits are noted, he is still in exalted company: "Stahr was an artist only, as Mr. Lincoln was a general, perforce and as a layman" (LaT:105–106). While on the one hand Stahr's creative role intimates the heights of a Rubens and the depths of communal archetypes, on the other it expresses an easy familiarity with the instinctive freshness of individual origins as he gets a scriptwriting team back on track by "feeling like and acting like and even sometimes looking like a small boy getting up a show" (LaT:107).

As for the critique implicit in pointing to the fissures through which the real world tends to seep into the realm of film fiction, no Pirandellian anguish hovers over Fitzgerald's characters. But intimations of tension between reality and film do crop up. We find such tension, for instance, when Stahr watches the daily rushes; we see it behind some of Cecilia's experiences. Those men who fight over and over are discovered somewhat incongruously "touching the opponent in a friendly gesture on the shoulder." The old Russian prince, now turned communist, cannot appear to the camera as something other than what he is (a Russian aristocrat), but since his convictions won't allow him to play what he is, Stahr condemns him to unemployment (LaT:57). Fitzgerald presents all this with a light touch, but at bottom the dilemma of the Russian émigré is no less tragic than the existential disorientation we find in the Berlin refugees of Nabokov's writings.

Stahr's half-finished house is a haunting metaphor for his world of partially sketched realities, as well as a striking example of narrative condensation of the cinematic apparatus (apparatus as setting, in fact). The action that takes place at his house also illustrates the need to complete the illusion created by such settings with acts of faith and imagination. Like a set in a studio ("odd effect of the place like a set" [LaT:151]), the house is merely a fuselage, surrounded by the materials of its creation—"concrete mixer, raw yellow wood and builder's rubble." And even the natural elements that surround it appear unfinished, in expectant subservience to what will be constructed: "Great boulders rose to what would be the terrace" (LaT:81). Within this approximation of a place, however, just as on a set in which a specific scene must be shot, one area is finished to the last detail: a salon with built-in book shelves, even curtain rods, and a porch with cushioned chairs and ping-pong tables. All of these details of completion jar unexpectedly with the unfinished state of the rest. As Stahr puts it, "I had some props brought out—some grass and things." In an apt solipsistic way, the room even contains "the trap in the floor for the motion picture projection machine" (LaT:82). But all of this approximation can be enhanced by a version of what E. H. Gombrich has termed "the beholder's share" (Gombrich 1969:181–202). "No use looking for what's not here," advises Stahr. "Think of it as if you were standing on one of those globes with a map on it." As Kathleen seems to know, the power of such compensatory projection can be powerful indeed: "When you do that, you can feel the earth turn, can't you?" (LaT:81).

As for Cecilia, the deep gap between her romantic expectations about a meeting with Stahr and the reality that she actually encounters is anticipated by Wylie White's ironic counterpoint to her cliché-laden anticipations (LaT: 68–71). She is not always as naïve about the gap. Her reaction to the cows, the Negro, and the sheep that she meets in Nashville is to be struck by their reality ("they were real cows," "the Negro grew gradually real") because her first experiences with this kind of reality occurred at the studio. Even the sheep had found themselves ill at ease "about being in pictures," she notes. Just as in Stahr's viewing theater, the sheep's absorption by the movies does not really provide a substitute reality. They hover disembodied in Cecilia's memory: "If I ever knew what picture they were in, I have long forgotten" (LaT:9), she says, making in a lighter vein the same point that Serafino Gubbio makes with heavy emphasis in talking about the film actors who lose their relationship to a total, living reality when being dismembered for the purposes of film reality. But for all the lightly implied criticism, Cecilia notices the positive aspect of the rift—the mythical, psychological functioning of film illusion as it recreates the enchantments of childhood, as it aids in the process of individuation: "Under the moon the back lot was thirty acres of fairyland—not because the locations really looked like African jungles and French chateaux and schooners at anchor and Broadway by night, but because they looked like the torn picture books of childhood, like fragments of stories dancing in an open fire. I never lived in a house with an attic, but a back lot must be something like that, and at night of course in an enchanted distorted way, it all comes true" (LaT:25).

The episode of Stahr's death as projected by Fitzgerald was to have encapsulated a range of individual reactions to the seductive illusion of film. What is more, the plan isolates the essence of this fascination from its proper setting (the darkened cinema) and foregrounds the abstract and disembodied hold of Hollywood films on the popular imagination in a way that no film novel studied so far has done. The film world appears here as a new mythology, with its own gods and goddesses who may briefly descend from heaven, as actually happens early in the novel when Cecilia's plane stops over in Nashville and she notes how the Hollywood-bound plane suggests to the local people that "high adventure might be among us, disguised as a movie star" (LaT:8). These "deities" even possess a kind of glamor and power that may be transmitted to mere mortals by fetishistic osmosis. See for instance the "sacred relics" that fall into the hands of the three children who discover the remains of the plane crash. The purse and suitcase of an actress, Stahr's briefcase and "travelling appurtenances," and a ruined producer's "rather disreputable possessions" have the power to "infect" the children with the qualities of their dead owners (LaT:157). Fitzgerald was well aware that in thinking of this episode he skirted the danger of heavy-handed moralizing, and he noted to himself that this should be (but not appear to be) a morality play (LaT: 156–158).

In previous film-novel explorations of that which reaches out from the dreams of screen fiction into the real world (in Pirandello's sad fragments of the actors' reduced reality; in Nabokov's contested shards of the viewer's own world) we have not encountered, as we do here, an actual crossing of the line, except perhaps in the demented attempt by the protagonist of Nabokov's *Despair* to escape the police by crossing into movieland (to convince all that this *is* a movie). In Fitzgerald's projected treatment of Stahr's death, however, the kind of influence that the selective scenarios of film have on an audience reaches beyond the mediated experience of cinematography and is expected to stamp in formative ways, and for the rest of their lives, the children who find "the dream made flesh" strewn about their mountain.

Almost like the astral influences that descend from the qualities represented by Greek deities, the qualities of actress, producer, and Stahr are reflected in the children who move within their aura. While to Frances the actress's belongings are "things that . . . represent undreamt of luxuries," very much in the way that film glitter is a seductive dream for most audiences, there is a suggestion that the children find the belongings of those who most resemble them in their fundamental nature (Frances is malleable and amoral, presumably like the Hollywood actress; Dan has a certain resemblance to the disreputable producer). Furthermore, the overall impression is that the episode is instrumental in deciding the future course of the children's lives. Thus Frances was to have been last seen as "faintly corrupted," going "in search of adventure" and turning "into anything from a gold digger to a prostitute." We can see in these notes that Fitzgerald was carefully thinking about the precise way in which the dreams purveyed by Hollywood encourage certain kinds of misplaced expectations in life to the point of causing people to act in certain ways. This was to have been the case with Frances ("Let the readers hope that Frances is going to be all right and then take that hope away by showing the last glimpse of Frances with that lingering conviction that luxury is over the next valley") as well as with Dan ("Dan has been completely corrupted and will spend the rest of his life looking for a chance to get something for nothing" [LaT:158]).

Fitzgerald's interest in the extension of cinema into the moral fabric of the real world is finally also reflected by the political dimension that the novel was to have had, especially in the sections he never got to write. These episodes were to have incorporated a fictionalized account of the union struggles that were instrumental in changing the face of Hollywood as an industry. As it is, only one episode was sketched out at all (a meeting Stahr requests with a prominent labor organizer), and the remaining notes can only hint at the course these materials would have taken. Clearly Fitzgerald intended this political dimension to be a pivot in the story: "Stahr is now being pushed into the past by Brady and by the unions alike," we find in a summary outline put together by Wilson. It continues: "The split between the controllers of the movie industry, on the one hand, and the various groups of employees, on the other, is widening and leaving no place for real individualists of business like Stahr, whose successes are personal achievements and whose career has always been invested with a certain personal glamor. He has held himself directly responsible to everyone with whom he has worked; he has even wanted to beat up his enemies himself. In Hollywood he is 'the last tycoon'" (LaT:131).

Although Stahr is presented on the whole as a benevolent paternalistic employer who is inclined to listen to union demands even if he is not sympathetic to the idea of a union, he seems caught in his old-fashioned role. As Wylie White puts it in an episode found in Fitzgerald's manuscript that is not present in Wilson's edition, "Two years ago most of the boys around here would have died for you, but times have changed and you don't read the signs." Aptly enough, White analyzes Stahr's problem in terms of film drama: "You're doing a costume part and you don't know it—the brilliant capitalist of the twenties. But these secretaries and typists that have been living on hay since '29—they don't see themselves as Joan Crawford characters anymore. They want to eat" (Bruccoli 1977:69). Stahr's success as well as failure was to have been traced to an identical root. Precisely because it had been so easy for him to succeed through industry and initiative, he sees no reason to assent to union demands. His natural sense of justice and fairness, addled at first by Brady's double-cross of the office workers, does not fully protect him from siding with his own when push comes to shove. Whatever the final form such conflicts would have taken in the novel, it seems that Fitzgerald would have explored the complexity of Stahr's situation so that the overly heroic and positive impression that we get in what we have of the novel would have been better nuanced. As we find in a note: "I want to show that Stahr left certain harm behind him just as he left good behind him. That some of his reactionary creations such as the Screen Playwrights existed long after his death just as so much of his valuable creative work survived him" (LaT:150).

It is possible that, in the political dimension as well, Stahr would have ultimately been shown to be more a prisoner of his own film-delimited world than in charge of it. After all, to prepare for his meeting with Harry Bridges the best he can think of doing is "running off the Russian Revolutionary films that he had in his film library at home." Apt as this may seem as textural color, it does little to provide Stahr with the fundamental preparation he needs for the meeting. And his fuzziness about what is what among the different components of European culture as well as his superficiality in dealing with its fundamental texts is compounded even further: "He also ran off *Doctor Caligari* and Salvator Dali's *Le Chien Andalou,* possibly suspecting that they had a bearing on the matter. He had been startled by the Russian films back in the twenties, and on Wylie White's suggestion he had had the script department get him up a two-page 'treatment' of the *Communist Manifesto*" (LaT: 118). As can be seen, even from these fragments, Stahr's political consciousness is a far cry from that of Isherwood's filmmakers, although in both novels Russian Revolutionary films get short shrift. The level of ideological subtlety may well be the single fundamental difference between American and European cinema as these novels represent them. *The Day of the Locust* tends to confirm this. Any political dimension West may attribute to cinema, or even whether he regards the industry as a cultural institution in the sense that we do now, must be laboriously wrested from the allegorical cacophony of his world.

West: "The Barber in Purdue"

Of the three novels in this section of my study (Isherwood's, Fitzgerald's, and West's), Nathanael West's *The Day of the Locust* is chronologically the first and probably the most famous representative of what is known as the Hollywood novel. I choose to examine it last because it touches upon fewer of the elements of the narrative genre I am outlining than the previous two novels, yet it is also the one novel that integrates most fully the genre-specific elements it does display into its narrative texture. Moreover, it anticipates, as we shall see, what became a major theme in film novels after the forties: the centrality and ambiguity of the spectator's role. It seems to me also useful to have looked first at Isherwood and Fitzgerald (despite the fact that both may have been influenced by West) because this order reveals clearly that such novels involve many more elements than those usually singled out in studies of novels inspired by the tackiness and metaphorical aura of Hollywood. Some of these elements we have found to be fully expressed in Pirandello's novel already, so that in terms of genre I would say that West's *The Day of the Locust* is more a particular case of a wider genre than the sole source and inspiration of novels such as Fitzgerald's. Which is not to say that in many cases West and Fitzgerald may well be known to writers (especially American) who have never read Pirandello's *Shoot!* My aim here, however, is not so much to trace specific influences as to explore the parameters of a narrative genre. For this purpose it is best to come upon *The Day of the Locust* at this point.

West's novel, as I said, integrates many of the elements of the film novel into its narrative structure far more smoothly than Fitzgerald (who left us merely a first draft of a novel) and far more dramatically than Isherwood, whose treatment of the film world remains poised between an expository, almost journalistic summary of the context and a narrative flow that is mostly abstract and intellectualizing. In West, by comparison, one gets the feeling that thoughts about the values of Hollywood, about the effect that film dreams have on participants and spectators, and about the metaphorical extrapolations one can make from Hollywood to the rest of America all emerge from the ebb and flow of events described with hallucinatory clarity, events that occur independently of generic constraints and expository needs. Given the extent to which the ideological codes of the film novel are thus integrated into the texture of its narrative flow, *The Day of the Locust* illustrates how "seamless" the narrative rendition of this kind of novel can be.

West does have a point to make, of course, and one needs only mention briefly the most memorable episode in the novel (that final riot which turns into an apocalyptic painting in front of the "eyes" of the reader) to underline that the corruptions and frustrations of the "watchers" throughout the novel are meant to depict an existential condition which, West implies, may well erupt upon society. The episode is closely related to film even if Tod's search for the "watchers" leads us to other forms of escape as well: cultural fads, fringe religions, real life disasters and tragedies. These are West's versions of the pre- and extracinematic anticipations of the apparatus we have discussed before. All of these spectacles are closely linked to the excitement of film (a link that West states more explicitly than was the case with his predecessors and contemporaries), since film incorporates them into its materials and often titillates the "watchers" by using such spectacles as building blocks for its own stories. More importantly, the medium breeds a toleration for the extremes located in such spectacles, without expecting the audience to bear responsibility for the consequences and to take an individual moral stand. Here West anticipates quite explicitly later commentators, such as Guy Debord, who write of a society that has institutionalized spectacle to the detriment of the individual. Debord could be talking about West's "watchers" when he points out that "the erasure of the personality is the fatal accompaniment to an existence which is concretely submissive to the spectacle's rules, ever more removed from the possibility of authentic experience and thus from the discovery of individual preference" (Debord 1990:32).

As far as West is concerned, it is the constant and overstimulated watching, coupled with a lack of access to the action, that leads to violence. The instigators of the final riot "every day of their lives . . . read the newspapers and went to the movies. Both fed them on lynchings, murder, sex crimes, explosions, wrecks, love nests, fires, miracles, revolutions, wars. This daily diet made sophisticates of them. . . . Nothing can ever be violent enough to make taut their slack minds and bodies. They have been cheated and betrayed"

(DoL:178). West stresses the anaesthetizing effect of surfeit and repetition, unaware as yet that it is also the very fact of "mediation," the effect of "generic trivialization," that aids in the moral and affective distancing. West is, however, eloquent in taking the first step in the evolution of an anatomy of this situation that leads to the television news (ripe with disasters) of Walker Percy's *Lancelot,* and in our present to Debord again, whose own "disasters," one notes, are updated to the final years of our century: "The spectacle makes no secret of the fact that certain dangers surround the wonderful order it has established. Ocean pollution and the destruction of equatorial forests threaten oxygen renewal; the earth's ozone layer is menaced by industrial growth; nuclear radiation accumulates irreversibly. It merely concludes that none of these things matter" (Debord 1990:34).

It is interesting that West's protagonist Tod is made to question the accuracy and relevance of extrapolations such as these (an unusual discursive articulation of the genre-specific cultural code and its activities offered by this particular film novel), as if the author wanted to make sure that the surrealism of these scenes not lead the reader to dismiss their relevance in the real world: "He only wondered if he weren't exaggerating the importance of the people who came to California to die. Maybe they weren't really desperate enough to set a single city on fire, let alone the whole country. Maybe they were only the pick of America's madmen and not at all typical of the rest of the land" (DoL:118). But ultimately Tod knows "that they had it in them to destroy civilization" (DoL:142), that "it was a mistake to think them harmless curiosity seekers. They were savage and bitter, especially the middle-aged and the old, and had been made so by boredom and disappointment" (DoL:177). As one can see in the light of what I have discussed before, this is at quite a distance from the rebellious but harmless rioting of Nabokov's young friends, deprived of the fulfillment promised by the screen.

It is not only the mob that suffers the pain of alienated voyeurism, that simmers with violence. Tod too, and Homer, as well as the film cowboy Earle and his Mexican friend Miguel, gravitate with unfulfilled desire around Faye Greener, who is meant to epitomize in her person the glittering promise and unfulfilled desire found in the experience of film. Faye, aspiring starlet and ravenous consumer of films herself, is no less unfulfilled than the others. Her violence is expressed by withholding her promise and torturing Homer Simpson. But her understanding of the medium she aspires to is very limited, stopping at its outer mechanics. She especially fails to perceive the elements that, in Fitzgerald's novel, Stahr is able to teach an aspiring scriptwriter like Boxley. Faye has turned the mechanical and inbred spiral of the popular imagination which Fitzgerald's producer controls so well into a "system" that echoes the mechanical alternation of images in film. Even her daydreaming has become conditioned by the mechanics of film, just as we found these mechanics in control of Gubbio's view of life or of the evasions of Nabokov's Albinus.

In its own way, West's narrative device brings out into the open the implicit formal and psychological structure of the film medium (its dreamlike nature) and thus turns what is usually a formal-mimetic element in film novels to the vicissitudes of plot and characterization.

Faye's "method" of daydreaming relies upon a generalized "mood" induced by stock soundtracks (she uses whatever happens to play on radio) and unreels generic scenarios inspired by the kind of iconic posters that obviously entice her as much as they do Albinus: "She would get some music on the radio," West tells us, "then lie down on her bed and shut her eyes. She had a large assortment of stories to choose from. After getting herself in the right mood, she would go over them in her mind, as though they were a pack of cards, discarding one after another until she found the one that suited." She admits that her mental deck shuffling is "too mechanical for the best result," yet she is touchingly aware that "any dream was better than no dream" (DoL: 104). The "story" of these dreams does never stray far from the stilted prefabricated modules chillingly reminiscent of the genre loops that we found entrapping Albinus. It may concern a variation on the "South-Sea shipwreck" story (this one seems inspired by the Tarzan movie poster on the wall), or it may unfold the tritest kind of back-stage "rise to stardom" scenario. All of the plots are derived from the movies and, in a comical solipsism, Faye hopes to sell her "dreams" back to the studios as new material for films. In this she is not too different from Fitzgerald's Cecilia when she plans to seduce Monroe Stahr by using lines out of his own movies. But difference there is, since Cecilia is aware of what she does, and her friends don't encourage her in doing it.

Tod, on the other hand, the studio designer who lusts after Faye, plays along to further his ends. He is well aware that in her imaginative life Faye is displaying a pathetic film-induced shallowness, one we have encountered before in characters such as Nabokov's Margot. An awareness similar to Nabokov's about the sadness of people's fascination with *poshlost* (here in the guise of the phony and shallow surface glitter of film dreams) is thus nicely integrated by West into the narrative texture of the story (Appel 1974:42–46). What Nabokov had left implied, Tod voices openly: "All these little stories, these little daydreams of hers, were what gave such extraordinary color and mystery to her movements. She seemed always to be struggling in their soft grasp as though she was trying to run in a swamp." But his better perspective on such matters moves him only to take advantage (an exploitation similar to that of the movie industry): "His impulse wasn't to aid her to get free, but to throw her down in the soft, warm mud and to keep her there" (DoL: 106–107).

With an attitude again very close to Nabokov's, West seems more upset with the readiness to exploit than moved to mock the attraction that *poshlost* holds for simple souls. "It is hard to laugh," he says, "at the need for beauty and romance, no matter how tasteless, even horrible, the results of that are" (DoL:61). This is said of the comical striving of eclectic plaster in Pinyon Canyon ("Mexican ranch houses, Samoan huts, Mediterranean villas, Egyptian and Japanese temples, Swiss chalets, Tudor cottages") but soon reveals itself applicable to the context-ignorant posturing of film hopefuls all over town. In the same way, the remark stirred by Harry Greener's loss of ability to tell acting from true experience (he repeatedly finds himself unable to tell whether he is really ill, really dying, or just giving a beautiful performance) applies to most of the characters in the novel: "Feeling is of the heart and nerves and the crudeness of its expression has nothing to do with its intensity" (DoL:119).

There is a whole industry within which Tod is working, of course, the purpose of which is to further the exploitation that he has learned so quickly. Its visible symbol in the novel is that studio lot in which discarded props and scenery are kept and which reminds Tod of Janvier's painting "Sargasso Sea":

> Just as that imaginary body of water was a history of civilization in the form of a marine junkyard, the studio lot was one in the form of a dream dump. A Sargasso of the imagination! And the dump grew continually, for there wasn't a dream afloat somewhere which wouldn't sooner or later turn up on it, having first been made photographic by plaster, canvas, lath and paint. Many boats sink and never reach the Sargasso, but no dream ever entirely disappears. Somewhere it troubles some unfortunate person and some day, when that person has been sufficiently troubled, it will be reproduced on the lot. (DoL:132)

In this narrative condensation of the cinematic apparatus, the archetypal nature of filmic storytelling that is the focus of Fitzgerald's Monroe Stahr meets with the formal-mimetic nature of its discourse. While the nuts and bolts of cinematic representation are strewn about this setting with the anecdotal vivacity found before in Pirandello and Isherwood, the considerable paradigmatic evocativeness of this industrial setting emerges too. Despite the discursive jumble that the empty lot seems to suggest, we are struck by the intense discursive coherence of the metaphorical subtext that is attributed to it.

Tod Hacket is part of this industry, is ready to play its game, but he shares with the other characters the limitations of initiative and insight that the movies encourage. He is not totally unaware: in planning his epic painting he even "began to wonder if he himself didn't suffer from the ingrained, morbid apathy he liked to draw in others" (DoL:141). At the very least he is aware of what it is that he sees, even if the "interpretation" is not always clear to him. He too, like Monroe Stahr, finds that the "dream dump" which contains the detritus of cultural fantasy and personal obsession preserves something (even if to betray it) that is close to the way people really dream, not merely the superficial and glittering fantasies so easy to dismiss with ironic shrugs.

It is significant that Tod gets lost in his attempt to reach Faye and in what way he does. As opposed to Homer who, as we shall see, loses his way into the grooves of regression, Tod loses his way quite literally, and among the fragments and false façades of the studio lot. All these barely concretized backdrops which are meant to evoke so many imaginary worlds are perceived by Tod with the run-on and illogical continuity that anticipates Homer's account of his last night with Faye. Both also suggest, of course, the syntax of film discourse that we have defined as the characteristic tropes of the film novel.[11] Tod pursues Faye past a canvas ocean liner, a papier-mâché sphinx, across a desert ("a desert that was continually being made larger by a fleet of trucks"), along "a Western street with a plank sidewalk," and through a jungle. Meanwhile water buffaloes moan, an Arab charges by on a white stallion, and a truck full of snow and several malamute dogs drives by. Paris streets, Romanesque courtyards, summer camps, and Greek temples lead to each other with the surrealistic continuity of dreams.

This fantasy romp may be just good, clean fun (as magic as Cecilia's storybook view of the studio lot in Fitzgerald) were it not for the fact that ultimately the real people who move among these props are hurt by the hollow weakness of the set as it collapses under them. But (stylistic irony meant as a commentary on the film industry) their human cries and their real wounds are appropriated by the phony canvas and wood: "When the front rank of Millaud's heavy division started up the slope of Mount St. Jean, the hill collapsed. The noise was terrible. Nails screamed with agony as they pulled out of joists. The sound of ripping canvas was like that of little children whimpering. Lath and scantling snapped as though they were brittle bones. The whole hill folded like an enormous umbrella and covered Napoleon's army with painted cloth" (DoL:134). Buried in this witty transference of cries and agony from victims to setting (nails, not people, scream; canvas, not children, whimpers; lath and scantling, not humans, break bones) is a commentary on the true interrelation of the real to the illusory, of the humanly significant as it falls victim to the illusions of the "cinemonkey."[12]

This melodramatic catastrophe is but an external concretization of the inner conflict between reality and illusion best exemplified by the character of Harry Greener (quite significantly it occurs right after his death). Harry allows us to see the way in which the film medium appropriates elements from other art forms only to exploit them and discard their shell. He also demonstrates how the continuous enticement of film success (eternally hoped for, eternally beyond one's grasp) will reduce a human being to a caricature of himself. Inherently what the vaudeville artist has to contribute to the art of film is quite valuable. As Bazin has pointed out, film was able to isolate what is most significant in the old theatrical routines and foreground the cosmic significance within the comic mayhem. "The majorities of these burlesques," he says, "are an endlessly protracted expression of something that cries from within the character. They are a kind of phenomenology of obstinacy" (Bazin

1967:80). Bazin could be talking about Harry Greener as he patiently runs his act in bars and on doorsteps, hoping to make a friend, to make a sale. Harry leaves us in no doubt, moreover, that pratfalls and "exploding stoves" are more than the baggage of old-fashioned comedy. They stand as thinly veiled versions of serious pain and touching misfortune. We are made to see that life often, as in Bazin's words, "no longer calls for plot, episodes, repercussions, misunderstandings, or sudden reversals." The action rather "unfolds implacably to the point at which it destroys itself. It proceeds unswervingly towards a kind of rudimentary catharsis of catastrophe" (Bazin 1967:80). Or, to put it in Harry Greener's terms: "His life had consisted of a lightning series of 'nip-ups,' 'high-gruesomes,' 'flying-W's' and 'hundred-and-eights' done to escape a barrage of 'exploding stoves'" (DoL:77).

The clown is a clue to something more universal in the human condition. To Tod he is just like Faye's film dreams which, as we saw, are also perceived to be meaningful in a wider perspective. Both dreams and clowning are moreover significant in the way that the film medium may be: through images and enactment (DoL:76). For one thing, the clowning can in itself become a protection, since "most people," Harry had discovered, "won't go out of their way to punish a clown" (DoL:77). Yet this mask can be a "double-edged" shield. And Harry is quite prepared to use the essence of his comic gift (his laughter) to punish and hurt rather than to give pleasure or enlightenment. But it is not only his daughter, against whom the laugh is turned, who suffers. Harry himself becomes almost possessed by it and cannot stop it from hurting himself as well (DoL:96–97). In its emblematic particularity the laugh epitomizes what has become of Harry's act as a whole: it keeps him a prisoner to a point where no one is sure what is real and what is illusion (Harry himself knows least of all). Tod even notices that years of "performance" at the expense of simple, genuine "being" have reduced Harry's head to a mask, a professional deformation that seems to have caused in real life what is said to happen to Pirandello's actors only in metaphor: "Harry . . . had very little back or top to his head. It was almost all face, like a mask, with deep furrows between the eyes, across the forehead and on either side of the nose and mouth, plowed there by years of broad grinning and heavy frowning." The price of this professional deformation is very high indeed since, as a consequence, "he could never express anything either subtly or exactly. [His features] wouldn't permit degrees of feeling, only the furthest degree" (DoL:119).

It is not surprising, therefore, that his daughter should display an even greater discontinuity between meaning and its outer manifestation. Even Homer (who knows very little about his own feelings, let alone those of others) notices the discrepancy as she tries to impress him with her worldly manners and sensual posturing. Her elaborate gestures are "so completely meaningless, almost formal, that she seemed a dancer rather than an affected actress" (DoL:94). The fact that she is encouraged in this is yet another instance of the exploitative attitude of men around her, an exploitation similar to that of the movies. Tod is charmed by her eroticism, rather than critical of her affectations, and the men at the party at Homer's house don't really care what it is she is saying:

> None of them really heard her. They were all too busy watching her smile, laugh, shiver, whisper, grow indignant, cross and uncross her legs, stick out her tongue, widen and narrow her eyes, toss her head so that her platinum hair splashed against the red plush of the chair back. The strange thing about her gestures and expressions was that they didn't really illustrate what she was saying. They were almost pure. It was as though her body recognized how foolish her words were and tried to excite her hearers into being uncritical. It worked that night; no one even thought of laughing at her. The only move they made was to narrow their circle about her. (DoL:158-159)

Leaving aside the existential tragedy of such discontinuity, even Faye's professional aspirations are compromised by it. At least in the one screen performance that we witness she suffers precisely from such a flaw: "She was supposed to look drunk and she did, but not with alcohol. She lay stretched out on the divan with her arms and legs spread, as though welcoming a lover, and her lips were parted in a heavy, sullen smile. She was supposed to look inviting, but the invitation wasn't to pleasure" (DoL:68). But for Faye confrontation with her image on screen does not lead to the kind of insight that was achieved by Nabokov's Margot or Pirandello's Nestoroff.

In the end neither father nor daughter have any success within the medium they aspire to (at best Harry gets odd jobs whenever a specific director needs his trademark laugh for a horror movie), and in their private lives everything is reduced to movie clichés. "The theater is in our blood," is the way Faye refers to her family "tradition," while Harry recaps for Tom his barroom "autobiography routine" full of the most trite conventionalities in substance ("see him start out in his youth to play Shakespeare in the auditorium of the Cambridge Latin School") as well as in form ("he even did the off-stage noises, twittering like birds to herald the dawn of Love and yelping like a pack of bloodhounds when describing how Evil Fate ever pursued him" [DoL:120]). This recapitulation is even inserted into the novel just before Harry's death—ultimate cliché of movie structure!

The lack of connection between actions and feeling in the name of "show biz" pervades the whole novel and pursues all characters in it. The child actor Adore is a singular example, strutting around like a Frankenstein monster (says his mother apologetically without realizing that it is into a monster—one to be gaped at indeed—that she has turned him) and singing a song totally inappropriate for his age with incongruously apt mimicry ("he seemed to know what the words meant, or at least his body and his voice seemed to know" [DoL:141]). Faye, by contrast, sings her songs with Miguel by injecting irrelevant sensuality into a revolutionary song, or by turning the upbeat "Dreamed about a Reefer" into a lugubrious dirge. The only character in the novel who is revealed to be exactly what he seems is (paradoxically) the female impersonator in the "Cinderella Bar." The song performed by this artist (who arouses the hostility of faker Faye) is true to his nature: "What he was doing was in no sense parody; it was too simple and too restrained. It wasn't even theatrical. This dark young man with his thin, hairless arms and soft, rounded shoulders, who rocked an imaginary cradle as he crooned, was really a woman" [DoL:146]).[13]

This coherence between the expression of feeling and its true presence is rare among the characters in this novel. More often than not the expression of feeling is inappropriate or "theatrical" precisely in the way that the female impersonator avoids. Such is the case, for instance, with the spectacular "film kiss" between cowboy Earle and Faye to which Tom is treated. In watching this Tom is reduced to the nonparticipating presence of a film spectator trespassing upon an elaborate, stylized, and erotically charged love scene. Faye, of course, is quite uninvolved (she offers to repeat the performance with Tom), but for the film designer (who refuses to participate) this posture is ultimately the one most frequently assumed. This is also because in his professional role as a graphic designer for the studio he tends to look at everything in the visual terms of sketches for film production.[14] This specialized professional deformation explains why the novel's formal mimetics rather than being those of finished films are those of pastel and pencil drawing. Formal mimetics here become as "specialized" as the protagonist. With a few exceptions in which the progression of narrative does remind us of cinematography (the sudden violence at the campfire occurring almost backwards because of its speed; the first appearance of the dwarf Abe Kusich, who emerges like a startling puzzle from visual clues at first incomprehensible), the visual texture of the novel is distinctly painterly. The intensity and simplifications of the visual effect enhance the impression of watching and transfer this experience to the readers too. We are thus pulled into this dimension of the novel with an immediacy that helps to support what seems to me the most idiosyncratic contribution to the genre that West's novel makes. This is the isolation of the theme of passive, frustrated, nonparticipatory voyeurism within the film experience.

In this West anticipates many subsequent film novels by making the topic into a pivotal turning point. Episodes, characterizations, action, and ultimately the motivation behind the rage of the crowds that finally explode in an orgiastic riot (the motivation clearly involves unfulfilled and unsatisfied watching) are controlled by various manifestations of voyeurism. Christian Metz has pointed to the way in which film watching reenacts in their essence all those occasions of curious, guilty watching that involve the urge to witness aspects of life usually shielded by privacy, taboos, and shame. "The cinema," he says, "retains something of the peculiar prohibited character of the vision of the primal scene (the latter is always surprised, never contemplated at leisure, and the permanent cinemas of big cities, with their highly anonymous clientele entering or leaving furtively, in the dark, in the middle of the action, represent this transgression factor rather well)—but also, in a kind of inverse movement . . . the cinema is based on the legalization and generalization of the prohibited practice" (Metz 1982:65). West anticipates Metz's insights when he describes the crowds that watch Harry Greener's funeral (and anything else that might produce the intense pleasure of sudden sensationalism). They always wait "for a dramatic incident of some sort, hoping at least for one of the mourners to be led weeping hysterically from the chapel." Moreover, Tod perceives their expectant voyeurism as distinctly threatening when they stare "back at him with an expression of vicious, acrid boredom that trembled on the edge of violence" (DoL:127–128).

In West's novel the connection between voyeurism and film as an industry is clearly illustrated. This link is made early in the novel by the pornographic movie that Tod and his friends go to see at Mrs. Jenning's. The pretentious madam's establishment is clearly meant as a metaphor for the film industry (Bergmann to Isherwood: "We are like two married men who meet in a whorehouse" [PrV:32]). The equivalence is also underlined by the two beautifully iconic metaphors (one for mercenary sexuality, one for the embarrassing conspicuousness of true love) that Claude suggests as movie images during the visit to the brothel and then rejects because "it's good, but it's not for pictures" (DoL:72). The two images in question aptly depict the opposite poles of sexual experience (in fact by the sixties they were used in films such as Joseph Strick's *The Savage Eye* and Roman Polanski's *Two Men and a Wardrobe*). But in Hollywood in the thirties they would not do. "You've got to remember the audience," Claude remarks. "What about the barber in Purdue? He's been cutting hair all day and he's tired. He doesn't want to see some dope carrying a valise [the icon for the embarrassing burden of true love] or fooling with a nickel machine [the visual concretization of sex as "industrial design"]. What the barber wants is amour and glamor" (DoL:72).

The film industry is quite prepared to forego effective and meaningful imagery in order to provide the tired barber with cheap thrills disguised as kitsch culture. Mrs. Jennings and her establishment are thus quite apt as analogues to producers and studios. She puts on a front of elaborate culture ("She ran her business just as other women run lending libraries, shrewdly and with taste") and she insists in voicing only those cultural topics which help to pretend that (as we shall see further on with the director Jacoby in Walker Percy's *Lancelot*) her business "is not just screwing" (Lanc:157). Like the double-text rationalizations of Jacoby about the sex flicks turned out in the later novel, Mrs. Jennings "insisted on discussing Gertrude Stein and Juan Gris" while the get-togethers at her house carry on at quite a different level.

In fact, "no matter how hard the distinguished visitor tried, and some had been known to go to really great lengths, he could never find a flaw in her refinement or make a breach in her culture" (DoL:73).

The pornographic film that Mrs. Jennings shows (both in its manner of affecting the audience and in its structure) seems also to be meant as a metaphor for film in general. Like Nabokov's juvenile contemporaries who react noisily to the deprivation imposed by a blank screen, Mrs. Jennings's audience imitates "the rowdy audience in the days of the nickelodeon" when the clumsy projectionist cannot seem to get the projector started. And when the film breaks just before the climax, they stamp and whistle, shouting "'It's a frameup.' . . . 'Fake!' . . . 'Cheat!' . . . 'The old teaser routine!'" One notices especially that the climax of this sexual romp is not (as expected) a sexual view of erotic action but a question that promises a revelation. We yearn for a clear view of what the intertitle asks: "Who can it be that wishes to enter now?" (DoL:74, 75). What this narrative condensation of the apparatus seems to be saying is that the identity of those behind the door is far more significant than the erotic goings-on. This is just what occurs in bona fide primal scenes and, as we shall see, the similarity between the child behind the door and the film spectator is a motif that tends to appear more and more in subsequent novels such as *Lancelot* (where the plot revolves around camera-aided trespassing upon sexual betrayal) and *Betrayed by Rita Hayworth* (in which the themes of a child's sexual curiosity and of film watching are beautifully intertwined).

The character who is the unmetaphorical object of the ambiguity of watching in West's novel is Homer Simpson, who carries his love for Faye Greener as clumsily and as visibly as the man in Claude's little film scene (Homer makes his exit from the novel, in fact, carrying clumsily two suitcases that cause him to lurch from side to side [DoL:178]). The *visus interruptus* which ends the porno show, moreover, foreshadows Homer's experiences in more ways than one. His own feelings (sexual especially) are just as stunted as the film turns out to be, something we find out from his flashback to the threatening hotel drunk who made sexual advances to him in Wayneville: "It was always like that. His emotions surged up in an enormous wave, curving and rearing higher and higher, until it seemed as though the wave must carry everything before it. But the crash never came. Something always happened at the very top of the crest and the wave collapsed to run back like water down a drain, leaving, at the most, only the refuse of feeling" (DoL:86–87). Moreover, Homer regards his own repeated voyeuristic intrusions into Faye's liberal ways around men with self-delusive naïveté and, ultimately, with regressive childlike innocence.

At first he stands behind Tod (himself a passive voyeur), "watching her through the opening between Earle and the Mexican" while she tells everyone in fantastic run-on style (imaginary concretizations and paradigmatic montage) what her professional future is going to be. Homer doesn't want to see the way things are, and Tod has to shout it in his face: "She's a whore!" (DoL:162). But he only elicits a withdrawal on Homer's part. Withdrawal ultimately causes Homer to respond to his discovery of Faye in bed with the Mexican by displaying the innocence of a child (in substance as well as in form). Tod's description of Homer's account of the episode reproduces the run-on style that a child would use in accounting for a traumatic experience, or just an exciting movie (as we shall see this is precisely the style that Puig's protagonist Toto will use in retelling the films he sees): "A great deal of it was gibberish. Some of it, however, wasn't. . . . A lot of it wasn't jumbled so much as timeless. The words went behind each other instead of after. What he had taken for long strings were really one thick word and not a sentence. In the same way several sentences were simultaneous and not a paragraph" (DoL:168).

The substance of what Homer has to tell is just as troubling and full of misunderstanding as the style of the telling. Even after Tod's blunt description of Faye, Homer looks in on her dancing: "She and the Mexican were doing a slow tango to music from the phonograph. He held her very tight, one of his legs thrust between hers, and they swayed together in long spirals that broke rhythmically at the top of each curve into a dip. All the buttons on her lounging pajamas were open and the arm he had around her waist was inside her clothes" (DoL:163). Confronted with this transparent revelation, Homer decides it is all just good clean fun. He even forgets this moment in his account to Tod the next morning, although a reconstruction of events reveals that he was there. He also does not understand why Faye, discovering him in the act of watching the party from the kitchen (present but separate), feels there is something nasty in this: "She wouldn't listen and just went on calling him all sorts of dirty things" (DoL:169).

When he gets to the crucial part of the episode, moreover, the skewed nature of his relationship with Faye is confirmed by the way she defines their connection as daughter to father. In the orgiastic aura of this episode one recalls immediately the incestuous daisy chain seen earlier at Mrs. Jennings's, when all the family members were linked through the erotic lust of the sexy maid. But with the fluidity of totally imaginary scenarios, the relationship between Homer and Faye is yet again reversed when Homer has to interpret the sexual sounds behind her closed door. As innocent as a child, he takes the sounds to be indexes of physical jeopardy:

> She called him Daddy and kissed him and said that she wasn't angry at him at all. She said there had been a fight but nobody got hurt much and for him to go back to bed and that they would talk more in the morning. He went back like she said and fell asleep, but he woke up again as it was just breaking daylight. At first he wondered why he was up because when he once fell asleep, usually he didn't get up before the alarm clock rang. He knew that something had happened, but he didn't know what until he heard a noise in Faye's room. It was a

moan and he thought he was dreaming, but he heard it again. Sure enough, Faye was moaning all right. He thought she must be sick. She moaned again like in pain. He got out of bed and went to her door and knocked and asked if she was sick. She didn't answer and the moaning stopped so he went back to bed. A little later she moaned again so he got out of bed, thinking she might want the hot water bottle or some aspirin and a drink of water or something and knocked on her door again, only meaning to help her. She heard him and said something. He didn't understand what but he thought she meant for him to go in. Lots of times when she had a headache he brought her an aspirin and a glass of water in the middle of the night. The door wasn't locked. You'd have thought she would have locked the door because the Mexican was in bed with her, both of them naked and she had her arms around him. (DoL:170)

By the time Tod absorbs all of this, Homer has reached the ultimate physical expression of regressive shock. He is lying on the couch, asleep or catatonic, coiled like a fetus. Tod observes that he was like "a steel spring which had been freed of its function in a machine and allowed to use all its strength centripetally" (DoL:171). Both in shape and in the solipsistic direction of its energy, the image applies equally well to the film reels that bear the stories which, through many analogies of content and form, are so close to the experience Homer has to confront. The analogy does not escape Tod, who concludes by tying together Homer's flight and Faye's dream scenarios (he alludes to her Pacific shipwreck card): "What a perfect escape the return of the womb was. Better by far than Religion or Art or the South Sea Islands. It was so snug and warm there, and the feeding was automatic. Everything perfect in that hotel. No wonder the memory of those accommodations lingered in the blood and nerves of everyone. It was dark, yes, but what a warm, rich darkness" (DoL:171). And to Tod, who has all along shared in Homer's passive voyeurism, the connection is all the more comprehensible since the fraudulent illusions of cinematography are his business.

Seeing implies a range of feelings, ambiguities, and centers of interest that endow it with the kinds of overtones that film tends to contain, even when the subject matter of what it represents does not deal with charged or forbidden subjects. Film seems to summarize many dilemmas of perception that face us today, from the implications of too easy, too potent, and too uninvolved viewing to the display of multiple levels of reality and the claims of a realized imaginary that is too concrete. By now we have access through our media to regions that boggle the mind as, over our TV dinners, we peer under the rings of Saturn or penetrate into the spirals of cochleas. We need to wonder where to place our footholds in order to stay with our own reality. We need to watch out for the contradictory motives guiding the illusions channelled to us: illusions designed to inform our minds, to move our feelings. But these can also turn out to be illusions meant to move our horses into "Indian territory," our pocketbooks to the next shopping mall. Not surprisingly, the act of seeing, with its wider cultural manifestations and its intensely personal ramifications, has become a central trope in characterizing our period.

This is probably why Nathanael West's stress on the viewer's end of the film medium anticipates a central motif of subsequent literature informed by the movies. To us today the subject is fraught with greater urgency than it was in the forties. But already then West could pick up the early signs. Film viewing, far from being the neutral, escapist, bland activity some may suggest, has revealed its voyeuristic overtones. Narrow definitions of clinical scopophilia notwithstanding, we seem to belong to a culture in which seeing ever more clearly the very objects that we want to know (objects we can never fully reach) leads to moral ambiguities. And it is just those same moral ambiguities that narratives centered around film thematics seem to favor more and more. This focus will culminate in such novels as Walker Percy's *Lancelot,* although many others treat the theme quite explicitly. In this novel, however, we will find that motifs first broached by West come to a head, as the protagonist uneasily juggles informed, aware "insight" with an ultimately passive liberalism. As we shall see in the next chapter, what starts as Lancelot's maniacal pursuit of visual evidence ultimately tips into impersonal destruction and madness.

But West's open discussion of these themes is not entirely new to the genre of the film novel. Voyeurism in its sexual and social dimensions, as well as the polar responses of impotence and violence that it often provokes, is in one way or another present in all the novels we are dealing with. We have discussed Gubbio's "peeping Tom" camerawork with Nestoroff and seen in Nabokov as well (his possessed voyeur in *Despair,* his sadistic ones in *Bend Sinister*) that the privilege of spectator privacy can be tainted. Bergmann's lurid and persistent inquiries into his secretary's most intimate affairs, as well as the "guilt" he attributes to the politically irresponsible audiences of romantic fluff, place *Prater Violet* as well at the outskirts of such questions, while Cecilia's embarrassing discovery in *The Last Tycoon* of a naked secretary in her father's office comes closer to an open treatment of this theme.

Yet all of these examples are at best an implicit treatment of the matter. It seems that as one moves beyond West, through novels that respond to the root motifs of cinematography, this theme becomes more insistent. In Moravia's novel about a scriptwriter, as we shall see, deeper ambiguities and personal consequences start to emerge. At the center of the protagonist's misunderstanding with his wife, in fact, is the moment (most cinematic in its structure) when he sees her kissing someone else through a lighted window, out of the protective darkness of night, and does nothing. His passive voyeurism is very much at the center of his wife's "disprezzo" for him (this contempt accounts for the Italian title of the novel). The protagonist of Manuel Puig's *Betrayed by Rita Hayworth,* as we shall see, also struggles with the mirroring that the cinematic apparatus provides of events (primal scenes, sexual fantasies) and the feelings they arouse that Toto finds displaced, displayed, and made into stories by Hollywood. For the protagonists of *Kiss of the Spider Woman,* finally, this deep and personally intense merging with the screen becomes a lifeline, ideologically "correct" or not as it may be.

8

The Eyes Have to Know

Moravia: "Ghost in the Cave"

Subconscious yearnings and individual fantasies have defined the characters in the novels studied so far, distorting Gubbio's view of reality and of his fellowmen, trapping Albinus in his limited capacity to work out his own destiny. But just as much as these idiosyncratic personal subtexts, the cultural and ideological presuppositions of life have also affected the way these characters see and interpret reality. Such extremes form but the alternating poles (private and public) of all interaction with creative texts (film texts among them). Any story and any vision, in the way it is "presented," reflects the personal needs (Gubbio's story), the cultural canons (Albinus's paintings), or the ideological bent (Bergmann's musical) of its maker and of the culture that s/he belongs to.

The potential interconnection between psychic subtexts and ideological ones is well captured by Alberto Moravia in his novel *Il disprezzo,* in which the protagonist is a scriptwriter at odds with the world both in his personal and professional lives. Translated into English as *A Ghost at Noon,* the novel reveals to what extent the art of filmmaking has, by the fifties, become part and parcel of a broad cultural perspective. The formal peculiarities of cinematography appear in this novel only side by side with Moravia's parallel interest in the structures of stage drama (Cottrell [1974] makes a valiant and only partly successful attempt to separate film structure from theatrical structure in Moravia's work, while Tessari [1977] manages to discover only very general film qualities in his work). Moravia's long-standing focus on moral ambiguity and existential isolation finds an ideal setting in the world of filmmaking for many of the reasons already outlined in this study.

The director with whom the protagonist, Riccardo Molteni, has to work is a German named Rheingold (somewhat in the mold of Isherwood's Bergmann, although—as opposed to Bergmann—the point is made that he is not in a class with such directors as Pabst and Lang). This collaboration forces Riccardo into a multiple reading of Homer's *Odyssey,* the filming of which is the project they share. These readings are quite contentious, not least because some of their implications soon reveal themselves as relevant to the realm of Riccardo's private life. In this area too, we soon find out, "seeing" and "interpreting" the surface of the visible world is fraught with contradictions and hampered by the same personal idiosyncrasies that delimit the "reading" of classical texts. Neither what is obvious to Molteni about the nature of actions nor what is canonical about standard texts turns out to be what it seems. Moravia's treatment of the interaction of film and life is innovative in that it thus makes explicit many of the connections that were embedded more tacitly in novels studied so far. Whereas the "parallel process" inherent in juxtaposing Albinus's life to the film snatches he sees at the movies is at best part of a sardonic literary game that Nabokov plays with the reader, and while the political rereading of *Prater Violet* by Bergmann is Isherwood's illustration of a procrustean attempt to justify work in an unworthy context, Moravia's treatment makes the multiple flow of "versions" and "visions" the core of his film novel. For one thing, we witness that in looking at life (just as at the movies) one "spectator" 's version of what is happening may well be rejected by others, causing much heat and controversy. Just as Gubbio's version of his own story is open to reconstruction (but it is up to us to perform it), and just as Albinus's torrid affair with Margot turns out to be her financial arrangement (a conventional but plausible ploy), so in this novel Riccardo Molteni's Troilus (after much debate and self-examination) turns out to have been Emilia's Pander. The "correct" versions of books turn out to matter so much because they imply the different possible versions of human life itself.

The range of subtextual interpretations articulated in Moravia's novel exemplify broadly cultural and individually subliminal readings such as those we have encountered before (but never in such tight juxtaposition) in the work of West and Fitzgerald. They also address the nature of a "classic" and place it in the context of a discussion of "realism" that is given a contemporary twist by introducing the perspective of film theory. These interpretations ultimately bind into a new narrative manifestation of this genre the intertwining of the cultural, the individual, and the mythopoeic codes.

According to the most general of these interpretations, the ostensible reason for making a film based on the *Odyssey* is the status of Homer's work as the archetypal subtext of Mediterranean culture, comparable to the role that the Bible plays in Anglo-Saxon culture. This is the substance of the director's pitch to the producer Battista, although we soon find out that in fact Rheingold does not believe in this "canonical" nature of the classic text. One notes immediately, however, that in this version the *Odyssey* functions as a mythopoeic text that belongs to all and is thus quite similar to the kind of materials that Fitzgerald's producer Monroe Stahr looks for since he considers his work to be a mediation of the archetypal values of his culture.

For Rheingold's venal producer the "interpretation" of the poetic subtext of this classic merely involves a search for the stereotypes of cheap genre films (Nausicaa and companions will make suitable "naked nymphs") and for the threatening giants (cyclopes and all) that he considers as the "classical" predecessors to King Kong. Dressed up in the typical evasions and pretentious patter of many movie moguls, Battista's concern for the appeal of his film leads him to insist that what is "poetic" in the poem is precisely what will appeal to the majority of viewers: adventure, spectacle, giants, marvels, storms, witches, monsters. Much as this may cleverly appeal to the present postmodern divestment from the poetics of canonical elitism, this is (in the context of Battista's cultural moment) run-of-the-mill special pleading. Yet if not pre-postmodern, Moravia is engaging here in another kind of cultural critique. He uses Battista to illustrate one of the standard polemics that took place in the fifties against neorealism, the then reigning manifestation of politically engaged and aesthetically uncompromising cinema. "The neo-realistic film," he has Battista state (echoing many of the comments heard in those years on the political right), "is not a film that inspires people with the courage to live, that increases their confidence in life. The neo-realistic film is depressing, pessimistic, gloomy. Apart from the fact that it represents Italy as a country of ragamuffins—apart from this fact which, after all, is of considerable importance, it insists too much on the negative sides of life, on all that is ugliest, dirtiest, most abnormal in human existence. It is, in short, a pessimistic, unhealthy type of film, a film which reminds people of their difficulties instead of helping them to overcome them" (GaN:80–81, Disp:86–87). While much of this apes (when it does not actually quote) the famous open letter that Giulio Andreotti addressed to Vittorio De Sica, Battista finds that what is "unhealthy" and defeatist in neorealism may be remedied by staying true to Homer's poem.[1]

The confrontation between the scriptwriter's reading and the director's, on the other hand, involves more serious and profound considerations. It ultimately leads to an *Odyssey* precariously balanced between two irreconcilable poles and to the cancellation of the movie project. On the one hand we have Molteni's view that the poem embodies the ancient roots of what is most positive in Western civilization; a sunny, optimistic pragmatism in which a world clearly "readable" by the individual is the rational (if dangerous) stage for human striving. On the other we find Rheingold's idea that the poem displays the cultural turning point towards troubled modern individualism. In Homer's text he finds an ideological and ethical subject painfully squirming through the confusing geography of meandering, intersecting byways of moral ambiguity, cultural indecision, ironic skepticism, and the dark depths of the Freudian subtext. Writer and film director are here ultimately engaged in a value-driven placement of this ancient text; in seeking the reasons for its continuing canonical status. Does it continue to live (deserve to do so further) because it mirrors the positive values of a lost innocence or because it anticipates the entropy of modernism? Rheingold and Molteni personify a fact noted by Barbara Herrnstein Smith when she writes that "literary evaluation is not merely an aspect of formal academic criticism but a complex set of social and cultural activities central to the very nature of literature" (Smith 1984:10).

The two views are debated as an integral part of the narrative by the protagonists, who assume that these are irreconcilable "readings" of the history of human culture. Yet ultimately, as the story develops through its own meandering byways, we realize that there is more: the "interpretation" and "evaluation" of universal cultural codes are driven by the personal, individual preferences of a Rheingold and a Molteni. The German proposes a personal reading of the great classic as seen through the optics of a moment in Middle-European culture that is personal because it is heavily influenced by his own formative years in a modernist Germany and by the upheaval of a war that has evoked the dangers of a cultural regression to the primitive roots of the nation. The scriptwriter, who resists this interpretation, insists on his own view for personal reasons that are more private and defensive. As Molteni states at the outset of the novel, "I was aware the whole time that I was being swayed by material, subjective factors, that I was transforming purely personal motives into universal reasons" (GaN:19, Disp:25). Said in this instance of his rationalizations about joining the Communist Party (political conviction has very little to do with it), this statement effectively characterizes Molteni's hesitations between the universal truths Rheingold finds in Homer's text and the personal motives which lead the scriptwriter to reject them.

The interpretation and the "making relevant" of cultural and personal evidence is thus just as crucial here in this novel as we saw it to be in the cases of Pirandello's Gubbio and of Nabokov's Albinus. Reconstructive reading is at work in Rheingold's version of the *Odyssey,* just as it is part of Molteni's slow realization that it would help to gloss his misunderstanding with Emilia. Especially in the case of this marital instance of discursive disjunction (Emilia's contempt turns out to be based on the incompatibility of her own cultural code with her husband's), the facts emerge only after a laborious process in which actions, words, and the interpretations of both are played out in a series of painstaking flashbacks (the story is told by Molteni in retrospect). As he tells us at the outset, "I reconstructed later . . . patiently retracing in memory a number of occurrences which—at least at the time—had seemed insignificant, and which had passed almost unobserved by me at the moment" (GaN:9, Disp:13).

This process is distinctly reminiscent of the reconstruction of significant truth from seemingly peripheral details that film vision tends to favor, calling into play even the film-mimetic mechanisms of syntagmatic segmentation and paradigmatic retrospective reintegration. Yet in this instance (illustrating the productivity of this narrative genre) the materials that are called into play go far deeper than those we found in previous examples. Interpretation and evaluation play a role now in reconstructions deeply personal and broadly public. Moravia, in this narrative juxtaposition of film-specific contexts that resonate with the work of culture and the work of the private, writes a film novel that gives narrative context to the view in current theory of textual interpretation (a view he clearly anticipates) that "a subject's experience of an entity [the entity Smith refers to in these words is, on the whole, that of literature] is always a function of his or her personal economy" and that it reflects "the variable products of the subject's engagement with his or her environment under a particular set of conditions." The variables, as we can see even just from Battista, Rheingold, and Molteni, are multiple and may well lead to an impasse since "not only is an entity always experienced under more or less different conditions, but the various experiences do not yield a simple cumulative (corrected, improved, deeper, more thorough, or complete) knowledge of the entity because they are not additive" (Smith 1984:16).

Admittedly, the intellectual rigor of the checklist Smith provides may not matter much in the context of moviemaking. But even a popular film needs coherence, so much so that on the set with Rheingold it does turn out to matter that "each experience of an entity frames it [we note the representational metaphor that to readers of any film novel evokes the director with his eye to the viewfinder] in a different role and constitutes it as a different configuration, with different 'properties' foregrounded and repressed" (Smith 1984:16). Battista is the one most aware of the impasse and most determined to stop it from entering his film. This is perhaps so because his view on the matter of the value-driven readings of a text voices quite explicitly, as we saw, the words of Minister Andreotti, who in those years was charged by the party in power with fostering or smothering particular aesthetic and ideological manifestations of Italian cinema. This view therefore rests upon the tacit and confident conviction that "the major effects of prohibiting or inhibiting explicit evaluation is to forestall the exhibition and obviate the possible acknowledgement of divergent systems of value and thus to ratify, by default, established evaluative authority" (Smith 1984:11).[2]

Yet even director and scriptwriter are aware that their own readings do not reconcile easily into one film version. Rheingold's Freudian reading of Homer is as broad in its yearning to use a story to explicate a culture (in fact, a paradigm shift) as Bergmann's political one of *Prater Violet*. He finds in the poem a fundamental stand against barbarism (albeit projected backwards onto Greek history) comparable to the brunt of Bergmann's own stand against the rise of National Socialism in Germany. Such "contemporary" meaning, however, has to be painstakingly dug out of the ancient poem. The story, in

Rheingold's hands, must change from its ostensible surface of epic narrative to a personal psychological drama (as Molteni says of this, a "dramma da *boudoir"*). Only thus can Homer's archetypal frame of reference yield its "modernist" subtext. In the director's view this is a perfectly permissible procedure. The "moderns," says Rheingold, "in order to resuscitate such ancient and obscure myths" must "discover the significance which they can have for us of the modern world, and then to fathom that significance as deeply as we can, to interpret it, to illustrate it . . . but in a live, independent way, without allowing ourselves to be crushed by the masterpieces that Greek literature has drawn from these myths" (GaN:134, Disp:142). Homer's geographical extension therefore must become an inner landscape (in-tension); the Mediterranean sea, Rheingold insists, *is* Ulysses's subconscious. If the hero takes so long in returning home, this is not because of the ostensible obstacles of external reality. It is because he does not *want* to return. The landscapes, colors, sensations of the setting that (Molteni maintains) are the very point of Homer's narration must be abandoned (insists Rheingold) for the depths that hide beneath their deceptive referentiality. It is thus that even the kind of literary source cinema uses routinely for the sake of spectacle and diversion can hide paradigms of "ironic" revelation and produce the same kind of modernist irony we have found to be at the heart of Pirandello's notion of film vision.

But Molteni objects that "if we don't believe Homer . . . I really don't see who we are to believe." To him the ancient poet seems the epitome of "reliable" narration, the most suitable source for the innocent referentiality of the film medium that is given voice, for instance, in the poetics of neorealism. One notes the absence of any political message and of a working-class milieu from Molteni's plea for what one might call neoclassical neorealism, yet this is how he wants to see Homer on the screen: "Upon that bright-colored sea, beneath that luminous sky, along that deserted shore, it would not have been difficult to imagine the black ships of Ulysses outlined between one wave and another, sailing towards the then virgin and unknown lands of the Mediterranean. And Homer had wished to represent a sea just like this, beneath a similar sky, along a similar coast, with characters that resembled this landscape and had about them its ancient simplicity, its agreeable moderation. Everything was here, and there was nothing else" (GaN:140, Disp:148). This, even more than Battista's self-proclaimed classicism, is a reading that tries to preserve the canonical integrity of a classic "as a witness to lost innocence, former glory, and/or apparently persistent communal interests and 'values' and thus a banner of communal identity; as a reservoir of images, archetypes and topoi" (Smith 1984:32).

Not so, retorts Rheingold. In reading this text we must employ the assumptions of a modernist poetics of narrative: the story is told in the gaps, in the hidden inconsistencies, in the silences of Homer's *Odyssey*. We the readers, he insists, must only believe "ourselves, men of the modern world, who know how to see right through the myth" (GaN:136, Disp:144–145). To the poetics of reception voiced by Molteni, Rheingold juxtaposes another: the view that, in the words of Hans Robert Jauss, "literary tradition is a dialectic of question and answer that is always kept going . . . from the present interest." As opposed to the scriptwriter, he believes that "a past text does not survive in historical tradition, thanks to old questions that would have been preserved by tradition and could be asked in an identical way for all times including our own" (Jauss 1982:65). Why does Ulysses go to war, Rheingold asks, and why does he take so long to return to Ithaca? Whether such questions are actually in the text, overtly or covertly, and whether they are relevant in the present "is decided first and foremost by an interest that arises out of the present situation, critically opposes it, or maintains it" (Jauss 1982:65). The director thus rejects the validity of the question asked by Molteni. It does not matter whether we are to believe Homer. In the context of a culture in which secularization has led to multiplicity of choices, one must deny "the authoritative or authoritarian reading that insists on its identity with the intention of the author, or on its agreement with the readings of his contemporaries," because such pluralism "has opened up the possibilities . . . of regarding the text as the permanent locus of change; as something of which the permanence no longer legitimately suggests the presence and permanence of what it appears to designate" (Kermode 1983:138–139).

For Rheingold, just as was the case with Pirandello before him, film can provide the perfect medium to achieve this better and more relevant vision for all. In fact, a modernist reading of the classical text emerges most clearly when the story is parsed to meet the discursive needs of this medium; when one looks at the story through the formative optics of cinematographic language. This kind of reading reveals that the central spring of the story is the fact that Penelope does not love Ulysses. He joins the war against Troy to escape her (a prudent, unwarlike man like him would otherwise merely send a token force headed by Menelaus), and once the war is over he deliberately delays his own return. The problem between Penelope and Ulysses, according to this reading, amounts to a cultural conflict between primitive archaic culture and the later Greek cultural evolution represented by the Sophists and their fellow philosophers: "Ulysses is a man without prejudices, and, if necessary, without scruples, subtle, reasonable, intelligent, irreligious, sceptical, sometimes even cynical," a regular Man Without Qualities, it seems (GaN: 181, Disp:192). When confronted, therefore, with the archaic challenge to his sovereignty that the suitors mount in his own house by wooing his wife, Ulysses prefers to deal with the situation by relying upon a rational assumption: his wife is faithful. He thus avoids a ritual bloodbath, the only acceptable archaic solution to such a challenge. Penelope herself, however, cannot free herself from "reading out" this kind of situation according to the primitive ritual framework that her cultural paradigm provides. She thus turns against her husband and tells him she cannot love him anymore. Thus Ulysses goes to war and afterwards delays his return as long as possible. Yet he comes back to Ithaca only to find that, while Penelope is still faithful, she can still give him her love only if he agrees to slay the "dragon." The hero finally accepts this regression to an older cultural subtext, and the happy couple can at last consummate their "bluthochzeit."

Rheingold's interpretation is triggered by a clue within the original poem that is most cinematic in its focus. To a modern cultural reading of the classical text, and to the film medium that tends to elicit such rereading merely because the poem seems like a "good property," the novel therefore adds a more specifically filmic way of looking at things. The "story" of Penelope and Ulysses looks as it does to Rheingold because cinema, by foregrounding bare action, forces one to face discrepancies hidden in the literary text. Such "editing" emphasizes elements that, in a written text, are obfuscated by the power of rhetoric and special pleading. This medium-specific editing of the text is, as we saw, what Serafino Gubbio sees through his own camera; it is what Monroe Stahr tries to teach his scriptwriters. Thus Moravia's German director notices, in the wake of his predecessor (if with different narrative and cultural reverberations), that the acts and words of Ulysses throughout the major part of the story are in stark contradiction with the "action scene" at the end:

> Ulysses might very well have politely shown the suitors the door. . . . he had the possibility of doing this; being in his own house, and being king, all he had to do was to show himself as such. As he doesn't do it, it is a sign that he has some good reason for not doing it. What reason? Obviously Ulysses wishes to prove that not only is he cunning, flexible, subtle, reasonable, cautious, but also, if necessary, as violent as Ajax, as unreasonable as Achilles, as ruthless as Agamemnon. And to whom does he want to prove this? Obviously to Penelope. (GaN:184, Disp:194–195)

"ACTION IS CHARACTER," wrote F. Scott Fitzgerald in a Jamesian reminder to himself in the notes for *The Last Tycoon,* and proceeded to develop a brilliant scene in which Monroe Stahr demonstrates to the writer Boxley the principle which Rheingold has applied here side by side with a rather ponderous Freudian apparatus. Boxley was treated by Stahr to the essence of nonverbal yet deeply engrossing, deeply meaningful cinematic action and proved Stahr's success by being caught up in it and wanting to know "what happened" and "why" in the most urgent way (LaT:32–33). In the same way, Riccardo Molteni finds himself enmeshed in the surface manifestations of outer action. Yet, as it turns out, they are the actions of his own life, not those in Homer's story. The scriptwriter feels the urgency to know "what" and "why" not as a curious spectator but as a party to the "script." His stubborn insistence that Rheingold's reading belies the cultural value of the *Odyssey* (a value that when he formulates it amounts, as we saw, to a rather drab if "high" cultural stereotype) is ultimately a refusal to merge personally significant archetypes with the ambiguous but accessible manifestations of actions and words. These are much like the actions and words that Gubbio misses deliberately; like the actions and words to which Albinus is helplessly blind.

For Riccardo Molteni, the surface evidence of actions and words he and his wife perform and speak should be sufficient to reach an understanding of Emilia's feeling of contempt for him. After all, as he points out, the precious little creative contribution he is allowed to make to film resides in his ability to articulate effectively "the action, the gestures and words of the actors." His talent as scriptwriter rests in this as well as in his ability to define how these elements should be seen through "the various movements of the camera" (GaN:36, Disp:41). One notes that Molteni's pride in this "professional" ability parallels Gubbio's, even if, more than Pirandello's cameraman, Molteni is aware of his own limitations. He can see himself clearly as he acts out the externalized stereotype of an anxious, struggling, and hungry journalist, "the contributor to cheap reviews and second-rate newspapers" (GaN:17–18, Disp:23). He is aware that he responds to the external manifestations of the conjugal harmony of others: "I am following in the footsteps of all husbands who are not loved by their wives—envying a perfectly ordinary couple while they kiss and hug their offspring" (GaN:54–55, Disp:60). And he can "read" the behavior of Emilia from the external signs that link her to background and class. Would that Nabokov's Albinus could apply his professional expertise so well.

But just like Albinus, Molteni cannot see well enough (another "professional" who fails to apply his expertise to his own life) and betrays the tendency to replace the hard facts of reality with the illusions that he prefers. We know that he is good at doing this from his professional performance, we have seen him materialize his deliberately simpleminded version of the poem with great evocative power. In the same way, he finally creates for himself (after the extent of his break with Emilia is clear, after she has in fact left him for good) a vivid illusion of his wife in the guise of a loving and understanding spouse. The evocation is in fact so vivid that it mimics the concrete illusion of cinematic experience (he is, after all "in the business") and illustrates nicely Metz's formulation of cinema as that "extra reduplication, a supplementary and specific turn to the screw bolting desire to the lack" (Metz 1975: 61). Precisely as we have seen happen in Pirandello and Nabokov, Molteni ties together the concrete power of imaginative scenarios (we know they are illusion but we perceive them as real), the insistent solipsism of the images we generate, and the ultimate dilemma that links reality with wish.

He does so by materializing Emilia in broad daylight as he rows towards the dark grotto on the walls of which only reflections of the outside light are projected. And in this setting, so reminiscent of the Platonic cave that the French film theorist Baudry identified as a perfect analogue to the setting of cinematic illusion and thus another manifestation of what I have called the apparatus as setting, Emilia is made to act in the most blatantly wish-fulfilling manner. The scriptwriter now become spectator accepts this illusion as readily as a filmviewer might accept the conniving projections of his most private wishes. Molteni's description of what happens (this is part of his own subsequent critique of the interaction between illusion and wish) points out that "proof" that it was "a hallucination and nothing more" is found precisely in the fact that "I had made Emilia say all the things I wanted her to say, and assume exactly the attitudes I wished her to assume." The very same solipsistic circle that we described as a principal characteristic of the "active" use of cinematic projections by spectators in such examples as Nabokov's personal appropriation of public screen images, is here described by Molteni. "Everything had begun and ended," he states, "with myself," voicing a view that argues for the ultimate subjectivity of the subject position. Given the implicit cinematic context of the novel in which this occurs, Molteni also seems to be addressing in his discussion of this "projection" the nature of an illusion which (although not strictly cinematic in nature) takes on the same concreteness of a film image. "The only difference from what usually happens in such circumstances," he notes, is "that I had not confined myself to a wishful imagining of what I wanted to happen, but, from the sheer force of feeling that filled my heart, had deluded myself into thinking it really had happened" (GaN:241, Disp:253). The unreal, we see once more, is realized, but at the cost (as happened to Serafino Gubbio) of wiping out reality.

This is perhaps why the novel, ostensibly about the world of filmmaking, is so spare in its visual imagery. In fact the phenomenon of formal mimetics, at least in the ways in which it was prominent in the previous novels studied here, is conspicuous by its absence, almost as if to underline that when the scopic regime takes over it is in some way tainted. In fact, to the extent that Moravia's novel is film-mimetic, it is only so in terms of the elements that Molteni describes as his own contribution to the process of filmmaking. Much like the texture of *The Day of the Locust,* in which the formal-mimetic nature of the text strives to reproduce the professional deformation typical of its own protagonist (a studio design artist), *Il disprezzo* is written so as to conform with Molteni's definition of his own domain: actions, gestures, words, and a strongly "framed" (and thus biased) perspective on them. Yet intensely visual imagery is also used in sudden flashes to illuminate the troubled feelings of Riccardo. Out of long paragraphs of abstract and convoluted reasoning vivid images suddenly emerge such as the heavy closing of a safe door that is used to describe the scriptwriter's dismissal of misgivings as he sends Emilia off in Battista's car, or the mountain climbers who appear twice, as analogues to tired scriptwriters at the end of their labor. Images also appear, more dramatically, as metaphors such as the one that describes (hanging perilously in one of those spots where going forward is too dangerous, going back is impossible, and staying in one spot too risky) Riccardo's final stalemate with his wife. The images are often realized as intensely and occur as abruptly as those peripheral images in film that comment on the action without actually being part of it. Such a one is the image of a fish watching with anxious eye as the water in its tank is lowered (the actual setting is an elevator from which Molteni is watching the floors pass by); another is the fly that continues to walk about and clean itself pedantically for a long time after a sadistic little boy has detached its head. Such images (rare as they may be) lend a sudden vividness to the text and manage to transform Molteni's confusion and travail into startlingly cinematic terms. As such, setting and the natural elements carry effectively much of the unpicturable inner swirl of feelings:

> All this passed through my mind with the swiftness with which, if a window is suddenly thrown open, a blast of wind rushes into the room, bearing with it leaves and dust and all kinds of rubbish. And just as, if the window is closed again, there is a sudden silence and stillness within the room, so my mind, in the end, became all at once empty and silent, and I found myself standing there in astonishment, staring into the darkness, with no more thought or feeling in me. (GaN:162, Disp:171)

The apparatus, it seems, has been turned off; the movie is over.

The image of the window, and the violence that bursts through its frame, does not occur by chance here. It is through a window that one of the most traumatic turning points in the novel is staged: the furtively voyeuristic look Molteni gets (hidden by the darkness of the terrace at night) of the brutal kiss that the producer tries to give Emilia. Very much as we saw in *The Day of the Locust,* a physical arrangement of setting is made to mimic the situation of a "transgressing" film spectator (Emilia is just as annoyed at Riccardo as Faye Greener is at Homer). This narrative condensation of the apparatus turns into explicit narrative articulation the ambiguity of watching from the protective darkness of the spectator's seat. In fact, at issue in Emilia's quarrel with Riccardo is precisely the kind of passivity that, while inevitable in the cinematic spectator, bespeaks a deep-seated problem if manifested in real life. The truth is that the manifestations of Riccardo's involvement with everything that surrounds him are very much of this passive kind. At the same time, his ability to mimic to himself the vividness of unreal imaginings is a further case of professional deformation that we may add to the thematic repertory of the film novel. In his case the satisfaction of the imaginary saps the subject's impulse to claim his place in reality.

Percy: "Monkey See, Monkey Do"

What ultimately may be a state of "clinical" passive spectatorship for Molteni seems to have become a choice (fraught with undefined existential overtones) for Lancelot Lamar, the protagonist of Walker Percy's *Lancelot* (1977). A novel that exemplifies the interpenetration of film and narrative in a most comprehensive manner (of all the novels covered in the third part of this study it does so as extensively as *Prater Violet*), we find at its center once again a phenomenology of spectatorship presented as symbol of a human condition wider than just moviegoing.[3] In this the novel parallels most closely Pirandello, suggesting that all the elements that the movies triggered in the writer's imagination in 1916 are still potent sixty years later. Similar combinations of theme, plot, and questioning pervade Percy's novel, making it a most complete descendant of the first film novel. Spectatorship turns out to be fraught with the same overtones of feeling and ambivalence, while a questionable confidence in the clearness of vision provided by the latest in technological aids characterizes the protagonist. Scientific observation and optical instrumentation turn out to be as crucial to the story, in fact, as the malevolent spider is to Gubbio, or the plethora of scientific instruments of vision are to Nabokov and his characters. The nature of what is seen in *Lancelot* is questioned as extensively as it is in the earliest examples of the genre, while the genuineness and honesty of imaginative representations remain for Percy as important an issue as we found it to be for Pirandello and Nabokov.

Personal authenticity and the truth of one's relationship to existence as it truly is matter to Percy, who has noted in one of his essays that "if we must speak of a 'need' in connection with human behavior, let us speak of it as Heidegger does." He continues in the philosopher's own words: "The need is: to preserve the truth of Being no matter what may happen to man and everything that 'is.'" This requires sacrifice and what Heidegger terms "that hidden *thanking* which alone does homage to the grace wherewith Being has endowed the nature of man, in order that he may take over in his relationship to being that guardianship of Being."[4] The presumably truthful views provided by an objective medium are thus contrasted by Percy's novel (just as they were in Pirandello but with renewed philosophical urgency) to the inauthentic fictions produced through the very same medium. *Lancelot* continues to provide narrative context to the ambiguities of reality and illusion, to the ostensible and subtextual meanings (ideological as well as psychological) of cinematic discourse. But he implicates human beings as responsible agents by articulating with greater precision and deeper fervor the cultural codes activated by film. Insight about the human condition most typical to our period continues to be handed to the protagonist steeped in the very medium that projects it, but such insight comes to be inseparable from the medium that carries its meanings.

It is therefore important to Lancelot Lamar (just as it was for most of the characters studied so far) to separate a human truth from the truths projected through a mechanical apparatus. Reading the true nature of people beneath the façade they present to the cameras, recognizing their true feelings behind the catalogue of emotional postures they project in their acting, and even simply communicating without the mediation of the cultural preconceptions that are carried by language, all of these actions are crucial to Lancelot. But he too seems ultimately trapped by the human limitations of culture and vision. His own vision turns out to be just as conditioned as that of the machine, just as charged with preconscious purpose as the preplanned notions of "correct" visual perspective that are built into our lenses and viewfinders. Finally for Lancelot (as was the case for Tod Hackett) the only alternative to this kind of vision seems to be an apocalyptic "vision" full of rage, bitterness, and destruction. The "progress" that this novel illustrates (in life as well as in the genre) is that of a shift from the violence of a painting to that in the streets of our cities.

The biases of the subconscious and those of culture merge in this novel into an unstable mix rather than being rationally juxtaposed as they are by Rheingold and Molteni in *Il disprezzo*. It is thus that the eroticism and violence that in West are relegated to Mexicans, out-of-work actors, pornographic movies, and watchers from the Midwest, move now to the center of moviemaking. If there is a watcher, it is Lancelot Lamar eavesdropping while his wife and her lover make a film in his Southern mansion. The apparatus, exposed as it laboriously moves towards the finished condition of a movie, explicitly and by itself provokes the spectator's inner conflicts. Since it is in process, it exposes the kind of conflict that the sutures of a "finished" film strive to cover up: in this particular case a rupture that pits against each other the new, open sexuality of the sixties and the fading older code of behavior to which Lancelot's name is a pointed allusion. His reactions are not too far from those that we will find, if more repressed and subliminal, in the character of Manuel Puig's Toto. The boy, as we shall see, is completely at the mercy of the apparatus and only slowly manages to free himself by appropriating it from within. Lancelot's fear and revulsion is far more articulate, equipped as he is with the jaded and somewhat facile ironic distance of an adult observer.

The binary oppositions of the cultural codes of the Age of Aquarius, as it turns out, invade the very interpretation of the film itself. What to Lancelot clearly looks like an exploitation film undergoes at the hands of the filmmakers the kind of double-text reading we have encountered in *Prater Violet*, in *Il disprezzo*, and in *The Last Tycoon*. The brutality and directness of the sex scenes being filmed by the crew and the means used to gloss them clearly allude to a particular genre of "sex films with a message" produced by the likes of Pier Paolo Pasolini and Bernardo Bertolucci. *Last Tango in Paris* (1973) is in fact clearly alluded to in the following: "Fifteen or twenty times he had her up against the library stacks performing 'simulated intercourse.' He was filmed from the rear doing something to Margot quickly and easily. He was clothed. . . . 'I want to hear the zipper,' Janos Jacoby told Dana" (Lanc:

153–154). The prominent role that the sound of Marlon Brando's zipper played on the soundtrack of Bertolucci's film has made movie history, it seems.[5] But the sardonic allusion to this new "film topos" is given a critical context by the fact that the liberation which flows from Dana's open zipper turns out to be more than the simple sexual release one might expect. The allusion this time is to Pasolini's *Teorema* (1968): "What we are trying to get across is that it is not just screwing," explains the director, "though there is nothing wrong with that either, but a kind of sacrament and celebration of life" (Lanc:157). If we perceive here the shade of Pasolini's seraphic screwer, this is only confirmed by the further glossing of the plot.[6]

The protagonist of the film, it turns out, has appeared in the midst of a decaying and impotent old society much as does the mysterious visitor in *Teorema*: "his eyes, there's an inner light, he's a creature of light. . . . He actually glows. Most important, he is free. Everybody else is hung up—as in fact everybody is, you're hung up, I'm hung up. Right?" (Lanc:155–156). He plies his angelic wares in a library heavily laden with cultural symbolism, fertilizing, as it were, the barren old canon with the textual flow of alternative classics. This is explained as a ritual of social healing and regeneration in a comical alphabet soup of cultural-code extrapolation:

> He fulfills people. He fulfills the longing of the sharecroppers for their own land—he discovers that Raine's, Ella's, family owns their land. He reconciles black and white—who discover their own common humanity during the hurricane. He even gets to the sheriff (God, I wish we could have got Pat Hingle), who despite himself is tremendously moved by this glowing nonviolent vibrant creature—actually there's a strong hint here of Southern sheriff homosexuality, right? He almost reaches Lipscomb, who has lost his ties with the land, nature, and his own sexuality. He does reach Sarah. He walks into the library and while her mouth falls open, he simply goes to the bookshelf, takes down the *Rig-Veda,* and reads the great passage beginning: "Desire entered the One in the beginning!" Then, again without saying a word, he takes her hand and leads her back into the stacks, where he takes her standing against the old musty books—Thackeray and Dickens, and so forth—representing the drying up of Western juices. There's a lovely tight shot of her face while she's making love against a dusty set of the Waverly novels. Great? (Lanc:156–157)

Lancelot's own view of all this, however, is just as troubled as Homer Simpson's perception of "who it is" behind that primal door, just as confused as we shall find Toto's to be of the films he watches at the side of his mother. The difference is that Homer and the child are overwhelmed by their respective immaturity, while the Southern gentleman is revolted by the moral hypocrisy of a whole age. Yet there is a common thread too, one that we recognize as belonging to the thematic repertory of the film novel.

In all these cases the deflection of troublesome images is aided by the instrumental mediation of optics and science, by what William Barrett (1979: 3–29, 196–223) has referred to as "the illusion of technique." Lancelot repeatedly refers to his wife's adultery (not with the figural fornicator who stars with her in the film but with the director who stages this charade) through the deceptive control and illusory distancing provided by scientific terminology. The language of microscopic observation is meant to shield him from the impact of his wife's adultery, just as Toto's "scientific" digressions at one and the same time will reveal (the bird) and will deflect (the film) his preoccupations and fears. "Why is it such an unspeakable thing," Lancelot asks, "for one creature to obtrude a small portion of its body in the body of another creature? Is it not in fact a trivial matter when one puts it that way? . . . Why should I worry about a small matter like Margot taking a small part of Merlin's body into her body? As a physician, wouldn't you say that nothing more is involved than the touch of one membrane against another? Cells touching cells" (Lanc:15–16).

When Lancelot finally obtains evidence of Margot's adultery by rigging up an infrared television system and hooking it up to all the mansion's bedrooms, what he obtains is a garbled picture that reveals the electronic translation of such an atomically elemental universe. The image provides no answers at all as to the identities and combinations of suspected adulterers (those have to be interpreted by the forcibly active initiative of the watcher). What the screen offers is an insightful and concretized ironic metaphor of a humanity (its true forms dissolved, its personal boundaries uncertain) groping and merging with amoebalike promiscuity in a primeval ooze of phosphorescent matter:

> Something was indeed wrong with Elgin's camera. The figures, tiny figurines, were reddish, like people in a film darkroom, and seemed to meet, merge, and flow through each other. Lights and darks were reversed like a negative, mouths opened on light, eyes were white sockets. The actors looked naked clothed, clothed naked. The figures seemed to be blown in an electronic wind. Bodies bent, pieces blew off. Hair danced atop heads like a candle flame. I stared. Didn't Elgin say the figures were nothing but electrons? (Lanc:198)

Staring at this unexpected view provided by the latest in optical technology, Lancelot is forced to confront with unintended but unavoidable insight the elementary atomic structure, the ultimately unindividualized and threatening amorphous foundation of human life in a manner clearly anticipated by Pirandello and his brood of skeptical relativists. Yet this will not do at all. What Lancelot needs to see is a truth available only at a higher level of picture resolution. What he was hoping for, one presumes, was a technical mediation that would merely reveal to him (with the classical balance of *physis* and *poiesis*) what is concealed: technique as the medium that stages the essence of Being.[7] The primitive, cellular truth enframed by Elgin's screen, on the other hand, is too brutal (as it was for Gubbio and Nuti and will be for Toto). It is anything but the revealed reality that modern technological control suggests it may provide: a world on "standby," like Heidegger's airplane (Heidegger 1977:17). "Ready for takeoff" (just as it was for Monroe Stahr and for the pilot who watches Albinus crash), it would serve Lancelot's need to exercise the delusion that he is able as William Lovittis says in his introduction to Heidegger's essays, "to impose order on all data, to 'process' every sort of entity, nonhuman and human alike, and to devise solutions for every kind of problem"—the illusion, in other words, that "he is forever getting things under control" (Heidegger 1977:xxxvi). On the other hand, the enframing Lancelot thinks is provided by Elgin's camera (a disclosure that "brings man and Being into their own in entrusting them to one another") produces only existential ooze. It is a frightening picture that effectively images forth the modern human bind balancing on the cusp of technology and Being: the existential "estrangement" that is the "photographic negative" of the "skeletal darkness of Enframing" (Heidegger 1977:xxxvii).

Lamar's view of things through the video monitor turns out to be a paradigm for the way he regards the crucial turning points of his life and that of others. The neutralizing intention inherent in the technological perspective on the world that is exemplified by looking through the monitor is thus not relegated to delimited occasions that are defined by a simple hermeneutic need. What Lamar "sees" and what he "does" about it pervades life as a whole and ultimately bears down on the life of others with catastrophic results. He reduces the act of lovemaking, for example, to an alienated, scientific abstraction. This way of achieving distance through scientific overdetermination was anticipated in the film novel tradition, as we saw, by Nabokov's Hermann (engaged in a "controlled" sexual reverie very similar to Lancelot's), and we will find it again in Puig's Toto. "Her fornication, anybody's fornication," Lancelot remarks, "amounts to no more than molecules encountering molecules and little bursts of electrons along tiny nerves—no different in kind from that housefly scrubbing his wings under my hair" (Lanc:94). As Lancelot's obsession with his wife's adultery grows, so does this demeaning refuge in abstraction. The elaborate setup that he arranges to observe his wife's assignations, despite the complex contingencies of architectural layout and the scopic sadness of sexual spying, is described as "more lines, lines crossing lines like electrons colliding" (Lanc:106). Ultimately even brutal murder (that of his wife's lover) is described so that the human implications may be dismissed with the vocabulary of "steel molecules entering skin molecules, artery molecules, blood cells" (Lanc:275).

The scientifically distanced alternative between two modes of vision is developed by Percy's protagonist in terms that are very similar to those used by Pirandello. On the one hand, astronomy is the central metaphor that Lancelot uses to express the kind of ironic insight we found before in Pirandello's telescope: "How strangely," he muses, "one's own life had turned out during these same thirty years while Arcturus' light went booming down the long, lonesome corridors of space" (Lanc:60). Most evocative and philosophical, one is led to comment. On the other hand, deeply personal trauma, such as the discovery that his daughter is not his own, is emptied of its human feelings by the same metaphor in such a way that one is led to wonder about the loss of connection with authentic human experience:

> I can only compare it, my reaction, to that of a scientist, an astronomer, say, who routinely examines photographic plates of sectors of the heavens and sees the usual random scattering of dots of light. He is about to file away one such plate, has already done so, when a tiny little something clicks in his head. *Hold on. Hm. Whoa. What's this? Something is wrong. Let's have a look.* So he takes another look. Yes, sure enough, one dot, not even a bright dot, one of the lesser dots, is a bit out of place. You've seen the photos in the newspapers, random star dots and four arrows pointing to a single dot. To make sure, the astronomer compares this plate with the last he took of the same tiny sector of the heavens. Sure enough, the dot is out of place. It has moved. What of it, thinks the layman, one insignificant dot out of a billion dots slightly out of place? The astronomer knows better: the dot is one millisecond out of place, click click goes the computer, and from the most insignificant observation the astronomer calculates with absolute certainty and finality that comet is on a collision course with earth and will arrive in two and a half months. In eight weeks the dot will have grown to the size of the sun, the ocean risen forty feet, New York will be under water, skyscrapers toppling, U.N. meeting on Mount Washington, etc. (Lanc:19)

This supposedly scientific analogy in fact reveals very quickly that the "illusion of technique" is an empty hope. It may seem to be just another way of "making up a story," as the discourse slides into a standard science-fiction movie mode padded with "stock footage" of natural disasters typical of this genre. Rather than show what film (and all the other mediating technologies of the modern world) "could" reveal that is genuine, Lancelot falls back upon the kind of vision that betrays. Embodied in the contrivances of film fictions, this kind of vision is usually denounced by Lancelot Lamar just as Gubbio decries the silly lies of fiction films, just as the ironic narrative voice of Nabokov mocks the clichés of genre films. The alternatives of vision are similar to those we heard voiced in Pirandello: an opposition between the essential revelations of film vision and the sanitized "versions" of reality found in stereotypes and film fictions. Lancelot is well aware that the narrative concretizations of film (those that give better image resolution than Elgin's monitor) may be false. This fundamental dishonesty he forcefully denounces in words that often echo those of West's Tod Hackett, who underlines that in the studio back lot filled with junked dreams something is being betrayed that is important to humanity, and those of Fitzgerald's Monroe Stahr, who tries to salvage that "something" from the disjointed rushes that he reviews in his screening room. It is a dishonesty, Lancelot suggests, that invades our very homes (topples our own skyscrapers).

The Southern mansion in which Lancelot Lamar lives, for instance, offers a fertile field to the imaginative concretizations of his wife Margot. This Margot turns out to have an imagination as media-bound as that of her homonymous predecessor in Nabokov. Thus, during the first few years of their marriage, she restores the house and installs Lancelot in it "according to some Texas-conceived image of the River Road gentry, a kind of gentleman planter without plantation, a composite . . . of Ashley Wilkes (himself a creature of another woman of course, an anemic poetic Georgia gent), Leslie Howard (another anemic poetic gent), plus Jeff Davis home from the wars and set up in style by another strong-minded woman at Beauvoir, parked out in a pigeonnier much like mine, plus Gregory Peck, gentle Southern lawyer, plus a bit of Clark Gable as Rhett. She even bought my clothes. She liked me to wear linen suits" (Lanc:127). Much of Lancelot's resentment has to do with the fact that he thus becomes one of those "agents of the spectacle" described by Guy Debord, who "is the opposite of the individual, the enemy of the individual in himself as well as in others." The problem with such commonly found individuation achieved on the basis of cinematic models is serious. It implicates (we have seen this before with characters such as Aldo Nuti, Margot, Faye) the authenticity of who we are, since "passing into spectacle as a model for identification, the agent renounces all autonomous qualities in order to identify himself with the general law of obedience to the course of things" (Debord 1983a:¶61).

Lancelot's passive compliance with his wife's staging of his life according to such stereotypes is very much like the average person's obedience to the "spectacle" as defined in broad sociopolitical terms by Debord. The fact that it is "film stars" who must be Lancelot's models causes him an uneasiness about being a performer in this spectacle that is even more "film-specific." It is an *angst* not dissimilar, in fact, from that felt by Nabokov on the film set with Mozzhuhine. For him too (and much of this is made explicit through his character Ganin) the sudden joining in real life of film star and human being redoubles awareness that "being a star means specializing in the *seemingly lived.*" Nabokov/Ganin in Berlin and Lancelot in New Orleans thus experience that "the star is the object of identification with the shallow seeming life that has to compensate for the fragmented productive specializations which are actually lived" (Debord 1983a:¶60). Lancelot is quite accurate in identifying the problem, and can be more explicit than the characters of Pirandello and Nabokov could ever be, devoid as they are of the fully articulated critical theory that is available to Lancelot.

The mansion itself has been for years a haunt for tourists who were taken around at first by Lamar's grandfather, and now by Elgin who, despite a degree from M.I.T., remains Lancelot's black manservant. It was made the setting for fanciful stories ranging from the one accounting for a fake Bowie knife—"my grandfather . . . claimed it was one of the originals made by Bowie's slave blacksmith (though it wasn't: the original was made from a rasp and still showed the grooves)" (Lanc:18)—to the one that provides background for the more authentic "hiding hole" in which "nineteen-year-old Private Clayton Laughlin Lamar home on leave in 1862 hid from a Yankee patrol" (Lanc:46). One notes that all of these stories, true or false, are the staple genre clichés of films such as those in which the actors favored by Margot play their parts. It is also that very hole in the wall, discovered to connect all the bedrooms through the chimney, that finally becomes the key to Lamar's attempt to exercise total scopic control through the technology of television.

The hole thus embodies the ambiguous meeting point between illusion and reality that mimics much of the confusion in Lancelot's experience as well as the effect that film has on people. It puzzles the young visitors to the mansion precisely for the same reasons that Manuel Puig's Toto will be so taken by screen images: "Children believe that a wall is a wall, that the word says what is and what is not, and that if there is something else there the word doesn't say, reality itself is tricked and a new magic and unnamed world opens" (Lanc:47). But this world that is and is not happens to be also what the film crew has come to create at the mansion. Symptomatically, they prefer the wind machine used to bring about an artificial hurricane despite the fact that a real hurricane is at hand. The effects of such preference for the apparatus reach beyond the mansion. For the town's inhabitants, seduced by the promise of magic and mystery embodied in these techniques, the effects are as unsettling as they are for Lancelot. The story that the film crew imagines taking place among them belies entirely their true nature, but this is not important to them as long as they are allowed to take part in the travesty.

The conflation of all these compromises with reality is summarized by Lamar in a way that illustrates that the limited insight about such experiences that was within reach of the wondering Russian extras we encountered in Nabokov's *Mary* has reached greater definition by the second half of this century. "What was nutty," he notes, "was that the movie folk were trafficking in illusions in a real world but the real world thought that its reality could only be found in the illusions" (Lanc:161). Such ontological progress is possible for the protagonist of this film novel due to his acquisition of a film culture (genre-specific erudition) that relies on the increased public knowledge of film history and on the increased articulation by film itself of such issues. He alludes, in fact, to a film that is notoriously eloquent about the very topic of reality and illusion in the context of mediating techniques of reproduction. "Somehow," he says, "they had dropped the ball between them" (Lanc:161), just as the protagonist of Antonioni's *Blow Up* (1966) does when confronted with the mime troupe that provides closure to the film with an imaginary game of tennis played with an imaginary ball (but how is it that we can "hear" the ball bounce?).

The learned allusion (proof that the genre-specific erudition that is typical of film novels has come to include actual movies as part of the apparatus) is significant because it represents the other side of the counterfeit coin of film fakery which is the subject of Lamar's anger. There is no reason, that is, why film should not be meaningful, no reason why it should not refuse to exploit. The high-culture allusions by the filmmakers at the mansion, after all, confirm this fact. Their explication of the closure of the project in progress, a final lynching of the sexy saint in the film that is made to echo the allegorical death of Montgomery Clift in *Suddenly Last Summer* (1959), goes like this: "The stranger is immolated by a town mob who think they hate him but really hate the life forces in themselves that he stirs. He is the new Christ, of course" (Lanc:163). And Merlin describes his next film, obviously striving for significance by alluding to high-art films like Antonioni's *Red Desert* (1964): "A story ... about the dying out of the wildebeest and the death too of human love" set in Africa and therefore about "greening and ... turning back of the goddamn advancing Sahara. ... The Sahara of the *soul* too" (Lanc:218).

But such possibly worthy reading out of the subtext of films must be measured against the sincerity of the ostensible surface of the plots. On this score, the one staged in front of Lamar fails badly. Yet the problem with the film is not just a matter of being dishonest about what is shown (exploitation sex and sentimental melodrama). The failure concerns the flawed identity of film characters as they try to represent authentic people:

> The movie was about some people who seek shelter in the great house during a hurricane, a young Cajun trapper, a black sharecropper, a white sharecropper, a Christlike hippie, a Klan type, a beautiful half-caste but also half-wit swamp girl, a degenerate river rat, the son and daughter of the house, even though there are no sharecroppers or Cajuns or even a swamp hereabouts and river rats disappeared with the fish in the Mississippi years ago. And I don't even know what a "half-caste swamp girl" is. (Lanc:26–27)

None of these storybook cutouts may be found, but there is a very real hurricane moving toward the mansion. Even in this case, as we saw, the film company prefers to use its own wind machine. This shocks Lancelot with a discontinuity (a narrative instance of the discursive disjunction we have defined as an element of the film novel) that rapidly spreads from Lancelot's pigeonnier to his demented outburst of violence. The split between reality and the architecture of Los Angeles that attracts Lancelot's attention in the Raymond Chandler novel he is in the process of reading (an allusion, one may assume, to the use made of this same split by Nathanael West in *The Day of the Locust*) is quite like the discrepancy Percy's protagonist notes from his high vantage point as "one window let onto . . . blue sky, sun shining, children already building Christmas bonfires on the levee" and the other "let onto a thunderstorm" (Lanc:26). For the film crew the real thunderstorm, when it finally explodes, is merely an occasion for a party. Such a facile and partial use of an awesome phenomenon of nature that they had just betrayed with their machines is a mystery to Lancelot, who describes his response to news of the party with self-deprecating mockery: "'They're going to have a party named Goodbye movie, hello Marie.' I must have looked blank for he explained: 'Goodbye movie hurricane, hello the real thing'" (Lanc:219).

Discursive discontinuity that is thematically genre-specific turns out in the case of this novel, as in Pirandello's prototype of the genre, to precipitate crisis and closure. For Lancelot the storm becomes a cover for the sexual aggression and vindictive murder that leads to his cell in the clinic. With penis poised, in a mockery of the subtextual rationalizations indulged in by the movie folk that surround him, he pursues thoughts philosophical. He stands over the naked body of Raine Robinette while the image of his teenage gym-dream Ava Gardner leads to the mystery of time and the nature of its perception. He then sits "gazing down at her, my thumbnail against my teeth, thinking of the queerness of the present here-and-now moment," and concludes that "other times belong to someone or something or oneself. The present is something else. To live in the past and future is easy. To live in the present is like threading a needle." And suddenly he is struck by the figural lesson shared by screenstar and locker-room longing: "It came to me: our great locker-room lust had no relation to the present. Lust is a function of the future" (Lanc:253).

And so it is, alas, for the man that he kills. Lost, as far as Lamar is concerned, in a timeless impersonation of movie roles, the victim is trapped in one of those film loops we have found to be so deadly for Nabokov's Albinus, so deadening in the eyes of Fitzgerald's Stahr. Grabbing a knife, Jacoby starts "making wary circling movements, feinting and parrying like a scrappy movie star being put to the blood test by Apaches" (Lanc:261). The human implications of Lamar's actions are thus hidden from his consciousness not just by the "molecular" impersonality of movie technology but also by the conniving shield of superficial movie roles and stereotypes.

The insights into time, space, and identity are again in this novel, as we found in *Quaderni di Serafino Gubbio operatore,* mediated through recording machines and optical refractions. The apparatus, in fact, undergoes narrative condensation in similar fashion as the individual *becomes* the machine which initially was only a metaphor of experience: "I am aware," Lancelot tells his visitor in the mental clinic, "of being the tape head. I am aware of this room being a tape head. That is why it is so simple and empty: so I can be aware. As you can see, it consists of nothing but a small empty space with time running through it and a single tiny opening on the world" (Lanc:111). Or else the individual is unexpectedly confronted with a reflection of himself which, as we have seen frequently before, he does not recognize at first. Lancelot dismisses the implications with revealing understatement:

> I forgot to tell you another thing that happened in the parlor, a small but perhaps significant thing. As I stepped into the parlor with its smell of lemon wax and damp horsehair, I stopped and shut my eyes a moment to get used to the darkness. Then as I crossed the room to the sliding doors, something moved in the corner of my eye. It was a man at the far end of the room. He was watching me. He did not look familiar. There was something wary and poised about the way he stood, shoulders angled, knees slightly bent as if he were prepared for anything. He was mostly silhouette but white on black like a reversed negative. His arms were long, one hanging lower and lemurlike from dropped shoulder. His head was cocked, turned enough so I could see the curve at the back. There was a sense about him of a vulnerability guarded against, an overcome gawkiness, a conquered frailty. Seeing such a man one thought first: big-headed smart-boy type; then thought again: but he's big too. If he hadn't developed his body, worked out, he'd have a frail neck, two tendons, and a hollow between, balancing that big head. He looked like a long-distance runner who has conquered polio. He looked like a smart sissy rich boy who has devoted his life to getting over it. Then I realized it was myself reflected in the dim pier mirror. (Lanc: 67–68)

While in Pirandello and Nabokov the unexpected appearance of oneself on screen leads to a deeper knowledge of that self, Lancelot finds that a self-conscious subsequent look at the mirror does not yield as deep an insight as it did when he thought he was watching a stranger: "I had seen more of myself in that single glimpse of a ghostly image in the pier mirror, not knowing it was I" (Lanc:68). His scopic interaction with his own mirror-mediated image, thus, is in fact a moment that objectifies Lamar (even if it does not quite turn him into language) and alienates him from himself.

Yet the mediation of the mirror yields greater insight into others than does direct observation. The view from the parlor, carefully refracted and framed and also, one may notice, safely distanced from the viewer by choice, reveals to Lancelot what the state of intimacy between his wife and Merlin is, and what they think of him (shades of Moravia's Molteni, echoes of West's Homer). And all this revealing insight is made possible because of the blessings of carefully analyzed instrumental mediation, as noted by Lancelot: "It was possible," he says, "standing with my back against the door, to hear the diners and by moving from side to side to see their reflection in the dim pier mirror on the opposite wall. The images traveled some fifty feet, thirty feet from diner to mirror, twenty feet back to me" (Lanc:51).

Yet seeing with such clarity gives rise to ambivalence and guilt. The mirror reverses its points, and Lancelot is aware that what seems clear, objective, and analogous to reality may in fact be the wrong way round. His clear view of himself, for one, leads to the realization that *this* modern day Lancelot does not look bad, as does the knight of yore banished to the woods, because he had been "discovered in adultery with the queen." If Lancelot du Lac looks as seedy as Lancelot Lamar, the cause is the opposite (a mirror image?): "It was not so much the case of my screwing the queen as the queen getting screwed by somebody else" (Lanc:68). However, finding out what is what, and whether an action externally similar but morally appropriate is in fact taking place, is not easy. The alternatives of love and lust obsess Lancelot, and a mirror mediation will not suffice to give him an answer: "I had to make sure of it. Love and lust should not be a matter of speculation. . . . Why is it so hard to make certain of a simple thing?" (Lanc:138).

One reason, of course, is that people (actors especially) do not behave in ways that reflect any true intention or genuine character: they cannot be "read" with certainty. Raine acts seductively towards him, but Lancelot cannot tell whether she means it. He cannot tell if she is even paying attention to what she does: "Raine kissed me with every appearance of pleasure—what is she? actress? flirt? wanton? nice affectionate girl?" (Lanc:158). Dana, in the process of embodying the outsider Christ, is "an optical illusion"; as a person, he is "a trick." Lancelot perceives that "his beauty was not only accidental and that he had no part in it but that he didn't even credit himself with it. He was like a hound dog wearing a diamond necklace" (Lanc:159). To Merlin who directs him Dana is an empty shell to be filled by a role: "Thank God for the movies, Dana gifted? He barely had sense not to drown when he fell off his surfboard in *Beach Blanket Bingo*. But look at him, isn't he something? We can create him from the beginning like a doll. I created Dana—Dana himself is nothing, a perfect cipher" (Lanc:155). For Margot, who is less gifted even as a blank cipher, the dilemma involves getting lost in a series of receding mirrors: "She was . . . not a good actress. What she was doing was not acting, that is, imitating someone else, but acting like an actress imitating-someone-else. She was once removed from acting" (Lanc:154–155). Readers of Plato know how far that is from true reality; readers of Debord how even further from the "seemingly lived."

The problem is far-reaching since it involves one's access to a full range of emotions, as well as one's ability to have a recognizable self-identity. It is a sad state of affairs when actors can register more emotions than ordinary people by now can experience: "Love . . . hatred . . . jealousy. What do those old words mean? Emotions? Were there ever any such things as emotions? If so, people have fewer emotions these days. Merlin's actors could register fifteen standard emotions and not share a single real feeling between them" (Lanc:95). Janos Jacoby's emotions are supposed to define his character, but do they? "He was either volatile fiery French-Polish or he knew how to act volatile fiery French-Polish or maybe both. Maybe he was from the Bronx. His accent varied—he had been an actor too and so didn't know what he was" (Lanc:115). This intercultural impersonator goes to great lengths in explaining his allegorical transposition of the film's plot by stressing the difficulty he is having in "translating" his thoughts into English:

> "What starts out as rape . . . comes from his own—how do say, being caught—"
> "Trapped," said Margot. . . .
> "The girl through her own femaleness, feminineness, what? . . . That's the nice swing, what you say, switch. . . . It is the aristocrat in this case who has the life-enhancing principle and not the sharecropper, as is usually the case, since he is usually shown as coming from the dirt."
> "Soil," said Margot
> Was he from the Bronx or Brno? (Lanc:119–120)

For Lancelot, apart from the fine social comedy involved in such impersonations, these acts of garbled communication are too removed from the fundamentals of human interchange. Therefore, once in the clinic, he starts an "experiment" in communication theory with the girl in the cell next to his. The basics of this process have to do with the basics of human feelings at their least ambiguous:

> She won't speak to anybody. And has to be force fed. Like me she prefers the solitude of her cell. But we communicate by tapping on the wall. . . .
> Communication is simple when you are "in love." Driving with Lucy Cobb through the Carolina summer night with the top down and the radio playing the "Limelight" theme, one could say to her simply:
> "I like that, don't you?"
> And she would say: "Yes."
> With the girl in the next room it is the same. Yesterday I tapped twice.
> She tapped back twice.
> It might have been an accident. On the other hand, it could have been a true communication. My heart beat as if I were falling in love for the first time. (Lanc:11)

But soon doubts start creeping into Lancelot's mind. As she answers more complicated patterns Lancelot realizes that even this kind of communication is not clear. "Was it communication? If so, what kind? Two chimpanzees could do as well." As with the double-text readings of the filmmakers in his mansion, a doubt lingers: is this a real message? Is it being understood or is the recipient's reaction just a passive response followed by mechanical imitation: "Is that communication or imitation? Monkey see, monkey do." The girl next door could be passively responding to the stimulus just as do the passive and uncritical film audiences of current film theory. "Perhaps the girl is lying there, a hopeless idiot, her eyes vacant, her knuckles straying against the wall, like a two-year-old child lying in bed" (Lanc:36–37). To resolve the issue Lancelot invents a complicated code designed to test his interlocutor, but the result is delayed and inconclusive.

The fundamental assumptions of communication are here contrasted unfavorably with any kind of mediated exchange of meaning. The mediating surface in Lancelot's experiment is a wall, but it might just as well be the movie screen that brought Lancelot to this clinic. The problem resides in the mediation itself, he explains: "You see that is the point. To *make conversation* in the old tongue, the old worn-out language. It can't be done" (Lanc:89). Finally, one has to assume the risky ambiguities of full, direct communication: "Yesterday I simply got up, went to my door, opened it, and went out in the hall—the first time I had done so voluntarily—and walked ten feet and there was her door. I knocked on it and went in. (Sometimes life is simple!)" (Lanc: 113). Face to face with each other, having chosen to shed the "screen" of the wall, having questioned the right of those rooms to function as an apparatus (be it tape recorder, be it measuring tape) in which humanity is but a Pirandellian cog in the machine, the two finally talk.

But life is not always this simple. The ambivalence and ambiguity that pervade human contact are not an attribute confined to the unpredictable interaction of multiple subjects. The same uncertainty characterizes individual human perception as well. We recognize this in the charged and guilt-ridden character that the act of "seeing" manifests in Percy's novel. The guilt of Lancelot's father, the violence of his society, his wife's adultery are all viewed with what he terms (in a most Augustinian fashion) "eye-lust." Of the evidence that his father took bribes during his tenure in political office, what Lancelot remembers most clearly "is the sight of the money and the fact that my eye could not get enough of it. There was a secret savoring of it as if the eye were exploring it with its tongue." He generalizes the act of seeing as a kind of self-sustaining act: "When there is something to see, some thing, a new thing, there is no end to the seeing." As it runs out, this way of looking applies to all kinds of horrible occurrences: "Have you ever watched onlookers at the scene of violence, an accident, a killing, a dead or dying body in the street? Their eyes shift to and fro ever so slightly, scanning, trying to take it all in. There is no end to the feast" (Lanc:42).

The fact that such curiosity is fraught with guilt and with punishing consequences is not surprising if we consider the Catholic mold of who it is that is writing this novel. While much of what Lancelot Lamar experiences can be read through the filter of modernist ideological and psychoanalytic filters, this particular eroticized generalization of the eye that seeks transgressive knowledge is steeped in far more ancient fears about seeing, far older questions about the "good faith" of an inquisitive eye. Much as St. Augustine warned, Lancelot's metamorphic metaphor (an eye that licks!) demonstrates that "lust of the eyes" implicates "sense-experience in general." All sense perceptions are "incorporated," now as they were then, into the language of sight. More tellingly, we still question in what seem to be Augustinian terms the consequences of such ocular lust. The lustful drive for knowledge leads to the forbidden zone. The man from Hippo could have been watching Lancelot's television screen when he asked, "What pleasure can there be in the sight of a mangled corpse, which can horrify? Yet people will flock to see one lying on the ground, simply for the sensation of sorrow and horror that it gives them" (Augustine 1961:242).

As I anticipated in my discussion of West, Percy is here also updating the lust of the watchers. His narrative articulation glosses further a situation in which a "critique which reaches the truth of the spectacle" allows us to notice that, while "the spectacle" seen on its own terms seems to be "*affirmation of appearance and affirmation of all human life, namely social life, as mere appearance*," in fact that same spectacle is nothing but "visible *negation* of life . . . negation of life which *has become visible*" (Debord 1983a:¶10). By placing Lancelot's guilty and lustful watching in the early sixties in the United States, Percy provides the historical moment that stimulated the formulation just quoted. Every day as Lancelot and the nation sat down to watch the evening news,

> We were wondering who was going to get assassinated next. Sure enough, the next one did get killed. There it was, the sweet horrid dread we had been waiting for. . . . One came home with the dread and secret expectation that the pace had quickened, so that when the final act was done, the killing, the news flash: the death watch, the funeral, the killing during the funeral, one watched as one watches a lewd act come to climax, dry-mouthed, lips parted, eyes unblinking and slightly bulging—and even had the sense in oneself of lewdness placated. (Lanc:74–75).

The conflation of human catastrophe, political violence, and erotic voyeurism is by now familiar in a context of filmlike vision. It seems, as we found before, that beyond the contingencies of historical circumstances, it is elicited by the very situation of watching.

But this "eye-lust" seems to be destined to remain unfulfilled: a secular and quite modernist update of the warning given by St. Augustine. When Lancelot finally *sees* through his video cameras the evidence that is contained in his version of *cinéma vérité* (it is he who gives this genre designation—one that describes the ultimate attempt to produce reality in film—to Elgin's pornographic "double feature"), he has obtained nothing at all:

> I didn't see what I wanted to see after all. What did I want to see? The money in my father's sock drawer? Why was it so important for me to see them, Margot and Jacoby? What new sweet-horrid revelation did I expect to gain from witnessing what I already knew? Was it a kind of voyeurism? Or was it a desire to feel the lance strike home to the heart of the abscess and let the pus out? I still don't know. I knew only that it was necessary to know, to know only as the eyes know. The eyes have to know. (Lanc:255)

9

You Can't Imagine

Puig: "Dark Inside the Movie House"

The experience of Moravia's Molteni illustrates the powerful ability of personal wish and individual projection to become "real" in our mind. With a great immediacy that affects life, so does the murderous fantasy of Percy's Lancelot Lamar. These instances of what might be thus termed the "mimetic-effect fallacy" are of a piece with what we have found from the outset of this study, be it in the ways Gubbio and his colleagues cannot keep the movies out of their lives, be it in the similar confusion of the characters in the novels by Nabokov. But more than in those instances, Moravia's scriptwriter and Percy's bystander illustrate the conscious yet self-deluding ambivalence inherent in the interaction between spectator and spectacle. Such instances (that of Molteni especially) lead us to consider that if personal projection is this powerful in the absence of contributing stimuli (the "ghost" image of Emilia in the boat is not even "present" through a mediation such as that of celluloid) subjective projection is that much stronger when activated and abetted by the experience of cinematic viewing. If Molteni, a self-conscious and educated adult, can fall prey to such imaginative concretizations, one should not be startled to find that a simpler audience (culturally unprepared and of lesser age) would come to see no distinction at all between individual inner stirrings and images on the screen.

Such a distinction between "educated" and "naïve" audiences was foreshadowed by Nabokov's film experiences as a child. Film spectators such as the latter may well ultimately see quite directly, as is the case with young Toto in Manuel Puig's *Betrayed by Rita Hayworth,* their own unformed, inchoate subconscious in projections on the screen. In fact, Riccardo Molteni's final conclusion about his own projection ("it seemed almost impossible to search out the dividing line between dream and actual reality") is just as applicable to the young Toto. Molteni, after spending a long and intense time in the presence of what seems to be his wife, is left puzzling out intangible distinctions among levels of reality: "What had really happened at the precise moment when I lay down on the little beach at the far end of the cave? Had I fallen asleep and dreamed that I had been with Emilia, the real Emilia of flesh and blood? Or had I fallen asleep and dreamed that I had been visited by Emilia's ghost? Or again, had I fallen asleep and dreamed that I was asleep and dreaming one or another of the aforesaid dreams? Like those Chinese boxes each one of which contains a smaller one, reality seemed to contain a dream which in its turn contained a reality which in its turn contained yet another dream, and so on *ad infinitum*" (GaN:243, Disp:225). Lancelot, as we saw, is just as explicit: "I didn't see what I wanted to see after all," he states. If he is able to qualify this experience with less subtlety than the Roman scriptwriter, Lancelot nevertheless realizes more clearly than Molteni that it is a particular kind of knowing that counts: "I knew only that it was necessary to know, to know only as the eyes know" (Lanc:255). If his guilt retains echoes of Augustinian suspicion about the pursuit of secular science, his modernism does not.

Isherwood, Fitzgerald, West, Moravia, and Percy set their stories in a world that is more or less actively engaged in the making of films, and some of their characters exemplify the film viewer's dilemmas by being aware of or even by resisting the spirals of solipsistic projection. Manuel Puig in his novel takes us to the opposite end of the spectrum, from producers to consumers. Like the Paris audiences in Isherwood, the midwestern watchers in West, the black man on the beach in Fitzgerald, and the target audience envisioned so differently by scriptwriter, director, and producer in Moravia's novel, the film audiences in Vallejos have very little to shield them from the aggressive claims of the screen.[1] In Puig's setting, far more extreme in its cultural deprivations than Rome, Berlin, London, or even Los Angeles and New Orleans, spectators lead a life so impoverished of hope and so devoid of imagination that the appeals of "one-dimensional ghosts" that "dance between their arclamps and our skull" come to them as a form of relief.[2] As week after week the latest musical, melodrama, or gangster movie makes its way from Hollywood to the far reaches of provincial South America, we find an audience that needs more than most to graft such dreams onto their lives. We find also one spectator who represents the ultimate in receptive posture. This is so not only because of education, social status, and cultural context. This particular spectator is unusual because of his age. Yet if at first young Toto may seem at the mercy of these cinematic projections (an argument against letting little children go to the movies), in the end we find him to be just as creative in his readings as we have found young Nabokov to be. Toto too makes a positive effort to gain control over the invasive nature of these materials.[3]

Toto (six years old when we first find him groping with images on screen) cannot tell where reality stops and imagination takes over. His reading of the images on screen is totally solipsistic. This is rendered mimetically by the run-on formal texture of his soliloquy (a stylistic choice that blends the free association of the stream-of-consciousness novel with the syntax of dream and of the cinema) and made explicit by the child's own words: "Mommy!" he says at one point, "did the movie begin already and is it dark inside the movie house?" (Betr:37). He does not possess the critical distance to notice to what extent his experience of everyday life is also "like a movie." It too is a stream-of-consciousness flow that reflects in its structure the total present and the undifferentiated presence of everything in the film text. The conflation of film perception and private experience is almost total in the unformed psyche of this child and turns him into the one spectator (among the many that we are examining) who displays an evenhanded perception of either side of the screen. He accepts as a given the situation that Pirandello's Nuti and Nabokov's Ganin took as extensions of consciousness. While such critical distance was made possible by their double role as actors and spectators, Toto achieves it in the end—more admirably it seems to me—from the singular subject position allowed to spectators.

The fact is that by introducing us to a spectator so young, Puig can exemplify to what extent the basic features of film discourse correspond to the primitive structures of childish perception. It is thus that in this novel we finally find a condensation of the cinematic apparatus that explicitly figures forth the analogy between the structure of film and the subconscious that at least since Münsterberg's 1916 monograph has been a leitmotif in the theory of the medium. More recent work on the nature of child development tends to illuminate some specific commonalities that explain young Toto's use of film quite well. In Piaget's theory of early child development, the subject is said to respond to everything in the surrounding world by turning it into a sign meaningful to the self. It has been pointed out that much of what Piaget says about an innocent experiencing of the world can be applied to a typical spectator's perception of the world as it appears on screen. Toto at the movies illustrates this, for instance, by adopting "the images on the screen as if they embodied his own pre-cognitive experience" (Andrew 1976:55–57). The stories that he watches, the documentary he sneaks a look at (despite his mother's warning), even the intertextual "montage" between musical and cartoon that he creates by himself—all of these turn out to be reflections of his own childish obsessions.

Even more specifically, the materials that derive from one particular documentary film that Toto sees, just as Piaget's description of perception in the child would suggest, "emulates as closely as possible the physical characteristics of that for which it stands" (Andrew 1976:56). While the ostensible content suggests the kind of run-of-the-mill footage we all recall from Disney to Cousteau, it soon becomes clear that the subaqueous fauna and flora of the nature film become for Toto the mysterious, threatening, and ambiguous genitalia he is trying to understand in real life. Nothing for him (in life and on the screen) is other than what it appears in its fully realized condition: what Piaget calls its "terminal state" (Andrew 1976:56). Life and the movies are a continuous "montage" sequence, and at most what the child can do to keep up with it is to tell it as he sees it. The "syntax of inner speech" which the cinema reproduces is indeed in control of Toto's life at age six: a collage of images decides the logic of its continuity; cause and effect are explained, as by Piaget's children, by "the visually associated elements in juxtaposition." Above all, the coherence of things "exhibits a basic 'synchretism' which clusters numerous elements into a single event" (Andrew 1976:57).

Totally unrelated facts such as the death of a bird, Toto's half-understood sexual worries, his guilt over playing at his uncle's funeral, his conflict about his parents' afternoon nap, in conjunction with the curious and aggressive sexual gropings of older children, the frustrations and displacements of adults (Toto's father's rage and aggression, his mother's disappointment and escapism), added to the maid's primitive understanding of sexuality and taboo and her threatening story of a gypsy kidnapping a child—all of these elements are made one in the image Toto sees on screen of sea plants swallowing a school of fish:

> Mommy didn't look, the murder movie is scary and somebody comes into a dark room and the murderer's behind the door and Mommy and me we didn't look because it's a scary movie and before the long movie once they showed a short movie about the bottom of the sea and Mommy lowered her eyes because there is a plant that moves in the nice clear water at the bottom of the sea and it has hairs that wave like streamers but "Don't look" and I looked, I was naughty when the little fishes with many colors came close and went right next to the carnivorous plants at the bottom of the sea. "Swear by your mother you don't know what big boys do" I swear it I don't "When the boy climbs up to the roof while I'm sleeping he takes off my blanket and fucks me." What does "fucks" mean? "It's a bad thing that you can't do, you can only make believe, because if a girl does it she's lost, finished forever." Instead of not looking I looked because in the nice clear water at the bottom of the sea those hairs like streamers that wave come together all of a sudden and the fishies coming in between the hairs get caught. "Don't ask any more, I'm not going to tell you" naughty Pocha doesn't want to tell me what the boys with the hairs did.... (Betr:32)

The filmgoing occasion fuses in a most "egocentric" manner several of Toto's crucial experiences: from the way that a perfectly conventional gangster movie reenacts for him the fears of crossing the threshold behind which his parents "nap" ("once I woke Mommy up during nap-time because I'm bored and Daddy 'I never slapped you but the day I put my hands on you I'll break you in two'" [Betr:29]), to the way in which the roles of masculine and feminine are fuzzily confused in his mind and the act of sex is fraught with overtones of menace and mutilation. But in dealing with the confusing materials, the boy does not lack initiative. He suggests that his friend Pocha reverse roles with him in order to learn. He manages to be slapped by the housemaid for trying to see what effect calling her "fucksface" will have. No information is available from adults, he finds out, only sudden violence. Thus he must in the end rely on his own immature resources and internalizes everything into a highly synchretic fantasy that radiates out of an imagined escape from the pointer-wielding schoolteacher whom he also has called "fucksface." His jump from the window, however, is prevented by his tail, grown when he told a lie to his father about going to the men's room at the movies and which is now entangled in the teacher's legs:

> Now the tail is longer than ever and I can't jump and the teacher's getting closer and closer with the pointer in her hand! If Felisa comes into the kitchen to give me another slap I'll jump out and get away because she doesn't have a pointer and I'll try so hard to make a giant jump out the window, so's not to fall into the park pond and you have to watch out since there may be fucks bushes at the bottom. And I jump . . . and I'm almost flying . . . the gypsy's corral is on the other side of the pond and do I land inside? (Betr:36)

In a series of footnotes to his subsequent novel, *Kiss of the Spider Woman*, Puig offers some explanations about his views on the early development of sexual identity. These throw "retroactive" light (ironic as these notes may at times be in the context of the later novel) on the character of Toto. The remarkable thing about this film viewer is indeed, as we have said, his extreme youth. But even more remarkable is his precocious understanding and his creative appropriation of what he sees. Toto *notices,* in life as well as on screen, far more than he is able to absorb at his age. This is what helps to form him (despite the difficulties in his environment) into what he becomes, as we follow him, at the ages of nine, fourteen, and fifteen. This instance of "individuation through cinema" is an extreme and extended case of a genre-specific theme we have encountered before. Puig's dramatization of the deep influence film may come to have for many as we evolve into who we are raises this particular thematic trope of the film novel to a new level. In *Betrayed by Rita Hayworth* it is at the core of the story.

In Toto's particular case, this kino-genetic ontogenesis intersects with a particular kind of family structure. In the home situation, as Anna Freud is quoted as saying in Puig's aforementioned notes, "it is generally the precocious development of the intelligence and sensitivity of the child which can actually induce too strong a repressive activity in the same" (Kiss 1979:130).

Toto does indeed notice far more than the average child would in the same circumstances. Such a child (his cousin Héctor is an example) would not register the discrepancy (pointed out by Anneli Taube) between a primitive and brutal father and a submissive mother. It is crystal clear, on the other hand, to Toto, who is thus drawn to a mother whose "world . . .—tenderness, tolerance, and even the arts—will turn out to be much more attractive to him, especially because of the absence of aggressivity" (Kiss 1979:208). His father Berto, while technically present, is as close to being an absent father as one could find. As his figure leaves its intermittent trace in the book, the little we know of him suggests qualities and behaviors that are characteristic of the kind of repellent father who, in this theory of sexual individuation, may impel a son into overidentification with the mother (Kiss 1979:137–138). The father thus presents an Oedipal threat to his son that confirms Berto's threat of physical violence when Toto interrupts the afternoon "nap" of his parents.

That outburst of violence, one should note, occurs in the context of an episode describing Toto's attempts at a sexual individuation that is characterized by a conventionally heterosexual scenario. From Toto's stream-of-consciousness flow one picks out, for instance, an image such as "the wedding pictures in the photographer's window and Mommy doesn't it make your mouth water?" Yet the Oedipal conflict, even before it is chillingly turned into fatherly threat, lurks all around. It appears in Toto's merging of filial rebelliousness with a sensory inquisitiveness that echoes Lancelot's licking eye: "Daddy called her and Mommy had to go in to take a nap. And the only thing I'm going to cover is my mouth. I don't want to cover my nose with the scarf, I won't obey." It also explains the boy's need to point out that the Norma Shearer that he imagines while the troubling smell of lovemaking emanates from the bedroom is "never naughty" and in her wedding dress looks like "a nun with a white costume." In the midst of this maelstrom of immature feelings Toto argues with a mirror that (surprisingly congruent with its individuating role in examples we have discussed before) prompts the child to ask, "Who's looking at himself in the glass?" Yet the other figure reflected in this mirror is not the reassuring mother in the act of supporting her individuating child. It is a threatening figure that Toto is prompted to reject. "It's not him," he says of his father's image (Betr:28–29).

The evidence of one's eyes is explained away at the prompting of one's feelings (don't we all do this at times?) by the use of an irrelevant peripheral element: the poncho that the father wears. Yet the rejection has more fundamental reasons. Berto's threat transforms him explicitly into an evil agent and in the child's mind he finally merges with the image of a murderous gangster, like in the movies. The flight of Toto from his father is reinforced further by reasons other than an Oedipal scenario that is quite common and usually transcended in the course of time. Berto alienates the boy where it really counts in the process of individuation, especially through his enthusiastic and invidious approval of Toto's insensitive and conventionally masculine cousin Héctor.[4] Toto's reaction is further active rebellion to this modeling, against what Anneli Taube calls a world of the father that is characterized by such things as weapons, competitive sports, and disdain for sensitivity because it is a feminine attribute. It is thus that the boy refuses to learn to ride a bicycle, to become a junior soccer-league ace, or to restrain himself from crying when his baby brother dies (Kiss 1979:207).

Traces of Toto's precocious awareness and of this primal scenario can be seen especially in the artistic manipulation of film materials in which he engages, even as early as age six. This is the other side of the coin in the nature of this remarkable film spectator who, beyond the immature inability to tell the real from the imaginary, finds the resources to take "writerly" possession of that which possesses him. This ability will culminate in his remarkable retelling, at age fourteen, of Julien Duvivier's *The Great Waltz*. But even his accounts of earlier film experiences (he is six at this point) are seen and understood by the young boy in their generic distinctions and for the imaginative role models they offer him. It is a writerly precocity that allows Toto to gain some control over their impact and to "use" the films to help with the impact of life.

The range of genres that Toto notes and that he is able to use in what characterizes their essence is striking. It spans musical film, cartoon, and documentary and offers a rich choice of possible relations to reality of which Toto is well aware. As he scrambles a musical with Fred Astaire and Ginger Rogers—*The Story of Vernon and Irene Castle* (1939)—with Disney's *Snow White* (1937), he also makes it clear that he knows full well that he is making it up:

> And Felisa "Tell me what happens in the musical" and I told her lies not that the two of them danced alone and the wind lifted up her dress and his coattails, but that some birdies came flying along slowly and lifted her dress and his coattails because Ginger Rogers and Fred Astaire rise in the air to music, and the air carries them high with the birdies who help them twirl faster and faster, what a pretty flower! I think Ginger wants it, a white flower high up in a tree and does she ask a birdie to get it? and the birdie makes believe he doesn't hear her, when I want to give them breadcrumbs they get frightened and I have to go far away. Are they afraid of me? And of Mommy too? but there's a birdie who's the kindest of all and when Ginger is not looking . . . he flies over and cuts the flower from the tree and puts it in her blond hair and then Fred Astaire sings to her that she looks pretty with the flower and she looks at herself in the mirror and has the flower that she wanted in her hair, like a barrette, and she calls to the good birdie to come to her hand and pets him a lot. Felisa believes every bit of it and it's a lie, just in *Snow White* all the birdies are friendly, because it's an animated cartoon, when it isn't an animated cartoon they can't make the birdies

come to their hands since they're afraid, Choli's pigeon is not afraid, but the birdies are prettier. (Betr:29–30)

The sober analysis of the limits of representational conventions in the staging of live actors and the drawing of cartoons is clearheaded and mature well beyond what one might expect in a six year old. Yet we can see the overdetermination caused by strong feelings and darker anxieties as the description slides from Ginger's wish to Toto's. If the introduction of the birds seems initially caused by the child's naïve need to account for the "special effects" of the musical that seem to be in contradiction with the "realist" contract that resides in the use of live actors, it reveals itself just as motivated by Toto's worry and guilt over the death of a real bird that he tends to equate with that of his mother's baby. Being "kindest of all" and "good" and "prettier" does not save baby or bird in real life, only in the wish of this youthful spectator as he appropriates the materials of film. Yet he knows, as Felisa does not, that it is a lie.

It will take several years for Toto to achieve some control over the slide of desire. Even by the time he submits at fourteen his retelling of Duvivier's *The Great Waltz* to the annual Literary Essay Competition, we discover the solipsism of sudden shifts to first-person perspective that characterizes the example above, as well as the unaccountable digression into the "science" of things that is lurking already here in the "explanations" about the difference in genre conventions and that links Toto to the technological distancing of disturbing subjects that we found in Percy's Lancelot. It seems to be Toto's trait to fall back on empirical overdetermination at moments of stress. It happens with greater explicitness than with the birdies from *Snow White,* for instance, when, at the age of nine, his zoology drawing of a bird transcends the decorum of his age group and of the pedagogical codex of his teacher to insist with great detail and embarrassing redundancy on the creature's genitals. This is a period of latency in Toto's life when he is groping to control the stresses of sexual and social identity. He continues to do so, one notes, by "making use" of cinematic materials.

In the same "montage" fashion that we have seen applied to *Snow White,* he grafts his emerging feelings for a young man (Raul) onto his need for a stable family and comes up with an imaginary scenario that mixes several film genres. This time (Betr:72–73), in order to create the credibility of a genre convention that is Raul's favorite and thus is most likely to be "inhabited" by the man that he likes, Toto ends up choosing a gangster film as one of these ingredients. The other genre in this "meeting" of Raul and Toto is the latter's own favorite: a film musical. Stereotypical feminine subservience to the leading man is evident in the third genre of this montage as Toto, fainting in the snow near "their" cabin in the Canadian wilderness, describes himself as a damsel in distress in the act of being rescued by Raul ("with all his strength he can kill the bears"). If this particular damsel is still offered a very masculine glass of beer to recover, it becomes clear that Toto at this stage of his development reveals culture-specific feminine traits that take refuge (perhaps to "explain" these impulses with a modicum of social decorum) in the manifestations of maternal caretaking functions. Given the conflict between what is expected of him by society and what he is obviously feeling about his sexual identity, it is thus not surprising that his self-narrative does clear violence to his beloved films more decisively than ever before. Note the radical rewrite of *The Great Ziegfeld* (1936), the result of which allows Toto to cast himself as a bellboy who takes care of an ailing Luise Rainer.

Is this boy becoming a writer under the stress of rending conflicts about "correct" and "true" sexual individuation? This seems to be so, and it seems, moreover, to be occurring at the intersection of verbal and film discourse. One notes that it is repeatedly in this chapter that Toto underlines what turns out to be the key narrative vehicle of Puig's *Kiss of the Spider Woman*: the extensive verbal account of movies. On the occasion of seeing the movie that is tagged in the novel's title (*Blood and Sand* with Rita Hayworth) Toto states, "We could talk all during supper about the movie, and isn't that like seeing it again?" (Betr:69). And even the Canadian cabin mentioned above is envisioned as an isolated and enclosed setting (does it anticipate a prison cell?) in which "every night I'd tell him the plot of a different play" (Betr:72).

Yet to reach the verbal authority of Molina, the protagonist of the later novel, Toto's creativity must transcend the guilt that at age six he feels about this kind of creative appropriation. His affective grasp must also grow beyond the latency-specific queasiness that hovers about the films associated with Raul, who, one notes, consummates his love for the girl in the movie with great explicitness, an uneasiness that characterizes the film in which Rita Hayworth, after all, is "a pretty actress but she's always betraying somebody." One notes that by age fifteen at last, Toto has fully claimed the liberating effect of imaginative appropriation. To some, such as the piano teacher who resents his fanciful "reading" of Chekhov's "The Madman," he still seems to be "lying" (Betr:234–235). She cannot understand "why a boy who has everything in life, or is going to have everything," has to change "a story that is already sad enough." But Toto by now knows better, as is shown by the film he recounts to Herminia and in which the Oedipal hate of a cruel father finds "adult" translation into the ideological codes of philosophy and religion. He may be in fact trying to teach the old spinster the "healing" functions of a textual interpretation that (transgressive as it may be to the literal surface) helps to transcend one's particular sadness by "reading out" the subtext of a story that (just like the roots we suppress of personal pain) "seems" to have nothing to so with us. It is a lesson that we can watch Toto learn in the most remarkable example of his creative appropriation of cinema.

The musical biography of Johann Strauss that he writes a year before these exchanges with his piano teacher is the most fully developed example of Toto's growing aesthetic control and of his understanding that genre provides a foundation for individuating role play. It seems as if by now he has understood that, submitted to "writerly" readings, the generic formulas of film stories are meant to provide models for coping and storyboards for living. Gubbio's stereotypical views of others, Albinus's genre-bound resolutions, and Faye Greener's cliché dreams are the kind of imaginative building blocks that Toto uses to make sense of life. The world of Duvivier's movie responds to Toto's genre-tuned descriptions with its lively details:

> That hot night in Vienna, the people didn't feel like going to sleep. Strains of a gavotte issued from the windows of a great ballroom but the heat was too much for even such a sedate dance as the gavotte, and the tenants of the neighboring houses, whether smoking a pipe, playing chess, or leafing through a newspaper, were gnashing their teeth they were so tired of listening to the same old music for twenty years straight. (Betr:207)

Setting, soundtrack, gestures, and further developments unfold in a "safe" genre-bound way to tell the story of the bold invention of the waltz by Johann Strauss and of his subsequent rise to fame.

But the scenario must also accommodate the sudden emergence of personal fears and insecurities that the love episodes in the film seem to trigger in Toto. As the famous Russian singer Carla Donner arrives unexpectedly in the company of "an officer of His Majesty's Armed Forces," we hear the words of Johann's song, of which she gives an impromptu rendition (Betr:209). These words may seem at first to conform closely to the saccharine verses typical of such music, but upon closer inspection they turn out to hide Toto's own "different and sad plot." He explains that "the poetic lyrics say that dreams sometimes come true and that a face so beautiful it can only be imagined may suddenly appear so close to you that you can caress it, her fair skin, her coral lips." But then he veers abruptly away from the ordered listing of this Petrarcan *blazon* into self-conscious quotation ("'her green eyes'"). The "real" words suddenly slide into what can be only the boy's own repertory of associations and questioning: "'—the emerald sea—where I submerged look for what? what is it lovers look for at the bottom of the sea?'" The question cuts like a knife to the core of Toto's (and our) cinematic memory. It turns into the lilting song of a present waltz that young Toto (too young to comprehend) saw long ago side by side with his mother. Deeply moved, we watch the emerging form of confused and unresolved Oedipal yearnings as Toto (like a demented editor who has dropped all his film strips on the floor) grafts the fragments of sea beds long gone to the demands of beds present that he cannot yet fully grasp.

Personal motifs such as his childhood mixup between lovers and "fishies" keep drifting into Toto's retelling of the film. Here is the son who does not eat and therefore may not love his family; here the baby who died as a consequence of this; here the pears his mother "was going to cut" from a tree on which the dead bird lives; and here is the kitchen wall covered with the same soot that the gypsy kidnapper had on his face. Finally the main conflict of the story brings matters to a head in a fashion we recognize from the previous times that Toto would "start telling . . . the stories in the movies." It reveals the boy's continued conflict with his father. Carla Donner turns out to be the mistress of the political figure most admired by Johann Strauss: "If he hadn't been what he is, a musician," Toto stops to explain, "Johann would have wanted to be a brilliant politician like Hagenbruhl" (Betr:211). Yet, as it turns out, he is the very same officer who beats Johann for making a drunken pass at the singer. In the figure of Hagenbruhl, "violent monster" and "political idol" coexist in the same uneasy balance that characterizes Berto. But Toto now can imagine that no more need he stay cowering outside the bedroom; no more need he nurse the ailing "good girl" after the fact. The boy who is choosing to be an artist rather than a man of power and politics elopes with the singer. As Toto recounts the story further (as we depart further and further, in fact, from the film by Duvivier), he clearly tries to make a stand by exposing Hagenbruhl's sexually degrading brutality as it starkly overwhelms his paternalistic role of "monarch who has done so much good for Vienna" (Betr:222–223). Yet Toto has problems of his own in the bedroom.

Toto executes these dizzying creative detours in a sequence that is notable for the use of highly controlled and stereotypical elements of genre films the detailed renditions of which slowly and subtly make space for his own concerns. We start with reassuring conventionality:

> Streaks of white light filter through the trees, trying to imitate the white of Carla's myriad gauzes, the tireless horse trots on rhythmically and the coachman turns round and says "good-day." "Good-day," they answer, and they've finally found the right words, "good-day," a good, beautiful, sweet day to come. Other dwellers of the woods announce their presence with sounds like the bleatings of sheep and the horn of their shepherd which grows louder in its echo. Goodday, day, day, day, day, and without a minute to lose the coachman pulls out a hunting horn answering with his not quite tuned notes "I love you" the coachman says to the woods, love you, love you, love you, and Johann frantically wonders what it is Carla expects from him, him, him, him, and Carla says "only one of your waltzes could make me forget the morning voice of the woods," woods, woods, and Johann already begins to feel inside a new melody, that is to say, the voice of a new waltz. (Betr:211–212)

Such control through form, such displacement through aesthetic activity cannot last forever. Toto's anxiety is nicely anticipated by Johann, as the composer is said to wonder "what it is Carla expects from him, him, him, him": sexual fear to the tune of an emerging waltz! This anxiety further colors Toto's rendition of the film whose innkeeper (in truth a charming Viennese) becomes "the malicious landlady" that "takes them to a shady apartment" (Betr: 213). But it is when Johann is finally confronted with the need to perform as a lover that the spectator's seemingly safe subject position collapses into the rift of failing sutures. The figure of Hagenbruhl appears in its absence to "take over" as a model of competence (to impose the traces of his brutality). "How should he act?" asks Toto, attributing telling doubts to a character that does not reveal any such thing. "They still haven't even kissed, Hagenbruhl must have kissed her, and perhaps also made her his, they've certainly been lovers, that harsh man, with abrupt manners, rough features contracted even more by his monocle, has put his paws on Carla's delicate body" (Betr:213–214). Finally Johann disappears altogether, as Toto's "script" breaks down in a paradigmatic paroxysm of cannibalistic fantasy. This is so close to his childhood conception of sexual consummation ("what is it lovers look for at the bottom of the sea?") that his ultimate slip from third-person narration to first-person questioning is not entirely unexpected:

> Will Johann have to kiss her like Hagenbruhl did? taking her forcefully by her slight shoulders, leaving purple marks on her white flesh, which means that the squeezing has hurt her skin from inside, has provoked wounds under the epidermis and the purple color comes from the breaking of veins and arteries which amounts to small internal hemorrhages. And that's only the beginning, when Hagenbruhl has become wild as an animal perhaps he has also used his teeth, and must have bitten her, and then better not to think of the final outrage, his fury certainly must not have calmed down till he saw blood run, and she, weaker and weaker, must have had little strength to defend herself, and was probably his victim several times, the victim of the raging executioner who wants to see blood flow. But how could Carla have given in to such a thing? There is something that escapes my understanding, some fatal secret. (Betr:214)

This is clearly *not* a sequence that belongs in the syntagmatic continuity of *The Great Waltz*. It is, rather, an imaginary sequence that exemplifies to what extent the character's inner obsessions take over in the midst of a formal exercise (the school composition) which is meant to reproduce the safe and controlled surface of a genre film. This safety, however, must make recourse to the resources of genre by reaching out beyond the confines of a single representational convention. Thus the objective details of the documentary genre in the scientific explanations that account for the red marks under Carla's skin and the wondrous theory and symbolic interpretation of the color white. They seem a bit incongruous, in this case, just as incongruous as the attempts at self-protection through technological distancing had been for Toto's predecessors in the film novel. Yet they make their point in their dissonance, just as mixed genres often make their point in their mutual enrichment through harmony.

The resources of film genre are thus used by Toto to cope with reality and provide a key to the articulation of his experience throughout the book. They help just as much (albeit at a much more primitive level) with the hopes and rages of other characters in the novel. Even with them films provide resources for the resolution of inner conflicts by opening up an imaginative arena that is wider than the characters' narrow horizon. As Michael Wood has aptly put it in his review of, among other books, *Kiss of the Spider Woman,* it is not so much that Puig considers movies "true . . . to the thin dreams of glamour we usually associate with them." They speak, in his view, "to the emptiness and solitude the dreams are supposed to disguise" (Wood 1980:43–47). Very much like the two-level critique of film we have found in Nabokov and in West (an overall skepticism about the flimsiness and anemia of film fantasies, but deepened by the awareness that the needs they speak to are not to be scoffed at), Puig's use of film articulates the seriousness of its role in people's lives. It is Wood again who phrases it pointedly when he discusses the protagonist of Puig's *The Buenos Aires Affair*: "Gladys, like everyone else in her world, is lulled and charmed by movies, songs, poems, and political promises which hide their truths even as they tell them. The point, of course, is not only that such consolations are part of the problem, but that they are the only consolation going."

With Toto we have seen, however, that this dependence on what Wood suggests to be the consolations of a popular culture (a consolation that has taken over the opiate sting of traditional religion) is anything but passive. It is as if the boy is able to incorporate the elements of film into his growth. He is able, in fact, to make the elements of film work for him as he would any element drawn from "real" life. A quick look at the other characters in the novel suggests that they do too, if with far less creativity than the talented Toto. This may take the form, for instance, of Héctor's contemptuous stream of invectives against the world, against girls, against culture, and against the homosexual boarding school teacher according to whom "French movies with those ugly sagging broads are the only ones for intelligent people." Nothing could be as different from Toto's almost too informed analysis of preferences and archetypal models found in film than his cousin's scoffing simplicity: "And he asked me what actress I liked the best and he almost shit in his pants laughing since I liked Ann Sheridan, because she has a good pair of udders he says, getting bugged because I was moving away on the edge of the bed while he read the *Kama Sutra* and bull Ann Sheridan is good all over and isn't she a good actress?" This is simpleminded, perhaps, yet Héctor seems to know that film is a referent for cultural preferences (sexual among them) and is stubborn in defending his own choices, mainstream machismic as they may be.

For Toto's boarding school companion Cobito Umansky (seething with rage, loneliness, and pain), films provide a very dangerous "consolation" indeed. They fuel his barely suppressed violence with uncontrollable images of grandiose brutality. Into these everything (even his justified suffering and his love and admiration for his dead father and for one of the school monitors) is subsumed. His monomaniacal dedication to gangster movies and his uncritical absorption of their modality is a study in contrast with Toto:

> I'm staying alone I don't give a damn, with my shoes dirty and the supervisor on Friday before class "So-o-o-, shoes unshined . . . and fresh answers" bastard, and right to Sunday black list, but at nine thirty and a half-minute when the doublecrossers are back, a bullet in their legs and they're goners, a kick in the belly and their mouths bleeding they kiss the dirt on the Chicago alley, and another harder kick right in the stomach so they'll spill out the secret of the metal gate and all they had for lunch at home I'll bet on top of it some jackass hit the soda fountain in the afternoon, what do you think they ordered? a triple-decker banana split, in *one* plate, for *one* guy, shoving it in, the bastard, and with one single kick I'll make him spill it out, yeah man, Joe will dash into the garage the minute they spill out the-secret-of-the-tightly-shut-metal-gate that only opens if you step on the key tile of the sidewalk. And I charge in while the doublecrossers are still twitching in agony, what a bunch of fucks, huh? with family in Buenos Aires and gorging themselves on Sundays and to top it all off they finked out on Deadly Joe, who stepping into the hideout carefully checks out the passageways and. . . . (Betr:168)

Rather than provide consolation, the films that furnish Cobito with his materials offer images of violence with which to dress up his individual brand of emptiness and solitude. They do indeed speak to it, but only to intensify the feelings and only to make it impossible for the boy to let the good feelings (hope, self-assurance, admiration, love) provide some balance. Even his burgeoning sexual fantasies end up in violence and brutality (not to speak of his attempted rape of Toto), and his attraction to the Monitor Big Chief as a role model ends up (we find out later) with an attack (he puts excrement in his shoes) that gets Cobito expelled.

But of course the point about the movies in Vallejo is that more or less everyone is affected by them. All the inhabitants depend on the distant glamor of the movies (the same "amour and glamor" that nourishes West's citizens of Purdue) to dispel the gloom of a dusty and depressed provincial town. But it is the creative and manipulative use of movie plots that we see in Toto (rather than the passive and escapist one of the others) that we find to be at the core of Puig's other major film novel, *Kiss of the Spider Woman*.[5] Its protagonists too, almost as if they were two alternative extensions of Toto's interaction with film, use the retelling of movies as a means to communicate and, as the story advances, to grow as human beings in real life through the mediation of films.

Puig: "Lots of Lovely, Lovely Films"

None of my previous chapters have included an extended comparison between the novels we are examining and their film versions. The main reason is that such comparisons are not likely to enlighten us about the literary source, other than by providing data about a thoroughly "cinematic" reading of texts. Since these, as my study has established, lay claim to the film-effect with greater intensity than most texts, one would expect such comparisons to yield consistent evidence about the dialogue between media-specific discourses. In fact, however, most film versions, rather than responding with consistency to the cinematic elements inherent in these novels, vary widely in their awareness of this aspect of their source or even in their emphasis on the nature of the cinematic apparatus. Most disappointing, in a way, is the version of *Laughter in the Dark* that Tony Richardson filmed in 1969. For reasons that should be clear after my reading of the novel, the film could easily have turned out to be a dizzying cinematic display without having to abandon a detailed reading of the text. As it is, the film is pedestrian and uncinematic in the extreme. By contrast, the "faithless" rendition of *Il disprezzo* by Jean-Luc Godard (1963) provides ample proof that what I have been discussing in this book is not just a twinkle in one watcher's eye. Despite Alberto Moravia's staunch insistence that the Godard version is a "good" film that unfortunately has little to do with his novel, there is ample evidence that in fact what Godard has done is to mine the literary text for some of the discursive elements that are at the center of the film novel as a genre.[6] A Moravia-Godard comparison, however, is not strictly necessary for the purpose of revealing what I am discussing in this book.

On the other hand, the case of Babenco's *Kiss of the Spider Woman* (a film I much admire) is far more revealing. The "failures" and "compromises" that are found in the film are of a kind that highlights what is new and original in Puig's most extensive attempt to incorporate film into his writing. A comparison thus allows us to examine this particular case of the intersection of film-specific discourses with more precision than would be the case if we looked at the novel just as literature. My reservations about the film version go to the heart of what I consider the particular feature that distinguishes Puig's novel from previous examples of the film novel: its representation of the "voiced narrative" of film.[7]

While some of this can already be seen in *Betrayed by Rita Hayworth,* where the stream-of-consciousness technique allows us to "hear" reports of film experience in the subject's "voice," it is only in *Kiss of the Spider Woman* that we find the narrative of film as a primary dialogic vehicle between two characters. Accounting for film experience matters here as much for what it "means" to each character as it does for what the films objectively contain. It is thus important, in the economy of the novel, that these films *not* be seen.[8]

They must be mediated in elaborate ways by Molina and (eventually) by Valentin. I realize that it would have been difficult to "sell" a film to a wide audience if it merely consisted of two characters retelling each other the plots of films. For one thing, and in view of what we have found about the film-effect in the film novel, this would cause an audience extreme anxiety since it would amount to a redoubling of the absence-effect of film. It would mirror, in fact, the doubling of frustrated desire that we have found at work in the film novel as genre.

Yet such a version would retain the representation (and actual experience) of a "desire for film" that is at the core of this genre and that is also an explicit theme in this individual manifestation of it.[9] While it would not be justified to reproduce this situation in a film on the grounds of its presence on "generic" grounds in the film novel, in this case the loss has to do with something that is present in Puig's novel as theme. What in fact is at issue in the exchange between Molina and Valentin is more than the "precise" version of one film or another. Showing the audience filmed realizations of Molina's accounts cannot but help provide "irrelevant" precision. It masks the fact that what matters to Puig is what the one (telling) derives from the film through his idiosyncratic reading and what the other (listening) may be able to perceive of it.

This structure of exchange raises the process of mediation that we have encountered throughout this study to new heights. The details of the exchange also make it clear that the nature of this mediation is now out in the open. See, for instance, how Molina responds to Valentin's objections to a film account that the latter considers to belie verisimilitude. Yes, Molina admits, of course he embroiders the films.[10] But the purpose is to convey more faithfully what it is he had seen. Molina could well say, in the words of Stephen Heath, "I have often been confronted by critical summaries that are unashamedly false to the manifest discourse—the body—of the film . . . but which nonetheless (and it is this that is significant) answer exactly to the narrative image, to the negotiable meaning: errors then, but correct errors, perfectly in accordance with the hold of the film, helping it to achieve and sustain consistency, coalescence" (Heath 1981:134). Molina, of course, lacks the critical vocabulary, but his point is well taken. In the film version of the novel it is this crucial verbal control over the filmic codes that is sacrificed.

A further telling difference between novel and film version (understandable perhaps on the grounds of "budget") is that of all the narrated accounts of films that we find in the first, only one (the Nazi film) remains in the second in its entirety.[11] This is a serious flaw because yet again it elides what is central in the novel and necessary to achieve its meaning. I am referring to the counterpoint created by the juxtaposition of various films. It is this that provides the precise kind of intertextual polyphony sought by Puig. It is only thus that the network of meanings (ironic, political, psychological, sentimental) speak out in this novel. It is in fact only through the discursive disjunction orchestrated by the tellings of films that Puig can underline how the genre-specific subtexts of different kinds of popular film may enrich the spectator's experience; how much one stands to lose by dismissing them in the name of high culture. The psychological and moral truths that are implicitly acknowledged in the parade of film genres that transect the literary discourse of this novel (a particular version of the intramedial character of film novels) cannot speak out if the gaggle of genres is mutilated. Much thus is lost. Take, for instance, the most effective discourse (and most accurate truth) that Valentin picks for Molina, despite the marxist's resistance (almost to the end) to the "poetics" I am describing. While Valentin starts out as the kind of genre-specific character who illustrates suspicion to film on ethical grounds (we have encountered his kind before in the film novel), he learns his lesson well if he can ultimately choose the spider woman to personify Molina. It is, alas, symptomatic again of the failure in the film version that this choice is transposed to Molina himself. Babenco thus evades the insight that it is through the mediation of film that the most comprehensive meeting occurs between the two cellmates. It is especially sad that it should be a *film* version that misses the point.

Beyond this, the reduction of Molina's verbal accounts to instances of specific film representation, and the excision of most of the films in favor of one, reduces the range of "possible stories" that this novel contributes to a tradition still closely wed to a wish for univocal and "precise" cinematic mimesis (I may, alas, be guilty of this myself in my impatience with the film version of *Laughter in the Dark*). The elimination of open-ended "reading" and of the "forking paths" of narrative flow also encourages a notion of spectatorship according to which cinema triggers merely one, individual "interior monologue."[12] Yet, as we have seen, both aspects of the film novel (be it formal mimetics, be it the "translation" performed by an internal voice) are ultimately just limited versions of the medium-specific syntax of film (as it reaches for reality, as it affects people). In a broader sense, this amounts to a new kind of paratactic compulsion as well as to a "specialized" kind of iconic intensity. It is a genre of discourse, in other words, that is ever after the trace, ever after an attempt to "put into words" cinematic experience in its raw form. What, if not this, are we to make of the verbal montages of crazed urban environments, of the word-driven tracks and cross-fades we have repeatedly found in these novels? What of the genre-specific "turning into words" of an experience (cinema) that is totally new to human experience? Thus if Puig, in the end, makes creative contributions to the poetics of this narrative genre, one of them resides in the transformation of Eichenbaum's interior monologue into a dialogue.

Puig elaborates, in fact, a veritable "poetics" of the act of narrating film. Initially this is still posited upon the private interior *monologue* of a single character, as found at the origin of this specialized form of storytelling. Witness the episode in which the two prisoners, momentarily at odds because of political disagreements and physical indisposition, plunge into their own personal film accounts. At moments such as these, the syntax and the iconography hark back to what we have found in previous novels: imitation of the synchretic nature of the apparatus-as-dream (a place within which we owes no whys and no wherefores to nuttin' and nosbodies). But even in these sections one can recognize the evolution from monologue to dialogue: Molina reacts, unwillingly as may be, to the critical conscience that Valentin has been demanding of him; Valentin, for his part, intersperses his private version of a film he heard from Molina with the kind of personal imagery he used to resent on ideological grounds. In a sense, however, the "private" nature of these moments intensifies the loneliness and imprisonment that characterize the condition of both protagonists in this film novel.

The prison (the cave) has become quite literal, at last. The only way out, paradoxically, is through the discursive disjunction that is implicit in film as it is in the kind of novel we are dealing with; disjunction that was used as a vehicle for closure in previous cases too. In the ending of this novel the very question of closure (is it just that, or is it an actual escape?) is left quite open. Yet at least the "need" for an opening is made explicit in *Kiss of the Spider Woman*, just as it is foreshadowed in Puig's earlier film novel. In *Betrayed* it is young Cobito (we met him but a few pages ago) for whom escape from this kind of prison is found within a film that reveals how to open the "tightly shut metal gate" which "only opens if you step on the key tile of the sidewalk." He, as the two cellmates in the real prison, needs to gain control and gain the initiative in a situation that will not allow him to. All of these characters thus share the need to exercise a modicum of control in situations in which the "materials" are recalcitrant. Often the imagination is the only way out.

Toto, as his version of *The Great Waltz* demonstrates, gains an almost masterful control over the materials of film by the time he is an adolescent. Lancelot, on the other hand, finds that the clarity and control he wishes to attain by the use of the medium escape him, even as an adult. Yet none of these characters are in a situation as extreme as that of the two prisoners in this novel. It is this extremity, it seems to me, that puts into question the viability of the notion that discursive coherence can ever make up for a pandemonium of empirical data. This may well be the implicit lesson of *Kiss of the Spider Woman*. Despite the interesting opposition between Molina and Valentin—a dialogue that tries to disguise the fact that they both hold to a version of the same notion of discourse over story (be it the discourse of film narration, be it that of ideology)—the outcome is the same. It confirms in both cases that escapes such as that of Nabokov's Hermann are made at the cost of entering entirely into the dimension of discourse. Such entry, Puig and his predecessors seem to imply, predicates individual disintegration: a loss of reality similar to the one that overtook Serafino Gubbio so many chapters ago on the train from Sorrento.

Puig's novel thus takes to new levels of complexity many of the genre-specific features we have encountered from the outset. If, to give another example, Lancelot discovers the conflation of medium and "look" to the point of identifying the ultimate complicity between the viewer's look and the look within the film, in *Kiss of the Spider Woman* this "psychology" of spectatorship becomes an element of plot endowed with the full complexity of recent film theory. Molina is in fact an example of audience (and so is Valentin) who comes to the screen fully aware of the reality of "subject position" and who is able to play along with it. If anything, as I pointed out, the notion of cinematic "entrapment" is unmetaphored and becomes the reality of a prison. It is film that promises the only way out. What in earlier novels in the genre had been a conceptual extrapolation becomes here primary material (empirical data) of story: a prison cell that entraps two individuals who seek to escape its confines by "generating" cinema; a spider woman who entraps in the webs of her film stories, not unlike the camera-spider wielded by Serafino Gubbio. The contradictory effect of seduction and aggression that cinema embodies (another kind of notion that more often than not needs to be extrapolated from the film novel) is here personified by the interaction of the main characters.

There are times, in fact, when in *Kiss of the Spider Woman* the distinctions between what is story and what is discourse blur into each other much in the way we have seen before in such moments as the ending of *The Day of the Locust*. One notable instance is the difficulty that Molina has in making a clear distinction between the discourse of self and the discourse of film. In this he is not unlike Toto, who, as we saw, tries, despite the odds, to maintain control over the pressure of contamination. As I put it for Toto, and Lancelot, and Molteni as well, we can say that the conflation of film perception and private experience is almost total. Just as with Toto, then, it is doubtful if even Molina can tell the difference. Valentin's critique of Molina's way with the discourse of film, promising as it might seem, is not undertaken in the name of maintaining the difference. He too, as we said, comes to films with the claims of an alternative discourse. Moreover, Valentin is just as vulnerable to the regressive invitation of film as is Molina.

Yet there is progress too, since Valentin's critiques do enter the medium in "writerly" fashion, without doing an injustice to the integrity of the films themselves. He discovers in films the kind of meaning that Isherwood's Bergmann and Moravia's Rheingold were seeking in clumsier ways. If Percy's Merlin and Jacoby provide a skeptical counterbalance that warns us about the need for good faith in such endeavors, we are still left with the fact that Valentin's critical interventions do affect Molina. He even shows some progress when compared to Puig's own Toto. Molina finds patterns *in* the films that respond to his sexual strains, rather than writing himself *into* the films as does Toto with the story of the bellboy and Luise Rainer.

The difference between Toto and Molina speaks of progress on another level too. It has to do with a process (a "story") that is central to *Kiss of the Spider Woman* and that illustrates the productive possibilities of a genre trope such as the one that links the mechanism of film with that of human individuation. I am referring to the journey of regression and reindividuation that is taken by Valentin, a journey that implicates and is implicated by film as well.[13] We have seen often, in fact, that the two are connected. Such is the case with Homer Simpson's film-structured primal scene trauma. Such is the case with Lancelot's allusions to his false individuation at the hands of a wife who assigns him his identity on the basis of movie roles, quite like a casting director. Percy in fact implies much the same (is it meant to be witty?) in his prefatory disclaimer to *The Moviegoer*: "every character, except movie stars . . . [is] fictitious." The cost, as is often stressed in the film novel, is high: in the case of characters such as Percy's Lancelot and West's Homer Simpson, the confrontation with the cinematic apparatus leads, as we saw, to clinical regression.

Valentin's regression is quite dramatic as well, although in his case it is only one half of a journey that provides a return ticket as well. It is also true that in his case the apparatus at cause (beside the enveloping one of cinematography) is explicitly that of political repression. Its violence forces the prisoner all the way back to the physical manifestations that often go with psychic regression: the loss of bowel control. Valentin is in fact reduced to a diapered and whiny baby, whimpering to his mothering caretaker: "I don't want to die." It is at this point that the reader finds out about Molina's (mother's) complicity with the political apparatus. What a shock to face betrayal at the very moment Valentin has regressed to the time when trust is absolute and caring must be true. Need I point out, at this stage in my study, the homology with the film apparatus that also "betrays" at the very point of deepest trust, while the subject is lulled into childlike regression?

Yet at the same time we also find out that Molina is shielding his cellmate from this betrayal, and at great personal risk. The ambivalence of the role here played by Molina certainly suggests (given Puig's stress on the political and developmental framework) that Valentin is confronted by the good and the bad confusingly embodied in one and the same person. This is indeed the inevitable split to be bridged at several points on one's journey from helpless baby to fully individuated adult ("I'm a big boy now, right?" [Kiss:192]). Is it possible that for Valentin, as for us all, nurturing and safety can derive from the same individual who is involved in complicitous embrace with his master's voice? In fact Molina, flawed parent as he may be, goes on to preside over a veritable healing that returns Valentin to his rightful identity—with a difference.[14] After feasts of food from Molina's "real" mother (the ambiguity of the split is maintained, however, at the level of story as well as that of subtext by the fact that the food may be either from Molina's real mother or from the jailer, whose role Molina may wish to hide from Valentin) and after a transition marked as "teens" by a first cigarette and a first random erection, Valentin seems to have changed. It is a small detail, but significant: for the first time he asks to hear the "end" of a film. His reindividuation has thus returned him to the status of a "normal" spectator prepared to play the appropriate game with the hermeneutic code. The journey, in other words, is a further step in the evolution of narrative situations such as the episodes that describe Nabokov's individuating teenagers at the movies. The continuity is confirmed by the flood of questions that follow and that culminate with Valentin's exhortation about the need to stand up, the right to demand respect for what one is. Here finally it is Valentin who validates Molina's wounded sense of self: fair exchange for the return journey his cellmate has nurtured.

From this true exchange of gifts (nurtured in its turn, it should be noted, by exchanges based on film) grows yet another result: the "role" reversal that, having endowed Valentin with some of the qualities of Molina, allows the latter to grow in his own right and leave (leave home?). This is the meaning of the scar that seems to transfer from Valentin to Molina after they make love: a "peripheral detail" that would have delighted Nabokov, Monroe Stahr, or Rheingold. It is now that Molina acquires the kind of enhanced perspective on himself that recalls previous specular shocks: his friends from before appear to him, in this new light, as merely "a bunch of mirrors." The process continues outside the prison, where Molina actually "grows" into Valentin's role. To individuate in this way on the basis of his new role model, he has to achieve separation for real: from his mother, from friends, from his beloved waiter to whom he explains that he is going away with "another boy." The other boy, of course, is none other than his new self. Yet Molina still "dresses up" for the part, like a character in a movie. This is not, however, so much a parody of Molina's limitations this time. Rather it seems to be an admission that wearing the right clothes is a "positive" element of individuation through modeling. Molina does not "lose" himself in an impersonation, this time; he does not enter a movie in which he is always the heroine. Yet his choice of the symbolic over the imaginary costs him his life. There is a final irony in the balanced way with which at the end of the novel Molina walks into Valentin's "dream" of political commitment (and dies) while in prison Valentin escapes from torture (it seems while dying) by walking into one of Molina's film dreams.[15]

If the film narratives themselves have contributed to this process of reindividuation, and if they have suggested a way out, it is in the terms described eloquently by Linda Dittmar. "From goddess to martyr, from panther woman to zombie woman," she points out, "Puig's women sustain the Molina-Valentin courtship; they enable teller and listener to form and reform their identifications" (Dittmar 1986:83). While Dittmar reads much of this as part of her thesis about the redefinition of female desire, she seems to reach beyond this focus to embrace a redefinition of identity as well. These women, as she says, "make essentialist definitions of Woman give way to a materialist analysis of oppression as it operates within socially constructed ideology. Puig's text sets in motion a prismatic speculation about the archetypal feminine and problematizes that same speculation. Undermining the possibility of an archetypal construction of gender, it exposes instead the complicity which locks victims and victimizers alike into the dominant ideology" (Dittmar 1986:83). Dittmar describes the process as it affects Molina and Valentin in terms of "identifications" between various cinematic female roles and the two protagonists. It seems to me that what she describes is in fact part of a process of "reindividuation" made possible by the "writerly" treatment of film plots by Molina and Valentin. Even conceding Dittmar's reservations about the success of such reindividuation for Molina, it seems to me that Valentin's challenges to Molina's narratives and Molina's "education" of Valentin's cinematic literacy illustrate her point about women's challenge to "readerly" texts (a point I would extend, as indeed Puig seems to do, to both genders). They illustrate, that is, how one's "first step toward self-definition as desiring and narrating subjects rests on the recognition that the prevailing theories of imaginative production and reception are, like all paradigms, culturally constituted and subject to change" (Dittmar 1986:84).[16]

As I mentioned above, the novel (written at a time that film theory has reached new levels of sophistication, a time when the subject position appears in explicit guise in such popular fare as *The Naked Gun* [1988]) presents us with a range of "cinematic presence" that transcends both *Lancelot* and *Betrayed by Rita Hayworth*. At the same time, it deepens the narrative articulation of issues raised by film theory. As in *Betrayed,* we don't have the presence of actual filmmaking. In a way that is closer to *Lancelot,* however, we find a strong insistence on the full range of the cinematic apparatus, be it as it appears on screen, be it in such discursive manifestations as the promotional Nazi pamphlet. As a novel, in fact, *Kiss of the Spider Woman* uses the juxtaposition (the disjunctions) of inconsistent discourses to forestall generic closure. We have even seen that this works across two texts in Puig's own production, since the footnotes to this novel throw a retroactive light on *Betrayed by Rita Hayworth*. The gap that is opened by the promotional pamphlet in juxtaposition with the lovingly told plot rendition of the Nazi movie that it promotes raises more questions, in fact, than it answers. Does the film itself "show clearly" what it is? In this sense the Nazi film could be seen as a subtle critique of "any" ideologically aware filmmaking, since the "value" of its reading depends entirely on which side one chooses. Being "ideologically aware," therefore, must not be allowed to become a "story" of its own, to paper over the "contradictions." Thus Puig takes the film novel one step further, since he questions the *nature* of what is seen not so much for its perceptual-existential dilemmas as for its ideological ones.

While it may seem at times that the novel articulates a narrative version of several film theories (we note the opposition between lack and desire inscribed into the exchange between the cellmates and in which Valentin insists that no food and no women be present in the movies recounted by Molina), the fact is that the novel mostly juxtaposes Molina's view of film (the gender-centered passion for genre) to that of Valentin (a conventional view of film as social critique).

If indeed, as Barthes has put it, "to tell stories" is "to engage in a search for one's origin" (Willemen 1974/75:69), Molina's retelling of films is a journey in search for the self that takes him beyond the level of plot. His choice of genre (and Valentin's perceptive casting of Molina's self in a horror movie) indicates that he is quite perceptive about the true meaning of conventional structuration. As Robin Wood puts it, "what is repressed (in the individual, in the culture) must always return as a threat, perceived by consciousness as ugly, terrible, obscene. Horror films, it might be said, are progressive precisely to the degree that they refuse to be satisfied with this simple designation—to the degree that, whether explicitly, consciously or unconsciously, they modify, question, challenge, seek to invert it." Were this to seem only peripherally applicable to the situation in the cell, we need go no further than Wood's earlier remark (about *Murders in the Rue Morgue*) that "it is as if the Monster were waiting to be released by the kiss" (Wood 1985:215, 207).[17] It is the radical subversion of sexual conformity adumbrated in these genres that attracts Molina, as well as the poetic rendering of "otherness." Paradoxically, the politically aware Valentin cannot read this at all (he who should be sensitive to texts that subvert conformity) until instructed by the spider woman herself.

Molina's use of genre (his film theory) assumes that it provides a gain, rather than reduction, in specificity, quite in the spirit of Nabokov's remark that details are always welcome. Moreover, the gain of details goes well beyond the schematic structure of "narrativity" as such offered by the genres that Molina admires. Puig thus articulates in narrative fashion yet again (and does so with a vengeance) the interesting paradox of theory we have discussed before: that genre is not necessarily an example of "lack" of originality or a betrayal of idiosyncratic uniqueness as long as we recognize its use value; as long as we acknowledge the radical relevance of the subject's appropriation of the structure. Molina's "tellings" are a unique narrative displacement of the theoretical notion that genre films (and by implication, of course, all genres in all media) function productively in the realm of their "reception." In this case, since the personal reading is actually staged (as opposed to fishy hypothetical journeys by readers of various kinds), one can see "in action," as it were, to what extent a critical view of genres that stops at their schematic, external patterns is insufficient.

Valentin's film theory, on the other hand, harks back to the double-text readings we have encountered before in *Lancelot* and in *Prater Violet,* with the difference again that we find it now well within the conscious reach of what one might regard as the general public. Even Molina eventually admits with exasperation that he knows perfectly well how to read fascism into a Nazi propaganda film—should he wish to do so, that is. The "optional" nature of such skill indicates (more than Valentin's indoctrinated Brechtianism) that what Isherwood had to explain gingerly to his family may be taken for granted by now. Yet the optional nature of such erudition opens up the very danger of trivialization that Molina avoids with his genres: to Valentin's angry point that the romantic lead of Nazi Germany is a torturer, no different from the men who are holding the cellmates now, Molina declares, "I can't imagine." "No, you can't," responds with chilling closure Valentin. Valentin's kind of film theory is there to point out that there are important and real consequences which the "storytelling" indulgence of Molina may well ignore. Fantasies are no escape, unless they provide a real key to open the real prison's gate (Cobito's "key tile").

The "story" of the dialogue of these two theories of film, however, turns out to be ultimately about the subtle exchange that takes place between the two extremes: Molina starts to question the nature of his own investment in the velvet trap, while Valentin becomes increasingly able to respond to a wider range of elements present in the cinematic exchange.[18] It is because of this that an ideological confrontation such as that between Percy's Lancelot and the screen is here raised to new levels. It starts to absorb into the actual details of narrative development some of the qualifications and ambiguities (as well as the contradictions) of recent film theory.

Part Five

Conclusion

10
The Return of Genre

Kiss of the Spider Woman illustrates a new stage in the articulation of film discourse (and discourse of the apparatus) into story. While Lancelot's television monitor provides an anticipation of the conflation (the inseparability) of discourse and story in the context of film; while it even illustrates a new awareness of this union in the protagonist's attempt to find a "genre" for what he has videotaped ("Friday Afternoon at the Movies: A Double Feature"), Lancelot's attempt to impose a "story" on the inchoate images that he finds on the monitor stops short of Puig's way of involving the readers in *Kiss of the Spider Woman,* where they find themselves personally implicated. Lancelot's balancing of story and discourse is one we observe from the outside. We must participate, on the other hand, as Molina's discourse aspires in itself to be genre. Genre-distinctive characteristics of the film novel thus occur in *Kiss of the Spider Woman* within the very flow of discourse that connects reader to story.

We too are "listening" to Molina's films and trying, just like Valentin, to let the triggering film-effect of narration bring them back to life. These films work as whole narrative entities (intertextual, intramedial) within the body of the novel. Rather than finding, as one did in earlier examples of the film novel, a discourse straining to suggest the cinematic apparatus, this novel presents films to us as such . . . just films. We as readers thus also come to share the full range of film-theory issues with the characters, as opposed to "watching them" (one does this in previous examples of the film novel) while they experience film and its theoretical implications as part of a narrative. In *Kiss of the Spider Woman,* the genre-specific reader posited by the film novel, rather than just being involved in working out genre-specific topics at the level of a "story," finds that s/he is being engaged at the level of "enunciation." Yet even this level becomes part of the narrative, for if the digressions into the "science of things" (the discourse of technology) plays an essential narrative role for Toto, for Molina and Valentin the "escape route" (the *Exit*) that Puig's later novel offers runs through the awareness and foregrounding of cinematic "enunciation" (camera, staging, music). It is in this film novel, finally, that the discourse of film actually seems to become the discourse of literature. One may well ask what kind of genre the film novel has finally become.

To Lancelot Lamar's words "the eyes have to know," this new stage in the evolution of the genre adds Valentin's focus on "hearing" Molina's movies. Once he is "educated," in fact, he insists in doing so to the very end: "Come on, what happens?" (Kiss:185). Embracing thus the two primary modalities of cinematic perception (vision and hearing), the film novel expresses with succinct eloquence and with narrative diversity a pressure characteristic of twentieth-century culture: the need to control closure in a universe the plot of which we cannot trust to contain consolatory coherence. Gubbio, as is clear by now, is not alone in his need; nor is this need confined to the immediate world of cinema.

Prater Violet illustrates in its opening moves the kind of extrageneric productivity that film novels encourage. Its thinly veiled simile between the components of the cinematographic apparatus and another means of mediation (the telephone) illustrates this very well. Within the general picture of the genre, as I explained, this occurs because the wide cultural effect of film makes it easier to detect, even in extrafilmic situations, significant components of the apparatus. But well beyond that, Isherwood catches the vitality and license that cinematic productivity tends to unleash. As he stands by in awe (and some embarrassment) at Bergmann's cinematic appropriation of his host country and of the people surrounding him, director and scriptwriter both invoke the specifics of formal mimetics to underline the nature of this productive outburst (PrV:68). In terms of the energy that such a thematic invocation of the stimulating energy of film transfers to the novel itself, witness the narrative strand that explores Isherwood's own fear of artistic castration at being exposed to such as Bergmann. Important areas of his first-person narrative are generated when he reacts to this, as we saw, with extensive segments that aspire to the state of discourse of film. The specific realizations of this aspect of the film novel that we encounter here raise issues of discourse-specific hermeneutics (is the "cinematic" reading-out of physical appearance reliable?) and illustrate the durability (productivity) of the culture-specific film style (UFA "Stimmung") we encountered before, but translated here (intertextual disjunction) to a London that accommodates it rather haltingly.

Thus, the mixture of genre-specific elements, as one can see, is quite original. It is even more so in the subtle introduction of several "witnesses" who in turn provide a filmlike foreshadowing of Bergmann. This overlapping film-effect provides a "typical character" inserted into the literary text through the agency of what might be called "second level" spectators. Thus, the narrative of spectatorship is clearly thematized as well as generalized to underline the relativity of multiple points of view, a relativity that undermines reliability further by emphasizing the clichéd nature of modern vision. This critical view of what spectators are able to see is, in this example of the genre, linked directly to the most explicit treatment of film theory found in our sample. Occurring, as it does, late in the novel (and therefore after the cycle of debates about what film is, could be, and should be—*better* be, given the political situation in Europe—has run its course), Lawrence's report about the Parisian spectators provides a significant "rear view mirror vision" of all the previous situations we have encountered in this genre in which the demands, pitfalls, and illusions of spectatorship were invoked.

In a way, the originality here derives, it seems to me, precisely from what may seem to some as a "lack" of narrative productivity: the bare explicitness of the debates. But in fact, what this shows is that some of the more specialized ("erudite") aspects of the cinematic apparatus are now available (have been incorporated) for the purposes of plain narrative dialogue. Film theory has ceased to be exotic. As a consequence, a story may well be just about it. It has also entered the contested territory of political choices that it maintains to this day. There is no need, I am sure, to reiterate the details of this particular narrative realization of film theory. I would just add that in terms of the correspondences between the evolution of the genre and the cultural history within which it takes place, *Prater Violet* is symptomatic of the meeting in European culture between cinema and a host of lively debates on the aesthetics of other arts. It also captures in a narrative format several strands of discourse about film and about film theory that are still lively and important today. The integration of such cultural, symbolic, and ideological codes into narrative is as tight as the representational instance of Bergmann's film-mimetic staging of a German political trial and its ideological implications; tighter still, if we consider the implicit commentary (parodic simile?) in the person of a British secretary who witnesses it all, and does not understand what it is she is seeing.

Genre-specific characters, it should be noted, are also becoming far more differentiated and "specialized." This goes hand in hand with the fact that the film-mimetic style in this last group of novels follows suit by narrowing down its "effect of cinema" to the specialized perspective of individual characters. The film editor Lawrence is an example of this specialization. In his case the result is not, as it might well be, a narrowing down of the focus on cinema (this occurs, for example, with Moravia's scriptwriter): Lawrence is the one who has the last word about the wider social implications of a political view of cinema (do the working-class crowds have any inkling of the "bomb" that is cinema in Bergmann's view?), and it is Lawrence around whom swirls (in a very dramatic narrative rendition, it should be underlined) the most contentious questioning about the fascist undertone of pure formalism clamoring about its own ideological neutrality.

Among these new genre-specific characters one should note the narrator himself: a curious conflation, it seems, of Nabokov's biographical involvement in the elements of the apparatus (but then, let us remember, that even Pirandello stages himself in his novel in the act of visiting Gubbio's film studio) and the fictional characters that have a professional role in the stories. Perhaps Bergmann's vividness is also due to the "real life" model that Isherwood had in mind, as well as to the vitality of the cultural code they both articulate. It is through this readily available "genre" of experience (one that, after all, is the foundation of Isherwood's own international reputation as Berliner) that a host of elements we have defined before as part of the poetics of this genre find their way into the novel: from the genre-specific "kind" of representation of reality that derives from distinctions about the qualitative range of Bergmann's previous work to the polyphony of discursive kinds (literature, theater, philosophy, music, ideology) as well as the plurilingual intertextuality that nourishes his filmmaking.

From the interaction between the two (Isherwood and Bergmann) derives also one of the most original idiosyncrasies of this particular rendition of the film novel. Isherwood's ambivalent identification with the director is articulated, we may recall, at the level of semic mimicry and even bodily merging ("How did it feel to be inside that stocky body, to look out of those dark, ancient eyes?" [PrV:154]). This appears to be a translation of the cinematic mechanism of subject position (wishing for, yet resisting, such merging with the dominant discourse of film) to the context of narrative story and setting. Isherwood is quite explicit about the fear he harbors at Bergmann's attempt to take him over *in whom he is*, something that happens, as we know, within the coordinates of the cinematic apparatus. The narrator proceeds to react, of course, in a genre-appropriate manner. He displays the kind of rebelliousness ("spectators" who do not cooperate with the director; "readers" who introduce their own code) that we have encountered before. Yet again, this particular novel turns this particular trope into narrative. Isherwood refuses in quite specific ways to lend his innermost self to this director, and, given the fact that what is at issue here is the nature of Isherwood's sexual involvement with another man, the "apparatus" (personified here by the director) is in fact attempting to delimit and define the sexual individuation that we have found before to be one of the intents of cinematic subject positioning.

The "writerly" reaction of Isherwood extends also to an immediate attempt (noted above in the context of the productivity of the discourse of film) to take over in the imagined style of the master. What this amounts to, of course, beyond the film-effect, is an instance of the psycho-epistemological yearning—a wish to break through to a vision of inner truth—that has characterized so many instances of the film novel so far. It is understood that Bergmann is endowed with a better vision similar to what Gubbio maintained "could" be had through the camera. As we have seen, it endows with eagle-like knowledge and control even such a representative of unenlightened Hollywood (light years away from the culture of Berlin) as Fitzgerald's last mogul.

A continuity in themes and form extends to many other features of the genre in Fitzgerald's novel, while at the same time giving it a distinctive flavor of its own. "Vision" (the genre-specific narration of spectatorship), for one, is articulated in two complementary ways by Fitzgerald in *The Last Tycoon*: as a narrative problem in the mediated and contested reconstitution of the story itself by Cecilia (the reconstructive challenge inherent in the writerly nature of these novels that we have identified before) and as a special talent that Monroe Stahr possesses and that transforms him into arbiter and controller of what the culture is to see. The specific theme of privileged and controlling versus passive and controlled vision (the theoretical distinction between "point-of-view" and "look") that has characterized the film novel from the outset is here orchestrated through the juxtaposition of two characters. Yet the treatment of the theme is richer still, since, as our discussion showed, the captive, star-struck spectator is able to articulate the opposition. Stahr-struck as she may be, Cecilia is also our readerly source of the symbolic (rather than imaginary) story organization.

On the other hand, Stahr as the novel's ostensible representative of point-of-view vision is often motivated by a merging with the imaginary, a disregard for the rational and the limiting that belies his claimed ability to "read out" the cultural and symbolic codes of America ("take people's favorite folklore and dress it up and give it back to them"). As we saw, his search for Minna's face in Kathleen is fraught with the same kind of ambiguities we have found in many of the writings examined since Pirandello (Gubbio and Nestoroff, Albinus and Margot). In Stahr's case it is clear that, even if his "professional" vision and medium-specific erudition is what it is said to be, the reality that is just beyond the studio gates is quite explicitly relegated to the status of special effects ("a good illusion").

This confusion of reality and film is worked out in a narrative way in the most transparent use so far of the genre trope we have defined as the use of setting as apparatus: Monroe's meeting with Kathleen at his unfinished home. It is not merely that the place is marked as cinematic apparatus by referring to it as a "set." As I noted above, the scene orchestrates elements that are medium-specific well beyond such explicit level. We find in this scene that the fragmentary and unfinished truth of the "reality" that contributes to a cinematic illusion "speaks" of the distinctly cinematic reality-effect; we discover that the subterranean presence of the actual mechanical apparatus ("the trap in the floor for the motion picture projection machine") alludes to the place in the human mind "to which," "from which" it speaks and—perhaps—to the biting pitfall that it represents; and we are encouraged to share (as genre-specific readers) what I called the power of compensatory projection that articulates (Kathleen in fact does so literally) the spectator's complicitous participation in the process of the apparatus.

One might feel that more explicit "settings as apparatus" are found in those instances (Albinus goes to the movies, say) in which the apparatus is apparent and complete. Yet these are not genre "tropes" in quite the same way as the examples above, since it is in cases where the apparatus is not immediately obvious that the power of conceptual productivity in the film novel is able to surprise us with greater (because unexpected) effectiveness. Thus, the extensive representations of Monroe "in" and "of" the apparatus (watching rushes, being the studio auteur) are indeed instructive and fascinating as some of the most articulated instances of the discourse on film and on film theory in the genre. Yet it is moments such as the projected death of Stahr that provide greater insight into the apparatus and its wider repercussions. I don't mean to belittle either aspect of the presence of the apparatus in this novel, however, since as in the articulated juxtaposition of character-vision mentioned above, Fitzgerald's originality in the genre consists in the balance and range that he musters.

It is hard to imagine a narrative episode more effective in outlining what is special about cinematic narrative (while being at the same time a masterful example of literary storytelling) than the "master class" that Stahr provides to Boxley. The very object (a nickel) that comes to be emblematic of the "hook" of hermeneutic questioning in the medium (as well as a characteristic counter of its proairetic momentum) recalls that aspect of genre-specific strategy that we found to be so central in Nabokov's *Laughter in the Dark*: the peripheral detail that turns out to be of central importance. This is an example of what might be termed a cine-semiotic literacy that at times ("pictures have a private grammar") is explicitly stated in this novel. The view from the chemist shop here is no different, in fact, than the view from Margot's window. As with *Laughter in the Dark,* moreover, it is obvious from Fitzgerald's notes that he conceived of episodes (if not the whole novel) in terms of a style that would trigger in the reader's mind a film-effect. Cecilia's description of her tentative wisdom about the movies (something she knew "dimly and in flashes") echoes directly, involuntarily as may be, the very "dark" in the title of Nabokov's novel. Her essay in film-mimetic description, as we saw, is quite literate in the semiotics of film language.

This is in addition to the fact that she stresses the nature of the apparatus (stories put together by committee) before taking charge (as Monroe does with his films) of this particular discursive version of the story. Fitzgerald balances, therefore, Cecilia's tendency to buy into the imaginary with a shrewd knowledge of the details of the medium. Both she and Kathleen, in fact, are given the ability to formulate what in previous treatments of these themes remained unspoken. Kathleen, as I pointed out, recognizes that her own image shares the same space in Monroe's head as the screen images he deals with daily. If anything, it is the producer who ultimately succumbs to the kind of professional deformation we have encountered before, stumbling over (date with the wrong girl) and remaining a victim of (Minna's face yet not) the metonymic syntax of film. He does so even if, as Albinus, he "should" know better: sensitive as he is to the genre loops that his films could become, were it not for his forceful insistence that rules of repetition be abandoned in the name of the different and the new. The realm of genre (or of "quality" film) may well be that of "code." As any code, this may be fixed and circumscribed. But even codes must be productive to sustain themselves. Addressing as he does what we would call the mythopoeic code (as opposed to the ideological code that is invoked in *Prater Violet* by Bergmann), Stahr insists that there is a distinct particularity that must always be sought precisely because one is dealing with convention.

What he is nurturing, in fact, is a public version of the personal individuation that we encountered in earlier examples of the genre. For this purpose he even provides the ultimate in omnipotent camera tropes (the elaborate crane-shot he insists be used). It will lend (as we may surmise from the film theory we have examined before) a subliminal thrill that can inscribe the cultural message into our minds and hearts by employing the muted speech of form. A "national" sense of who we are and where we come from can thus be re-enforced, articulated, and validated by such moments as two children, two books, and a tree. Monroe Stahr's kino-genesis aims to do far more than Nabokov's: it wishes to recapitulate phylogenesis!

It would be tempting to suggest that the same is true of West's final apocalypse. Yet in *The Day of the Locust* we have to deal with the fact that the formal process of story development and the discursive generation of a reality-effect owes more to painting than it does to film. I have stated before that this should be considered a kind of film-effect, narrowed down as may be to the "professional specialization" of the protagonist in this novel. It is a sign of maturity in the genre if the genre-specific characters of the outset (cameraman, director, actor) can give way to those endowed with far narrower professional deformation. In a sense, Nabokov's Albinus anticipates the very same "specialized" professional deformation (although he is not a practitioner in the process of filmmaking as is Tod Hackett). Yet the painterly mimesis of

West's novel does more than that of Albinus: it provides an insightful discursive disjunction and ultimately offers the most spectacular instance in the group of novels we are examining of a plot that finds closure on a discursive rather than narrative plane.

Much as the more conventional discursive disjunction that characterizes Bergmann's wealth of cultural sources, West's rests on the introduction of a wide variety of discursive kinds, each accompanied by its own proairetic imperatives. Thus, the revealing existential wound that is exposed by Harry Greener's "biography as vaudeville act" is "seen to be" (and thus is not quite) sutured by the effective (genre-appropriate) comedy of his act. Do we laugh at the wonderful routine? Do we weep at this man's alienation from the appropriate discourse of identity and personal history? Similarly, Faye's revolutionary song and Adore's blues reveal the true, substantive disjunctions of character and role. Even more, they up the ante since they redouble disjunction: once as disjunction from the main discourse of the narrative, then twice (and more importantly) as disjunction between the substance of the songs (their story, as it were) and the particular discursive realization of those who interpret them. It is only a female impersonator's rendition of a song that paradoxically heals such disjunction, making, as it were, "true" story and "true" discourse homologous.

This is a homology that is, of course, yearned for and missed by West's "watchers," a veritable crowd of genre-specific characters (typical character here expands to a crowd of extras) who yet again confirm a central characteristic of these novels: their nature as narratives of spectatorship. Some of West's spectators may not care that disjunctions exist, happy to be carried along in the hope that discourse and story may eventually come together. Such is the case with the crowd that watches Faye Greener at her party, as we have seen. But other crowds are beyond this kind of delusion. For these "professional" watchers the film-specific fixation has spilled back into life. For them real events have become "genres," canceling out the distinction between "genres of experience" and discursively focused manifestations of film genres. Yet they continue to pursue and to plumb "lynchings, murder, sex, crimes, explosions, wrecks, love nests, fires, miracles, revolutions, wars" for the remaining ounce of sensation they may provide. We find here a curious apocalypse of a genre-specific feature that we noted before: the presence, that is, of elements of the apparatus in extracinematic contexts. The particular nature of its rendition, in this novel, is important and quite new because for the first time it becomes explicit subject matter for cautionary social commentary. The productivity of this evolution of a genre-specific trope can be recognized from its reappearance in Walker Percy's *Lancelot,* where, as we saw, the guilty sensationalism that the protagonist derives from the litany of disasters on the television news is not unlike the catechism of horrors listed by West.

West's version of the film novel thus makes the personification of spectatorship tainted by the apparatus a central theme. It is thematized in the variety of voyeurisms (implicit as well as explicit) that go from Homer's physical placement in the house during the party (Faye articulates its significance in a way that leaves no doubts) to the projection of a pornographic film. It is inscribed in its components into the attitudes of the characters, from Faye Greener's deliberate performance as fetish (stimulating yet frustrating an audience of male watchers) to Hackett's dispassionate yet eager participation in her performances. It is even explored in its psychoanalytic manifestation, more openly than in previous novels, in the person of Homer, who, as we saw, is made to recapitulate the typical childhood trauma of guilt-inducing voyeurism (kino-genesis recapitulates retro-genesis?). The film-effect can thus be found beyond the "painterly" vision of a set designer. It is the kind of discourse of film that reiterates, as we saw before, the similarities between the discourse of the subconscious and that of movies. If the vivid simile (noted by West) between Homer's coiled body and the film reels of the cinematic apparatus is not enough to make the point, we have other iterations of this relationship in such things as the syntax of Homer's traumatized report, the splice-induced censorship at the porno movie (a rupture of the filmstrip that reveals as no other case in these novels the presence of suture in the composition of the imaginary), and the explicit analysis that Hackett makes of the role that Faye Greener's generic vicious circles play in nurturing (anorectically as may be) her dreams.

Apparatus in this novel, therefore, as perhaps in no other, is both explicit in its presence and repeatedly linked to the texture (the syntax) of our inner, less visible lives. Only with Puig we shall find a similarly strong connection (Toto too is lost among the medium-specific discursive confusion of reality and illusion). But lacking in Puig is West's explicit exploration of the reality of the apparatus at its "productive" as well as its "receptive" end. In Puig, as we have also just seen, Toto can make use of the apparatus in the opposite way than Homer. While the apparatus destroys Homer, it brings Puig's little boy to life (*apparatus ad partum*). In West the film machine is also, more than in the other novels, merged with the story as a whole (apparatus as story, rather than just as setting). This all-encompassing presence (as in the case of the thematic code that Barthes maintains one fails to notice because it is so "visible") tends to make us discount what in fact is a wealth of genre-specific components that we have encountered before but that in this case we might tend to overlook. They are so well integrated into the story that they often become invisible unless West makes a point of them: the use of a megaphone, for example, as in the collapse of the set during the filming of Napoleon's battle, or muted sotto voce, as when Faye kisses the cowboy for the benefit of Tod. What this leads to, however, apart from such occasional foregrounding, is a novel in which the narrative articulation of what is particular to the film novel becomes as transparent as the elements that stand for "reality" in classical realism.

It is this realism that is found at the center of the discourse on film and on film theory that characterizes Alberto Moravia's *Il disprezzo*. Moravia's is a novel that produces its distinctive effect by emphasizing three areas of the genre in particular: the inherent gravitation of the art form towards "strong" coding, the "semic" dilemma inherent in "reading" reality as it is circumscribed by film language, and the narrative setting as apparatus.

The debate about film theory that, as we saw, pits notions of realism against each other and advances the apparatus as a possible framework for everything from poetry, to realism, to cheap thrills, is the foundation upon which the novel builds a sophisticated drama of writerly intertextuality. This is one of the aspects that Jean-Luc Godard caught well in his film adaptation of the novel (*Le Mépris,* 1963) by actually "personifying" intercultural translation and intertextual interpretation in the character of the script girl. This contribution by Godard is congruent with Moravia's own staging of a varied cast of genre-specific characters engaged in a narrative articulation of film-specific discursive alternatives. They personify the struggle for supremacy among various cultural and symbolic codes (silly as this may sound when the flick at issue is a salacious version of the *Odyssey*), the poignancy inherent in the individual drama of reading the signs of human behavior through the imaginary, and the consequences of collusion with the invasion of our very landscape by the apparatus.

It can be seen that the novel is thus a complex and inventive synthesis of elements we have encountered before in the genre. Especially when it comes to the narrative articulation of codes, we find that the intertwining of discursive strands that we have met separately in works by Isherwood, Fitzgerald, and Puig are here orchestrated into a single story. Contrasting readings of the source-text thus give a skeptical twist to the monolithic interpretations of a Bergmann or a Stahr, colored as the multiple interpretations of Homer are by the doubts that arise when we notice that the producer's mythopoeic appeals to "poetry" are made in the name of exploitation, that the scriptwriter's insistence on the classical transparency of reality is motivated by subjective defensiveness, and that in its broadness the director's "modernist" psychoanalysis may well represent the kind of overdetermination that Brechtian aesthetics recommends.

Yet in a way, it is Rheingold who at least tries to "read out" in the name of cultural relevance, and does so by using the appropriate cinematic method. It is the method that his scriptwriter claims for himself as well but, as we saw, is unable to apply in his misunderstanding with his wife. Her "semic" interpretation of her husband's actions is, after all, quite cogent within the cinematic manifestations of this code (it is the explicit kind of element that Nabokov's Margot misses, we may recall, when she fails to identify Axel Rex despite his telltale rubbing of hands). It is the very same element that seduces Boxley during Stahr's lesson in cinematic literacy.

But most of the genre-specific productivity in Moravia occurs in the exploration of the voices that juggle culture, myth, politics, greed, suspicion, and lust. It is not just a matter of articulating the existence of conflicting interpretations. Moravia illustrates the need to decide what can derive from them as well. Reading out, we find through the drama that unfolds, is not a neutral process at all, even when we identify the frame of reference to which we hold. After all, the very "gaps" within which Rheingold insists that we find the true story of Penelope and Ulysses (the discursive disjunctions that are true to the irreconcilable differences of cultural symbolic oppositions) is the territory of Molteni's own "story." In other words, what "covers up" for the scriptwriter, "reveals" the truth as far as the director is concerned, and vice versa. As we said, even the ostensibly value-free individual "scores" that constitute the polyphony of this story are in fact tainted by individually colored leitmotifs. It is thus that we find the reconstructive procedure that film production forces upon this cast of characters (a genre-specific feature we have found before) reaching down to the deeper level of canonical reintegration, but also to the ever so slow revelation of "readings" that work their way back into life, and even to distinctly film-mimetic ways of reconstituting personal events after the fact in flashbacks. Ultimately, it is only film-as-a-medium (see Rheingold's cogent defense of it) that is said to provide an effective way to achieve a relevant contemporary recasting of classical texts.

Yet juxtaposed to this pro-active approach to the medium we find, as I said, one of the most dramatic realizations of setting as apparatus in the genre: a cave that harks back to the very same "classical" canon (Plato's parable of the cave) that contemporary film theory has employed to illustrate its theory of the apparatus as locus of passive subjection. I have analyzed this example at length. May I just add, in the light of the current recapitulation in the key of genre and narrative theory, that it is significant that this blatant joining by the protagonist with an admittedly self-indulgent subject position ("modal" as it may be both because it is extracinematic in the strict sense and because it is all about the subject's lack of power) occurs after the other spokes*men* for cinema (for they are always men in these novels) and their alternative views of the medium have left the scene. It is true that the apparatus appears in this guise elsewhere in *Il disprezzo*. Molteni's voyeuristic experience when he watches his wife through the frame of a window as she is kissed by his producer anticipates the final moment in structure if not in content (in content the ending is in fact a compensation). Yet that window is also as controlling and dominant as the window that figures in Molteni's metaphorical recapitulation of the turmoil that he carries within, a window that finally shuts, leaving "darkness, with no more thought or feeling in me" (GaN:162, Disp:171). The apparatus has indeed been turned off; the movie is over.

Lancelot's landscape, by contrast to Molteni's, seems utterly devoid of suitable spokesmen for cinema. This is one of the reasons, perhaps, that leads one to feel that Percy's novel harks back so strongly to Pirandello's prototype. The protagonist's tone of relentless denunciation, as well as the openly "clinical" reaction inherent in his behavior, is but a minor amplification of Gubbio's complicity and final mutism. It may even seem, due to the many similarities between *Shoot!* and *Lancelot,* that Percy's novel does not reward attention. Yet it plays, it seems to me, a very important role in the evolution of the genre precisely for this reason: more than any other of the examples so far, it *confirms* a continuity and a consistency over a long period of time.

In fact, one could wish for no better implementation of the genre inaugurated by Pirandello and his cameraman than Walker Percy's *Lancelot*. It almost speaks for itself (if it is the genre-specific narrative elements that are almost "invisible" in West, in Percy it may be the genre itself), ringing the changes of themes and ideas we have found again and again. It thus provides the genre with a renewed vitality as an update of the full range of the genre (for in this *Lancelot* is indeed quite new) and thus injecting it with renewed vitality at a time that, as we shall see, the tendency has been to emphasize only the spectator's end of the equation. In some ways the distance between Lancelot Lamar and Serafino Gubbio (oceans, epochs, film history notwithstanding) seems very small indeed as they hide behind the deceptive protection of technological visions, and as they try to gain a measure of control over a life that seems too threatening by absorbing the habits (not the best ones at that) fostered by cinematic spectatorship.

Lamar recapitulates the dilemmas of spectatorship in the passive mode, but at the same time confronts and implicates (something his kind of genre-specific character has not done before) the ostensible producers of that apparatus (cinematic and extracinematic) that holds him in place. For it is with them, ultimately, that responsibility lies. Isherwood's Bergmann comes to stand, as we saw, for all those figures we have encountered who through their access to the mechanism of illusion (real or just imaginary) can imprint their vision on the rest of us. They may be self-delusive as Gubbio or self-serving as Axel Rex and Margot, but they always raise questions for those who perceive their "projections": questions of social responsibility posed by Monroe Stahr or questions of ethical sincerity relevant to Merlin and Jacoby in *Lancelot*.

But such "foreigners" may also be like the photographer in the bedroom of Proust's grandmother, "the witness, the observer with a hat and traveling coat, the stranger who does not belong to the house, the photographer who had called to take a photograph of places which one will never see again" (Kracauer 1960:14). Such a witness may help us to see things as they are, or as we do not want to see them at all. We may find that this critical privilege threatens our own subjective and emotional right to interpret our own vision. If with Gubbio we found that such a dilemma threatens the very telling of a story, the same opposition informs Nabokov's autobiographical and fictional work, and the historical context of Bergmann's musical, the personal one of Molteni's *Odyssey,* and Lancelot's "scientific" observations. The exploration of film in these works outlines a dilemma that, as we said, applies to areas beyond the movies, that implicates a broader apparatus. It submits to culture as a whole questions such as what is the value and need to see as clearly as a camera, as truthfully as an objective, uninvolved observer? Is film representative of a technological vision that is better than unaided human perception? What are the limits of subjective vision and objective observation? What is it, in fact, that we are seeing? *Lancelot* returns us with a vengeance to the full range of such questions, confirming that the film novel as a genre is well suited to explore them because of the inherent implications of its themes, characters, and setting. They easily lead us to explore the human dimensions and experiential intricacies of such moral and epistemological questioning.

While philosophical thinking has by now transcended the faith that "technique" (in the guise of logical positivism, for instance) may improve the human lot, William Barrett observes that "the belief in the decisive role of technique had not vanished; it has become a general faith, widespread even when it is unvoiced, that technique and technical organization are necessary and sufficient conditions for arriving at truth; that they can encompass all truth; and that they will be sufficient, if not at the moment, then shortly, to answer the questions that life thrusts upon us" (Barrett 1979:10–11). If Isherwood (the "scriptwriter" in his fictionalized persona) and Tod Hackett exemplify the faith in a conscious and creative use of film and art to "interpret" reality, Lancelot Lamar clearly entertains an overly naïve expectation of the ability of technology to reveal the truth, and of that truth to be the one that will satisfy his needs. We have found such an expectation at the back of Serafino Gubbio's mind (he assumes that the "truthful" use of the medium is possible and would be satisfying), while Nabokov the scientist and the artist reveals a more contemporary skepticism.

But Lancelot Lamar also represents the modern doubt that questions the *kinds* of truth we may view and their all-encompassing nature. It is a doubt expressed in denouncing what K. Michael Hays refers to as "the mirage of organic realist unification"[1] and given concrete manifestation by often noted frustrations with the wealth of image types that new technologies provide. Fuzzy newspaper prints of astronomical observations as well as infrared video scans of darkened bedrooms raise questions similar to those voiced by Nabokov when faced with the different levels of observation open to the scientist. At what level of image-definition does reality reside? The grainy images facing Lancelot are, after all, just as puzzling and "mediated" as the fuzzy visions of Berlin (and his aunt's interiors) that face Nabokov's Franz in *King, Queen, Knave*. And even if we could decide, the doubts expressed by Pirandello's Cesarino about the need of mankind to see too clearly stands as a warning. Tod Hackett is at least caught in the ambiguities of his refusal to face its implications (layers of allegorical paint will not cover his voyeuristic connivance), while Nabokov's displaced personas (his friend viewing a home movie, his character Ganin facing himself on the screen) find that seeing with distance and clarity gives no pleasure. Yet it is Lancelot who pays the price of this clearer vision: it drives him to a mental clinic.

Lamar, however, puts himself in charge of his *cinéma-vérité* production, despite the fact that he is wise to the ways of those who are usually in charge of putting the world on film. He even attributes supernatural powers of vision and wisdom to his own manservant-cameraman Elgin, despite the fact that he knows it is foolish to expect this of him (just like Gubbio, another "slave" to the camera). Technical defects and human failures of vision do affect what we see on screen. The unreliability of those who control our visions (technologically gifted as they might be) thus remains central in *Lancelot* as in the other novels we have examined, from Gubbio's unreliable narration to the questioning of the technological apparatus itself in Nabokov's skeptical viewings. The mechanical failure of Lancelot's television rig is only the most explicit example of this. Since the apparatus involves more than just nuts and bolts, the questioning here extends to all the ways in which camera, filmmaker, screen, viewer, cinema, and culture come into contact with each other.

One question thus remains, as the pornographic context invoked by *Lancelot* suggests: how is it that the film apparatus, at the opposite extremes of exploitation films and home movies, calls up some of our murkiest memories, deepest fears, and most urgent curiosities? These genres too have to do with vision and its miraculous extensions by modern technology. If the notions of the subconscious and the readiness to admit its importance vary greatly among the novelists we have studied (what Nabokov rejects outright Rheingold uses intellectually and Homer Simpson suffers in the flesh as part of the action) the personal enthrallment to a primal viewing situation that borders on voyeurism is with *Lancelot* firmly at the center: the "story" is articulated around the charged, ambiguous, guilty, painful connection between what is seen and what is experienced by its protagonist. This morally ambiguous voyeurism is just as much a part of the definition of such novels as the interpretations of ideology, the responsibilities of active viewing, the illusions of reality, the realities of illusion, the doubts and expectations vested in technological ways of seeing, the reliance on superior stage-managers, and the wish to control reality and its representations.

Manuel Puig, at least for the moment, represents a point of arrival for the film novel. As my opening conclusion to this chapter suggests, it may well be that with the increased integration of film into culture (into our consciousness, into our discourse) a new relationship will emerge between narrative protocols in film and in literature. One hears less and less that a film cannot "do" what literature does, and literature (as well as the study of it) has become increasingly supple in reaping the benefits of film culture without compromising its essence (without seeming odd). Puig, thus, has confirmed the shift of attention to those who are at the receiving end of film, while at the same time raising the level at which thinking about film is articulated in narrative fashion. Film theory within the film novel started out by being anticipated. Then, as it was evolving, the film novel followed film theory's progress, sometimes implicitly, sometimes explicitly, sometimes without the apparent awareness of the novelists, sometimes with total and sophisticated knowledge. Finally, with *Kiss of the Spider Woman,* film theory can be said to "generate" the story itself. What if not derived from the cultural critique of film are the dialogues between Molina, who refuses to consider the historical context of the films he retells with such love and in the name of their "emotions," and Valentin, who tries to educate his cellmate in the acquisition of a critical conscience even as film spectator, yet learns in his turn that there are circumstances in which the opiate dreams of the screen are the only refuge—the only way out.

Puig represents a point of arrival also because, given the dialogic structure of *Betrayed by Rita Hayworth* (in which dialogue is meant in its Bakhtinian sense, given the "choral" nature of the novel) and of *Kiss of the Spider Woman* (in which, as we saw, film-specific interior monologue has developed into dialogue proper), he makes evident what I consider to be one of the central aspects of the film novel as genre (the discourse on and of film) more explicitly than ever before. What Puig also "makes evident" at the end of our journey is the fact that, while film discourse as such has been evolving along its own path, a parallel evolution of film discourse "in another genre" has taken place within the institution of literature. Taken together with the integration into film discourse of what literature and other forms of written discourse have to offer, such mutual referentiality (a referentiality that includes, of course, self-reference of a kind that by now has ceased to seem extradiscursive) indicates that the film novel is but one of the examples in contemporary culture of the interpenetration of discourse "on" and "of" film.

We need go no further, for confirmation of this, than to the videogame entitled *Space Quest Four: Roger Wilco and the Time Rippers* (notorious for its outrageous need for space on one's hard disk) in which, as one vaults into the future, one may enter a computer store and find there, in a bin dedicated to "old" computer games, a future version of yet another disk-hungry game entitled *King's Quest [nnn]: The Search for More Disk Space.* This kind of thing clearly indicates that the productive currency (philosophical, psychological) of self-reference has been co-opted by pop culture. Does this mean that the kind of insights achieved by characters from Gubbio to Molina are thus neutralized? Not so, it seems to me. I would argue that such instances remain productive even when incorporated in such a fashion. They indicate that a culture that only yesterday needed the impact of shock techniques to discover that the conditions of its living were to be questioned can now incorporate in its gaming the nature of the universe (highly technological, circumscribed by extremely complex symbolic systems) in which we live and play. It is no longer disorienting or traumatic to look at the "code" and its outrageous demands for ever more space, while traveling through the universe. Yet only yesterday this was not so, and the film novels I have examined trace the journey from then to now.

Yet when all is said and done, it seems that for other reasons we must always return with Molteni (with Toto) to the bottom of the cave in Capri. It is characters such as they, it seems, who best represent the condition of most of us who do not yet play *The Quest for More Disk Space* without a sense of dread. In the seminal case of Pirandello, it turns out, the link between the illusory vision of perfect love, the brutal discovery of betrayal, and the charged views of Nestoroff through Gubbio's camera may ultimately derive from a very specific traumatic experience that took place in early childhood when (it is said) in the darkness of a morgue, as the rustling of amorphous forms assumed outline and identity, young Pirandello discovered a couple in each other's arms: a death-tinged primal scene.[2] But even without such a remarkable coincidence (or are coincidences indeed, as Chesterton maintained, a form of spiritual pun) what Homer Simpson, what Lancelot, what Toto see would have become part of the structure of expectation in the watching of films: "Cinema plays on the hidden visible to be suggested, glimpsed, revealed, plays on the shown and the expectations and the pleasures produced in the displacement and use of those limits" (Heath 1981:184–185).

The danger-fraught voyeurism, the sexual betrayals, the stylized song-and-dance routines, the discoveries, and the murders that characterize almost all the novels we have studied are the thematic material typical of this narrative realm not entirely by chance. Below the obvious aptness of such plot devices for stories that take place in the world of the movies, they reflect, in popularized and externalized form, deeper disappointments, more personal wishes, and idiosyncratically individual anger and rage of a kind we all experience at some level or other. The "detectives" of such plots reflect the sleuthing with which we pursue our most personal obsessions. As the Fat Man on the radio used to say of his own work, "It's a chancy job that makes a man watchful and sometimes a little lonely."

Notes

Preface

1. Excellent studies that raise such problems are, for instance, McConnell (1975), Spiegel (1976), and Cohen (1979). In a more "European" vein see Clerc (1985) and Morrissette (1985). For an interesting study that approaches the problem in a "reverse angle" from mine (verbal narratives within films), see Fleishman (1992).

2. See Baudry (1976:113) and (for Baudry's link between the movable camera and the "transcendent subject") Baudry (1974/75:43–44). A recent study in the field of art history seems to confirm that one can also find a cinematic sensibility in painting that precedes the institution of cinematography. See Hollander (1989). For the history of mechanical realizations of the "wish," see Milner (1982) and Costa (1983).

3. For a discussion of this way of looking at genre, see Brooke-Rose (1981).

4. An illustration of the "state of the art" in genre studies is given by Bordwell (1989:147–148): "Interpreters no more have strict definitions of genre than speakers of English have definitions of *game* (to take the most famous example in the philosophical literature). Genre would seem to be an 'open textured' concept, and genres are treated as 'fuzzy' categories, definable neither by necessary and sufficient conditions nor by fixed boundaries. The processes by which people construct a fuzzy category do not define it but rather provide a loose set of more or less central, more or less strongly linked expectations—default hierarchies—that are taken to hold good unless contradicted by other information."

Chapter One: Man Makes Movies Make Man

1. The novel was originally published in the literary periodical *Nuova antologia* (1915). The English translation by C. K. Scott Moncrieff was published in 1926. The mimetic intent of the novel is most often the one noted by commentators, as is the as-

sumption that Gubbio, rather than representative of wider cultural views, is merely a foil for Pirandello's own views on the cinema. See Barilli (1972:206–207) and Crespi (1967:849). On the novel see also Nulf (1970/71:40–48), Maira (1972:187–223), Cohen-Budor (1974), Angelini (1975, 1977, 1978), Sogliuzzo (1977), Cudini (1978), and Dombroski (1978:103–118). On Pirandello and the cinema see also the whole volume edited by Enzo Lauretta (1978) and the more recent and beautifully produced double volume edited by Nino Genovese and Sebastiano Gesù (1990). Additionally, see Aristarco (1984), Grignani (1985), Barlusconi (1985), Barberi Squarotti (1986), and Artioli (1988). Finally, see now also Angelini (1990) and Càllari (1991).

2. Dziga Vertov in 1929 described the process of filmmaking in a manner that stresses the operations of "selection" and "combination" and the criteria of choice by "similarity" and "contiguity" which the Russian formalist critics were trying to apply to literature and art at about the same time. As he puts it, "Kino-eye is: Montage, when I select a theme (choosing one from among thousands of possible themes); Montage, when I make observations for a theme (choosing what is expedient from thousands of observations on the theme)." Both of these are aspects of the "selection" of possible materials from the continuum of life in terms of (a) thematic suitability and (b) semantic appropriateness. Vertov continues: "Montage, when I establish the viewing order of the footage on the theme (selecting the most expedient from thousands of possible groupings of shots, proceeding from the qualities of the film footage as well as from the requirements of the chosen theme)" (Vertov 1984:90). This exemplifies the process of "combination" according to the two possible criteria of association by similarity/opposition or by contextual relevance. It is notable that Roman Jakobson, as early as 1933, was writing about film language in ways related to this: "*Pars pro toto* is a fundamental method of filmic conversion of things into signs. Scenario terminology with its 'mid-long shots,' 'closeups,' and 'mid-closeups' is sufficiently instructive in this respect. Film works with manyfold fragments of objects which differ in magnitude, and also with fragments of time and space likewise varied. It changes their proportions and juxtaposes them in terms of contiguity or similarity and contrast; that is, it takes the path of metonymy or metaphor (two fundamental kinds of cinematic structure)" (Jakobson 1987:459–460).

3. For street scenes, the visual rendition of the flow of city life, and the character who just floats along with it as the Baudelairian *flaneur* (all as film subjects), see Kracauer (1960:72, 50–51).

4. It is notable that Luciani talks also about the structural process of putting a film together in terms very similar to Dziga Vertov's and Roman Jakobson's. The succession of particular parts of a whole situation is very much like the view of film as inherently metonymic. Elsewhere Luciani points again to the fact that a setting will be presented cinematically by accumulation of fragmentary views (Luciani 1928:42) and draws a parallel between film and the novels of Joseph Conrad, where characters are built up in similar metonymic fashion (Luciani 1928:28).

5. "It ought to be understood that the fantastic cannot acquire reality except by means of art, and that the reality which a machine is capable of giving it kills it, for the very reason that it is given it by a machine, that is to say by a method which discovers and exposes the fiction, simply by giving it and presenting it as real. If it is mechanical, how can it be life, how can it be art?" (Sh:87–88, Quad:53). This statement

anticipates the notion of the destruction of the "aura" of unique, unreproduced works of art referred to by Walter Benjamin. In his essay "The Work of Art in the Age of Mechanical Reproduction," Benjamin draws on this and other ideas from Pirandello's film novel (Benjamin 1969:219–251). I have dealt in detail with the connection (Moses 1988a:57–62). For the history of this essay and both extant versions, see Snyder (1983/84).

6. Traveling shots were part and parcel of early Italian cinema at least since 1906, when we have documentary evidence that the cameraman Giovanni Vitrotti would place the camera on the back of a moving trolley car and produce a comic routine with the actor Vaser in the process of "missing the train." In 1909, he placed the camera on a raft and followed tree trunks floating downstream (Brunetta 1972:8–10). Kracauer points out that it was photography (and then cinematography) which made the relativity of viewpoints and perspectives into a major "period topic" (Kracauer 1960:8–9).

7. This is a good example of the "dramatic collision" typical of *formal mimetics* referred to by Michael Głowinski, who remarks, "In this process, the form performing the 'imitation' plays an active part, for under the guise of more or less total reproduction, it introduces the 'imitated' elements into the limits of the rules peculiar to itself." It is this attempt at domestication that allows *formal mimetics* to highlight features not always clear in the product imitated without the tension that occurs by this transfer. Głowinski concludes: "Thus, formal mimetics never relies upon the total assimilation or entire transferring of structural principles from one type of expression to another. Formal mimetics rather resolves itself into a set of analogies which ought to suggest identity but, at the same time, attest to the impossibility of achieving identity" (Głowinski 1977:106).

8. Kracauer in a *positive* vein points to the ability that the camera has of "disintegrating familiar objects and bringing to the fore . . . previously invisible interrelationships between parts of them" (Kracauer 1960:54, see also 19–20).

9. Christian Metz has applied this classical term designating the recital of facts in judiciary discourse to film discourse to mean the "film's *represented* instance . . . the sum of a film's denotation: The narration itself, but also the fictional space and time dimensions implied in and by the narrative, and consequently the characters, the landscapes, the events, and other narrative elements, in so far as they are considered in their denoted aspect" (Metz 1974:98).

10. This is typical of film as a medium, in which the metaphoric is nearly always *seen* as part of an illusion of nonsymbolic reality. It also tends to be typical of a lot of modern fiction, as has been shown in such studies as Ullman (1957), Ullman (1960), Genette (1972), and Lodge (1977).

11. The process of "unmetaphoring" is an artistic strategy very apt in overcoming the "secondarization" that occurs to figures once they become part of the traditional, expected repertory of literary discourse. On secondarization Genette remarks: "The figure is a divergence—écart—in relation to normal usage, yet this divergence is also part of usage itself: this is the paradox of rhetoric" (Genette 1966:209, my translation). Unmetaphoring, it seems to me, manages to recreate the shock inherent in the actual creation of the figures (that unique moment when the figure had not yet become part of a convention) by reversing the process. In this novel by Pirandello we witness such a process within the context of one work rather than, as is more often the case, a

whole literary tradition. See, for example, Rosalie L. Colie's discussion of unmetaphored Petrarchan tropes in *Othello* (Colie 1974: chap. 3).

12. It can be shown, in fact, that all of Gubbio's most cogent thoughts and pieces of information derive from what others tell him. This contributes further to undermine his credibility as narrator.

13. For an example of a critical account of the novel based on the assumed reliability of Gubbio as narrator, see Cuminetti (1967). One consequence of such a misreading is that Cuminetti, as well as de Castris (1962) and Barilli (1972), cast Gubbio in a "saintly" mold.

14. In fact Gubbio openly admits to Ferro that his own philosophy of human relations is based on duplicity: "As I look at it, people invariably lie" (Sh:157–158, Quad: 90). He is here merely extending this principle—usually regarded as a "Pirandellism" with existential import—into his action.

15. Notably Gubbio manages to deny both kinds of feeling. See Emile Benveniste quoting Freud on negation as "a way of taking cognizance of what is repressed" (Benveniste 1971:73).

16. For Gubbio as executioner, see Pirandello (Sh:104, Quad:62).

17. See Benveniste: "For it is style rather than language that we would take as term of comparison with the properties that Freud has disclosed as indicative of oneiric 'language'" (Benveniste 1971:75). Thus we need not lay Gubbio down upon the analyst's couch, for his style in itself reveals to us the nature and structure of his "dream" logic. For a fragmentary attempt to psychoanalyze the characters in this novel, see Barilli (1972:212–216).

Chapter Two: Icons Unreal Irony

1. In suggesting a connection between irony and the film image one must be careful to qualify: irony as utterance involves an *intention* which the image and its mediating apparatus does not inherently contain. Following the ground rules for recognition of stable irony suggested by Wayne Booth, one would have to ask in what way the camera *in itself* leads to an *intended* rejection by the viewer of the structure of belief which it implies. In the specific context of Gubbio's statement that such an inherent, essential (if not consciously intended) absence of coherence (if not active rejection) exists within the medium, we find the modernist doubt about the reliability and even the very possibility of objective representations. In modern culture this applies to all representations, but more than to any to photographic representations, since it is these that claim greater reliability than most. It is a common cultural assumption that if objective representation is possible, photography is "the method that least lends itself to deception." It does as such carry the claim that it *shows* things *as they are*. See Booth (1974:29–39). See also Kracauer (1960:4, 21) about the general notion that photography reproduces reality as is and on this as one of its basic appeals. On irony see also Muecke (1969) and (methodologically quite different) Muecke (1978). An issue of *Poétique* 36 (1978) dedicated to the topic of irony extends this bibliography both historically and methodologically. As far as Pirandello is concerned, see Pagliaro (1970) and Guglielmi (1974). See also Barlusconi (1985) in the light of Moses (1981a).

2. Before Barthes, André Bazin had already noted that "the realism of the cinema follows directly from its photographic nature. Not only does some marvel or some

fantastic thing on the screen not undermine the reality of the image, on the contrary it is its most valid justification" (Bazin 1967:108).

3. Pirandello defines rhetorical irony as "a fictitious contradiction between what one says and what one means." It derives from "a contradiction that is merely verbal, from a rhetorical dissimulation." He notes that this is "absolutely contrary to the nature of genuine humor" (Hum:34–35, 125; Lum:52, 139).

4. For this supposed "neorealist" aesthetics of Pirandello see Mario Apollonio, cited in Crespi (1967:850). See also Verdone (1952:226).

5. At the simplest level this attitude is in harmony with ads such as the 1913 one by Louis Feuillade cited by Henry Agel in which the fantastic adventures of characters set in a hyperrealist urban setting are touted as showing "life as life." But ultimately even for a "modern" realist photographer such as Edward Weston the precise factual rendition of reality which is made possible by the photographic image amounts to a "better" view, one that takes us "behind" appearances. As Kracauer puts it, "Weston refers to camera revelations rather than representations of familiar sights. What thrills us today then is the power of the medium, so greatly increased by technical innovations and scientific discoveries, to open up new, hitherto unsuspected dimensions of reality" (Kracauer 1960:8).

6. But see della Terza (1972) and Ragusa (1977).

7. Kracauer anticipates these notions, as well as those of Roland Barthes's "effet de réel" and Christian Metz's "faire vrais," when he says that "cinematic films evoke a reality more inclusive than the one they actually picture. They point beyond the physical world, he explains, to the extent that the shots or combinations of shots from which they are built carry multiple meanings. Due to the continuous influx of the psychophysical correspondences thus aroused, they suggest a reality which may fittingly be called 'life'" (Kracauer 1960:71).

8. For these notions, see Bazin (1967:9–16). See Bazin (1967) also for the notions of "depth of field" (p. 92), "time-space perimeter" (p. 98), "death mask" (p. 12), and "transfer" and "photo album" (p. 14). For the notion of "motivation," see Fónagy's definition of motivated sign as "a sign which admits the partial presence of reality, which incorporates that portion of reality in its signifier, rather than being content with denotation pure and simple" (Fónagy 1972:414–431, my translation)—a definition most apt to the filmic sign. Gérard Genette has also noted that "the motivation of a sign, particularly of a 'word,' is in linguistic consciousness a typical case of the illusion of reality" (Genette 1968:19). Thus the notion of "motivation" as it applies to film signs is particularly attractive if we regard the film image as a "transfer" of reality.

9. But note that Mitry (1963/65:I, 209) already refers to the term "faire vrais" in his section on veristic painting (chapter 19), and in a rather negative context at that.

10. See, for instance, Prolo (1951:10–11). Ricciotto Canudo also initiated "genre" subdivisions in film criticism. See Aristarco (1963:80) on Canudo's "recensioni."

11. In Nuti's case too the fall into folly is characterized by a *montage* of images that Gubbio describes as "imaginings [*immagini,* or images, in Italian] accumulated in years past and now wandering unconnected" which "burst in tumultuous, with diabolical fury, roaring like wild beasts" (Sh:217–218, Quad:122).

12. Christian Metz does not see that film images and mental images are similar in this way. He posits an opposition between perception and presence on the one hand and imagination and dream on the other (Metz 1976:80, 83). While, strictly speaking,

Metz's points that film is not like the imaginary or like dream are well taken, it seems that the narratives we are studying stress over and over again that film, at least in a metaphorical way (and often in the way it is experienced), does conform to these models.

13. Note that the discontinuity between image and space, as well as that between image-time and *real* time-space, is also explored in this passage and corresponds in its articulation to Sartre's discussion of these subjects elsewhere (Im/E:180–188, Im/F: 243–254).

14. All translations of Pirandello's "Ironia" are my own.

15. Speaking of this determination to cling to the illusory, della Terza writes: "It could be said that the humoristic technique used by Pirandello, in revealing the truth of the game underneath the illusion, ends up vigorously underlining the pathetic consistency of the very illusion, its power of survival" (della Terza 1972:31).

16. Pirandello describes this attitude as the "irony which, according to Schlegel's definition, reduces the literary material to a perpetual parody and consists in the writer's not losing, not even in the moments of pathos, his awareness of the unreality of his own creation" (Hum:58, Lum:75). This conception, very close to the "transcendental clowning" of German Idealism, is introduced here as description of Pulci's Morgante. It is then extended by Pirandello to Ariosto (Hum:76 ff., Lum:92 ff.).

17. For an application of such notions to cinematography, see Baudry (1974/75), who recalls Freud's comparison of the "instrument which serves in psychic productions" to a "microscope or camera" and points out that "this optical choice seems to prolong the tradition of Western science, whose birth coincides exactly with the development of the optical apparatus which will have as a consequence the decentering of the human universe, the end of geocentrism (Galileo)" (Baudry 1974/75:39–40). For a more skeptical critique of the metaphorical application of advances in optical instrumentation to human history, see Barfield (1977:65–78), who questions whether the instruments which are usually considered as "an emblem of that species of Copernican Revolution in the human psyche which was quite as much the cause as it was the consequence of the Copernican Revolution in astronomy" (Barfield 1977:69) have not come to be accepted as such emblems too readily. He suggests that "in the age of the movie, the student of words who is unfashionable enough to examine their history as well as their current use, is not perhaps so impressed as some others are by the universal practice of projection not only in movie houses and on the television screen, but also, as a concealed metaphor, in the ingenious fancies of men. Is projection itself being projected?" (Barfield 1977:74). He continues with a useful if brief summary of the application of such notions by scientists, philosophers, psychologists, anthropologists. The evidence of the novelists examined in the present study suggests that in their works at least (film novels and not) such metaphorical applications do take place.

18. I cite and summarize the earlier, longer version of the poem which appeared in *Nazione letteraria,* June 1893. The editors of Pirandello (1960) print it as footnote number 73 to the later version, published in *La riviera ligure,* August 1905.

19. It is also a polemic against such spiritualist metaphors as that contained in Niccoló Tommaseo's poem "La piccola mia lampana" (Tommaseo 1958:77).

20. Kracauer puts it thus: "This is then modern man's situation: . . . He touches reality only with the fingertips" (Kracauer 1960:294). For Rudolf Arnheim, who adds a moral twist, modern man

is immensely better informed about the epidermis of the world at large, the appearance of what goes on; but we have good reasons to call him less wise than his counterpart of the pre-photographic era. The addicts of photography seem highly distracted. They think less well. Their ever stimulated curiosity makes them lose themselves in the capillaries of the particular rather than move on the mainstream of life. Photographic information, potentially a magnificent source of knowledge, seems to serve as a powerful distraction from insight. The mere exposure to the visible surface of the world will not arouse ideas unless the spectacle is approached with ideas ready to be stirred up. (Arnheim 1966:187)

21. Pirandello also remarks,

Beyond so called rhetorical irony . . . [there is] another irony: a philosophical one, derived by the German Romantics directly from the subjective idealism of Fichte, but which at bottom has its origin in the whole post-Kantian German idealist movement. . . . Hegel used to explain that the I, only the reality, can smile about the evanescent appearances of the universe: the way he puts it, he can also wipe them out; he can take his own creation with no seriousness at all. It is from this that we derive irony: that power—according to Tieck—which allows the poet to dominate the matter which he is dealing with. This matter—according to Frederich Schlegel—because of irony is reduced to a perpetual parody, a transcendental farce. (Ir:994)

Rudolf Arnheim sees another type of parallel between a romantic view of the world and the kinds of views which are akin to the film image: "What cinema is so well equipped to redeem is . . . the view of a boundless, indeterminate, unfathomable world . . . a Romantic image obtained by photographic realism!" (Arnheim 1966:183).

22. Jean-Louis Baudry echoes this in saying that "the world [in cinema] is no longer only an 'open and unbounded horizon.' Limited by the framing, lined up, put at the proper distance, the world offers up an object endowed with meaning, an intentional object, implied by and implying the action of the 'subject' which sights it." He goes on to talk about the "apodicity of the ego" and of Husserl's "aspects" and "unity," all in relation to the film viewing situation (Baudry 1974/75:43).

Chapter Three: Memory Unreals

1. Gilbert Ryle also points out that people tend to take literally the colloquial reference to imaginative operations as "picturing" and "visualizing": "If a person says that he is picturing his nursery, we are tempted to construe his remark to mean that he is somehow contemplating, not his nursery, but another visible object, namely a picture of his nursery, only not a photograph or an oil painting, but some counterpart to a photograph, one made of a different sort of stuff" (Ryle 1949:247). See, for precisely such a way of looking at things, Nabokov's memory of his parents' bedroom discussed later. For an argument against Ryle, see Hannay (1971:27–60).

2. This point was made most recently by Roland Barthes: "The image, phenomenology tells us, is a nothing as an object. Now in photography what I posit is not merely the absence of the object; it also says, with the same movement, with the same power, that this object existed, that it was there where I see it. And in this resides the madness because until today no representation could reassure me about the past of things, other than by indirect links; but with photography my certainty is immediate: no one in the world can disenchant me. Photography then becomes for me a bizarre

medium, a new form of hallucination: false at the level of perception, true at the level of time" (Barthes 1980:115, my translation). See also Metz (1975:47–48) and (in French) Metz (1977:65), where he points out that "the unique position of the cinema lies in this dual character of its signifier: unaccustomed perceptual wealth, but unusually profoundly stamped with unreality from its very beginning. More than the other arts, or in a more unique way, the cinema involves us in the imaginary: it drums up all perception, but to switch it immediately over onto its own absence, which is nonetheless the only signifier present."

3. For the phenomenologist, of course, "imaginative" seeing is only valid if it occurs as a "first time" experience.

4. *The Compact Edition of the Oxford English Dictionary* (New York: Oxford University Press, 1971), I:323.

5. *The Compact Edition of the Oxford English Dictionary,* I:323. The citation is of Ephraim Chambers, *Cyclopaedia; or, An Universal Dictionary of Arts and Sciences; Supplement* (1753).

6. Jean-Louis Baudry extends such cinematic images to parallels in Freud (microscope and camera as the instruments of psychic production) as well as to implications of perceptual stance: *camera obscura* as "a displacement of the center (which settles itself in the eye)" and which "will assure the setting up of the 'subject' as active center and origin of meaning" (Baudry 1974/75:39–40).

7. See Jean Epstein on "slow-motion" and "time expansion," cited in Kracauer (1960:53). See also Arnheim (1969:116–117).

8. For further discussion of photography and the distinction between depiction and denotation, see Goodman (1968:9, 40).

9. The kind of films described by Nabokov could well be some of the most interesting productions of prerevolutionary Russian cinema. This is so especially in the case of Yevgeni Bauer's films, which, Mitry points out, represented a "state of the art" summa and which in my view have intriguing similarities to Nabokov's work (Mitry 1963/65:I, 230). I will just mention the snow-bound exhilaration of the kiss in Nabokov's short story "Spring in Fialta" and the snow-framed seduction in Bauer's stunning film *Yurii Nagornyi* (1916).

10. This is the title of a story in Seán O'Faoláin (1949:114–120).

11. This is André Bazin's point in comparing theatrical and cinematic identification (Bazin 1967:98 ff.).

12. In the case of the genre-cliché appearance of the country mansion on the screens young Nabokov watched, the general point about the tantalizing illusion of the presence of the cinematic image (desire) and its paradoxical unreality (lack) is concretized into a biographical image that is experienced in and of itself and which, due to the vagaries of life and history, happens to be the image of a specific and personal lack and desire. Describing the feelings he retained for a house lost since childhood, Rainer Maria Rilke said, "As I see it now the way it appeared to my child's eye it is a building, but it is quite dissolved and distributed inside me" (Rilke, cited in Bachelard 1969:57). In Nabokov's passage the identification of setting with actor is extended by the actor's interaction with the houses to involve a sense that lost possession causes the house itself to be internalized. Rilke again points out that the very notion of rootedness and tradition in Western European civilization can be represented by the "melting" of one's human self into the forms, the vessels, represented by human habitations:

"To our grandparents a 'house' . . . was still infinitely more intimate: almost . . . a vessel in which they found something human and into which they set aside something human" (Rilke 1962:134). Psychoanalytic thinkers have pointed out many uses of the image of one's very own house such as Nabokov's. The "white-pillared mansion" with its "wildwood and peatbog" is, ultimately, the house as image of one's body (Freud 1965:117), the fortress "surrounded by marshes" symbolizing the "I" (Lacan 1977b:5). The cellars and attics function as "image[s] of the psyche" (Jung 1965:160), as "centers of condensation of intimacy . . . of simplicity" which come to embody the unconscious as well as the rational in all of us (Bachelard 1969:29). As the latter concludes, "the unconscious is housed" (Bachelard 1969:10).

13. Means such as the distortion of image and wipes are precisely the ones used by early experimental filmmakers. Rudolf Arnheim sees such "defects" of film as the foundations of its artistic potential (Arnheim 1969:3). For Russian film theory, see Sergei M. Eisenstein (1943) on "synchronization of senses." For more detailed application of this principle to Nabokov's narrative technique, see chapter 4 here.

14. "Sound and picture each run on independently, without uniting in an organic whole. It is important to keep in mind that our conception of synchronization does not presume consonance. In this conception full possibilities exist for the play of both corresponding and non-corresponding 'movements,' but in either circumstance the relationship must be *compositionally controlled*" (Eisenstein 1943:72).

Chapter Four: Albinus Fakes Movies

1. In direct quotation, and also in the general thrust of my discussion of irony and its "reconstructions" in this chapter, I am beholden to Wayne Booth's useful extension of the traditional notions on irony.

2. While Bazin, writing originally in 1948, derives his notions from theories of realism that hardly apply to Nabokov's position on these matters, it has been clear for some time that the power and significance of the camera styles described by the French critic go beyond the limited and sometimes mistaken applications he makes of his own terms. See Vernon Young on Orson Welles's deep-focus expressionism (Young 1978/79:140–144). Filmmakers such as Antonioni—who can hardly be regarded as a realist—have taken Bazin's notions well beyond their original context. Michelangelo Antonioni's last sequence of *The Passenger* (1975) is a good example. See also the discussion of the relation of this camera style to the American novel in the last section of Bazin (1971). Bazin is here echoing Magny (1948), whose book was published in the same year as Bazin's original essay. Renoir spoke very early (in *Point,* 1938) about his own deep-focus aesthetic. See also Henderson (1980:6–11).

3. This is, by the way, remarkably similar to the ending of Max Ophuls's 1932 film *Liebelei,* in which the protagonist's suicide is followed by a track through the empty apartment that is thus allowed to tell its own story.

4. Albinus's eye damage is described thus: "The optic nerves had been damaged at the point of their intersection in the brain" (L:250). This is very similar to the description of the television image as an "apparatus" that reproduces "the simultaneousness of . . . random events . . . optically within the frame of one screen" (SO:154).

5. Kracauer has pointed to this as an example of thematic material that has emerged in the twentieth century due to the peculiar ways of seeing (the "inherent affinities")

of film (Kracauer 1960:18–19, 130–131). The idea is found already in Brecht's writings on cinema.

6. As Kracauer points out, "The affinity of film for haphazard contingencies is most strikingly demonstrated by its unwavering susceptibility to the 'street,'" including the street's "various extensions, such as railway stations, dance and assembly halls, bars, hotel lobbies, airports, etc." This region of human experience, so favored by film, is "a region where the accidental prevails over the providential, and happenings in the nature of unexpected incidents are all but the rule" (Kracauer 1960:62).

7. In the "closed" story structure that, as I said, *Laughter* seems to exemplify, Braudy (1976:47–48) points out that such elements are usually used to increase the sense of closure which grips the characters. On open and closed form see also Wölfflin (n.d.:24–154), Adams (1958), and Klotz (1960).

8. The street as a thematic context of its own is, Kracauer points out, the natural center for a cinematic perspective on the world: "Since the days of Lumière there have been only few cinematic films that would not include glimpses of a street, not to mention the many films in which some street figures among the protagonists." Such films were in fact legion at the time Albinus went to the movies, and it is therefore of little surprise that his own story, so close to conventional story clichés in its outline, is not so different from the prototype of the German "street" films, Karl Grune's *Die Strasse* (1923). The film's protagonist is, Kracauer reports, "a middle-aged *petit bourgeois* possessed with the desire to escape from the care of his lifeless wife and the prison of a home where intimacy has become a deadening routine" (Kracauer 1960:62, 72). This is indeed very reminiscent of the way Albinus sees his own life with Elizabeth, a life epitomized by a striking cinematic image as "one of those long, dim, dusty passages where one finds a nailed-up box—or an empty perambulator" (L:178–179).

9. Béla Balázs talks about this: "Every shape makes a—mostly unconscious—emotional impression on us, which may be pleasant or unpleasant, alarming or reassuring, because it reminds us, however distantly, of some human face, which we ourselves project into it. Our anthropomorphous world-vision makes us see a human physiognomy in every phenomenon" (Balázs 1952:92).

10. As Kracauer points out, "The cinema in this sense is not exclusively human. Its subject matter is the infinite flux of visible phenomena—those ever changing patterns of physical existence whose flow may include human manifestations but need not climax in them" (Kracauer 1960:97).

11. This is a muted example of Hans Richter's notion of "activated sound," according to which sound fulfills narrative and expressive functions (Richter 1955a). See also Eisenstein's (1943:60–91) notion of the creative use of separate tracks.

12. See also C. Carrà (1920:72). The Montale lines are from the second part of "Spesso il male di vivere ho incontrato": "Bene non seppi, fuori del prodigio / che schiude la divina Indifferenza: / era la statua nella sonnolenza / del meriggio, e la nuvola, e il falco alto levato" (Montale 1948:63).

13. Braudy (1976) points out that

> from their own resources films lend to twentieth-century visual art the portentousness of detail, any detail, with no specific historical or traditional symbolic scheme to justify it. In the works of Giorgio de Chirico, René Magritte, and other surrealists, for example, we see isolated and arrayed objects whose meaning goes beyond the cultural expectations we have brought to our viewing. The idea of meaning has become more important than the

articulation and specification of meaning, and the ability to evoke the dread of unreachable truth more important than the ability to express it with clarity and order. This effect owes its existence to the cinematic attitude toward objects and their invisible potential (Braudy 1976:40).

14. Individual focusing and framed setting thus echo the kind of images held up for observation by young Nabokov during magic lantern shows and which we saw as analogous to Bachelard's miniatures. The French philosopher observes that "to use a magnifying glass is to pay attention, but isn't paying attention already having a magnifying glass? Attention by itself is an enlarging glass" (Bachelard 1969:158). We have seen how the film image derives from and is related to the optically isolated views of "reality" seen through microscope or telescope. In this regard it is important to note that Nabokov is on record as estimating Robbe-Grillet (that practitioner of the hyperrealist description) the "best" of French writers (NW:329).

15. Braudy points out that such details "form a plot in both the aesthetic and the conspiratorial sense" (Braudy 1976:48).

16. Considering the theoretical perceptiveness Nabokov and Eisenstein shared about the structure of film, it is comical that Nabokov should have doggedly garbled Eisenstein's name as, I presume, a show of hostility (NW:195, 323). For *audition colorée,* see Nabokov (SpM:24–26) and Eisenstein (1943:74–79). Of the need to suggest sound by visual means Eisenstein says: "The scene [in *Strike* (1924)] ended with a sequence in which we tried to convey the idea of sound by purely visual means" (Eisenstein 1970:115). See also the following examples from *October* (1927). Needless to say, these are the kind of films that Nabokov would have hated: "I have also a hunch that the general idea that avant-garde literature and art were having a wonderful time under Lenin and Trotsky is mainly due to Eisenstadt [*sic*] films—'montage'—things like that—and great big drops of sweat rolling down rough cheeks" (NW:195). Obviously it is only deep down in the realm of essential cinematic sensibility that the two shared an affinity.

17. See Arnheim (1969:106 ff.) on the "gain" inherent in the visual transposition of sound.

18. As Arnheim points out, "The enrichment and unity that may result in art from the cooperation of several media are not identical with the fusion of all sorts of sense perception that is typical for our way of experiencing the 'real' world. Because in art the diversity of the various perceptual media requires separations among them—separations that only a higher unity can overcome" (Arnheim 1969:202–203).

19. This is a notion akin to Eisenstein's description of the film shot as a collection of "attractions" (a term he drew from an analogy between the elements in the shot and the bright spotlit centers of audience attention in the circus). This notion holds that "all elements of cinematic expressiveness must participate in the making of a film as elements of dramatic action" and that "in its place, at a given moment, each [element] is the protagonist of the moment, occupying the leading place in the general chorus of expressive elements" (Eisenstein 1970:121–122).

20. The skinlike quality of that garment is stressed soon after its appearance on the beach, when Margot "snake-like, shuffled off her black skin" (L:115) in a sensual striptease aimed at Albinus.

21. Nabokov never uses the term "revolver" for the gun. He does, however, depict

Albinus intensely "revolving" the chamber and feeling the bullets before his final blind confrontation with Margot.

22. The same paragraph contains another clue pointing to synaesthetic translation in the noise of the heating element that echoes the visual notation about a similar object in visual terms. Pattern for pattern, moreover, Rex and Margot too are linked by Wagner, in the guise of a Lohengrin joke. But in their case it is a pattern centering on a joke that they share across occasions: very apt given Rex's propensities for farce.

23. Just as in Eisenstein's view of the use of color in film (an element as changeable and developmental as a musical motif), we can say that in *Laughter in the Dark* the color leitmotif unfolds "an inner drama, weaving its own pattern in the contrapuntal whole, crossing and recrossing the course of action, which formerly music alone could do with full completeness by supplementing what could not be expressed by acting or gesture" (Eisenstein 1970:128). For a fuller discussion of the analogy between music and color, see Eisenstein (1943:72–77, 88–91). Obviously, as in the case of flashbacks in narrative structure, color motifs are not new in literature at all. It is in the complexity of the use of such a device, and in the stress on its visual quality, that Nabokov is more filmlike than, say, Flaubert. We shall soon see, however, that even his treatment of color and light becomes easily cinematic in ways that go beyond the previous use of color in literature.

24. The nonreferential use of color in film was already adumbrated by Ricciotto Canudo in "Reflexions" (cited by Aristarco 1963:80). But this was by no means a universally accepted view. See Balázs (1952:242–245) and Balázs (1938).

25. This range (and color sensitivity in general) may also be a by-product of the fact that there is actually no word in Russian which is equivalent to plain blue. See Lyons (1968:56–57).

26. "The artistic reason for colour cinematography can be only in the experience and expression of colour in motion" (Balázs 1952:242).

27. Kracauer is writing here about the film *Menschen am Sonntag*. Susan Sontag (an alliterative happenstance that would have pleased Nabokov) comments on this film in a manner that illuminates the deadening effect of looking at life in this way, a lack of vitality that is implicit in Albinus's self-destructive affair with Margot: "One by one they step before the itinerant photographer's black box—grin, look anxious, clown, stare. The movie camera lingers in close-up to let us savor the mobility of each face; then we see the face frozen in the last of its expressions, embalmed in a still. The photographs shock, in the flow of the movie—transmuting, in an instant, present into past, life into death" (Sontag 1979:70). See also Sontag's references to Nabokov's *Invitation to a Beheading* (Sontag 1979:167, 178). It must, of course, be pointed out that Sontag's (as well as Barthes's) views on photography and death are found already in Aldo Nuti's meditation upon photography and film in Pirandello's *Quaderni*.

28. See Arnheim (1969:102–103) on the relation of movement to point of view.

29. Nabokov here seems indeed to be toying with the inherent qualities of the camera that have enabled recent film criticism to regard camera views similar to that found in the novel as manifestations of the "transcendental subject" (Baudry 1974/75:43–44).

30. Baudry's elaboration of the tendency of the film-viewing subject to identify himself with the camera (to see the camera as a medium that concretizes the transcendental possibilities of subjectivity and consciousness) provides added poignancy to

Albinus's failure in seeing the trap that is closing down upon him. This character's lack of freedom, direction and purpose stands out against the promise of a camera which suggests that "to seize movement is to become trajectory, to choose a direction is to have the possibility of choosing one, to determine a meaning is to give oneself a meaning" (Baudry 1974/75:43).

31. See on this Balázs (1952:55): "Blurred outlines are mostly the result of our insensitive short-sightedness and superficiality." One great contribution of film cameras is the access they provide to "the hidden mainspring of a life which we had thought we already knew so well."

32. Albinus here makes a choice very similar to the one made by Martha Dreyer in *King, Queen, Knave,* who works so very hard at making "real" the kind of romantic clichés current in movies. He shows the same disregard for the continuities of real life that one finds in such dream scenarios. The connection to characters from *King, Queen, Knave* is more than casual, by the way. Their presence is inscribed into the novel at the very point at which Albinus goes back home to face the consequences of his night with Margot: "Some opened letters lay on the desk. Ah, there it was—what childish handwriting! Bad spelling, bad spelling. An invitation for lunch from the Dreyers. How nice" (L:86).

33. "Continuity" is the function in filmmaking that ensures a semblance of "real world" logic despite the fact that consecutive moments in the film may be shot at different times. Albinus thus is trying to impose upon life a logic that is inherent to the limited and controlled conditions of filmmaking.

34. Albinus, in this episode, is given a chance to review his mistaken image of Margot by the inherent effect of estrangement and alienation typical of cinematography. Exploited most commonly for the amusing or critical purposes of comedy or satire, the ability of the camera to reveal with candid directness what people look like beneath the aura of feeling we impose upon them or the impression they themselves try to project, was noted in a text which could not have escaped Nabokov's attention. What Albinus fails to realize as he watches Margot on screen is stated most clearly by Proust in *The Guermantes Way* in the way the protagonist seems to absorb for a moment the distanced view of the photographer in his grandmother's room: "There was present only the witness, the observer with a hat and travelling coat, the stranger who does not belong to the house, the photographer who has called to take a photograph of places which one will never see again. The process that mechanically occurred in my eyes when I caught sight of my grandmother was indeed a photograph." This is an unexpected and unwelcome experience, for in both Proust and Nabokov what counts is the inner emotional investment of one's personal involvement with an image: "We never see the people who are dear to us save in the animated system, the perpetual motion of our incessant love for them, which before allowing the images that their faces present to reach us catches them in its vortex, flings them back upon the idea that we always had of them, makes them adhere to it, coincide with it" (Proust, cited in Kracauer 1960:14). Albinus's behavior in the cinema illustrates this conflict dramatically.

35. Parker Tyler reflects that "animating a given plastic composition by a great artist may strike one as not only a vulgar but also a criminally absurd idea" (Tyler 1954:12). On this topic see Kracauer (1960), Bazin (1967:164–169), and Mitry (1963/65:I,195–198). See also Lindsay (1970), Durgnat (1971), and Cavell (1971). Most recently we find a whole study dedicated to the study of film and painting in Hollander

(1989). Finally, see also the rather odd (but surprisingly apt in view of Albinus's project of animating medieval stained-glass windows) study by Poncet (1952).

36. As Tyler points out, this kind of technique displaces completely the painting from its aesthetic center since it "actually treats plastic images . . . as though they were live performers and not as the central forms in works of a two-dimensional art." In a more positive vein, however, he sees how the technique may recreate the dynamic vision that precedes painting since "among other things, what such animation accomplishes is a 'flashback' impression of the dynamic elements which temporally went into the making of the work" (Tyler 1954:12).

37. In concluding his discussion of films that "represent" and "interpret" famous paintings, Mitry does point out that such films "offer a demonstration *per absurdum* of the essential principle of filmic expression: montage." He explains, echoing Bazin and Kracauer, that "through fragmentation, through *découpage,* through the juxtaposition of successive images which are yet immobile, film creates, through successive images, the *idea of movement*." In other words, it is through the application of what is most specific to cinematic language that painting yields up its own essence to that of a different medium. But Mitry goes well beyond the thinking of his theoretical predecessors in maintaining that it is through this cinematic essence too that the appearance of causality is created: "Ordered in time these images implicate each other and inscribe themselves into a causal chain. To be more exact, the continuity itself *creates* a causal link among the things which are shown to us in succession; they incite us to believe in some relation of cause and effect between acts which on the canvas are nevertheless simultaneous." Mitry draws radical consequences from this insight, foregrounded and isolated as it is by the interaction of painting and film. One notes that the consequences echo substantially the fictional fate of Albinus the character. As the French critic says, from all of this "it is apparent that causality, as much as it might be subject to logical implications, is in cinematography (more than in literature and anywhere else) the exclusive domain of the all-powerful filmmaker who holds up and directs the duration of the world and of all things and who impresses upon them the laws that he wishes." The ultimate consequence Mitry draws from this is radical indeed, since cinema (more than literature or any other medium) demonstrates how "causality . . . is just an illusion due to the temporal unfolding of things. Since it can be fabricated, it does not exist in absolute terms" (Mitry 1963/65:I, 264).

Chapter Five: Film Theory as Narrative

1. I am alluding to earlier views about this novel such as Brunetta's, who maintains that "the choice of setting seems a matter of happenstance" and to Tessari's strong contention that "the world of cinema is, in *Quaderni,* essentially a pretext for arguing a case that touches upon matters far more important" (Brunetta 1972:23; Tessari 1973:321).

2. Much work has been done in trying to define what the state of film theory was at the time the novel was written and about Pirandello's own notions of film theory. Apart from the studies by Brunetta, Tessari, Angelini, and Cudini mentioned above (and my own earlier versions of materials now in this book), see also Petronio, Farassino, Angelini, Bettettini and Fink in Lauretta (1978), Marra (1976), Brunetta

(1982), Romeo (1988), and Welle (1988), and the studies by Raffelli and Comuzio in Genovese-Gesù (1990:I).

3. This episode also serves to underline the separation between author and narrator in the novel, something that has not been recognized by critics such as Leone de Castris and others, who tend to assume that Gubbio functions essentially as a mouthpiece for Pirandello. What in fact is occurring at this point is a clear separation between the limited import of the "visitor"'s remark and the appropriation of its contents followed by their idiosyncratic extension by Gubbio. In the long run Pirandello in fact warns us of the limits of Gubbio's abilities to handle in practice the theoretical objections to the dehumanizing effects of mechanized society. But even here on the studio floor, while the face is Pirandello's, and the original observation may be too, Gubbio's answer is his alone, reacting as he does to the visitor's words with the assumption that they are laden with malice (a recurring feature of Gubbio's own character). He manages at once to concede the point yet claim that it is he who can "regulate movements." Gubbio thus claims some measure of control in the process of filming, a control that depends on critical empathy with the nature of the action involved—for under- and overcranking depends on a feel for the inherent dynamics and affect of the action. These are important abilities in the performance of his job, but they are crucial also to his role as narrator of this book (Sh:7–8, Quad:11–12).

4. That Gubbio's statement supports neorealism is suggested by Mario Apollonio, cited in Crespi (1967:850). See also Verdone (1952:226) and Marra (1976). I note that my alternative suggestion, first published in 1981, has meanwhile gained some currency; see Barlusconi (1985).

5. For a brief description and evaluation of the results of *Acciaio,* however, see Brunetta (1979:479) and references in his footnote. See also Comuzio in Genovese-Gesù (1990:I).

6. While the critical literature on this topic is by now quite vast, let me just indicate the following: Laura Mulvey's seminal essays first published in 1975, 1981, and 1985, now all gathered in Mulvey (1989). See also Hansen (1986). That what men actually fear is female power, and not castration as such, is suggested by Gabbard and Gabbard (1989) and before them by Lurie (1981/82:52–74). For further questioning of what by now might be called the "classical" version of the subject position, see Clover (1992).

7. A type of film in which the thrilling events—mostly deaths and torture—are known to be unsimulated. While this may seem to be the first such case in fiction, this is not so if we look beyond novels and consider a 1907 story by Apollinaire entitled "Un beau film," in which a group of friends who run a film company arrange for a real murder to be performed for their camera. They achieve a huge success by letting the truth be known to a viewing public greedy for sensationalism while at the same time denying their guilt to the police. When an innocent is finally executed for the murder, they film that too and add the execution to the film. Need I underline the contemporary relevance of such issues (well beyond the seamy cubicles of porno establishments) as seen in the use of "true" execution footage in Antonioni's *Professione: Reporter* (1975)? See Heath (1981:113).

8. References to this famous commonplace that pits the merits of one art form against those of another, a theme debated with great passion over the centuries by

the likes of Leonardo and Lessing, can be traced all the way back to Horace and Simonides. It is still with us (mutatis mutandis) when we debate whether it is film, literature, painting, the theater that can best represent truth and reality; that best captures our essential humanity. Thus, when Gubbio dissects the materials of filmmaking and points out that red light and celluloid strips reduce us to less than human dimensions he is part of the old tradition. He is merely updating Leonardo's judgment that a sculptor, say Michelangelo, cannot be the ideal human being envisioned by the philosophy of his day, working as he does with brutal physicality, covered as he is by sweat and marble dust and chips (Leonardo 1966:5). For background on this subject see Hagstrum (1958), Lee (1967), and Lessing (1965). See also Moses (1981b).

9. Tangential to my treatment of the "discourse on film theory" in *Quaderni,* but important nevertheless in the history of modern cinematic culture, is the effect Pirandello's views have had on film theory. In most cases it would be difficult to attribute direct derivations, although it is often clear that, Pirandello's influence being what it is, his views spread seamlessly into the literature. His anticipations must have been influential, and at the very least they are intriguing in their perceptiveness and for their timeliness. In some cases, however, one can see the derivation quite clearly. It is remarkable, for instance, to what extent traces of Pirandello's novel can be found throughout Walter Benjamin's famous essay "The Work of Art in the Age of Mechanical Reproduction," well beyond the specific reference that Benjamin makes to Pirandello as a source. I have given more details about this topic than I can accommodate here in Moses (1988a:57–63). See also Snyder (1983/84) and Hansen (1987).

10. In dealing, for instance, with what will come to be a key opposition (the formative and mimetic views of cinema), he is most subtle in anticipating the recent awareness that the two are not either/or positions, but should be combined. See Earle (1968) and Mast (1974). Kracauer is on record about this: "The formative tendency, then, does not have to conflict with the realistic tendency. Quite the contrary, it may help substantiate and fulfill it" (Kracauer 1960:16).

11. I say this being fully aware, of course, that even autobiography is a rhetorical convention (and all the more so one written by Nabokov, one might add). Yet the "contract" does contain what is necessary to make relevant what even an autobiographer as stylized as Nabokov has to say about how we go on to experience our lives.

12. Hermann's escape becomes possible only by crossing right into an imaginary screen-space. His is a final and maniacal attempt to impose a totally "cinematic" explication on his actions by convincing bystanders that they are watching the making of a film (D:222). Smurov comes to see his own manipulation of what he perceives in reality, as filtered through his own application of cinematic "special effects." This amounts to a metaphorical control of a mediating cinematographic apparatus: "Whenever I wish, I can accelerate or retard to ridiculous slowness the motions of all these people, or distribute them in different groups, or arrange them in various patterns, lighting them now from below, now from the side. . . . For me, their entire existence has been merely a shimmer on a screen" (Eye:100).

13. For an extensive discussion of the novel, including its cinematic aspects, see Bienstock (1982:125–138).

14. The one filmmaker who seems to have struck a note with Nabokov is Federico Fellini, and he may have done so because of an affinity that emerges most clearly if

we take note of how the personal implications of watching home movies led to the obvious presence of filmlike form in some of Nabokov's most personal childhood memories. The affinity is most striking with Fellini's *8½*, a film Nabokov thought "wonderful." It seems likely that the novelist's sympathetic recognition was triggered by many of the stylistic film innovations Fellini devised to convey the direct experience of memory, of fantasy, and of a totally personal appropriation by the subject of the facts, objects, and people that surround him now and in the past. The haunting effect of a simple gesture (the mother's farewell in the opening of *Speak, Memory*), which is both commonly understandable yet mysterious in its function, is visible repeatedly in *8½* (there too Guido's mother appears waving a handkerchief in a familiar but incomprehensible way). And so are many of the devices which form Nabokov's memories. His English governesses, like the different actors tested for one part in *8½*, fade in and out, repeating their identical characterizing gestures, "some of them wringing their hands, others smiling . . . enigmatically" (SpM:86). They are displayed in parallel vignettes that isolate their actions in paradigmatic film loops, just like the characters from Fellini's past. Both artists (the one working in the medium itself and the other bending another medium to the forms of film) foreground the technical and aesthetic peculiarities of the film medium in order to emphasize the ritual self-enclosedness of remembered details.

15. See, for more details, Moses (1987).

Chapter Six: The Film Novel as Literary Genre

1. Fowler (1982) and Rosenmeyer (1969) subscribe to this classical notion of the evolution of genres.

2. See also Boyd (1990:368, 569). The film novel is somewhat analogous, if more far reaching in its ambition, to the short-lived experiment in "roman cinéoptique" described by Clerc (1985:179 ff.). According to the founder of this film-influenced narrative genre, A. Marchard, the reader was to be put in the same position as a film spectator. The novels in question first appeared between 1926 and 1928.

3. See especially Christine Brooke-Rose (1981) and Todorov (1990). See also Todorov (1970) and Ceserani (1983).

4. I evoke Hoffmann who is not, as the well-read know, the true protagonist of a story by E. T. A. Hoffmann called "Der Sandmann" (1816–1817), and to glasses that, the erudite will insist, are not the optical instrument that causes a mechanical doll named Olimpia to appear human. In doing so I validate the most influential of several versions of this famous episode which, as happens at times, has assumed a life of its own in cultural discourse. In abandoning the philological accuracy of character Nathanael for autobiographical frame narrator Hoffmann, by superseding the mechanics of "perspective" for the convenience of eyeglasses, I address the fact that this particular moment in the evolution of cultural attitudes about illusion and its apparatus is epitomized by the 1881 opera version that Jacques Offenbach derived from the enormously successful theatrical version staged by Jules Barbier and Michel Carré in 1851 in Paris. The influence of both, as well as the later exigencies of theatrical mise-en-scène, have obliterated from this topos the fact that Hoffmann's protagonist Nathanael actually refuses to buy the eyeglasses offered to him by Coppola and instead succumbs to the

mystification of a small kaleidoscopic telescope, one that actually makes no mystery of its "special effects." Thus, kaleidoscopes, telescopes, opera glasses, pince-nez, and eyeglasses take over from one another as versions go by (a veritable minihistory of optical evolution), and Hoffmann's hapless student is replaced by the self-referential author. It is he, and his eyeglasses, who is now enshrined in the popular imagination: precocious personification of a subject position that all too readily submits to the *effect of real* provided by deceptive and malevolent optical mediation.

5. For this classical example of the meeting of the two discontinuous discourses of literature and painting in an atmosphere in which one was seen as inferior to the other (much like cinema was for a long time to literature), see Alpers (1960:190–215).

6. In the following I rely on Alpers (1973). For a discussion of the more traditional concept of "mode" that stresses the enunciative situation and the tendency of theory to confuse it with "genre," see Genette (1979:65 ff.). See also Société des Anglicistes (1986) and Ceserani (1989).

7. As Angus Fletcher argues, "the term 'mode' is appropriate because in each of the five [periods] the hero is a protagonist with a given strength relative to his world, and as such each hero—whether mythic, romantic, high mimetic, low mimetic, or ironic—is a *modulator* for verbal architectonics; man is the measure, the *modus*, of myth" (Fletcher 1966:34–35).

8. Quoted by Todorov (1984:92), who adds that in Bakhtin's overlapping and catch-as-catch-can lists of genres and subgenres the "mode of representation of the main character" provides a strong focus. He adds that "Bahktin's work does not consist in the establishment of genres, but, having found them, in their submission to analysis (which can be stylistic as well as chronotopic, or related to the conception of man revealed in them)" (Todorov 1984:93).

9. The film novel exhibits, in other words, the kind of textual productivity that Barthes gathers into the proairetic code.

10. The desire to transcend the limits set by life (temporal, epistemological, and so on) is given as possible motivation for the creation of genres by Gumbrecht (1992: 50): "If the limits of the life world are regarded as anthropologically constant, then it can be assumed that their transgression either backward or forward in time is an equally constant anthropological fascination. The fascination of simulating the transgression of the life world's limits in either direction would have to be regarded as part of that anthropological basis for individual genres that we have sought as a parallel to the types of experiential style."

11. I am not trying to suggest, of course, that we can determine with certainty that materials found in autobiography may be less "fictional" than those found in fiction (whatever that term may mean). Especially in the case of Nabokov, one tends to feel that the materials in *Speak, Memory* may well deserve the skepticism reserved for some of Freud's "case histories" by readers such as Peter Brooks. With Nabokov too one feels that what matters is "another kind of referentiality," and that "tales may lead back not so much to events as to other tales, to man as a structure of the fictions he tells about himself" (Brooks 1985:277). Disheartening as this may sound to those of us who need to believe in the "unaffectedness of the real," Brooks's elucidation of this mechanism actually helps to set in perspective, when applied to our context, the significance of Nabokov's use of the "primal" cinematic event: "Such primal phantasies

[the actual event of which may not have happened to the individual] may be a phylogenetic inheritance through which the individual reaches back to the history of mankind, to a racial 'masterplot'" (Brooks 1985:276).

12. Genre studies, like studies in other areas, have in recent years advanced with greater boldness in film studies than in literary ones. It is thus that one may find useful, if initially opaque, a monograph such as Neale (1983), from which I draw in this as in other passages. As Neale puts it,

> It is the specific inscription of music into the plurality of discourses that constitute the text which ultimately shapes, determines and marks the register in which equilibrium and disequilibrium achieve their most intense expression and in which narrative resolution finally occurs. In other words, sequences of song and dance represent a shift in the regime of the narrative discourse, marked, for example, by a different articulation of body and voice. These sequences, this 'other' regime, woven into the narrative, allow a particularly intense and coherent statement of the conflicts, tension and problems that traverse the narrative as a whole. They also, at certain points in some musical films, represent the terms of a resolution to these conflicts, tensions and problems.... Whether such a resolution occurs in all song and dance sequences or not, the point here is that these musically determined sequences, in their completion and perfection, represent the discursive mode in relation to which resolution or lack of resolution are to be measured and through which stability and equilibrium are ultimately to be achieved. (Neale 1983:23)

13. Neale insists that "the organization of a given 'order' and of its disruption should be seen always in terms of conjunctions of and disjunctions between multiple sets of discursive categories and operations" (Neale 1983:21). His examples of physical violence are derived from the western, gangster, detective, and horror film, respectively.

14. See the useful summary on writerly text in Silverman (1983:146–150). Useful suggestions about a more differentiated articulation of such responses are found in Gumbrecht (1992:47).

15. I am modifying what Elaine Showalter, quoted by Culler, has stated as "the way in which the *hypothesis* of a female reader changes our apprehension of a given text, awakening us to the significance of its sexual codes" (Culler 1988:204). See also Culler (1982:43–64).

16. Neale's somewhat concise formulation is that narrative "binds together, implicating the subject as the point where its binding mechanisms cohere, the point from where the deployment and configuration of discourses make 'sense'" (Neale 1983:25).

17. Note that—independently of a preconceived Lacanian theory of the subject as discussed, for instance, by Silverman (1983)—the film novel has a tendency to derive the essence of the existential experience of lack from a character's confrontation with the discursive clash of film discourse and literary discourse.

18. For a short while, of course, Albinus gets his "dream," but, as we said, his very way of looking at it (filmlike in its generic impersonality) dooms him to ultimate deprivation: "With nothing but the deep blue above, Margot lay spread-eagled on the platinum sand, her limbs a rich honey-brown, and a thin white rubber belt relieving the black of her bathing-suit: the perfect seaside poster" (L:112). As Nabokov points out at the outset, "detail is always welcome" (L:7).

19. When MacCabe, in an essay on "principles of realism and pleasure" first pub-

lished in 1976, talks about the "complicated circulation which ensures that I am not only a spectator in the cinema but also, by a process of identification, a character on the screen," he could be offering an "explication" of *Laughter in the Dark* as it moves from the darkness of the Argus to that of a blinded Albinus groping (like a masked man) for the girl he is trying to kill (MacCabe 1985:68).

20. Such distinctions are currently still undergoing theoretical evolution. See, for instance, the discussion of "look" and "gaze" in Silverman (1992:129–130).

21. "It is the mother's look that confirms the validity of the infant's image and with this look we find that at the very foundation of the dual imaginary relationship there is a third term already unsettling it. The mother verifies the relationship for the child, but at the cost of introducing a look, a difference where there should be only similitude" (MacCabe 1985:66).

22. Thematic clustering is what Todorov essentially seems to mean when he discusses the concept of thematic proliferation.

23. See Tomashevsky's "Thematics" in Lemon-Rees (1965), as well as a longer version in Todorov (1965). Concerning Barthes's view of thematics, Silverman puts it thus: "Thematization involves a quite complex operation, in which the semic code plays an important role. It is in effect the definition of character, object or place in ways which signify 'mystery'" (Silverman 1983:258).

24. Note that Lesage stays with the Barthes/Lévi-Strauss model based on the relationship between language and kinship or sex and commercial economy and points to "antithesis" as the main rhetorical figure that carries the code. She then defines narrative as follows:

> In the classical narrative, representation depends on an order of just equivalencies, by means of which we can regularly distinguish contraries, sexes, and possessions. Yet it is only when an excessive element enters which interrupts the normal circulation of the antitheses, sexes, property relations, or contracts that the narrative begins. It is the transgressor that impels the narrative toward its climax or catastrophe. Symbolic and narrative requirements in a work of fiction finally merge, for narrative resolution not only means the final irreversible "predicating" of the subject and the end of the story (for there is no more to say) but also the end of the symbolic search, what Barthes calls a symbolic closure or return to order. (Lesage 1985:494)

See on this also Silverman (1983:272), especially her discussion of Barthes. For a broader overview of what is implicit in such oppositional semantic fields see Bordwell (1989:105–128).

25. I am aware, of course, that above I gave as the reason for the death of Albinus his loss of point of view and look. As we find that the productivity of this text provides multiple determinations for his death, Albinus may well be the man who dies the death of a thousand tropes!

26. The novel, first published in 1986, clearly owes something to the final moments of Michelangelo Antonioni's film *Blow Up* (1966). For more on this and the multicultural travels of this trope, see Moses (1991).

27. Julia Kristeva considers such microscopic discursive manifestations to be "dynamic predicates" endowed with the "power to form a story" (quoted in Culler 1975: 204). On the movement from this fundamental textual level to that of genre, Neale

comments: "The *marks of generic specificity as such* [my emphasis] are produced by an articulation that is always constructed in terms of particular 'combinations' of particular types or categories of discourse" (Neale 1983:21).

28. On the dependence of the subject on discourse, see Benveniste in Silverman (1983:199).

Chapter Seven: The Hollywood Novel

1. On these novels, see many of the essays in *Cinema & Cinema* 11:40/41(1984) in which my chapter on Fitzgerald first appeared. See also Millar (1979/80). On the Hollywood novel in general (apart from Alfred Appel's study on Nabokov), see Cowley (1951:237–240), Wilson (1956:24), Lokke (1961), Fiedler (1964), Pisk (1967), Powell (1971), Schulberg (1940), Schulberg (1960), See (1968), Wells (1973), Widmer (1961), and Widmer (1973). For comparison of West with Fitzgerald, see Bittner (1960) and Galloway (1963/64). For comparison of Fitzgerald and Evelyn Waugh's *The Loved One*, see Aaron (1951). On the Wilson edition of *The Last Tycoon*, see Bruccoli (1977).

2. Isherwood's homosexuality is here hinted at by the teasing Shakespearian allusion that Bergmann makes: "Is it Mr. W. H. you seek, or the Dark Lady of the Sonnets?" (PrV:50).

3. Paradoxically, *Die Weltbühne,* when founded in 1904 by Siegfried Jacobsohn under the name *Die Schaubühne,* was indeed a stage magazine. Only in 1918, renamed *Die Weltbühne,* did it broaden its coverage to political issues (Friedrich 1972: 345–347). The paper was closed down in 1933, the year Bergmann was in London.

4. See also Willemen (1972). See, for an example of Brecht's own double-text reading, Brecht (1970:221–225).

5. Bruccoli (1977) throws some light on Wilson's procedure.

6. He read it while working with Schulberg on a film and writing his own novel (Bruccoli 1977:20–21). See also Schulberg (1978) and Rapf (1988).

7. That Fitzgerald's notion of auteurship entails a conscious counter-marxist coloring is suggested by Callahan (1978:205), who quotes Fitzgerald's advice to his daughter to "read the terrible chapter in *Das Capital* on *The Working Day*" and suggests that the chapter is the subtext of Stahr's day at the studio. It "is geared to show," Callahan contends, "how crucial the gifted individual is to the collaborative enterprise of movies." On Fitzgerald and the communist view of Hollywood, see also Rapf (1988: 78–79).

8. One must note that even Bachelard concedes the amorphously rhetorical use of literary topoi that are like "a schoolboy's habit of writers with no imagination."

9. I. Lloyd Michaels, in a paper that, while discussing Elia Kazan's film adaptation, says a lot that illuminates the novel as well, underlines that this episode is used in brilliant fashion by Kazan to advance the agenda of a film that "seeks to return us not merely to the golden days of Hollywood, but to the very essence of the cinema itself." In this Kazan's film seeks to achieve the same ultimate aim of many of the film novels I discuss. "In its most positive light," Michaels states, "the scene with Boxley confirms Stahr's ability as movie-maker to generate a spontaneous reality and to captivate

the most sophisticated of viewers under its sway. Stahr's is the 'vital illusion' of Jay Gatsby, the apprehension of an aesthetic dream which Fitzgerald in his earlier novel described as a 'heightened sensitivity to the promises of life,' a 'romantic readiness'" (Michaels 1982:113–114). On the adaptation see also Rapf (1988).

10. See Bruccoli (1977:20). For Fitzgerald's note on Huxley, see Bruccoli (1977: 130).

11. Allmendinger (1988:108, 110) makes an interesting case based on his observation that, commonplace as it is to say that novels have "a film-like quality," it is necessary to ask further: "What kind of film *is* it which informs the novel?" In the case of West's novel, Allmendinger suggests it is silent movies.

12. Appel (1974:29) cites this Nabokovian tag for the ultimate in mimetic arts.

13. It has taken until now, it seems, for mainstream film theory to catch up with themes that seem to have been obvious to West. See, for instance, Silverman (1992).

14. Dan Millar, while noticing this as others have done before, misses the connection between the pictorial visual style and Tod Hackett's role as visual designer. In Millar's view, West's novel "tries to turn words into the stasis of a painting, moments of vision, perhaps narrative painting, still photography, the ordered and limited movements of a stage act—anything but the driving narrative flow of the well-made '30s movie, which West refuses to produce out of office hours . . . except on the 'soundtrack,' which is brilliantly complex and varied, including the dialogue." As my discussion shows, West's relationship to what is and is not cinematic is far more complex than Millar (and others) allows for. It is best revealed by keeping in mind the full range of possibilities inherent in the film novel as derived from Pirandello rather than (as happens in Millar's hurried observations) by measuring West's prose against the narrow standard of the "well made '30s movie" (Millar 1979/80:19).

Chapter Eight: The Eyes Have to Know

1. Mira Liehm, who notes the similarity between what Battista says and political polemics by the right, quotes what Moravia had to say about this kind of attitude in 1950, as well as parts of the famous open letter that Andreotti addressed to De Sica in *Libertà* (February 24, 1952) (Liehm 1984:91, 334). See also Brunetta (1982:87, 102) for Giulio Andreotti's large influence on Italian cinema in the fifties.

2. On the effective control that censorship had on Italian cinema in these years, see the cautious chapter in Brunetta (1982:83–104) and the somewhat less cautious bibliography cited within. For a lighter, if not less serious, cinematic treatment of the matter, see Ettore Scola's *We Loved Each Other So Much* (1974), in which one of the characters loses his job when he shows De Sica's *Ladri di biciclette* (1948) at the local film club and dares stand up and defend it against the objections of the local Andreottis.

3. While little has been written on film in this novel—see Freshney (1982) and Bugge (1983)—there is a more extensive bibliography on Walker Percy's first novel *The Moviegoer*. While I do not consider *The Moviegoer* a film novel in the sense that I am discussing in this study, see Henisey (1968), Thale (1968), Byrd (1972), Pindell (1975), Vauthier (1975), Vauthier (1978), Lawson (1980), Zamora (1984), and Lawson (1988).

4. This quotation from Martin Heidegger's *Existence and Being* concludes Walker Percy's essay entitled "Naming and Being" (Percy 1992:137–138).

5. After saying in 1985 that he did not consider *Last Tango in Paris* a very good film, Walker Percy continued:

> I do not think it pornographic, either. In this film two people who remain strangers throughout perform a series of sexual operations on each other, mostly in dead silence, and in the end one kills the other. Two things happen, an impersonal sex and a dispassionate violence. Perhaps these are the only two things that can happen. A case might be made that, given a certain urban environment and an educated class of laymen alienated from each other and from themselves, only two real options remain, genital sex and violence, and perhaps the realest of all, death. (Percy 1992:215)

6. For a more extensive exploration of the intertextual intercourse of Pasolini and Percy, see Moses (1985).

7. See Heidegger (1977:10). My frame of reference here is Martin Heidegger's contrast of Greek and modern attitudes about technology, spectacle and the way in which they call upon human awareness of self.

Chapter Nine: You Can't Imagine

1. A recent essay that makes important observations about this novel in the context of verbal as well as iconic semiotics is Zamora (1984). While Zamora obviously touches upon some of the features that are also part of my discussion, the ultimate focus of the essay is to consider the presence in Puig and Percy of certain semiotic notions put forth by Juri Lotman—natural and secondary sign systems, "transcodage," among them. The novels thus come to be seen not as instances of a narrative mode in its own right, but as further instances of the fact that "the singularity of these works is the product of systems created within the text, and furthermore by the relationship of those systems to systems outside the text. Their uniqueness results not from the absence of norms and systems but from their abundant presence, and from the interaction of these various systems, both internal and external to the novel" (Zamora 1984: 63–64). Perhaps.

2. The verses come from Dylan Thomas's magnificent "film poem" "Our Eunuch Dreams" (Thomas 1957:16–18). For more on this genre that does for lyric poetry what the film novel does for narrative, see Moses (1992) and Goldstein (1994).

3. My reading of Toto's interaction with the movies thus differs from Worley (1983), who concentrates on the lack of control over the escapist fascination with movies by Toto and the other characters in the novel. As Worley puts it, the power of Puig's novel resides in his "skill in revealing the fantasy underlying each character's life and presenting that fantasy to us in common terms—the shorthand of film dreams" (Worley 1983:51–52). For a list of films Puig alludes to in this novel, see Campos (1985:181–183).

4. It is a measure of Puig's subtle artistry that both Berto and Héctor, despite their negative effect on Toto, still emerge from the chorus of voices in this novel to reveal their own pained humanity and deep need for affection and understanding.

5. The novel was first published in 1976 and translated into English in 1978. Apart

from the well-known film version, Puig wrote a stage version that was first performed on 18 April 1981, at the Sala Escalante della Diputación in Valencia under the direction of José Luis García Sánchez (Puig 1988).

6. Moravia had stated this view before, but again made this claim during a television interview recorded with me in April 1981. Godard, on the other hand, set out to do what he refers to as "a chapter-by-chapter adaptation" (Baby 1972:37). Walter Korte regards the novel merely "as the *pre-text* which provides the catalytic elements for an entirely new creation" (Korte 1974:284). More aware that the film incorporates in its structure the very problem of adaptation is Kinder (1981). She concludes, however, that "*Le Mépris* implies that it is impossible to make a film that is faithful either to Homer's autonomous unity or to Moravia's psychological analysis because in each case the time, medium, and artistic consciousness are different" (Kinder 1981:105).

7. My comparison of novel and film is strictly governed by my concern with the film novel as genre and was first presented at the Seventh "Convegno Internazionale di Studi sul Cinema e gli Audiovisivi" (Urbino, 1988). For comparisons independent of my views, see Fontenot (1985), Boccia (1986), Dittmar (1986), Karetnikova and Barber (1987), Cheever (1987), Bost (1989), and Mistron (1989)—a study that by its own admission is unaware of the preceding bibliography. Fontenot discusses what he calls "the creative integration of the reader with the text" (Fontenot 1985:5), without, of course, relating this feature to the fact that *Kiss of the Spider Woman* belongs to a narrative genre that overdetermines this integration in genre-specific ways. He discusses its use of reported film plots, for instance, in Bakhtinian terms. Boccia goes too far, it seems to me, in maintaining that "the nature and meaning of the films are irrelevant because the embellished retellings represent the world according to Molina and are more indicative of his world view than any cinematic tradition" (Boccia 1986:419). Without the actual films "as they are," there would be no meaning in Molina's and Valentin's writerly intervention. The fact is that "the films Molina relates" are *not entirely* "his own inventions." Dittmar addresses the loss inherent in simplifying the structure of the novel for the cinema as a "political" as well as a "formal" loss. More specifically, she complains that "the film cuts back on the discourse of gender and on the role of gender within capitalism" (Dittmar 1986:83). Karetnikova-Barber, after claiming that the entire book is "cinematic" because it appeals to visual perception, is written in the present tense, shows only what people say and do, and contains no authorial digressions and abstract concepts (they also provide examples of cutting, montage, and moving camera), reaches the puzzling conclusion that the film version is a failure because "Puig's novel *is* an accomplished 'film' in itself." This is apparently based on the dubious logic that, since scriptwriting has become as important as shooting and editing was in earlier times, "today . . . a film could be fully visualized without any shooting or editing" and that "*Kiss of the Spider Woman* is a quintessential example of that" (Karetnikova and Barber 1987:165). Cheever feels that "the movie version so distorts and transmogrifies Puig's exploration of [the theme of 'abysmal alienation'] as to render it barely recognizable," but that "such distortion and transmogrification are *inevitable* in any attempt to transfer Puig's story from one medium to another" (Cheever 1987:14). Among other things, Cheever seems to feel that film by definition cannot challenge the reality of familiar worlds, while literature can: "The viewer of the movie sees what he recognizes as a story projected upon a screen, and his task is thus that of interpreting that story in terms of what he knows about the fa-

miliar world. But the reader of the novel holds in his hands a document which *itself* demands interpretation before any story can emerge at all. In other words, the reader must *discover* the book's story before he can hope to *recognize* it, and this very complex and difficult task of discovery is precisely what the movie version cannot show" (Cheever 1987:19). It is not obvious to me that film as a medium cannot provide a process of "discovery" to its spectators, nor that it could not find ways of articulating the narrative voices suggested by Cheever. The fact that Babenco does not do so says nothing about what would be possible.

8. David H. Bost also notes, in agreement with my remarks at the Urbino conference in 1988, that "we must remind ourselves that Molina is a narrator, not a director or cinematographer, and that his evocation of visual data appears in the novel as narrative, not as real movie" (Bost 1989:94). Bost, however, does not question the elimination of this dimension from the film version of the novel. It is not clear why, as Deborah E. Mistron contends, "the act of Molina's describing films indirectly . . . can be recreated on the screen for a short time, but eventually the images being described must be *shown*" (Mistron 1989:110). She is right, I believe, in her conclusion that the problem resides in Babenco's decision to adopt "traditional narrative strategies which cannot express fully Puig's concern with power and control in artistic discourse as well as in society" (Mistron 1989:111).

9. Thus, rather than just representations of desire as suggested by Echavarren (1978), film also embodies the very experience of desire itself.

10. For specific discrepancies, see Wyers-Weber (1981:167–170).

11. Boccia (1986) notes this too. He also makes the point that "there could be no way to show his sources" (Boccia 1986:419) because of Molina's tendency to embroider and conflate. One fails to see why this is so, since a variety of technical solutions (including the option of merging existing old footage with new material) are state of the art today. The problems, of course, were also quite practical ones, as indicated by Puig himself in an interview cited by Sloan, in which the writer indicates that "they couldn't show *The Cat People* [sic] because of the rights problems" (Sloan 1987:24).

12. We have remarked on this notion of Eichenbaum's before. It should be noted that he meant it to apply to silent cinema. Stern warnings, still current today, about speaking out loud during the show suggest that a verbal response (not always silent) continues to be triggered by sound movies too. Because of this, it seems to me that the sections that depict the narrative appropriation of films by Molina and Valentin have more to do with Eichenbaum's notion that film generates an instinctive retelling in words than with "the return of the oral tradition in postliterate society" (Sloan 1987:23) or with an updated version of the "inserted tale" (Bost 1989:93). For a wide-ranging discussion of Eichenbaum (1981), see Bordwell, Levaco, and Willemen in *Screen* (vol. 15, no. 4), and Bordwell in *Screen* (vol. 16, no. 1).

13. Molina's own self-identity and its interaction with the films he retells have been addressed by Bost (1989).

14. For frame of reference, apart from a dusting of post-Freudian ideas made inevitable by the cinematic framework, see views of "separation" and "individuation" in Mahler, Pine, and Bergman (1975), Blos (1962), and Bowlby (1973).

15. This point is made also by Boccia (1986). A reading that ignores such considerations, on the other hand, and confines itself to the schematic framework of conventional ideological distinctions, will tend to condemn the two protagonists as unregen-

erate reactionaries. See Merrim (1985:309–310). This disregards the potential inherent in the writerly subject position available to spectators at the movies, B-grade as may be. In fact, for both Molina and Valentin film provides, as it does nowadays in culture at large, one of the means of individuation. As with all other such means (parental role models and the like) successful individuation requires an "active" and "critical" role on the part of the individual. It seems to me that bad films, as opposed to bad parents, can hardly be accused of intentional child abuse (filmmakers are not in a parental role). Passive and compliant audiences, by the same token, are as responsible for their own "repression" as insufficiently "rebellious" teenagers. What Linda Dittmar says about women applies just as much (mutatis mutandis) to all film viewers: "Only deliberately interventionist, resisting and disavowing readings can protect women from weaving their identifications into the web of patriarchal repression which *Gilda* spins for its audience" (Dittmar 1986:82).

16. Dittmar describes some of the problems inherent in Molina's construction of a psychological identity at odds with his physiological one. "His definition of femininity," she points out, "colludes with the patriarchy." She concludes that, "for him, loving and being loved 'as a woman' means an erasure of self." Sloan (1987) concurs.

17. It seems to me that Bill Nichols's objections that "the political effect of this representation of contradiction is not necessarily obvious" (Nichols 1985:196) is essentially met by Wood (1985:202). Sloan applies Wood on horror movies (specifically *Cat People*) to Puig in a way somewhat different from mine: "The horror movie serves the function of collective dream or nightmare in which repressed desire is transferred to a double (the monster). The desire is acted out and then relegated back into the unconscious. Wood sees that one of the key forces suffering from 'surplus' repression in our culture is sexuality, and the greatest threat to patriarchal control is female sexuality" (Sloan 1987:25).

18. The other "story" in this novel is, of course, the one suggested by the juxtaposition of film plots with the situation of the two prisoners. Masiello (1978) has made seminal suggestions about this, later developed in some detail by Worley (1983), Sloan (1987), and Bost (1989). She stresses the predictability and "patterned experiences" of these parallels as well as what she regards as a smooth continuity between films and prison. Masiello considers Molina a "traditional reader" who "identifies with the plight of the heroes" (Masiello 1978:20). Yet Molina, as he tells us himself, is a male reader who always identifies with the heroine. He is thus the kind of reader who, rather than establishing a traditional identification, "reads" from "difference." It seems to me that, in similar fashion, the parallel between films and story is not that smooth. The films don't "emplot" an unproblematic analogy with the lives of the two prisoners. Rather, they highlight experiences in the characters' lives that are painful, disjointed, and chaotic. The films thus provide "form" and "glamor" to the subtext of life and aim at providing an "ending" that in life remains ever elusive and filled with anxiety. See Masiello (1978) and Worley (1983). For a psychoanalytic juxtaposition of the film plots with Molina and Valentin, see Merrim (1985). As she puts it, "while the characters themselves supposedly encode the films with their personal circumstances, the author has built an extra dimension into each film which addresses matters of homosexuality, sex roles, repression, and so on" (Merrim 1985:305). Bost also discusses how the movies "deal with issues like identity, political consciousness, relationships, and self-sacrifice" (Bost 1989:93).

Chapter Ten: The Return of Genre

1. Applied by Hays to the realm of current "representation" theory, this formulation nicely captures the element that is contributed to the genesis of this "mirage" by the delusion of instrumental cinematic synthesis we have encountered often in this study (Hays 1992:295).

2. The episode, reported by Nardelli (1932), is also discussed in a psychoanalytic perspective by Ferrario (1978:25 ff.).

Bibliography

Primary Sources

Alther, Lisa. 1976. *Kinflicks*. New York: Knopf.
Dürrenmatt, Friedrich. 1989. *The Assignment: or on the Observing of the Observer of the Observers*. Tr. Joel Agee. New York: Vintage Books.
Fitzgerald, F. Scott. 1970. *The Last Tycoon*. New York: Scribner's. [LaT]
Hollander, John. 1962. "Movie-Going." In *Movie-Going and Other Poems*, 2–6. New York: Atheneum.
Isherwood, Christopher. 1978. *Prater Violet*. New York: Avon Books. [PrV]
Montale, Eugenio. 1948. *Ossi di seppia*. Milan: Mondadori.
———. 1970. *Provisional Conclusions: A Selection of the Poetry of Eugenio Montale*. Tr. Edith Farnworth. Chicago: Henry Regneri Company.
Moravia, Alberto. 1955. *Il disprezzo*. Milan: Bompiani. [Disp]
———. 1955. *A Ghost at Noon*. Tr. Angus Davidson. New York: Farrar, Strauss and Young. [GaN]
Nabokov, Vladimir. 1960. *Laughter in the Dark*. New York: New Directions. [L]
———. 1964. *Bend Sinister*. New York: Time Incorporated. [Bend]
———. 1965. *The Eye*. New York: Phaedra. [Eye]
———. 1966. *Speak, Memory: An Autobiography Revisited*. New York: Putnam's. [SpM]
———. 1968. *King, Queen, Knave*. New York: McGraw-Hill. [KQKn]
———. 1973. *Mary*. Harmondsworth: Penguin. [M]
———. 1973. *Strong Opinions*. New York: McGraw-Hill. [SO]
———. 1979. *Despair*. New York: Putnam's. [D]
———. 1979. *The Nabokov–Wilson Letters: 1940–1971*. Ed. Simon Karlinsky. New York: Harper and Row. [NW]
———. 1980. *Lectures on Literature*. Ed. Fredson Bowers. New York: Harcourt Brace Jovanovich. [LoL]

O'Faoláin, Seán. 1949. *The Man Who Invented Sin, and Other Stories*. New York: Devin-Adair.
Percy, Walker. 1977. *The Moviegoer*. New York: Noonday Press. [Mov]
———. 1978. *Lancelot*. New York: Avon Books. [Lanc]
———. 1992. *Signposts in a Strange Land*. Ed. Patrick Samway. New York: Noonday Press.
Pirandello, Luigi. 1920. "Ironia." *L'idea nazionale* (27 February). Reprinted in Lum: 992–995. [Ir]
———. 1926. *Shoot! (Si Gira): The Notebooks of Serafino Gubbio Cinematograph Operator*. Tr. C. K. Scott-Moncrieff. New York: Dutton. [Sh]
———. 1954. *Quaderni di Serafino Gubbio operatore*. Milan: Mondadori. [Quad]
———. 1960. *L'umorismo, Saggi, Poesie, Scritti varii*. Ed. Manlio Lo Vecchio Nusti. Milan: Mondadori. [Lum]
———. 1974. *On Humor*. Tr. Antonio Illiano and Daniel P. Testa. Chapel Hill: University of North Carolina Press. [Hum]
Puig, Manuel. 1971. *Betrayed by Rita Hayworth*. New York: Avon Books. [Betr]
———. 1979. *Kiss of the Spider Woman*. New York: Knopf. [Kiss]
———. 1988. *Stelle del firmamento e altre commedie*. Tr. Angelo Morino. Turin: Einaudi.
Rilke, Rainer Maria. 1962. *Sonnets to Orpheus*. Tr. M. D. Herter Norton. New York: Norton.
Thomas, Dylan. 1957. *Collected Poems*. New York: New Directions.
Tommaseo, Niccoló. 1958. *Opere*. Ed. Aldo Borlenghi. Milan: Ricciardi.
West, Nathanael. 1969. *Miss Lonelyhearts* and *The Day of the Locust*. New York: New Directions. [DoL]

Secondary Sources

Aaron, Daniel. 1951. "Writing for Apocalypse." *Hudson Review* 3(Winter):634–636.
Adams, Robert M. 1958. *Strains of Discord: Studies in Literary Openness*. Ithaca: Cornell University Press.
Agel, Henri. 1957. *Esthétique du cinéma*. Paris: P.U.F.
Allmendinger, Blake. 1988. "The Death of a Mute Mythology: From Silent Movies to the Talkies in *The Day of the Locust*." *Literature/Film Quarterly* 16(2):107–111.
Alpers, Paul. 1973. "Mode in Narrative Poetry." In *To Tell a Story: Narrative Theory and Practice*, 25–56. Los Angeles: William Andrews Clark Memorial Library.
Alpers, Svetlana. 1960. "*Ekphrasis* and Aesthetic Attitudes in Vasari's Lives." *Journal of the Warburg and Courtauld Institutes* 23:190–215.
Andrew, J. Dudley. 1976. *The Major Film Theories*. New York: Oxford University Press.
Angelini, Franca. 1975. "Serafino Gubbio, la tigre e la vocazione teatrale di Luigi Pirandello." In *Letteratura e critica: studi un onore di Natalino Sapegno*, 2:855–882. Rome: Bulzoni.
———. 1977. "*Si gira* . . . : l'ideologia della macchina in Pirandello." In *Il romanzo di Pirandello*, ed. Enzo Lauretta, 143–160. Palermo: Palumbo.
———. 1978. "Dal 'teatro muto' all' 'antiteatro': le teorie del cinema all'epoca del

'Si gira. . . .'" In *Pirandello e il cinema,* ed. Enzo Lauretta, 65–83. Agrigento: Centro Nationale di Studi Pirandelliani.

———. 1990. *Serafino e la tigre.* Venice: Marsilio.

Anon. 1925. "Notizie bibliografiche: letteratura contemporanea." *L'Italia che scrive* (Rome) 8(September):171.

Appel, Alfred, Jr. 1974. *Nabokov's Dark Cinema.* New York: Oxford University Press.

Appel, Alfred, Jr., and Charles Newman, eds. 1971. *Nabokov: Criticism, Reminiscences, Translations and Tributes.* London: Weidenfeld and Nicolson.

Aristarco, Guido. 1963. *Storia delle teoriche del film.* Turin: Einaudi.

———. 1984. *L'utopia cinematografica.* Palermo: Sellerio.

Arnheim, Rudolf. 1966. *Toward a Psychology of Art.* Berkeley: University of California Press.

———. 1969. *Film as Art.* Berkeley: University of California Press.

Artioli, Umberto. 1988. "*L'itinerarium* di Serafino Gubbio: motivi e struttura di una rielaborazione pirandelliana." *Rivista di studi pirandelliani,* 3d series, 1(December):9–30.

Augustine, Saint. 1961. *Confessions.* Tr. R. S. Pine-Coffin. Harmondsworth: Penguin Books.

Baby, Yvonne. 1972. "Shipwrecked People from the Modern World: Interview with Jean-Luc Godard on *Le Mépris.*" In *Focus on Godard,* ed. Royal S. Brown, 37–39. Englewood Cliffs, N.J.: Prentice-Hall.

Bachelard, Gaston. 1942. *L'Eau et les rêves.* Paris: Corti.

———. 1969. *The Poetics of Space.* Tr. Maria Jolas. Boston: Beacon Press.

Balázs, Béla. 1938. "Il film a colori." *Bianco e nero* 3(2).

———. 1952. *Theory of the Film: Character and Growth of a New Art.* London: Dennis Dobson.

Barberi Squarotti, Giorgio. 1986. "La sfida di Serafino Gubbio operatore." *Arel* 1(3): 189–210.

Barfield, Owen. 1977. "The Harp and the Camera." In *The Rediscovery of Meaning and Other Essays,* 65–78. Middletown, Conn.: Wesleyan University Press.

Barilli, Renato. 1972. *La linea Svevo-Pirandello.* Milan: Mursia.

Barlusconi, Giovanna. 1985. "Pirandello: l'arte e la macchina." In *Il novecento letterario in Italia,* 159–171. Milan: Vita e Pensiero.

Barrett, William. 1979. *The Illusion of Technique.* New York: Anchor Books.

Barthes, Roland. 1968. "L'Effet de réel." *Communications* 11:84–89.

———. 1980. *La camera chiara: nota sulla fotografia.* Turin: Einaudi.

Baudry, Jean-Louis. 1974/75. "Ideological Effects of the Basic Cinematographic Apparatus." *Film Quarterly* 28(2):39–47. Originally in *Cinétique* 7/8:1–8 (1970). Also in Nichols (1985) and Rosen (1986).

———. 1976. "The Apparatus." *Camera Obscura* 1(Fall):97–126. Original appeared as "Le dispositif," *Communications* 23:56–72 (1975). Also in Rosen (1986).

Bazin, André. 1967 and 1971. *What Is Cinema?* 2 vols. Berkeley: University of California Press.

Benjamin, Walter. 1969. *Illuminations: Essays and Reflections.* Ed. Hanna Arendt. Tr. Harry Zohn. New York: Schocken.

Benveniste, Emile. 1971. "Remarks on the Function of Language in Freudian Theory." In *Problems in General Linguistics,* tr. Mary Elizabeth Meek, 65–75. Coral Gables, Fla.: University of Miami Press.

Bienstock, Beverly Gray. 1982. "Focus Pocus: Film Imagery in *Bend Sinister*." In *Nabokov's Fifth Arc: Nabokov and Others on His Life's Work,* ed. J. E. Rivers and Charles Nicol, 125–138. Austin: University of Texas Press.

Bittner, William. 1960. "A la recherche d'un écrivain perdu." *Les langues modernes* 54(July–August):274–282.

Blos, Peter. 1962. *On Adolescence: A Psychoanalytic Interpretation.* New York: Free Press.

Boccia, Michael. 1986. "Versions (Con-, In-, and Per-) in Manuel Puig's and Hector Babenco's *Kiss of the Spider Woman,* Novel and Film." *Modern Fiction Studies* 32 (Autumn):417–426.

Booth, Wayne C. 1974. *A Rhetoric of Irony.* Chicago: University of Chicago Press.

Bordwell, David. 1974/75. "Eisenstein's Epistemological Shift." *Screen* 15(4):29–46. See also his "Response," *Screen* 16(1):142–143 (1975).

———. 1989. *Making Meaning: Inference and Rhetoric in the Interpretation of Cinema.* Cambridge: Harvard University Press.

Bost, David H. 1989. "Telling Tales in Manuel Puig's *El beso de la mujer araña*." *South Atlantic Review* 54(2):93–106.

Bourget, Jean-Loup. 1977. "Social Implications in Hollywood Genres." In *Film Genre: Theory and Criticism.* Methuchen, N.J.: Scarecrow Press.

Bowlby, John. 1973. *Separation: Anxiety and Anger.* New York: Basic Books.

Boyd, Brian. 1990. *Vladimir Nabokov, The Russia Years.* Princeton: Princeton University Press.

Braudy, Leo. 1976. *The World in a Frame.* New York: Anchor Books.

Brecht, Bertold. 1970. "Le film parlant *Panses glacées ou On verra bien á qui le monde appartient*." In *Sur le cinéma,* tr. Jean-Louis Lebrave and Jean-Pierre Lefebre, 221–225. Paris: L'Arche. Original German in Brecht, *Kuhle Wampe: Protokoll des Films und Materialien,* ed. Wolfgang Gersch and Werner Hecht (Frankfurt: Suhrkamp, 1969), 89–92.

Brooke-Rose, Christine. 1981. "Historical Genres/Theoretical Genres: A Discussion of Todorov on the Fantastic." In *A Rhetoric of the Unreal.* New York: Cambridge University Press. Originally in *New Literary History* 8(1):145–158 (1976).

Brooker-Bowers, Nancy. 1985. *The Hollywood Novel and Other Novels about Film: An Annotated Bibliography.* New York: Garland.

Brooks, Peter. 1985. *Reading for the Plot.* New York: Random House.

Bruccoli, Matthew J. 1977. *"The Last of the Novelists": F. Scott Fitzgerald and* The Last Tycoon. Carbondale: Southern Illinois University Press.

Brunetta, Giampiero. 1972. *Intellettuali cinema e propaganda tra le due guerre.* Bologna: Pàtron.

———. 1976. *Letteratura e cinema.* Bologna: Zanichelli.

———. 1979. *Storia del cinema italiano: 1895–1945.* Rome: Editori Riuniti.

———. 1982. *Storia del cinema italiano: 1945–1980s.* Rome: Editori Riuniti.

Bugge, John. 1983. "Merlin and the Movies in Walker Percy's *Lancelot*." *Studies in Medievalism* 2(4):39–55.

Byrd, Scott. 1972. "Mysteries and Movies: Walker Percy's College Articles and *The Moviegoer*." *Mississippi Quarterly* 25(2):165–181.

Callahan, John F. 1978. "The Unfinished Business of *The Last Tycoon*." *Literature/Film Quarterly* 6(3):204–213.

Càllari, Franceso. 1991. *Pirandello e il cinema*. Venice: Marsilio.
Campos, René Alberto. 1985. *Espejos: la textura cinematica en* La traición de Rita Hayworth *de Manuel Puig*. Madrid: Editorial Pliegos.
Carrà, Carlo. 1920. "Misticità e ironia nella pittura contemporanea." *Valori plastici* 2(7/8):69–73.
Carrà, Massimo, ed. 1968. *Metaphysical Art*. Tr. Caroline Tisdall. New York: Praeger.
Catania, Corrado, ed. 1988. *Pirandello e d'annunzio nel cinema: atti di un convegno*. Agrigento: Centro di Ricerca Narrativa-Cinema.
Cavell, Stanley. 1971. *The World Viewed*. New York: Viking Press.
Ceserani, Remo. 1989. "Primo approccio alla teoria critica di Frye: riflessioni attorno al concetto di 'modo.'" In *Ritratto di Northrop Frye,* ed. Agostino Lombardo, 17–38. Rome: Bulzoni.
Ceserani, Remo, et al. 1983. *La narrazione fantastica*. Pisa: Nistri Lischi.
Cheever, Leonard A. 1987. "Puig's *Kiss of the Spider Woman*: What the Movie Version *Couldn't* Show." *Publications of the Arkansas Philological Association* 13(2): 13–27.
Cinema & Cinema. 1984. Issue devoted to "Il romanzo di Hollywood," 11(40/41).
Clerc, Jeanne-Marie. 1985. *Ecrivains et cinema*. Metz: Presses Universitaires.
Clover, Carol J. 1992. *Men, Women, and Chain Saws: Gender in the Modern Horror Film*. Princeton: Princeton University Press.
Cohen, Keith. 1979. *Film and Fiction: The Dynamics of Exchange*. New Haven: Yale University Press.
Cohen-Budor, Dominique. 1974. "Les *Quaderni di Serafino Gubbio operatore* ou le refuge dans l'écriture." *Revue des etudes italiennes* 1/2:7–29.
Colie, Rosalie L. 1974. *Shakespeare's 'Living Art.'* Princeton: Princeton University Press.
Costa, Antonio, ed. 1983. *La meccanica del visibile: il cinema delle origini in Europa*. Florence: La Casa Usher.
Cottrell, Jane E. 1974. *Alberto Moravia*. New York: Ungar.
Cowley, Malcolm. 1951. *Exile's Return: A Literary Odyssey of the 1920s*. New York: Viking Press.
Cremonini, Giorgio. 1988. *L'autore, il narratore, lo spettatore*. Turin: Loescher.
Crespi, Stefano. 1967. "L'esperienza cinematografica in Pirandello." *Vita e pensiero* 50:847–853.
Cudini, Piero. 1978. "Elementi di una 'teoria del cinema' in Luigi Pirandello." In *Pirandello e il cinema,* ed. Enzo Lauretta, 85–103. Agrigento: Centro Nationale di Studi Pirandelliani.
Culler, Jonathan. 1975. *Structuralist Poetics*. Ithaca: Cornell University Press.
———. 1982. *On Deconstruction*. Ithaca: Cornell University Press.
———. 1988. *Framing the Sign*. Norman: University of Oklahoma Press.
Cuminetti, Benvenuto. 1967. "Indicazioni su *Quaderni di Serafino Gubbio operatore*." *Vita e pensiero* 50:857–865.
Debord, Guy. 1983. *Society of Spectacle*. Detroit: Black and Red.
———. 1990. *Comments on the Society of the Spectacle*. Tr. Malcolm Imrie. London: Verso.
de Castris, Arcangelo Leone. 1962. *Storia di Pirandello*. Bari: Laterza.

de Chirico, Giorgio. 1968. "On Metaphysical Art." In *Metaphysical Art,* ed. Massimo Carrà, 87–91. New York: Praeger. Originally in *Valori plastici* 1(4/5):15 (1919).

della Terza, Dante. 1972. "On Pirandello's Humorism." In *Veins of Humor,* ed. Harry Levin, 17–33. Cambridge, Mass.: Harvard University Press.

Dittmar, Linda. 1986. "Beyond Gender and Within It: The Social Construction of Female Desire." *Wide Angle* 8(3/4):79–88.

Dombroski, Robert S. 1978. *Le totalità dell'artificio: ideologia e forma nel romanzo di Pirandello.* Padua: Liviana.

Durgnat, Raymond. 1971. "The Cinema's Art Gallery." In *Films and Feelings,* 115–132. Cambridge, Mass.: MIT Press. Originally in *Burlington Magazine* (February 1967).

Eagle, Herbert. 1981. *Russian Formalist Film Theory.* Ann Arbor: University of Michigan Slavic Publications.

Earle, William. 1968. "Revolt against Realism in the Film." *Journal of Aesthetics and Art Criticism* 27(Winter):145–151.

Echavarren, Robert. 1978. *"El beso de la muier araña* y las metáforas del sujeto." *Revista Iberoamericana* 44:65–75.

Eichenbaum, Boris. 1974. "Problems of Cinema Stylistics." *Screen* 15(3):7–32. Also in Eagle (1981) and Kraiski (1971).

Eisenstein, Sergei M. 1943. *The Film Sense.* Tr. Jay Leyda. London: Faber and Faber.

———. 1970. *Notes of a Film Director.* New York: Dover.

Erlich, Victor. 1955. *Russian Formalism: History—Doctrine.* 'S-Gravenhage: Mouton.

Ferrario, Eduardo. 1978. *L'occhio di Mattia Pascal.* Rome: Bulzoni.

Fiedler, Leslie. 1964. *Waiting for the End.* New York: Dell.

Field, Andrew. 1977. *Nabokov: His Life in Part.* Harmondsworth: Penguin.

Fleishman, Avrom. 1992. *Narrated Films: Storytelling Situations in Cinema History.* Baltimore: Johns Hopkins University Press.

Fletcher, Angus. 1966. "Utopian History and the *Anatomy of Criticism.*" In *Northrop Frye in Modern Criticism,* ed. Murray Krieger, 31–73. New York: Columbia University Press.

Fónagy, Ivan. 1972. "Motivation et remotivation: comment se dépasser?" *Poétique* 11:414–431.

Fontenot, Ronald. 1985. "Theory and Subjectivity in the Novels of Manuel Puig." *Spectator* 5(Fall):5–7.

Fowler, Alastair. 1982. *Kinds of Literature: An Introduction to the Theory of Genres and Modes.* Cambridge, Mass.: Harvard University Press.

Freshney, Pamela. 1982. *"The Moviegoer* and *Lancelot:* The Movies as Literary Symbol." *Southern Review* 18(4):718–727.

Freud, Sigmund. 1965. *The Interpretation of Dreams.* Tr. James Strachey. New York: Avon.

Friedrich, Otto. 1972. *Before the Deluge.* New York: Harper and Row.

Gabbard, Glen O., and Krin Gabbard. 1989. "The Female Psychoanalyst in the Movies." *Journal of the American Psychoanalytic Association* 37:1031–1049.

Galloway, David D. 1963/64. "Nathanael West's Dream Dump." *Critique: Studies in Modern Fiction* 6(Winter):46–64.

Genette, Gérard. 1966. "Figures." In *Figures I,* 205–221. Paris: Seuil.

———. 1968. "Vraisemblance et motivation." *Communications* 11:17–21.

———. 1972. "Metonymie chez Proust." In *Figures III*, 41–63. Paris: Seuil.
———. 1979. *Introduction à l'architexte*. Paris: Seuil.
———. 1983. *Nouveaux discours du récit*. Paris: Seuil.
Genovese, Nino, and Sebastiano Gesù, eds. 1990. *La musa inquietante di Pirandello: il cinema*. 2 vols. Palermo: Bonanno.
Głowinski, Michael. 1977. "On the First-Person Novel." *New Literary History* 9(1): 103–114.
Goldstein, Laurence. 1994. *The American Poet at the Movies: A Critical History*. Ann Arbor: University of Michigan Press.
Gombrich, E. H. 1969. *Art and Illusion: A Study in the Psychology of Pictorial Representation*. Princeton: Princeton University Press.
Goodman, Nelson. 1960. "The Way the World Is." *Review of Metaphysics* 14(53): 48–56.
———. 1968. *Languages of Art*. Indianapolis: Bobbs-Merrill.
Grignani, Maria Antonietta. 1985. "*Quaderni di Serafino Gubbio operatore*: sintassi di un'impassibilità novecentesca." *Rivista di studi pirandelliani* 5(June):7–24.
Guglielmi, Guido. 1974. *Ironia e negazione*. Turin: Einaudi.
Gumbrecht, Hans Ulrich. 1992. *Making Sense in Life and Literature*. Tr. Glen Burns. Minneapolis: University of Minnesota Press.
Hagstrum, Jean H. 1958. *The Sister Arts*. Chicago: University of Chicago Press.
Hannay, Alastair. 1971. *Mental Images: A Defense*. New York: Humanities Press.
Hansen, Miriam. 1987. "Pleasure, Ambivalence, Identification: Valentino and Female Spectatorship." *Cinema Journal* 25(4):6–32.
Hays, K. Michael. 1992. *Modernism and the Posthumanist Subject*. Cambridge, Mass.: MIT Press.
Heath, Stephen. 1981. *Questions of Cinema*. Bloomington: Indiana University Press.
Heidegger, Martin. 1977. *The Question Concerning Technology and Other Essays*. Tr. William Lovitt. New York: Harper and Row.
Henderson, Brian. 1980. "The Long Take." In *A Critique of Film Theory*, 48–61. New York: Dutton. Originally in *Film Comment* 7(Summer):6–11 (1971).
Henisey, Sarah. 1968. "Intersubjectivity in Symbolization." *Renascence* 20(4):208–214.
Hollander, Anne. 1989. *Moving Pictures*. New York: Knopf.
Jakobson, Roman. 1987. "Is the Film in Decline?" In *Language in Literature*, ed. Krystina Pomorska and Stephen Rudy, tr. Elena Sokol, rev. by Jakobson, 458–465. Cambridge: Harvard University Press. Originally "úpadek Filmu," *Listy pro Umeni a Kritiku* (Prague) 1:45–49 (1933).
Jauss, Hans Robert. 1982. *Toward an Aesthetic of Reception*. Tr. Timothy Bahti. Minneapolis: University of Minnesota Press.
Jung, C. G. 1965. *Memories, Dreams, Reflections*. Recorded and ed. Aniela Jaffé, tr. Richard and Clara Winston. New York: Vintage Books.
Karetnikova, Inga, and Susanna Barber. 1987. "Cinematic Qualities in the Novel *Kiss of the Spider Woman*." *Literature/Film Quarterly* 15(3):164–168.
Kermode, Frank. 1983. *The Classic*. Cambridge: Harvard University Press.
Kinder, Marsha. 1981. "A Thrice-Told Tale: Godard's *Le Mépris* (1963)." In *Modern European Filmmakers and the Art of Adaptation*, ed. Andrew Horton and Joan Magretta, 100–114. New York: Ungar.

Kinnear, G. K. 1969. "Ingmar Bergman, Master of Illusion." In *Man and the Movies*, ed. W. R. Robinson, 161–168. Baltimore: Penguin.

Klotz, Volker. 1960. *Geschlossene und offene Form im Drama*. Munich: Carl Hanser Verlag.

Korte, Walter. 1974. "Godard's Adaptation of Moravia's *Contempt*." *Literature/Film Quarterly* 2(Summer):284–289.

Kracauer, Siegfried. 1960. *Theory of Film*. London: Oxford University Press.

Kraiski, Giorgio. 1971. *I formalisti russi nel cinema*. Milan: Garzanti. Also in Eagle (1981).

Lacan, Jacques. 1970. "The Insistence of the Letter in the Unconscious." In *Structuralism*, ed. Jacques Ehrmann, 101–137. New York: Anchor. Original French published in 1957. Also Lacan (1977a).

———. 1977a. "The Agency of the Letter in the Unconscious or Reason since Freud." In *Écrits: A Selection*, tr. Alan Sheridan, 146–178. New York: Norton.

———. 1977b. "The Mirror Stage as Formative of the Function of the I." In *Écrits: A Selection*, tr. Alan Sheridan, 1–7. New York: Norton.

Lauretta, Enzo, ed. 1977. *Il romanzo di Pirandello*. Palermo: Palumbo.

———. 1978. *Pirandello e il cinema*. Agrigento: Centro Nazionale di Studi Pirandelliani.

Lawson, Lewis A. 1980. "Walker Percy's *The Moviegoer*: The Cinema as Cave." *Southern Studies* 19:331–354.

———. 1988. "Cinematography in *The Moviegoer*." In *Ambiguities in Literature and Film*, ed. Hans P. Braendlin, 42–49. Tallahassee: Florida State University Press.

Lee, Rensselaer W. 1967. *Ut Pictura Poesis: The Humanistic Theory of Painting*. New York: Norton.

Lemon, T., and Marion J. Rees. 1965. *Russian Formalist Criticism*. Lincoln: University of Nebraska Press.

Leonardo da Vinci. 1966. "Fragments from the Treatise on Painting." In *Italian Art 1500–1600*, ed. Robert Klein and Henri Zerner, 4–9. Englewood Cliffs, N.J.: Prentice-Hall.

Lesage, Julia. 1985. "S/Z and *The Rules of the Game*." In *Movies and Methods*, ed. Bill Nichols, 2:476–500. Berkeley: University of California Press. Originally in *Jump Cut*, no. 12/13 (1976).

Lessing, Gotthold Ephraim. 1965. *Laocoön: An Essay upon the Limits of Painting and Poetry*. Tr. Ellen Frothingham. New York: Noonday Press.

Levaco, Ronald. 1975. "Eikhenbaum, Inner Speech and Film Stylistics." *Screen* 15 (4):47–58.

Liehm, Mira. 1984. *Passion and Defiance: Film in Italy from 1942 to the Present*. Berkeley: University of California Press.

Lindsay, Vachel. 1970. *The Art of the Moving Picture*. New York: Liverlight.

Lodge, David. 1977. *The Modes of Modern Writing: Metaphor, Metonymy, and the Typology of Modern Literature*. Ithaca: Cornell University Press.

Lokke, V. L. 1961. "A Side Glance at Medusa: Hollywood, the Literature Boys, and Nathanael West." *Southwest Review* 46(Winter):35–45.

Luciani, Sebastiano Arturo. 1928. *L'antiteatro: il cinematografo come arte*. Rome: La Voce.

Lurie, Susan. 1981/82. "The Construction of the Castrated Woman in Psychoanalysis and Cinema." *Discourse* 4(Winter):52–74.
Lyons, John. 1968. *Introduction to Theoretical Linguistics*. Cambridge, U.K.: Cambridge University Press.
MacCabe, Colin. 1985. *Tracking the Signifier*. Minneapolis: University of Minnesota Press.
Magny, Claude Edmonde. 1948. *L'age du roman americain*. Paris: Seuil.
Mahler, Margaret S., Fred Pine, and Anni Bergman. 1975. *The Psychological Birth of the Human Infant: Symbiosis and Individuation*. New York: Basic Books.
Maira, Salvatore. 1972. "Ideologia e tecnica nella narrativa di Luigi Pirandello." *Nuovi argomenti* 29/30:187–223.
Manser, Anthony. 1966. *Sartre: A Philosophic Study*. London: University of London, Athlone Press.
Marra, Claudio. 1976. "Estetica cine-fotografica come recupero della realtà." In *Estetica e società tecnologica,* ed. Renato Barilli, 149–174. Bologna: Il Mulino.
Martin, Wallace. 1986. *Recent Theories of Narrative*. Ithaca: Cornell University Press.
Masiello, Francine R. 1978. "Jail House Flicks: Projections by Manuel Puig." *Symposium* 32(Spring):15–24.
Mast, Gerald. 1974. "What Isn't Cinema?" *Critical Inquiry* 1(December):373–393.
———. 1980. "Kracauer's Two Tendencies and the Early History of Film Narrative." *Critical Inquiry* 6(3):455–476.
McConnell, Frank D. 1975. *The Spoken Seen: Film and the Romantic Imagination*. Baltimore: Johns Hopkins University Press.
Merleau-Ponty, Maurice. 1947. "Le cinéma et la nouvelle psychologie." *Les temps modernes* 26(November):930–943.
———. 1964. "The Film and the New Psychology." In *Sense and Non-Sense,* tr. Hubert L. Dreyfus and Patricia Allen Dreyfus, 48–59. Evanston, Ill.: Northwestern University Press.
Merrim, Stephanie. 1985. "Through the Film Darkly: Grade 'B' Movies and Dreamwork in *Tres tristes tigres* and *El beso de la mujer araña*." *Modern Language Studies* 15(Fall):300–312.
Metz, Christian. 1968a. "Le dire et le dite au cinéma." *Communications* 11:22–33. Also in Metz (1968b) and Metz (1974).
———. 1968b. *Essais sur la signification au cinéma,* vol. 1. Paris: Klincksieck.
———. 1974. *Film Language*. Tr. Michael Taylor. New York: Oxford University Press.
———. 1975. "The Imaginary Signifier." Tr. Ben Brewster. *Screen* 16(2):14–76. Originally in *Communications* 23:3–55 (1975). Also in Metz (1977) and Metz (1982).
———. 1976. "The Fiction Film and Its Spectator." Tr. Alfred Guzzetti. *New Literary History* 8(1):75–105. Originally in *Communications* 23:108–135 (1975). Also in Metz (1977) and Metz (1982).
———. 1977. *Le signifiant imaginaire*. Paris: Union Générale d'Editions.
———. 1982. *The Imaginary Signifier: Psychoanalysis and the Cinema*. Tr. Celia Britton, Annwyl Williams, Ben Brewster, and Alfred Guzzetti. Bloomington: Indiana University Press.
Michaels, I. Lloyds. 1982. "Auteurism, Creativity, and Entrophy [sic] in *The Last Tycoon*." *Literature/Film Quarterly* 10(2):110–119.

Millar, Dan. 1979/80. "California Graffiti: The 'Hollywood Novel'—A Posthumous Phase." *Sight and Sound* 49(Winter):18–21.

Milner, Max. 1982. *La fantasmagorie: essai sur l'optique fantastique*. Paris: Presses Universitaires de France.

Mistron, Deborah E. 1989. "Narration in Literature and Film: Intertextuality in *Kiss of the Spider Woman*." *West Virginia University Philological Papers* 35:104–111.

Mitry, Jean. 1963/65. *Esthétique et psychologie du cinéma*. 2 vols. Paris: Editions Universitaires.

Morrissette, Bruce. 1985. *Novel and Film: Essays in Two Genres*. Chicago: University of Chicago Press.

Moses, Gavriel. 1979. "*Gubbio in Gabbia*: Pirandello's Cameraman and the Entrapments of Film Vision." *MLN* 94(1):36–60.

———. 1981a. "Irrealtà ed ironia del fatto filmico in Pirandello." *Inventario* 1(1):74–96.

———. 1981b. "Philosophy and Mimesis in Michelangelo's Poems." *Italianistica* 10(2):162–177.

———. 1984. "Sogno incarnato: la Hollywood di Francis Scott Fitzgerald." *Cinema & Cinema* 11(40/41):13–23.

———. 1985. "Teoremi all'argine del Mississippi: Pasolini in Percy." *Cinema & Cinema* 12(43):35–42.

———. 1986. "La camera lucida di Vladimir Nabokov." *Belfagor* 41(March):125–142.

———. 1987. "SPECULATION on Pirandello and Nabokov on SPECULARITY." In *Pirandello 1986: atti del simposio internazionale (Berkeley)*, 135–148. Rome: Bulzoni.

———. 1988a. "Film Theory as Literary Genre in Pirandello and the Film Novel." *Annali d'Italianistica* 6:38–68.

———. 1988b. "Pirandello ed il cinema nei generi letterari." In *Pirandello e d'annunzio nel cinema: atti di un convegno,* ed. Corrado Catania, 31–45. Agrigento: Centro di Ricerca Narrativa-Cinema.

———. 1991. "As We [They] See [Hear] Them [Us]." *VIA: Voices in Italian Americana* 2(Spring):1–8.

———. 1992. "Opus a Hollywood: Daffy Duck e Montale tra letteratura e cinema." In *Bologna: la cultura italiana e le letterature straniere moderne*, Atti del congresso internazionale, Bologna 1988, ed. Vita Fortunati, 2:193–199. Ravenna: Longo.

Muecke, D. C. 1969. *The Compass of Irony*. London: Methuen.

———. 1978. "Irony Markers." *Poetics* 7:363–375.

Mulvey, Laura. 1989. *Visual and Other Pleasures*. Bloomington: Indiana University Press.

Münsterberg, Hugo. 1970. *The Film: A Psychological Study*. New York: Dover.

Nabokov, Dmitri. 1979. "On Revisiting Father's Room." In *Vladimir Nabokov: A Tribute,* ed. Peter Quennell, 126–136. London: Weidenfeld and Nicolson.

Nardelli, F. V. 1932. *L'uomo segreto*. Milan: Mondadori.

Neale, Stephen. 1983. *Genre*. London: BFI.

Newhall, Beaumont, ed. 1980. *Photography: Essays and Images*. New York: The Museum of Modern Art.

Nichols, Bill, ed. 1985. *Movies and Methods*, vol. 2. Berkeley: University of California Press.
Nulf, Frank. 1970/71. "Luigi Pirandello and the Cinema." *Film Quarterly* 24:40–48.
Pagliaro, Antonio. 1970. *Ironia e verità*. Milan: Rizzoli.
Pifer, Ellen. 1981. *Nabokov and the Novel*. Cambridge: Harvard University Press.
Pindell, Richard. 1975. "Basking in the Eye of the Storm: The Esthetics of Loss in Walker Percy's *The Moviegoer*." *Boundary 2* 4(1):219–230.
Pisk, George M. 1967. "The Graveyard of Dreams: A Study of Nathanael West's Last Novel, *The Day of the Locust*." *South Central Bulletin* 27(Winter):64–72.
Poétique. 1978. Issue devoted to *Ironie*, 36(November).
Poncet, Marie-Thérèse. 1952. *Étude comparative des illustrations du moyen age et des dessins animés*. Preface by Louis Réan. Paris: Nizet.
Powell, Lawrence Clark. 1971. "*The Day of the Locust*: Nathanael West." In *California Classics: The Creative Literature of the Golden State*, 344–356. Los Angeles: Ward Ritchie Press.
Prolo, M. A. 1951. *Storia del cinema muto italiano*. Milan: Il Poligono.
Pudovkin, Vsevolod I. 1960. *Film Technique and Film Acting*. Tr. Ivor Montague. New York: Grove Press.
Puppa, Paolo. 1978. *Fantasmi contro giganti: scena e immaginario in Pirandello*. Bologna: Pàtron.
Ragusa, Olga. 1977. "Correlated Terms in Pirandello's Conception of *Umorismo*." In *The Two Hesperidas: Literary Studies in Honor of Joseph G. Fucilla on the Occasion of His 80th Birthday*, ed. Americo Bugliani, 291–307. Madrid: Ediciones José Porrúa Turanzas.
Rapf, Joanna E. 1988. "The Last Tycoon or 'A Nickel for the Movies.'" *Literature/Film Quarterly* 16(2):76–81.
Richter, Hans. 1955a. "8 x 8." *Film Culture* 1(5/6):17–19.
———. 1955b. "Eight Free Improvisations on the Game of Chess." *Film Culture* 1(1):36–38.
———. 1955c. "The Film as an Original Art Form." *Film Culture* 1(1):19–23.
Robinson, Robert. 1979. "The Last Interview." In *Vladimir Nabokov: A Tribute*, ed. Peter Quenell, 119–125. London: Weidenfeld and Nicolson.
Romeo, Carlo. 1988. "Da 'specchio' a 'occhio': il cinema nella poetica pirandelliana." *Cristallo* (Bolzano, Italy) 30(3):81–86.
Rosen, Philip, ed. 1986. *Narrative, Apparatus, Ideology*. New York: Columbia University Press.
Rosenmeyer, Thomas G. 1969. *The Green Cabinet: Theocritus and the European Pastoral Lyric*. Berkeley: University of California Press.
Ryle, Gilbert. 1949. *The Concept of Mind*. New York: Barnes and Noble.
Sartre, Jean-Paul. 1972. *The Psychology of Imagination* (*The Intentional Structure of the Image*). Tr. Bernard Frechtman. Secaucus, N.J.: Citadel Press. Published in French as *L'imaginaire, psychologie phénoménologique de l'imagination* (Paris: Gallimard, 1940). [Im/E] [Im/F]
Savinio, Alberto. 1968. "Anadyomenon: Principles in the Evaluation of Contemporary Art." In *Metaphysical Art*, ed. Massimo Carrà, 155–162. New York: Praeger. Original Italian in *Valori plastici* 1(4/5):6–14 (1919).

Schulberg, Budd Wilson. 1940. "Literature of the Film: The Hollywood Novel." *Film* 1(2):68–78.
———. 1960. "The Writer and Hollywood." In *Writing in America,* ed. John Fisher and Robert B. Silvers, 95–107. New Brunswick, N.J.: Rutgers University Press.
———. 1978. *What Makes Sammy Run?* Harmondsworth: Penguin.
See, Caroline. 1968. "The Hollywood Novel: The American Dream Cheat." In *Tough Guy Writers in the Thirties,* ed. David Madden, 199–216. Carbondale: Southern Illinois University Press.
Shklovskij, Viktor. 1979. "Letteratura e cinema." In *I formalisti russi nel cinema,* ed. Giorgio Kraiski, 99–144. Milan: Garzanti.
Silverman, Kaja. 1983. *The Subject of Semiotics.* New York: Oxford University Press.
———. 1992. *Male Subjectivity at the Margins.* New York: Routledge.
Sloan, De Villo. 1987. "Manuel Puig's Kiss of the Spider Woman as Post-literature." *International Fiction Review* 14(1):23–26.
Smith, Barbara Herrnstein. 1984. "Contingencies of Value." In *Canons,* ed. Robert von Hallberg, 5–39. Chicago: University of Chicago Press.
Snyder, Joel. 1983/84. "Benjamin on Reproducibility and Aura: A Reading of 'The Work of Art in the Age of Its Technical Reproducibility.'" *Philosophical Forum* 15(1/2):130–145.
Société des Anglicistes de l'Enseignement Superieur. 1986. *Mode(s): actes du XXIII congrés de Reims, 1983.* "Études anglaises," no. 93. Paris: Didier Erudition.
Sogliuzzo, Richard. 1977. "'Si gira . . .' un'amara parabola della tecnologia moderna." In *Il romanzo di Pirandello,* ed. Enzo Lauretta, 169–181. Palermo: Palumbo.
Sontag, Susan. 1979. *On Photography.* New York: Dell.
Spiegel, Alan. 1976. *Fiction and the Camera Eye: Visual Consciousness and the Modern Novel.* Charlottesville: University of Virginia Press.
Stuart, Dabney. 1975. "The Novelist's Composure: *Speak, Memory* as Fiction." *Modern Language Quarterly* 36(2):177–192.
Tessari, Roberto. 1973. *Il mito della macchina.* Milan: Mursia.
———. 1977. *Alberto Moravia: introduzione e guida.* Florence: Le Monnier.
Thale, Mary. 1968. "The Moviegoer of the 1950s." *Twentieth-Century Literature* 14(2):84–89.
Todorov, Tzvetan, ed. 1965. *Théorie de la littérature.* Paris: Seuil.
———. 1970. *Introduction à la littérature fantastique.* Paris: Seuil.
———. 1976. "The Origin of Genres." Tr. Richard M. Berrong. *New Literary History* 8(1):159–170. Also in Todorov (1990).
———. 1984. *Mikhail Bakhtin: The Dialogical Principle.* Tr. Wlad Godzich. Minneapolis: University of Minnesota Press.
———. 1990. *Genres in Discourse.* Cambridge, U.K.: Cambridge University Press. Published in French as *Les genres du discours* (Paris: Seuil, 1978).
Tyler, Parker. 1954. "The Film Sense and the Painting Sense." *Art Digest* 28(February):10–12, 27–28.
Ullmann, Stephen. 1957. *Style in the French Novel.* Cambridge, U.K.: Cambridge University Press.
———. 1960. *The Image in the Modern French Novel.* Cambridge, U.K.: Cambridge University Press.

Vauthier, Simone. 1975. "Title as Microtext: The Example of *The Moviegoer.*" *Journal of Narrative Technique* 5(3):219–229.

———. 1978. "Narrative Triangle and Triple Alliance: A Look at *The Moviegoer.*" In *Les Américanistes: New French Criticism on Modern American Fiction,* ed. Ira D. Johnson and Christiane Johnson, 77–221. Port Washington, N.Y.: Kennikat Press, National University Publications.

Verdone, Mario. 1952. *Gli intellettuali e il cinema.* Rome: Ateneo. New edition, Rome: Bulzoni, 1982.

Vertov, Dziga. 1984. "From Kino-Eye to Radio-Eye" (1929). In *Kino-Eye: The Writings of Dziga Vertov,* tr. Kevin O'Brien, 85–92. Berkeley: University of California Press.

Viazzi, Glauco. 1949. "Cinema sovietico del dopoguerra." *Bianco e nero* 10(7).

Welle, John P., ed. 1988. Issue devoted to "Film and Literature," *Annali d'Italianistica* 6.

Wells, Walter. 1973. *Tycoons and Locusts: A Regional Look at Hollywood Fiction of the 1930s.* Carbondale: Southern Illinois University Press.

Widmer, Kingsley. 1961. "The Hollywood Image." *Coastlines* 5(1):17–27.

———. 1973. "The Last Masquerade." In *Nathanael West: The Cheaters and the Cheated, A Collection of Essays,* ed. David Madden, 179–193. Deland, Fla.: Everett/Edwards.

Willemen, Paul. 1972. "Distanciation and Douglas Sirk." In *Douglas Sirk,* ed. Laura Mulvey and Jon Halliday, 23–31. Edinburgh: Edinburgh Film Festival.

———. 1974/75. "Reflections on Eikenbaum's Concept of Internal Speech in the Cinema." *Screen* 15(4):59–70.

Wilson, Edmund. 1956. *A Literary Chronicle: 1920–1950.* New York: Doubleday.

Wölfflin, Heinrich. n.d. *Principles of Art History.* Tr. M. D. Hottinger. New York: Dover.

Wood, Michael. 1980. "The Claims of Mischief." *The New York Review of Books* (24 January):43–47.

Wood, Robin. 1985. "An Introduction to the American Horror Film." In *Movies and Methods,* ed. Bill Nichols, 2:195–220. Berkeley: University of California Press.

Worley, Joan Yvonne. 1983. "Film into Fiction: Thomas Pynchon and Manuel Puig." Ph.D. dissertation, Ohio University.

Wyers-Weber, Frances. 1981. "Manuel Puig at the Movies." *Hispanic Review* 49:163–181.

Young, Vernon. 1978/79. "Dry Welles." *American Scholar* 48(1):140–144.

Zamora, Lois Parkinson. 1984. "The Reader at the Movies: Semiotic Systems in Walker Percy's *The Moviegoer* and Manuel Puig's *La traicion de Rita Hayworth.*" *American Journal of Semiotics* 3(1):50–67.

Index

Allmendinger, Blake, 296
Alpers, Paul, 133
Alther, Lisa, 43
Andreotti, Giulio, 209, 211, 296
Apollinaire, Guillaume: "Un Beau Film," 289
Apparatus, 120, 129–130, 134–135, 149, 214, 226, 250, 252, 260, 262, 271. *See also* Apparatus, specific types; Film apparatus; Genre specific discourse
   and cinema, 66–67
   as culture code, 120–121
   its history, 10, 33, 40, 44, 46, 48, 56–57, 130, 132, 136, 141, 163, 202, 275, 282
   and ideology, 103, 172–173, 207, **209–211**, 231, 241, **247–256**, 282; in film, 125, **170–174**, **181–183**, 218, 299–300; in print news, 4, 167, 223, 242, 295; in television news, 194, 232, 266
   instrumental, 67, 169, 301; attitude, 187; mediation, 20, 103, 151, 155, 228; perception, 154, 184
   and memory, 7, 41–42, 47–49, 51–52, 54, 56, **58–60**, 65, 80–82, 101, 104–105, 107, 115, 117–118, 136, 152, 189, 204, 210, 272, 291
   as metaphor, 267–268
   its narrative condensation, 20, 120, **129–130**, 163, 168, 188, 196, 202, 217, 227, 235
   its narrative productivity, **130–132**, 165, 211, 260–262, 264, 266, 269, 292, 294
   its power, 204
   as setting. *See* Genre specific settings
   and technology and technique, **44–45**, 70, 77, 104, 111, 168, 218, 271, 274
Apparatus, specific types
   optical mediation, 31–33, **44–51**, 90, 110–112, 129–130, 150–152, 158, 218, 220–223, 227–229, 280; glasses, 74, 84, 87, 126, 151, 167; microscope, 45–46, 48–49, 113, 280, 282, 285; telescope, 31–33, 49, 104, 151, 222–223, 285; window reflection, 70, 90, 158
   radio, 195, 230, 274
   telephone, 168–169
   television, 39–40, 42, 44, 51, 65–66, 113, 194, 221–222, 225, 231–232, 259, 266, 271–272, 280, 283, 298; its image resolution, 221
   theatre, xvii, 9, 55, 59–60, 64, 69–70, 115, 133, 151, 164–165, 167, 172, 182, 188, 195, 199, 200, 207, 212, 262, 272, 282, 295, 296, 298; burlesque, 197, 200; play, 187, 199, 241; opera, 60, 151; variety, 69; vaudeville, 197, 266
   video games, 273
Appel, Alfred, Jr., 195, 296
Archetype, 110, 183, 188, 214; and discourse, 208. *See also* Myth; Mythopoeic
Augustine, Saint, 232
Awareness. *See* Knowing

Bachelard, Gaston, 43, 46, 48–49, 134, 155, 183–184, 283, 285, 295
Bakhtin, M. M.: and dialogue, 125, 165, 247–248, 250, 262, 269, 273; and genre, 134, 292
Barber, Susanna, 298
Barilli, Renato, 278
Barlusconi, Giovanna, 289
Barthes, Roland: absence, 281–282; code and closure, 155; and codes, 294; effect of real, 21, 76, 278, 279; narrative and origin, 255; photography and death, 286; proairetic code, 292; thematic code, 267
Baudelaire, Charles, 4, 276

Being. *See also* Self; Subject; Subjectivity
and alienation, xx, 50, 59, 116, 146, 151, 222, 266, 287, 298, 300
and authenticity, 16, 21, 23, 26–27, 30–31, 35, 41, 93–94, 193, 196, 218, 223, 263
awareness: of being, 103, 119; of being in time, 20, 44, 54, 115, 266, 282; of lack, 56, 58, 148, 152, 166, 193, 215, 255, 282, 293; of loss, 9, 40–41, 53, 55, 57, 107, 115, 131, 148–149, 223, 250, 252; of void, 23, 27, 30–31, 33, 42–43, 107, 132, 138, 217, 223, 227, 229, 245–246, 284
identity, 23, 30, 35, **59–61**, 73, 114–115, 120, 229, 255, 283, 299; and film, 86, 93–94, 105, 119, 136, 146–147, 193, 224, 262; and film roles, 13, 15–18, 23, 59–61, 93–94, 173–174, 180, 187, 198–200, 210, 214–215, 224, 227–229, 252–255; and houses, 7, 17–19, **55–61**, 117, 138, 147, 180, 183, 188, 196, 224, 267, 270, 282–283, 287; and mimesis, 166; and mirror, 146–147, 150–152, 206, 227–229, 238, 253; and photographs, 132; and stereotype, 167. *See also* Genre specific themes; Self; Subject; Subjectivity
individuation, xx, 42, 73, 139, 147, 151, 210, 221, 238–239, 241–242, 246, 252–255; child development, 235; and discourse, 251; and education, 134; and film roles, 55–56, 189–190, 238–243, 252–254, 300; Margaret S. Mahler et al. on, 299; and mimesis, 166, 249; and mirror, 19, 238; ontogenesis, 147; Jean Piaget on, 235–236; sexual, 238–239; Anneli Taube on, 238–239. *See also* Genre specific themes; Self
Benveniste, Emile, 160, 278
Bloodmark, Vivian, 41
Boccia, Michael, 298, 299
Booth, Wayne C., 63, 278, 283
Bost, David H., 299
Brecht, Bertolt, 151, 173, 256, 268, 284–285, 295
Brook-Rose, Christine, 275, 291
Brooks, Peter, 292, 293
Butterflies, 49, 70, 76, 132, 137; as camera, 52–53, 117; epistemological, 45

Callahan, John F., 295
Campos, René Alberto, 297
Canon, 25, 122–123, 129, 130, 141. *See also* Genre specific themes
Canonical authors and works: Ariosto, 31, 133, 280; Cervantes, 31, 141; Raymond Chandler, 226; Anton Chekhov, 241; *The Communist Manifesto*, 192; Charles Dickens, 220; Ralph Waldo Emerson, 181; Gustave Flaubert, 286; Galileo, 280; Juan Gris, 201; E. T. A. Hoffmann, 126, 291–292; Homer, 208–215, 268; Aldous Huxley, 187, 296; Janvier, 196; *The Kama Sutra*, 245; Mihail Yurievich Lermontov, 56, 136; Michelangelo, 187; John Milton, 133; Eugenio Montale, 75; Francesco Petrarch, 242; Marcel Proust, 46, 110, 130, 270, 287; Luigi Pulci, 280; Rembrandt, 86; *The Rig Veda*, 220; Peter Paul Rubens, 188; William Shakespeare, 169, 199; Gertrude Stein, 201; William Makepeace Thackeray, 220; Leo Tolstoy, 41, 129, 169; Richard Wagner, 81, 286; Jean Antoine Watteau, 26
Cast: Fred Astaire, 239; Marlon Brando, 74, 220; Montgomery Clift, 226; Joan Crawford, 191; Clark Gable, 55, 224; Greta Garbo, 71, 132, 186; Oliver Hardy, 22; Pat Hingle, 220; Leslie Howard, 224; Stan Laurel, 22; Ivan Mozhukhin, 55, 59, 115, 117, 140, 146, 224; Gregory Peck, 95, 224; Luise Rainer, 241, 252; Ginger Rogers, 239; Norma Shearer, 238; Anne Sheridan, 245; Rudolf Valentino, 176, 183
Ceserani, Remo, 291, 292
Cheever, Leonard A., 298, 299
Chesterton, Gilbert Keith, 274
Cochleas, 240
Code, 152, 175, 264, 297; and artifice, 6, 18, 26, 44, 105, 140, 158, 176, 185, 195, 200, 225, 227, 274, 280, 290; and nature, 25, 32, 34, 50, 75, 78, 88, 109, 112, 128, 139, 154, 155, 171, 188, 195, 200, 208, 217, 220, 223, 225, 227, 236, 297, 298; and suture, 139, 219, 244, 266, 267
Codes, specific
autism, 155–156
communication: objectified, 168–169; and truth, 230–231; in visual archetypes, 183–184
culture, 125, 181–182, 192, 196, 212, 214, 223; and counter culture, 220, 245; and discourse, 173, 184; erudition, 44–45, 49–50, 52, 85, 87, 94–95, 102, 113, 120, **132**, **134–136**, 171, 174, 177–178, 185, 200, 215, **225–226**, 256, 261, 263, 265, 273; expressionism, 72, 88–89, 101, 130, 158; geocentrism, 280; Juan Gris, 201; High art, 163, 187–188; interpretation, 201, 211; Janvier, 196; kitsch, 201; Michelangelo, 187; paradigm, xix, 24,

126, 132, 196, 211–213, 222, 254; personified, 134, 165, 187, 210, 231–232, 263, 268–269; poshlost, 195; Rembrandt, 86–87; Peter Paul Rubens, 188; Gertrude Stein, 201; topos, 109, 110, 111, 126, 128, 148, 176, 183, 212, 220, 277, 295; triviality, 103, 113, 115, 184, 194; Jean Antoine Watteau, 26; zipper as, 219. *See also* Film theory: and ideology
  hermeneutic, 14, 51–52, 81, 100, 105, 128, 138, 142, 147, **155–156**, 160, 167, 177, 186, 203, 208, 210, 222, 226, 253, 264, 300
  ideological, xx, 102, **125–126**, 140, 143, **153–154, 163–165**, 167, **170–175**, 181–183, **190–196**, 200, **206–212**, 218–219, 224, 226, 230–232, 241, 243–245, **248–256**, 261–262, 265–266, 269, 272, 282, 295, 298, 299, 300; of society personified, 185, 191; subtext, 139, 163, 172, 173, 174, 181, 182, 196, 207, 208, 209, 210, 212, 214, 218, 226, 241, 249, 295, 300. *See also* Genre specific
  opposition, 4–11, 16, 20–22, 24, 27–33, 45–46, 50, 76–79, 86, 88–93, 100, 105–108, 110, 114, 116, 118, 123–124, 126, 134–135, 138–143, 146–150, 154, 156, 163, 167, 172, 177, 182–183, 191, 197, 199–201, 204–205, 207–208, 211, 212–213, 219, 223–224, 230–231, 238, 240–241, 243, 245, 250–251, 254–256, 263, 266–271, 275, 276, 277–278, 279, 282, 287, 290, 293, 294, 297, 300
  proairetic, 5, 7, 10, 17–18, 66–68, 92–95, 101–102, 109–111, 130, 138, 142–145, 149, 153, 155, 159–160, 177, 185, 197, 200, 212–215, 226, 236, 243–244, 260, 264, 266, 269, 287, 288. *See also* Plot
  semic, 153, 159, 165, 167, 262, 268, 294. *See* Genre specific thematization
  symbolic, 3, 8, 9–10, 17, 28, 34, 55–56, 72, 77, 81, 95, 134, 139, 144, 150, 152, 154–155, 157, 163, 165, 196, 201, 207–210, 215–216, 218–220, 223, 230, 235, 241, 244, 253, 256, 261, 263, 268–269, 274, 277, 283, 284, 285, 294, 300; personified, 268
Colie, Rosalie L., 278
Color, **83–85**, 89–90, 95, 136; and apparatus, 47, 286; and audition colorèe, 77–78, 81, 285; and black and white, 78, 81, 228; as convention, 26; and feeling, 53; as interference, 81; as leitmotif, 286; as metaphor, 69; as metonymy, 6, 180, 244; and movement, 83, 118, 286; and music, 286; and objectivity, 16; and polyphony of the apparatus, 56–57; and reality, 70, 148, 212, 286; and subjectivity, 72; and synaesthesia, 118
Color in literature and film, 286; blue as "protagonist" and "plotter," 65, 72–74, **79, 81–83**, 90, 227, 286, 293; red as formal displacement of plot elements, 89, 158
Conrad, Joseph, 276
Costa, Antonio, 275
Cottrell, Jane E., 207
Cremonini, Giorgio, 136
Culler, Jonathan, 138, 140, 156, 159, 160
Cuminetti, Benvenuto, 278

Dance, 64–65, 141, 198, 239, 274, 293; erotic, 15–14, 54, 107; gavotte, 242; pas de deux, 80; as social ritual, 177, 242, 284; tango, 203; waltz, 239–240, 242–244, 250
Dandieu, Arnaud, 46
De Castris, Arcangelo Leone, 289
Della Terza, Dante, 24, 35, 280
Diegesis. *See* Representation
Discourse, 143, 166, 197, 213, 218, 241, 247–251, 254, 266, 268, 273, 277, 290, 293, 294, 295, 298, 299
  cinematic, 9, 20, 44, 66, 73, 83, 108, 112, 128, 137, 147, 150–151, 158, 166, 169, 175, 180, 185, 197, 249, 264–265; and fiction, 21, 23, 58, 66, 68, 107, 143, 218, 223; and language, 64
  and closure, 117, **140–145**, 149, 154, 155, 179, 223, 225–227, 250, 254, 256, 260, 266, 284, 294
  and disjunction, **140–145**, 149, 179, 210, 226–227, 249–250, 260, 266, 269, 293
  and enunciation, 260, 292
  and experience, 271, 292
  and extrapolation, 93, 104, 109, 125, 130, 135, 141, 144, **153–154**, 165, 193, 194–195, 220, 251
  of fiction: and autobiography, 43, 49, 51, 58, 61, 112, 115, 117, 119, 132, 137–139, 143, 146–147, 164, 171, 262, 271, 292; and ideology, 142–143, 191; and intertextuality, 138; and philosophy, 29, 39–40, 44, 49, 51, 75, 107, 117, 119; and progress of technology, 31; and reality, 102, 104, 107, 117, 188, 190, 223, 276, 289
  and film effect, **152–153**
  fragmented, 6, 58, 85, 136, 142, 148–149, 150, 153, 155, 159–160, 168, 178, 180, 183, 187, 189, 190, 192, 197, 224, 263, 276, 278

320 Index

Discourse *(continued)*
  and genre, 25, 122–124, 125–128, 137–139, 195, 247, 249, 254, 259, 268, 273, 293. *See also* Bakhtin; Genre specific discourse
  and ideology, 174, 254
  and illusion, 30, 151, 169, 202, 233, 267, 270. *See also* Knowing
  intercultural, 229–230, 268
  interior, 52, 79, 108, 115, 137, 147, 166, 235, 250, 267
  of interior speech, 102, 125, 236, 249, 273, 299
  intertextual, 138–140, 184, 248, 259, 262, 268
  intramedial, 80, 124, 140, 143, 166, 249, 259
  of literature, 160, 166, 249, 293
  mixed, 3, 8, 64, 108, 276, 279
  and narrative, xx, 24, **129–132, 137–139, 140–145, 159–160,** 175, 250, 255, 266, 293
  and overdetermination, xxi, 135, 222, 240, 268
  paradigmatic, 9–10, 17, 41, 55, 58, 108, 130, 136, 157–158, 202, 211, 244, 291
  paratactic, 4
  and perception, 128, **149–152**
  and productivity, 130–131, 165, 211, 260, 261–262, 264, 266, 269, 292, 294
  and reader, **145–149,** 259, 260
  and reality, 117, 265, 267
  and representation, 25, 165, 196–197
  of science, 143
  and selection, 3, 8, 18, 22, 35, 55, 64, 71, 108, 156, 167–168, 276
  of self, 166, 235, 251, 266–267, 298
  and signified, 25, 146
  and signifier, 25, 279, 282
  and spectator, 102, 125, 185, 249, 273, 299
  and story, 3, 5–6, 8, 10–11, 17–19, 55, 66–69, 71–72, 78–79, 85, 91, 93, 101, 110–112, 116–119, **130–131, 136–138, 141–142, 144, 146, 155–156, 157–160,** 166, 169, 175, 177, 180–182, 191, 195–197, 207–208, 210–215, 223, 225–226, 236–237, 239, 241–243, 246, 250–252, 254, 256, 259–269, 271–273, 283, 284, 294, 298, 299, 300; and genre, xviii, 85, 91, 118, 126, **137–138,** 148, 154–156, 159, 187, 195–196, 240–242, 250, 284; and narrator, 11, 78–79, 135, 146, 175, 177, 181, 223, 247, 256, 263, 271, 299
  and subtext, 139, 163, 172–174, 181–182, 196, 201, 207–209, 212, 214, 218–219, 226–227, 230, 241, 249, 256, 295, 300
  syntagmatic, 3, 9–10, 41, 57–58, 108, 157, 159, 179–180, 183, 244
  of technology, 110, 260
  and theme. *See* Genre specific thematization
  and transcodage, 297
  and vision, 149–152
Discursive polyphony, 140, 262, 269, 297; of apparatus, 56–57, 74, 78, 81, 195, 284; personified, 165, 210, 268–269
Dittmar, Linda, 253, 254, 298, 300
Dürrenmatt, Friedrich: *The Assignment,* 157, 294

Ecárt, 277
Echavarren, Robert, 299
Erlich, Victor, 122
Estragon, 22. *See also* Vladimir, not Nabokov

Feeling, xvii, 6–7, 9–19, 22–24, 27, 30–31, 34–35, 41, 42–43, 45–46, 53–57, 59–60, 66, 68–69, 76–77, 82–83, 89, 91, 94, 100, 109, 115–116, 119–120, 130–131, 133–135, 138, 143, 146, 149, 160, 168, 172, 176, 178–180, 187–188, 194, 196, 198–206, 215–219, 223, 229, 232, 238–241, 246, 262, 269–271, 273, 278, 282, 287, 297; authenticity, 13–19, 22–24, 62, 87–88, 93–94, 120, 133, 140, 143, 151, 173–174, 176, 182, 187, 193, 196, 198–202, 213–219, 223, 229–230, 241, 243, 273; cosmic indifference, 35, 75, 184, 284; intentionality, 68, 76–80, 284
Feelings: aggression, 13, 16, 23, 92, 114, 141–142, 169–170, 191, 193–194, 200–201, 205, 214, 219, 220, 226–227, 231–232, 236–238, 243, 246–247, 251–252, 293, 297; anger, 13, 164, 184, 200, 203, 219, 226, 236, 244–246, 256, 274; anticipation, 24, 58–59, 69, 114, 132, 176, 189, 201, 227–228, 232, 243–244, 274, 287; contempt, 13, 205–206, 210, 215, 245; delight, 4, 51, 53, 84, 87–88, 94, 132, 165, 184; desire, 59, 107, 179, 202, 232; disappointment, 69, 182, 189, 194, 201, 219, 236–237, 274; empathy, 22, 64–65, 289; fear, 15–16, 23, 42, 53, 75–77, 92, 94, 113–114, 148, 155, 166, 219, 221–222, 224, 231–232, 236–237, 239–240, 242, 244, 260, 262, 272, 274, 284–285, 289; hate, 77, 174, 226, 241; indifference, 13, 172; revulsion, 15, 94, 147, 219; shock, 10, 15, 23, 25, 144, 147, 167, 170, 192, 198, 200, 203–204, 217, 223, 226, 252–253, 267, 274, 277, 286; subjective, 89, 168. *See also* Genre specific themes; Perception; Sensations

Index 321

Field, Andrew, 59
Film
  and genre, 21–28, 54–55, 87, 91–94, 117, 124, 140–146, 183, 186, 195, 199, 236, 239–240, 242–244, 254–255, 265, 267, 284, 293; genre films, 25–26, 43, 68, 93–95, 141, 172–173, 209, 223, 240, 242, 244–245, 249, 255, 266; and the reader, 255; stock footage, 91; stock sets, 197. *See also* Film genres and types
  and literature. *See* Literature and film
  and reality, 4–6, 8, 11, 18, 44–45, 55, 57–58, 60–61, 64, 68–69, 71–72, 78, 81, 83, 85–86, 91–94, 104–112, 117, 120, 139, 142, 149, 186–190, 197, 204, 208–209, 217, 223, 232, 240, 245–246
Film apparatus, 3, 32, 34, 35, 39, 40, 42, 44–46, 48–49, 51, 54, 57, 65–69, 89, 99, 100, 102, 107, 114–116, 118–120, 125–127, 129–130, 131–136, 139, 144–145, 147, 156–160, 163, 166, 168–169, 177, 181–182, 187–189, 190, 193, 196–197, 202, 206, 215–219, 221–222, 225, 227, 233–235, 247, 250, 252, 254, 259–262, 264, 266–270, 272, 278, 280, 282, 289, 290. *See also* Film technology and technique; Genre specific setting as apparatus; Philosophical aspirations, of the film apparatus
  camera, 3, 5, 10–11, 17–18, 20, 24, 33, 44, 46, 48, 50, 58–59, 65–68, 70, 82, 85–86, 100, 105, 112, 113, 116, 119, 127, 136, 150–151, 156–157, 171, 179, 182, 184, 188, 202, 205, 218, 221–222, 232, 251, 263, 271–272, 274, 275, 277–280, 282, 286, 287, 289; handle, 9, 11–12, 100, 110; lens, 126; obscura, 44, 282; shutter, 48; tripod, 14, 18; viewfinder, 26, 211. *See also* Film form: and camera
  components, xvii, xix–xxi, 124, 129–130, 141, 158, 192, 260, 266
  darkroom, 9–10, 127, 221
  film image, 3, 21, 23–25, 29, 31, 36–37, 42, 49–50, 56, 58–60, 62–63, 65, 80, 85–86, 94, 105–106, 109, 111, 114–115, 117, 120, 152–153, 177–178, 194, 201, 216, 278, 279, 281, 285; negative, 158, 228
  film stock: black and white, 78, 81, 228; color, 47, 57, 286; grainy, 43; as metaphor, 10, 158; microfilm, 49; and movement, 83, 118, 286
  human component: director as, 5, 25, 68, 137, 173; interior speech, 102, 125, 236, 249, 273, 299; spectator as, xviii, 21–22, 42, 53–58, 62, 64, 67, 82, 94, 103–105, 108, 111, 113–115, 118–119, 126, 131, 133, 145–146, 148–150, 152, 158–159, 166–167, 169, 174, 182–183, 185, 192–193, 200, 202, 205, 208, 214, 216–217, 219, 233–235, 239–240, 244, 249, 253, 261–264, 266, 270, 273, 289, 291, 294, 299, 300; spectatorship, xx, 85, 103, 108, 145–146, 217–218, 249, 251, 261, 263, 266–267, 270; spectatorship personified, 267
  intertitles/subtitles, 5–6, 116
  lighting, 16, 18, 60, 71, 113, 127, 131, 135, 151, 158, 160, 165, 176, 205, 215, 223, 243, 286, 290
  megaphone, 60, 113, 135, 267
  movie theatre, xv, 31, 51, 54–57, 59, 61, 85, 89–91, 107, 111, 131, 147, 160, 172–173, 176, 215–216, 235–236, 280; nickelodeon, 202; penny arcade, 141
  production, 25, 40, 57, 75, 93, **101–104**, 107, 113, 125–127, 133, 135, 137, **163–168**, 172–173, 175–176, 179, 181, 183–185, 188, 190, 194, 201, 209, 217, 234, 254, 265, 268–270. *See also* Genre specific character: film director; Genre specific character: producer
  projection, 3, 34, 39–40, 46, 48, 50, 54–57, 73, 86, 90, 93, 107, 114, 130, 131, 136, 147, 178, 215–216, 234, 267, 280, 298; ideological, 171–172, 211, 218, 270; imaginative, 89, 92, 101, 131; as metaphor, 3, 48–49, 136, 280; slide show, 56, 136; special effect, 56
  projector, 3, 45–46, 56–57, 118, 132, 147, 189, 202, 218, 264, 287, 298; camera lucida, 46, 130, 132; celluloid, 233; lens, 46, 126, 129; light cone, 131; magic lantern, 40, 48, 56, 130, 136; praxinoscope, 44; shutter, 158
  reception, 51, 102–103, 113–115, 125, 170, 172, 213, 254–255. *See also* Spectator
  screen, 3, 8, 18, 29, 39, 42, 45, 48, 55–56, 59–61, 66, 68, 88, 91, 93, 94, 103, 105, 114, 115, 117, 119, 127–129, 132, 135, 142, 145–149, 151, 158–159, 178–180, 187, 202, 212, 234, 235–236, 237, 251, 254, 265, 272, 279, 280, 282, 283, 298, 299; and codes, 55–56, 58, 181, 192, 206, 212, 235–236, 256; as escape, 93, 95, 114, 190, 273, 290; and memory, 29, 52, 54, 65; personified, 90; and philosophical insight, 9, 15, 20–21, 23–24, 26–27, 29–32, 36, 61, 93, 100, 107, 119, 126, 135, 199, 221, 228, 231–232, 251, 272, 287; and self, **54–61**, 94, 108, **114–117**, 119, **146–149**, 159, 166, 194, 199, 202, 206, 216, 225, 228, **233–236**, 282,

Film apparatus *(continued)*
screen *(continued)*
294; as trope, 28, 40, 54, 58, 117, 202, 227, 280; and voyeurism, 54, 202
script, 25, 104, 133, 164, 180, 182, 188, 192, 205, 209, 210, 214, 216, 233, 244, 268, 269, 271, 276
set, 60, 64–65, 75, 183, 186, 188–189, 197, 211, 224, 263, 267
setting as, 9–10, 131, 157–160, 188–189, 215–216, 227, 231, 263–264, 267–269
sound, 4, 6, 9, 47, 53, 56–57, 74, 76, 78, 81, 86, 169; and dreams, 108; epistemological, 260; and film structure, 18, 101, 118, 136, 169, 283, 284; and formal mimetics, 74; and hermeneutic code, 53; and interior monologue, 102, 125, 236, 249, 273, 299; montage, 4, 118; pro-airetic, 77, 92, 141, 151; representation, 47, 57, 70–71, 243; silence, 64; and symbolic code, 9, 138, 140, 167, 197, 203, 199, 220; as synaesthetic trope, 81; theory of, 86, 108; and vision, 77–78, 80, 101, 118, 283, 285; voice, 9
sound machine, 57
soundtrack, 6, 47, 74, 195, 220, 242, 296
studio, 7, 9, 12, 60, 65, 158, 164, 168, 169, 177, 181–182, 185, 187, 188, 189, 196–197, 216, 223, 262, 263, 264, 289, 295
viewing theatre, 23, 127, 186, 189
Film apparatus personified, 12, 14, 19, 110, 113, 134, 141, 165–166, 186–188, 200, 210–211, 249, 251, 262, 267–268, 289, 296
Film apparatus troped: apparatus ad partum, 267; bomb, 170, 262; brothel, 164–165, 201; butterfly, 52–53, 117, 137; cave, 57, 80, 146, 215, 234, 250, 269, 274; cine-monkey, 197; desk drawer, 158; exile, 59; immanence, 29; incarnation, 190; kinflicks, 43; machine from hell, 170; mechanical piano, 10, 241, 242; monotype printer, 10; pornography, 202; spider, 10, 24, 251; subjectivity, 85; symphony, 169–170; telephone, 168–169, 260; tree leaves, 47–48, 158; windowpane, 70, 158
Film directors: Michelangelo Antonioni, 225–226, 283, 289; William Asher, 229; Hector Babenco, 247–249, 299; Yevgeni Bauer, 55, 282; Ingmar Bergman, 151; Friedrich Bergmann, 172; Bernardo Bertolucci, 219–220, 297; Maya Deren, 157; Vittorio De Sica, 209, 296; Walt Disney, 239–240; Alexander Dovzhenko, 82; Ewald André Dupont, 69; Marguerite Duras, xx; Julian Duvivier, 239–245; Sergei M. Eisenstein, 57, 77–78, 81–82, 283–284, 286; Morris Engel, 73; Jean Epstein, 47, 50, 282; Federico Fellini, 116, 290–291; Louis Feuillade, 75, 279; Jean-Luc Godard, 151, 247, 268, 298; Karl Grune, 72, 284; Sir Alfred Hitchcock, 68, 157; Elia Kazan, 73–74, 295; Fritz Lang, 68–70, 116, 187, 208; Robert Z. Leonard, 241; Marcel L'Herbier, 59, 101; Ernst Lubitsch, 173–174; Louis and Auguste Lumière, 284; Rouben Mamoulian, 241; Joseph L. Mankiewicz, 226; Vincente Minnelli, 173; Max Ophuls, 283; Georg Wilhelm Pabst, 208; Pier Paolo Pasolini, 219–220; and Walker Percy, 297; Roman Polanski, 201; H. C. Potter, 239; Yakov Protozanov, 55; Jean Renoir, 68, 70, 283; Tony Richardson, 247; Hans Richter, 33, 284; Walter Ruttmann, 70, 101, 169–170; Ettore Scola, 296; Robert Siodmak, 286; Douglas Sirk, 173, 182; Joseph Strick, 201; Dziga Vertov, 50, 70, 84, 101, 108, 116, 171, 276; Charles Vidor, 300; Robert Wiene, 192
Film form, xix, 4, 25, 67, 78, 85, 158, 168, 170–172, 175, 177, 181, 187, 202–203, 207, 212, 214–217, 224, 228, 260–264, 269, 276, 278, 281, 282, 283, 285, 292, 296, 297, 299
and camera: angle, 65–66, 73, 115–116, 165, 177; close-up, 5, 17, 51, 84, 111, 165, 220, 276; composition, 116; crane shot, 182, 184, 265; detail shot, 108; double-exposure, 20; establishing shot, 18; extreme close-up, 276; eyeline shot, 73; focus, 47, 63–65, 83, 89, 116; focus length, 115; framing, 17–18, 22, 33, 35, 39, 45, 66, 73, 76, 83, 86, 128, 131, 136; freeze frame, 84, 129; long shot, 5, 51, 84, 108, 111, 184–185; middle shot, 276; movement, 5; and narrative style, 63; pan, 18; point of view shot, 8, 12, 150, 167, 177, 180; position, 5–6, 8; reverse motion, 42; reverse shot, 8, 73, 150; stop-motion, 105; style, 63–64, 66, 75, 260, 283, 298; subjective camera, 168, 175, 286; superimposition, 20, 52, 116, 117, 159, 166; and technique, 116, 175, 247, 283; tracking shot, 47, 64, 108; traveling shot, 7, 20, 108, 110, 277, 298; variable speed, 100, 110, 127, 129
and lighting. *See* Vision: light
and meaning, 85

and memory, 7, 29, 39–40, 52, 89, 101, 110, 130, 136
mise-en-scène, 64–65, 157, 177, 260
personified, 198
primitive, 118
and style, 51, 53, 67–68, 70, 72, 83; evocative, 17–18; realist, 21–23, 68, 100, 123–124, 209, 212, 279; stimmung, 89, 168, 170, 260; UFA, 124, 260
and syntax, 5; decoupage, 288; editing, 3, 127, 279; fade-in, 47; fade-out, 47; flashback, 7; fragment, **142**; jump-cut, 53, 116, 151; lap dissolve, 52; metonymic, 19, 35; montage, 3, 4, 6, 7, 17, 20, 28, 52, 56, 63–65, 78, 81, 108, 118, 136, 158, 170, 175, 180, 202, 235, 236, 240, 276, 279, 285, 288, 298; sequence, 52; synecdochic, 6

Film genres and types. *See also* Film: and genre
adventure, 3–19, 189–190, 279
animated, 94–95, 113, 239–241, 287–288
avant garde, 70, 84, 101, 129, 169, 192, 201, 283, 286
backstage drama, 195
beach, 84–85, 129, 229, 286
biography, 239–244, 250
comedy, 22, 42, 80, 154, 167, 197–199, 277; parody, 27
crime, 144–145, 234, 236, 238, 240, 246, 293
didactic, 26, 64, 116
documentary, 235, 239, 244
erotic allegory, 219–220, 226, 297
expressionist, 88, 101, 192, 283
foreign art, xx, 69, 72, 219–220, 225–229, 245, 247–249, 283–284, 289, 290–291, 296, 297, 299
historical costume drama, 26, 191, 197, 295
home movie, 42–43, 60, 112, 119, 136, 138, 156, 272, 291
horror, 26, 255–256, 293
ideological, 172, 191, 285; propaganda, 248, 254–256
melodrama, 12, 15, 24–26, 54–55, 70, 92–93, 115, 141, 143–144, 146, 165, 183–185, 197, 226, 234, 247, 300
musical, 141, 163–174, 239–241, 271, 293
office movie, 191
pornographic, 43, 202, 219, 232, 267, 297
"quality," 265
realist, 73–74; neorealist, 21–23, 68, 100, 123, 209, 212, 279, 296; neue Sachlichkeit, 124
Russian, pre-revolutionary, 55, 282
science fiction, 68, 223

sea adventure, 173, 195
silent, 6, 9, 25, 40, 43, 59, 68–69, 77, 80, 100–101, 110, 127, 136, 138, 296, 299
snuff, 116, 289
spy, 68
street, 72, 124, 284
suspense serial, 65
Tarzan, 195
toga, 208–215, 268–269, 271
western, 194, 197, 200, 205, 227, 229, 267, 293

Film history, 24–25, 44, 127, 187–188, 191–192, 224–225, 270; and art history, 75, 115, 275; and Brando's zipper, 220; Ernesto Vaser and Giovanni Vitrotti, 277

Film technology and techniques, xix, 4, 39, 43, 47–48, 53–54, 56–57, 63–66, 68–69, 74, 84, 100, 102–104, 106–108, 116–118, 127–129, 131, 134, 167, 169–170, 225, 227, 271–272, 277, 288, 291, 297
effect on humanity, 5, 31–33, 42, 44, 47, 53–54, 104–105, 107, 120, 126, 128, 133–134, 180, 183, 221–223, 225, 240, 244, 260, 270–272, 274, 279; limits of, 112, 127, 271–272
of film and beyond, 34, 39, 66, 110, 118–121, 129, 153, 184, 221, 225

Film theories and concepts. *See also* Film theorists; Film theory
apparatus, xv, 5, 8, 10, 12, 14, 19–20, 31–33, 42, 44, 47, 51, 53–57, 59–61, 65, 68–69, 77–78, 82, 85–86, 89–91, 94–95, 104–105, 107, 110–111, 113–114, 116, 120, 126–128, 130–131, 133–134, 141, 146–147, 158, 160, 165–166, 170, 172–173, 176, 179–183, 186–188, 200, 202, 210–211, 215–216, 221–223, 225, 235–236, 240, 244, 249, 251, 260, 262, 267–272, 274, 279–280, 287, 289, 296
archetypal, 55–56, 183, 184, 188, 208–209, 212–213
attraction, 71, 137, 186, 193–194
auteur, 5, 25, 60, 62, 68–70, 102, 104, 109–110, 113, 116, 137, 164–168, 170–174, 176, 181–182, 185–187, 201, 208–213, 220, 262, 264, 268
constructivist, 50, 70, 84, 101, 108, 116, 171, 276
dominant, 65, 71–74, 79, 81–83, 90, 227, 286, 293
existential, 3–4, 9–10, 15, 18–19, 23, 27–28, 31, 42, 50, 52, 99, 107–108, 111–112, 117, 126, 128, 135, 138–140, 148, 154, 179, 188, 193, 199, 207, 217, 222, 255, 266, 278, 293

Film theories and concepts *(continued)*
  expressionist, 72, 88–89, 101, 130, 158, 168, 170, 260, 283
  feminist, xx, 15–16, 23, 30, 54, 94, 103, 107–108, 115, 119, 126, 178–180, 195, 199–200, 202–203, 205, 219–220, 263, 265–266, 289, 293, 294
  formalist, 6, 9–10, 20, 44, 56–57, 66, 73–74, 78, 81, 83, 100, 108, 110, 112, 122, 127–128, 129, 137, 147, 150–151, 158, 166–167, 169, 170, 172, 175, 180, 185, 197, 249, 264–265, 275, 284
  formative, xxi, 22–23, 27–28, 33, 47, 50–52, 67, 70, 75–76, 83–84, 86–87, 95, 100–101, 106, 109–112, 116–118, 119–120, 124, 127, 132, 134–136, 147, 152, 156, 183–186, 211, 213, 217, 223, 233, 247, 260, 264, 265, 276, 281, 282, 283, 285, 290, 291, 298
  ideological apparatus, 64, 102, 109, 112–113, 125–126, 140, 143, 153–154, 163–165, 170–175, 190–192, 181–183, 193, 205–209, 211–212, 218, 221, 224, 231–232, 241, 245, 248–250, 252, 254–256, 261–262, 265, 269–272, 277, 280, 282, 290, 296, 298, 299–300
  ideological montage, 63–64, 78, 170, 276, 285
  immanentist, 24–25, 29, 55, 63, 68, 105–107, 145, 197–198, 278–279, 282–283
  mentalist, 7, 40–43, 47–49, 51–52, 54, 56, 58–60, 65, 74, 80–82, 89–90, 101, 104–105, 107, 115, 117–119, 136, 138, 152, 178–180, 189, 204, 210, 235, 272, 291, 299
  mimetic, 43–44, 50, 52, 71–74, 105–106, 109–113, 118, 120, 128–129, 138, 166, 212–213, 270, 277, 278, 279, 280, 283–284, 290, 296
  musical, 101, 169–170
  neorealist, 21–23, 68, 100, 123–124, 209, 212, 279, 296
  phenomenological, 36, 51, 58, 76, 107, 111, 119, 279, 282, 288
  polyphony of apparatus, 56–57, 74, 78, 81, 195, 284
  post-structuralist, xix–xxi, 5–8, 12, 15–16, 19, 25–26, 29–32, 42, 43–44, 46, 48–50, 52, 54, 56–58, 62, 68, 72, 84, 86, 90, 93, 100, 105–108, 111–113, 117, 119–120, 132, 139, 142–144, 148–152, 154, 156–157, 167, 175–177, 180, 182, 184, 200–201, 203, 212, 215–217, 219, 231–233, 236, 238, 244, 248, 251, 263, 266, 267, 274, 277, 278, 280, 281, 282, 286, 287, 293–294, 295
  psychoanalytic, 3, 15–20, 26, 30–31, 39, 43, 44, 54–56, 58–61, 63, 68–69, 79, 84–87, 88, 90, 93–94, 101, 105, 107–108, 113–115, 117, 119–120, 126, 132, 136, 138, 141, 142, 146–152, 155, 156, 165–166, 168, 175–176, 178, 181, 183–184, 186, 189–190, 193–205, 215–216, 219–224, 227–229, 231–235, 237, 239–240, 242–245, 248–249, 250, 252–255, 262, 264–267, 269, 272–274, 278, 279–280, 282, 284, 286, 287, 289–291, 292, 297, 299, 300
  subjectivist, 85, 104, 118, 149, 236, 239–240, 242–244, 248, 299
  subject position, 107, 114–115, 125, 150, 160, 166, 216, 234–235, 244, 251, 254, 262, 269, 289, 293, 294, 300
Film theorists: J. Dudley Andrew, 64, 235; Rudolf Arnheim, 33, 47, 50–51, 67, 86, 109–112, 118, 120, 127, 135–136, 281, 283, 285; Béla Balacz, 83; Owen Barfield, 280; William Barrett, 221, 271; Jean-Louis Baudry, xix, 44, 46, 52, 57–58, 86, 107–108, 111, 113, 120, 215, 280–282, 286–287; André Bazin, 24–25, 55, 63, 68, 105–107, 145, 197–198, 278–279, 282–283; Walter Benjamin, 109, 277, 290; David Bordwell, 275, 294, 299; Jean-Loup Bourget, 173; Leo Braudy, 68–70, 165, 170, 187, 284–285; Stanley Cavell, 51, 58, 119; Carol J. Clover, 289; Guy Debord, 193–194, 224, 229, 232; Alexander Dovzhenko, 82; William Earle, 290; Boris Eichenbaum, 249, 299; Sergei M. Eisenstein, 57, 77–78, 81–82, 283–284, 286; Jean Epstein, 47, 50, 282; Glen O. and Krin Gabbard, 289; Stephen Heath, 248, 274; Marsha Kinder, 298; Siegfried Kracauer, 43–44, 50, 71–74, 105–106, 109–113, 118, 120, 128–129, 270, 277, 278, 279, 280, 283–284, 290; Ronald Levaco, 299; Mira Liehm, 296; Sebastiano Arturo Luciani, 5, 276; Colin MacCabe, 149–151, 293–294; Gerald Mast, 290; Christian Metz, 6, 25–26, 54, 105, 108, 115, 200–201, 215, 277, 279, 280, 282; Max Milner, 275; Jean Mitry, 36, 58, 76, 107, 111, 279, 282, 288; Laura Mulvey, 289; Hugo Müstenberg, 115, 235; Vladimir Nabokov, 39–47, 111–112; Stephen Neale, 142–144, 149, 154, 293, 294, 295; Luigi Pirandello, 99–102, 169–170, 288–290; Vsevolod I. Pudovkin, 52; Hans Richter, 284; Alberto Savinio, 75–76; Victor Shklovskij, 122; Kaja Silverman, 293,

294; Dziga Vertov, 50, 70, 84, 101, 108, 116, 171, 276; Edward Weston, 279; Paul Willemen, 299; Michael Wood, 245; Robin Wood, 255; Vernon Young, 283

Film theory, xx–xxi, 24–25, 33, 35, 67–68, 75, 103–108, 114–115, 125–126, 143, 163, 165, 181, 196, 210, 225, 230, 254, 261, 265, 268–269, 270, 273, 275, 277, 283, 290, 293, 296; articulated by characters, 9–11, 21–22, 27, 30, 33, 67, 69–70, 86, 100–101, 106–107, 109–110, 112–113, 135, 165, 169–173, 175–177, 181–182, **185**, 201, 209, 211–212, 215, 241, 250, 255–256, 261–264, 268, 272–273; and discourse, xxi, 109–111, 118–121, 125–126, 170–171; its history, xix, 4–5, 7, 99, 130, 101, 127, 168, 288, 290; and ideology, 102, 113, 125–126, 140, 143, 153–154, 163–165, 170–174, 175, 190–192, 181–183, 193, 205–206, 207, 208–209, 211–212, 218, 224, 231–232, 241, 245, 248–250, 252, 254–256, 261–262, 265, 269, 272, 282, 296, 298, 299–300; and Nabokov, 39–47, **111–112**, 290–291; as narrative, xix–xx, **99–121**, 129–130, 171, 261; and Pirandello, **99–102**, 169–170, 288–290; and the reader, 101, 259; its representations in film, 65–66, 88–89, 168

Film titles: *8½* (Fellini, 1963), 290–291; *Acciaio* (Pirandello/Ruttmann, 1933), 101, 169; *Beach Blanket Bingo* (Asher, 1965), 229; *Berlin, die Symphonie der Grosstadt* (Ruttmann, 1927), 70; *Blood and Sand* (Mamoulian, 1941), 241; *The Cabinet of Doctor Caligari* (Wiene, 1919), 192; *Le Camion* (Duras, 1977), xx; *Un Chien Andalou* (Buñuel/Dalí, 1928), 192; *Gilda* (Vidor, 1946), 300; *The Great Waltz* (Duvivier, 1938), 239–245, 250; *The Great Ziegfeld* (Leonard, 1936), 241; *Kiss of the Spider Woman* (Babenco, 1985), 247–249, 299; *Ladri di biciclette* (De Sica, 1949), 296; *Last Tango in Paris* (Bertolucci, 1972), 219–220, 297; *The Last Tycoon* (Kazan, 1976), 295; *Laughter in the Dark* (Richardson, 1969), 247; *Liebelei* (Ophuls, 1932), 283; *The Little Fugitive* (Engel, 1953), 73; *The Man with a Movie Camera* (Vertov, 1929), 70, 84, 101, 171; *Die Melodie der Welt* (Ruttmann, 1929), 101; *Menschen am Sonntag* (Siodmak, 1929), 286; *Le Mépris* (Godard, 1963), 247, 268, 298; *On the Waterfront* (Kazan, 1954), 73–74; *The Passenger/Professione Reporter* (Antonioni, 1975), 283, 289; *The Pirate* (Minnelli, 1947), 173; *Prater Violette* (Bergmann, 1934), 172; *The Red Desert/Il Deserto Rosso* (Antonioni, 1964), 226; *The Savage Eye* (Strick, 1959), 201; *Snow White and the Seven Dwarfs* (Disney, 1937), 239–240; *The Story of Vernon and Irene Castle* (Potter, 1939), 239; *Die Strasse* (Grune, 1923), 72, 284; *The Student Prince in Old Heidelberg* (Lubitsch, 1927), 173–174; *Suddenly Last Summer* (Mankiewicz, 1959), 226; *Teorema* (Pasolini, 1968), 220; *Two Men and a Wardrobe* (Polanski, 1958), 201; *Variété* (Dupont, 1925), 69; *We Loved Each Other So Much* (Scola, 1974), 296; *Yurii Nagornyi* (Bauer, 1916), 282

Fitzgerald, F. Scott, xviii, xx, 163, 164, **174–192**, 193–197, 208–209, 214, 223, 227, 234, **263–265**, 268, 295; *The Last Tycoon*, 163, 164, **174–192**, 205, 214, 219, **263–265**; and Edmund Wilson edition, 295

Fletcher, Angus, 292

Fónagy, Ivan, 279

Fontenot, Ronald, 298

Form, xviii–xix, 3, 19, 34, 41–42, 44, 49, 52, 64–68, 74–75, 78–79, 83, 85–86, 91, 99, 106, 108–110, 112–114, 117–118, 120, 122–124, 129, 132, 137–139, 148, 152–153, 156–158, 163, 165–166, 170–172, 177, 179, 195–196, 198–200, 204, 207, 213, 216, 221, 235, 243–244, 249, 260, 262, 263, 265, 274, 277, 282–283, 290–291; and ideology, 172; juxtapositions of, 67; patterns, 41, 53, 78; repetition, 65. *See also* Representation

Formalism. *See* Film theories: formalist; Representation

Formal mimetics. *See* Genre specific style

Formative, xvii, xxi
  aspect of painting, 86–87
  genre of experience, 139
  individuation, 134
  nature of film, xxi, 106, 110, 117, 127, 147, 183, 185, 213, 265, 290; like dreams, 235; in literary discourse, 109, 118; personified, 110; and professional deformation, 4, 11, 117, 132–133, 179, 198, 200, 215–217, 265–266; like the subconscious, 235; and view of reality, 86–87, 134

sadism, 70

view of reality, 86–87, 134

326 Index

Foucault, Michel, xx
Fowler, Alastair, 122, 123
Freud, Sigmund, 19, 209, 211, 214, 237, 280, 282, 283

Genette, Gérard, 24, 277, 279, 292
Genovese, Nino, 276
Genre, 85, 91–94, 115, 119–120, 123, 193–194, 248, 254, 260, 295
 and cinematic condensation: of epistemological uncertainty, 50; of factual truth, 26, 223; of imagination, 20, 40, 43, 179, 196–197, 224; of irony, 21, 23, 34, 39, 100, 221; of memory, 40, 43, 54, 179; of pragmatic code, 183; of subjective consciousness, 86; of supernatural, 26; of time and death, 27, 41, 111, 138; of transcendental ego, 44, 54, 113, 286
 as contract, 107
 and convention, 34–35, 56, 80, 139–140, 146, 240, 244, 284, 290
 its history, 122–124
 kernels, 135
 mixed, 12, 114, 124, 131, 158, 245
 and narrative, 21, **99–105**, 127–128, 134–135, 143–145, 148, 152, 255; conflict, 24, 89, 92, 114, 140, 141, 143, 146, 152, 163, 197, 213, 219, 236, 238, 241, 243, 287, 290; of film, 34, 78, 90, 99–100, 102–103, 107, 138, 247; of film theory, 99–101, 104–105, 107, 145; foregrounding, 66, 71, 74, 76, 82, 110, 124, 129, 130, 185, 197, 214, 260, 267, 291; foreshadowing, 6, 81, 103, 115, 149, 261; of mind, 153; proairetic elaboration, 59, 119, 131, 135, 145, 156; of spectatorship, 103, 107–108, 145, 217, 261, 266
 and narrative condensation: of apparatus, 20, 120, **129–130**, 163, 168, 188, 196, 202, 217, 227, 235; of culture code, 128, 136, 201; of epistemological experience, 8, 20; of existential experience, 9, 128; of discourse, 143; of discursive manifestation of film and film theory, 127, 157; of filmmaking, 63, 65, 104; of genre specific themes, 202, 282; by imagination, 29; of subconscious, 283; of subjectivity, 88, 90, 197, 233
 and narrative theory, 137, 147
 and pattern, 18, 24, 40–41, 48, 52–54, 56, 63, 65, 70, 77, 79, 80–81, 86, 91, 93, 95, 117, 129, 137, 142, 144, 156, 166, 178, 186, 194, 200, 202, 248, 265, 284, 286
 and proliferation, 127, 136, **153–154**, 163, 167, 294
 and reader, 101
 and reality, 132–133, 143, 262, 266
 and repertory, 72, 109, 120, 123, 132, 135, 153, 176, 217, 220, 242, 277
 and resolution, 105, **141, 143–144**, 154, 155, 221, 223, 245, 293, 294. *See also* Discourse: and closure
 stereotype, 26, 42, 72, 84, 152, 174–175, 189, 199, 242, 282
 and story discourse, xviii, 85, 91, 118, 126, **137–139**, 148, 154–156, 159, 187, 195–196, 240–242, 245, 250, 284; and narrator, 11, 78–79, 135, 146, 175, 177, 181, 223, 247, 256, 263, 271, 299
 and story manifestations, 85, 125–126, **137–139**, 150, 153–154, 185, 200, 205, 211, 214–217, 241, 252, 254, 266, 269, 284, 286, 294
 and structure, 280
 theoretical, xx
Genres
 and discourse, **122–124**
 of discourse, **125–128**
 of experience, **132–133**, 262, 266; genre specific, 143
Genres, literary: autobiography, xix, 40, 45, 49, 51, 58–59, 74, 85, 110, 112, 117, 120, 132, 134–135, 137–139, 143, 146, 164, 171, 199, 262, 266, 271, 282, 290, 292; Bildungsroman, 132, 135, 139, 170, 173, 254, 260, 273; blazon, 242; chivalric romance, 31, 126, 133, 141, 280; comedy, 31, 34, 54, 69, 80, 167, 198, 230, 266, 280, 281, 287; ekphrasis, 128; epic, 126, 133, 208–215; factory novel, 123; fairytale, 62, 124, 137, 141–142, 167; fantastic, 26, 125–127; farce, 34, 80, 281, 286; film novel, xviii–xix, 67, **122–160, 259–274**; film poem, xv, 32, 297; Hollywood novel, **163–206**; novel, 31, 41, 129, 169, 141, 220, 286; parody, 26–27, 34, 41, 63, 131, 163, 166, 172, 200, 253, 261, 280, 281; pastoral, 141; piscatory eclogue, 123; Prüfungsroman, 134; roman cinéoptique, 291; satire, 43, 63, 67, 84, 172, 287; tragedy, 31, 34, 132, 133, 149, 167, 188, 193, 199
Genres, musical: musique concrète, 6; song, 199–200, 242–243, 245, 266, 274, 293. *See also* Dance
Genres, narrative, 99–100, 143
Genre specific, 103, 125, 135, 137, 145, 152, 156–157, 159, 168, 177, 251, 260, 264, 266, 267, 268, 298
Genre specific author, 6, **43–48, 51–61, 62–65, 74–79**, 85, 100–102, 133–134, 136–137, 140, 145–148, 152, 156, 159–160,

175, 193–195, 207–208, 259–260, 262–264, 267–268, 270, 272–274, 291, 298
Genre specific character, 132, 135, 139, 160, 164, 167, 170, 179, 249, 261, 262, 265–266, 268, 270
  actor, xvii, 3, 5–7, 9, 13–18, 26, 43, 55, 59–61, 74, 91–93, 101–104, 115, 117, 145–146, 152, 164, 177–179, 181, 189–190, 196, 198–199, 215, 219–221, 225, 227, 229, 235, 240–241, 245, 255, 282, 286, 291; colors as, 82
  art director, **192–206**, 230, 267, 277, 296
  art historian, 114–115, 124, 154, 275
  as bolt in apparatus, 54, 115
  cameraman, xviii, **3–19**, 25–26, 100–104, 107, 109–110, 114, 119, 141, 145, 171, 215, 265, 270, 272, 277
  clown, 172, 198, 280
  editor, 164, 169–173, 183, 261–262
  film director, 11–13, 25, **101–104**, 110, 113–114, 133, 135, **163–174**, 186, **208–214**, 221, 226, 229, 251, 260, 262, 265, 270, 299; as auteur, 181–182, 185, 187, 264; character as, 67, 77–78, 94, 102, 112–113, 148, 165–166, 262, 269; and control, 102, 104, 109–110, 113, 165–166, 170, 187, 262; and culture code, 164–165, 209–210, 212; as gangster, 69; as God, 68–69; and ideological code, 171–174, 213, 268; and insight, 186; and moral responsibility, 116; and point of view, 62, 168, 170; as sadist, 69, 116, 165, 170; and symbolic code, 211, 220; transcendental, 70; types of, 60, **68–70**, 102, 104, 113, 165–167, 170, 176, 187, 201, 208; writer as, 65, 68, 70, 113, 116
  flaneur, 4, 59, 70, 76, 88–89
  inanimate objects as, 10, 14, 18, 64, 66, 71–73, 84, 87, 89, 91–92, 137, 141, 158, 168, 204, 216, 220, 226
  motopictum vir, 120
  paparazzo, 114
  producer, **174–192**, 201, 208–212, 219–220, 229, 251, 270, 296
  scriptwriter, 25, 101, 103–104, 133, 137, 164, 176, 180, 185–189, 194, 205, 207–217, 233, 234, 260, 261, 264, 268, 269, 271; and "writer," 185–188, 194
  as spectator, 67, 78
  stage-manager, 69–70, 90, 272
Genre specific closure, **140–145**
Genre specific codes, 134–135, 139, 155–157, 163, 167, 172, 177, 194. *See also* Code; Codes, specific
  autism, 155–156
  culture, **134–135**, 169
  hermeneutic, **155–156**, 160, 177, 222, 253, 264
  ideological, **125–126**, 140, 143, **153–154**, **163–165, 167, 170–175, 190–196, 206–212, 248–256**, 261–262, 265
  opposition, 106, 107, 110, 123, 134, 139–140, 142, 146, 150, 154, 156, 163
  proairetic, 66–68, 92–95, 101–102, 109–111, 130, 138, 142–145, 149, 153, 155, 159–160
  semic, 153, 159. *See also* Genre specific thematization
  symbolic, 72, 77, 81, 95, 134, 139, 144, 150, 152, 154–155, 157
Genre specific death, 141
Genre specific desire, 142
Genre specific discourse, 139, 142–143, 152, 249; of apparatus, 56, 114, 118, 126, **129–130**, 139, 144, 157, 159–160, 163, 168, 193, 202, 217, 219, 226, 250, 259–260, 262, 264, 266–267, 269, 282; on apparatus, 129, 130; dialogue, 6, 78, 153, 247, 250, 256, 261, 273; and disjunction, **140–145**; and extrapolation, **153–154**; of film, **104–109, 116–118**, 259, 260, 262, 273; on film, **102–104, 112–116**, 157, 261, 264, 268, 273; of film theory, xx, 100, 101, **105–111**, 119, 125–126, 170–171, 256, 261, 288; on film theory, xx, **109–111, 118–121**, 129, 143, 261, 264, 268, 290; interior speech, 102, 125, 236, 249, 273, 299; and synaesthesia, 128
Genre specific effects
  alienation, 151
  effect of: film, xix, 59, 76, 107, 116, 120, 152–153, 160, 166, 186, 247–249, 259–261, 263–265, 267; film vision, 149–152; new, 130; real, 21, 57, 76, 106–107, 139–140, 141–142, 146, 148, 166, 264–265; space, 158
  mimetic, 233
  shutter, 48, 158
  subject, 107
Genre specific erudition, 44, 52, 132, 134–137, 171, 177, 185, 225–226, 256, 261, 263
Genre specific mode, 133–134, 176, 246, 269–270, 292
Genre specific narrative, 134–135, 139, 142, 155, 167, 177, 179, 192, 263, 269–270
Genre specific narrator, 5–8, 68, 82, 136, 140, 150, 168, 175, 247–256, 262, 278, 289, 299; and reliability, xvii–xviii, 10–19, 100, 103, 236–237, 239–244, 248, 251
Genre specific novelist as director, 114–115

Genre specific personification of: apparatus, 12, 14, 19, 110, 113, 134, 141, 165–166, 186–188, 200, 210–211, 249, 251, 262, 267–268, 289, 296; culture code, 165, 167, 210, 268; discursive polyphony, 165, 210, 268; epistemological awareness, 134–135; formative power of film, 110; mimetic individuation, 166, 249; production/reception, 113; seduction/aggression of film, 251; society, 185, 191; spectatorship, 267; symbolic code, 268

Genre specific productivity, 130–132, 153–154, 165, 211, 260–262, 264, 266, 269, 292, 294

Genre specific props: airplane, 189–190, 222; baby carriage, 42–43; dagger, 15; doors, 64, 72, 92, 131, 137, 145, 151, 173, 186, 198, 202–204, 216, 220, 228, 231, 236; elevators, 137, 217; fire engine, 71; glove, 64, 185; horses, 95, 176; mirrors, 18–19, 36, 40–41, 50, 72, 77, 79, 87, 90, 129, 130, 131, 137, 150–152, 227–229; projector, uncooperative, 114–115, 202; telephone, 168–169, 185, 260; tennis ball, 226; tennis racket, 71–72, 137; tennis shoes, 92; tennis sock, 82; window, 18, 42, 52, 55, 70–71, 76, 79–81, 83, 94, 158, 178, 186, 205, 217, 227, 237, 242, 264, 269, 288

Genre specific reader, 64–65, 75, 101, 139, 145–149, 152, 160, 259, 264

Genre specific representation, 167, 262

Genre specific roles
and discourse, 11, 78–79, 135, 146, 175, 177, 181, 223, 247, 256, 263, 271, 299
as pragmatic functions, 69, 85, 103, 113, 115, 148, 165, 192, 235
shaped by apparatus, 31–32, 163, 170
specific: bellboy, 137, 241; coachman, 243; concierge, 173; doorman and wife, 80, 84; driver, 145; extras, 61; landlady, 244; lift-boy, 71; maids, 92, 141, 203, 236–237; mailman, 80; news vendor, 167; photographer, 110, 270, 286–287; pilots, 65, 82, 150, 222; policemen, 54, 145; secretaries, 165, 174, 185, 191, 205, 261; strangers, 93, 165, 180, 226, 228, 270, 287, 297; typists, 191; waiter, 253

Genre specific setting as apparatus, 9–10, 131, 157–160, 188–189, 215–216, 227, 231, 263–264, 267–269

Genre specific settings
airplane, 65, 81–82, 150, 184
automobile, 4, 7–9, 65, 71, 75, 81–82, 90, 110, 136, 145, 149–150, 156, 159, 175–176, 180, 183–184, 186–187, 216, 230

ballroom, 177, 242, 284
beach, 82–84, 181–182, 226, 229, 293
bedroom, 72–73, 77, 150–151, 221, 225, 238, 243, 270, 271, 281
brothel, 201–202
bus, 59, 93, 165
carriages, 7–9, 17, 74–75, 126, 128, 243
elevators, 137, 217
home, 17–19, 42–43, 47–48, 55–56, 72–73, 79, 270–271, 282–283, 287; as film set, 64–65, 188–189; as film studio, 224–229; as Oedipal apparatus, 202–204
hotel, 64, 91–93, 167, 202, 204, 284
ice rink, 73–74, 82
laboratory, 7, 9, 20, 134, 151, 282
at the movies, 54–55, 57, 60–61, 91, 93–94, 116, 159–160, 172, 185–187, 195, 199, 202, 221–222, 235–236, 239–240
movie set, 60, 75, 183, 186, 188, 197, 211, 224, 263, 267
museum, 20, 54, 134, 165
office, 4, 185, 187, 191, 205
prison, 69, 144, 158, 247–256, 284, 300
restaurant, 167–168; dining room, 81, 228
road, 8, 40, 65, 81, 183, 186
stage, 59–60, 64, 195, 199, 207
stairs, 72, 77, 81, 118
street, 4, 59, 61, 70–72, 75–76, 80–81, 89, 108–109, 112–113, 118, 124, 165, 197, 219, 231, 284; its extensions, 284
train, 27–28, 30, 61, 101, 108, 158–159, 250–251, 277

Genre specific style: formal mimetics, xviii, 3–4, 6–7, 19, 24, 42, 47, 52–53, 63–64, 66–68, 70, 73–74, 76, 79, 81, 83, 85, 91, 99, 101, 105, 108–109, 112–114, 117, 122–123, 126–127, 130, 137, 139, 144, 148, 152, 156–158, 165–166, 168, 172, 175, 177, 195–196, 200, 210–211, 216, 235, 249, 260–261, 264, 266, 269, 277; and reader, 146, 148. See also Tropes

Genre specific thematization, xviii, 3, 7, 59, 67, 70, 73, 85, 90, 99, 103, 109, 112–113, 115, 117, 123, 125, 127–128, 136, 143–144, 147, 153–154, 156, 163–166, 171, 174, 177, 192, 200, 202, 205, 217–220, 226–227, 237, 248, 256, 260–267, 270–271, 274, 276, 283, 284, 294, 296, 298; overdetermined, 135; semic, 159

Genre specific themes, 75–76, 141–142, 145, 154–155, 165, 167–168, 183, 187, 193, 197, 199, 231, 266, 269, 284, 294. See also Apparatus; Being; Film; Knowing; Vision
absence and film, xix, xxi, 7, 29, 30, 42, 43, 57, 100, 106, 107, 117, 119, 139, 148,

152, 177, 180, 212, 216, 233, 238, 244, 248, 278, 281, 282. *See also* Being: awareness

authenticity: of experience, 15–16, 21, 23–24, 26–27, 30–31, 35, 41, 93, 193, 196, 210, 218, 223, 263; and identity, 9–11, 16, 35, 60, 91, 93–94, 112, 116, 124, 187, 197, 200, 218–219, 224–226, 229, 241, 266; and reality, 22, 24, 26, 80–81, 140, 166, 210–211, 225, 229, 280, 284–285, 289; in representation, 12, 16, 21, 25–26, 28, 31, 45–46, 51, 62, 76, 87, 100, 102, 106, 116, 120, 124, 156, 166, 201, 209, 218, 221–224, 229, 232, 245, 249, 263–264, 269, 271, 281–282. *See also* Genre specific themes: professional deformation

control, **102–106**, **113–118**, **133**, **148–150**, 160, 248, 250–251, 260, 263; by apparatus, 87, 22; by cinematic apparatus, 8, 20, 60, 65, 68–69, 77–78, 82, 86, 90–91, 94–95, 114, 116, 130, 146, 158, 160, 165–166, 170, 172, 179, 187, 269–270, 287; claim to, 100, 289, 290; culture code, 182, 263; and desire, 148, 150, 156, 200, 240, 246, 270, 272; illusion of, 50, 104, 106, 133, 222; and imaginary, 150, 194; and knowledge, 134; lack of, 12, 59, 80, 87, 91, 104–106, 115–116, 130, 133, 297; by memory, 104; of narrative, 6, 17–19, 53, 68, 78, 86, 117, 170, 175, 186, 208; need for, 95, 110, 113, 149, 235, 250; and painting, 170; and photography, 130, 160; physiological, 252; and power, 191, 252, 299, 300; by spectator, 104, 118, 149, 236, 239–240, 242–244; of symbolic code, 183–184; by technology, 8, 104, 133, 170–171, 221–222; and television, 225; transcendental, 69–70, 157

death, xvii, 9–10, 13–15, 18, 27, 42–43, 58–59, 60–61, 68–69, 79–81, 91–93, 103, 139, 141–144, **149–152**, **155**, **159–160**, 171, **189–191**, 197, 199, 226–227, 231–232, 239–241, 243, **252–253**, 264, 274, 276, 286, 289, 294, 297; gun as pun, 285–286; invisible, 64–65

desire and film, 19, 43, 44, 56, 58, 90, 107, 113, 115, 120, 126, 136, 141, 142, 148, 150, 152, 155, 156, 184, 194, 215, 220, 232, 240, 248, 254, 255, 282, 284, 292, 299, 300

dream and film, 31, 58, 88, 93–94, 101, 107–108, 166, 178, 181, 183, 186, 190, 193–198, 204, 223, 227, 234–235, 242, 245, 250, 253, 267, 273, 278, 279, 280, 287, 297, 300; their discourse, 79, 108, 166, 235, 250; and science, 46, 49; and sound, 108

existential aspects of film, 3–4, 9–10, 15, 18–19, 23, 27–28, 31, 42, 50, 52, 99, 107–108, 111–112, 117, 126, 128, 135, 138–140, 148, 154, 179, 188, 193, 199, 207, 217, 222, 255, 266, 278, 293

identity: and apparatus, 39, 227–229; and authenticity, 60, 116, 187, 218, 224, 226, 266; and film, 86, 93–94, 105, 119, 136, 146–147, 193, 224, 262; and genre, 124; and mask, 91, 141, 149–150, 152, 198, 294

illusion, 21–22, 25–26, 28–35, 49–50, 52, 57–58, **103–106**, 118, 131, 133, 138, 149, 158, 177–179, 188–189, 197, **215–218**, **221–225**, 261, 277, 280, 288; awareness of, 103, 138, 169, 171, 204–205, 225; and filmmakers, 60, 69, 204, 215–216, 270, 295; and immanence, 29, 41, 43, 131, 216, 282; and reality, 86, 105–106, 131, 152, 177, 197–198, 215–216, 218, 229, 263–264, 267, 272, 279

individuation and film, 39, 54, 59, 63, 114, 134, 136, 138–139, 146–148, 166, 176, 183–184, 189–190, 224, 237, 242, 244, 249, **252–255**, 262, 265, 267, 300; and film roles, 55, 199, 229, 239, 242–243, 300; and genre, 26, 132; and regression, 43, 114, 139, 151, 176, 197, 202, 204, 251–252

irony, xix, 3, **20–36**, 39, 50, **60–67**, 75, 86, 94, 100, 106, 111, 120, 151, 197, 209, 212, 219, 221, 222, 248–249, 278, 279, 280, 281, 283, 292; avvertimento del contrario, 22; Johann G. Fichte, 281; Friedrich Hegel, 281; Immanuel Kant, 281; and reading, 62–63; G. P. Richter, 33; Friedrich von Schlegel, 34, 280, 281; sentimento del contrario, 22; Ludwig Tieck, 281

literary canon and the movies, 141, 165, 169, 181–182, 185–187, 199, **207–215**, 220, 226, 268, 269

memory, 7, 39–61, 73–74, 102, 124, 143, 149, 168; and apparatus, 7, 41–42, 47–49, 51–52, 54, 56, **58–60**, 65, 80–82, 101, 104–105, 107, 115, 117–118, 136, 152, 189, 204, 210, 272, 291; its cinematic condensation, 40, 43, 47, 52, 54, 74, 89–90, 101, 115, 119, 138, 178–180; and imagination, **28–29**, 40, 136, 152, 178–179; and reality, 51, 58, 89–90, 119; and visual literacy, 45, 87, 132

330 Index

Genre specific themes *(continued)*
  movie kiss, 200, 205, 217, 229, 244, 255, 267, 269, 282
  movie love, 5–6, 13, 15–17, 26, 62, 80, 87–88, 93, 115–116, 130–131, 140, 147, 165–166, 174, 176–177, 183, 187, 193, 199, 201–202, 213–215, 222, 229–230, 238, 241–244, 253, 274, 300
  musical canon and the movies, 10, 70, 78, 81, 101, 165, 169–170, 241–245, 262, 286
  nickel, for the movies, **185**
  professional deformation, 4, 11, 86–87, 117, 132–134, 179, 198, 200, 215–217, 229, 265–266. *See also* Genre specific themes: authenticity
  sea, 57, 72, 79, 82–84, 129, 180, 187, 195–196, 204, 212, 236, 142, 241, 244, 293
  seduction and sex, 15–16, 54–56, 60, 72, 89, 107, 113–114, 141–142, 146, 148, 151, 154, 166, 193, 195, 199–200, 201–203, 205–206, 219–220, 222, 227, 229, 232, 236–238, 240–241, 243–244, 245–246, 251–252, 255, 262, 269, 274, 294, 300
  thrills and spills, 45, 51–52, 65–66, 71, 104, 137, 140, 142, 149, 180, 197–198, 201, 232, 265, 268, 272, 274, 279, 289, 293–294. *See also* Sensations
  visual arts canon and the movies, 26, 48, 86, 94–95, 113, 188, 287–288
  voyeurism, **15–16**, 18, 20, 30, 54, 56, 59–61, 68–69, 80–81, 84–85, **114–116**, 117, 127, 135, 138, 148–149, 150–151, 153, 159, 165, 167, 176–177, 185–186, 188, **193–194**, **199–205**, 217, 219–220, 222, 228, **231–232**, 234–236, 260, 264, **266–267**, 269, 272, 274, 287, 290–291
  women in film, xx, 15–16, 23, 30, 54, 94, 103, 107–108, 115, 119, 126, 178–180, 195, 199–200, 202–203, 205, 219–220, 263, 265–266
  vision, **149–152**. *See also* Vision
Gesù, Sebastiano, 276
Głowinski, Michael, 122, 277
Gombrich, E. H., 45, 189
Goodman, Nelson, 51, 118
Gumbrecht, Hans Ulrich, 182, 292, 293

Hays, K. Michael, 271, 301
Heidegger, Martin, 185, 218, 222, 297
History of culture, 35, 100, 196, 210–211, 261, 280, 293; and regression, 210, 214
Hoffmann, E. T. A.: *The Tales of Hoffmann*, 126, 291
Hume, David, 40

Humor, xix, 22, 23, 24, 27, 28, 31, 32, 33, 57, 100, 169, 279
Husserl, Edmund, 281
Hyde, Mr., 114–115. *See also* Jeckyll

Illusion, 21–22, 25–26, 28–35, 49–50, 52, 57–58, 103–106, 118, 131, 133, 138, 149, 151, 158, 169, 177–179, 188–189, 197–198, 202, 215–218, 221–228, 233, 261, 263–264, 267, 270, 277, 280, 288
Imaginary, 18, 22, 59–60, 88, 92, 152, 168, 185, 196–197, 202–204, 217, 239, 244, 255–256, 268, 270, 279–280, 282, 290; Lacanian, 150, 200, 240, 253, 263, 265, 267, 294
Imagination, 29–31, 40–49, 105, 188, 218, 239; concretized, 20, 29, 40, 43, 179, 196–197, 224; and knowledge, 39, 45–48, 107, 120, 279–280; and memory, 28–29, 40, 136, 152, 178–179; metaphor for, 196; popular, 39, 43, 75–76, 134, 163, 181–184, 189, 194–195, 245, 249, 254, 274; and reality, 28, 40–41, 45, 88–90, 92, 115, 118–119, 166, 177–179, 196, 215, 224, 233–235, 239, 241, 245, 250, 279–280, 281; and representation, 39–40, 42, 46–48, 56, 66, 68, 78, 90–91, 131, 176, 195, 224, 254
Isherwood, Christopher, xviii, xx, 110, 133, **163–174**, 181, 183, 187, 192–193, 196, 201, 208, 234, 251, 256, **260–263**, 268, 270, 271, 295; *Prater Violet*, xviii, **163–174**, 205, 208, 211, 218, 256, **260–263**, 265

Jakobson, Roman, 10, 108, 276
Jauss, Hans Robert, 213
Jeckyll, Dr., 114–115. *See also* Hyde
Jung, C. G., 283

Karetnikova, Inga, 298
Kermode, Frank, 213
Knowing, 39, 44–45, 49–50, 52, 85, 87, 94–95, 99, 102–103, 111, 113, 120, **132**, **134–137**, 148, 165, 168, 171, 174, 177–178, 185, 187, 200, 210–211, 215, **225–226**, 231–232, 256, 261, 263, 265, 268–269, 271, 273, 292
  awareness and effect of apparatus, xvii, 5, 29–32, 47, 51, 53, 56–57, 65, 68, 71, 77–78, 89, 91, 103, 109, 113, 117–119, 124, 127, 130, 136–137, 146–148, 164, 168–169, 174–178, 180–182, 223, 225–226, 239, 254, 260, 273, 280–281
  awareness of contradiction, 22, 211

awareness of effect of apparatus on the self, 9, 19–20, 23, 25, 27, 29–32, 34, 41–46, 49–50, 54, 56, 58, 60, 62, 67, 72, 83, 85–86, 88–89, 102–103, 105, 107–108, 111–112, 114–115, 117–121, 144, 147–148, 152, 165–166, 172, 178, 180, 182, 184, 190, 194–196, 215, 219, 224, 227–228, 233–235, 238–239, 247, 251, 255–256, 259, 267, 271–273, 278, 279, 284, 286–287; and illusion, 21–22, 25–26, 28–35, 49–50, 52, 57–58, 103–106, 118, 131, 133, 138, 149, 151, 158, 169, 177–179, 188–189, 197, 202, 215–218, 221–225, 233, 261, 267, 270, 277, 280, 288
  awareness of self, 8, 12, 15, 31, 35, 88, 90, 94, 105, 132, 134, 150, 172, 192, 205, 207, 210–211, 215, 238–239, 245, 297
  epistemological awareness personified, 134, 165, 187, 210, 231–232, 263, 268–269
  and imagination, 39, 45–48, 107, 120, 279–280
  omniscience, 68, 82, 86, 157, 175
  visual education, 45, 87; and memory, 132, 136
Korte, Walter, 298

Lacan, Jacques, 19, 150, 283
Lauretta, Enzo, 276
Leitmotif, 81, 269; in *Lohengrin*, 286
Lesage, Julia, 155, 294
Lévi-Strauss, Claude, 294
Literature and film, **4–10**, 19, **39–40**, 46–47, **51–54**, 79–81, 103, 120–121, **125–130**, **136–139**, 150, 152–157, 159–160, 165, 174, 181, 208–215, 219–221, 230–231, 236, 241, 247–250, 263–265, 268–269, 275, 276, 278, 279, 280, 288, 292, 294, 297, 298–299
Locations, xviii; airborn roundtrip French Riviera–Berlin, 65–66; airborn via Vologda to Boulder, Colorado, 52–53; American midwest, airplane crash site in, 190; Berlin, 42, **59–65, 69–77, 79–82, 86–95**, 116, 131, 169–170, 224, 272; Biaritz, 54–55, 57; Buenos Aires, 217–232; Capri, 5, 17, **207–217**, 274; Cinecittà, **207–217**; Cornell University, 45, 130, 134; French Riviera, **65–66**, 71, 78, 92–93; Harvard University, 45–46, 130, 132, 134, 136; Hollywood, xviii, xx, 163–164, **174–206**, 234, 263–268, 295; Italy, 45, 156; London, xviii, 75–76, **163–174**; Nashville, 189; New England, 40–41, 130; New Orleans, xviii, **217–232**; Saint Petersburg, 54–55, 57; Sargasso Sea, 196; Solfi, 77, **82–85**; Sorrento, 17–19, 27–28; Vallejo, Argentina, 233–246; Vyra and vicinity, 40–42, 47–48, 52–53, 55–56, 74, 130
Lotman, Jurij, 297
Lurie, Susan, 289

Magny, Claude Edmonde, 53, 283
Manser, Anthony, 40, 41
Masiello, Francine R., 300
Merleau-Ponty, Maurice, 35, 76, 111
Merrim, Stephanie, 300
Meyerhold, Vsevolod Emilievich, 55
Michaels, I. Lloyds, 295, 296
Millar, Dan, 296
Mistron, Deborah E., 299
Moravia, Alberto, xviii, xx, 133, 144, 205, **207–217**, 228, 233, 234, 247, 251, 261, **268–270**, 296, 298; *Il disprezzo/A Ghost at Noon*, xviii, **207–217**, 219, 247, **268–270**
Myth, 181–182, 189–190, 212–213, 169, 192, 269, 292. *See also* Archetype
Mythopoeic, 208–209, 265, 268

Nabokov, Vladimir, xviii, xix, xxi, **39–95**, **111–121**, 123–140, 143–148, 150–152, 154–157, 159–160, 163–166, 168, 170–171, 178, 182–184, 186, 188, 190, 194–195, 199, 202, 205, 208, 210, 215–216, 218, 222–225, 227–228, 233, 235, 245, 250, 253, 255, 262, 264–265, 269, 271, 272, 285, 286, 287, 290, 291, 292, 293; *Bend Sinister*, 116, 205; *Despair*, 66, 113, 139, 140, 145, 150, 190, 205; *The Eye*, 113, 139, 290; *Invitation to a Beheading*, 286; *Laughter in the Dark*, xviii, **62–95**; *Mary*, 59, 113, 117, 130, 131, 132, 146, 158, 225; *Speak, Memory*, xix, **39–61**, 52, 110, 114, 130, 138, 143, 147, 291, 292; "Spring in Fialta," 282; *Strong Opinions*, 135
Narrative of film theory, **99–121**. *See also* Genre: and narrative
Narrator, 5–8, 10–12, 17–19, 68, 78–79, 82, 135–136, 146, 150, 168, 175, 177, 181, 223, 247–256, 262–263, 271, 278, 289, 299; and reliability, xvii–xviii, **10–19**, 100, 103, 236–237, 239–244, 248, 251

Objectivity, 7, 10, 12, 15, 20–21, 24, 45–46, 48, 51–53, 62, 64, 71, 87–89, 123, 151, 175, 177, 180, 218, 228, 244, 247, 271, 278

Paradox of the apparatus, 4, 9, 27–28, 45–46, 50, 93, 105–106, 108, 116, 118, 126, 135, 183, 277, 282; and identity, 200, 266; and imagination, 29–30; and individuation, 147–148; personified, 177; proairetic, 138; and the spectator, 21–22, 46
Parker, Dorothy, 156, 287
Perception
  its discursive structure, 128
  instrumental, 154, 184
  multisensory, 76–77, 106, 231, 283, 285
  sensory, 50, 70, 204, 238; and apparatus, xix; limited by apparatus, 11; in producing illusion, 30
  its subject, 82, 86, 105, 131, 157, 286
Percy, Walker, xviii, xx, 110, 133, 194, 201, 205, **217–232**, 233–234, 240, 251–252, 256, 260, 266, **270–272**, 296, 297; *Lancelot*, xviii, xx, 156, 194, 201–202, 205, **217–232**, 254, 256, 266, **270–272**; *The Moviegoer*, 252, 296; and Pasolini, 220, 297
Phenomenology, 40, 43, 46, 103, 111, 120, 128, 197, 218, 281, 282
Philosophical aspirations, of the film apparatus, 33, 43–44
Physiogenesis, 237, 265
Pifer, Ellen, 63
Pine, Fred, 299
Pirandello, Luigi, xvii–xxi, **3–36**, 39–42, 45, 49–50, 59–60, 67, 75–76, 79, 81, 86, 90, 93, **99–111**, 112–121, 123–129, 133, 137, 139, 144, 152, 154, 157, 163–166, 168–170, 177–178, 182, 184, 190, 192, 196, 198–199, 210, 212–213, 215, 218, 221–224, 228, 235, 262–263, 270, 272, 274, 276, 279–281, 286, 289–290, 296; "Globo," 32; *Il fu Mattia Pascal*, 59–60, 101; *Quaderni di Serafino Gubbio operatore (Shoot!)*, xvii–xix, 3–19, 22–28, 85, 99–111, 122–123, 125, 127–128, 134, 137, 139, 144, 192, 227, 270, 288, 290; *L'umorismo*, xix, **20–36**, 100. *See also* Genre specific themes: irony
Plot, xvii, xxi, 8, 11, 25, 58, 60, 63, 66–68, 72, 77–82, 88, 99, 105, 113, 118, 126, 148, 173, 195, 198, 202, 220, 226, 230, 241–242, 246, 248, 251, 274, 285, 293, 298, 300. *See also* Codes, specific: proairetic
Poncet, Marie-Thérèse, 288
Propp, Vladimir, xvii–xviii
Psychological projection, 3, 26, 86–87, 101, 114, 147, 151, 166, 183–184, 189, 216, 219, 233–234, 264, 280, 284
Puig, Manuel, xviii, xx–xxi, 110–111, 133, 139, 144, 171, 176, 203, 206, 219, 222, 225, **233–256**, 259–260, 267–268, 272–273, 297, 298, 299; *Betrayed by Rita Hayworth*, xx, xviii, 202, 206, 233–246, 247, 250, 254, 273; *Kiss of the Spider Woman*, xviii, xx, 144, 154, 156, 171, 206, 237, 241, 245–246, 247–256, 259, 273, 298
Puppa, Paolo, 101

Reader, 51, 252; and alienation effect, 151; and canon, 181, 208, 269; and carpets, 137; cinematic, 147, 152, 156, 211, 247, 264, 291; and cinematic memory, 65, 81; collared, 137; and control of narrative, 6, 17, 53, 68, 78, 175, 208; and cultural competence, 136; and discourse, 145–149, 259, 260; and discursive disjunction, 142; and double text, 173, 219, 230, 256; and education, 130, 135; and extrapolation, 153; female, 293; and film theory, 101, 259; and formal mimetics, 43, 53, 63, 65, 74–75, 77–78, 80, 116, 127, 146, 148, 152, 193; and genre films, 255; genre specific, 64–65, 74, 139, **145–149**, 152, 160, 259, 264; and hermeneutic awareness, 88, 147, 156, 160; and ideology, 208; individuating, 147; and intention, 213; and interpretation, **209–214**, 241, 268; male, 300; mode, 133; and narrative aspect of genre, 101; and narrative reliability, xvii, 14, 100, 103; and omniscience, 68, 78; and proairetic code, 159–160, 259; readerly, 146, 254; and reading out, 213, 241, 260, 269; and reconstructive reading, 64–65, 87, 210; and selection, 186; and self, 147, 211; and solipsism, 80; and subjectivity of the apparatus, 85; and subtext, 139, 226, 241; and symbolic code, 182–183, 263; and synaesthetic shudder, 128; and verisimilitude, 194; and visualization, 128; and voyeurism, 200; writerly, 140, 145–146, 212–213, 242, 262
Realism, 7, 12, 39, 51–52, 62, 64, 87–89, 101, 151, 180, 218, 244, 278, 279, 285; versus formativism, 86–87, 134, 290; neorealism, 21–23, 68, 100, 123, 209, 212, 279; neue Sachlichkeit, 124
Reality, xvii, 3, 7, 10, 50–51, 56, 58, 70, 102–104, 115, 157, 178–179, 216–217, 271–272, 280, 282; and apparatus, 39, 46, 48–51, 120, 131, 267; and authenticity, 22, 24, 26, 60–61, 80–81, 87, 140, 166, 200, 210–211, 224–225, 229, 249, 280, 284–285, 289; and film, 4–6, 8, 11, 18,

44–45, 55, 57–58, 60–61, 64, 68–69, 71–72, 78, 81, 83, 85–86, 91–94, 104–112, 117, 120, 139, 142, 149, 186–190, 197, 204, 208–209, 217, 223, 232, 240, 245–246; and genre, 132–133, 143, 262, 266; and illusion, 198, 215, 218, 225–228, 263–264, 267, 270; and imagination, 28, 40–41, 45, 88–90, 92, 115, 118–119, 166, 177–179, 196, 215, 224, 233–235, 239, 241, 250, 279–280, 281; and subjectivity, 50, 76, 103, 107, 123, 184, 207, 233; and surrealism, 53, 60, 76, 194, 197, 284; and the unreal, 9, 11, 16, 20–36, 56, 104–105, 107–108, 117, 148, 152, 154, 166, 177–178, 216–217, 234, 250–251

Representation, 7, 9, 20, 23, 24, 30, 34–35, **55–59**, 70, 79, 82, 102, 107, 118, 136, 142, 144–145, 154, 165–166, 183, 211–212, 249, 278, 279, 281, 286, 294, 301
  and alienation, 59, 94
  and authenticity, 12, 16, 21, 25–26, 28, 31, 45–46, 51, 62, 76, 87, 91, 100, 102, 106, 116, 120, 124, 156, 166, 201, 209, 218, 221–224, 232, 245, 249, 263–264, 269, 271, 281–282
  and convention, 24
  in film, 65–66, 88–89, 168
  and form in painting, 86–87, 265
  and formalism: ideology, 262; Russian, 122, 170–172, 276; structural, 66; theory, 210
  and genre, 26, 135–136, 165, 262
  and imagination, 39–40, 42, 46–48, 56, 66, 68, 78, 90–91, 131, 176, 195, 224, 254
  and memory, 47
  and metaphysical implications, 67
  and verisimilitude, 24–25, 31, 105, 126, **139–140**, 144, 175, 194, 212, 240, 244, 248, 265, 268, 279. *See also* Visual representation

Representational mimesis: as aspect of modes, 292; and desire, 249; of film world, 125, 275–276; and mimetic effect fallacy, 233; and power of film, 138, 166, 296; and sound, 76; and technology, 68

Rilke, Rainer Maria, 282, 283
Robbe-Grillet, Alain, 285
Rosenmeyer, Thomas G., 123
Ryle, Gilbert, 281

Schulberg, Budd Wilson, 174, 175
Self, 23, 30–31, 35, 42, 44, 59, 77, 86, 88, 105, 114, 146, 173, 183, 229, 235, 244–245, 253, 282–283; and authenticity, 9–11, 16, 35, 60, 93–94, 112, 116, 124, 187, 197–198, 200, 210, 218–219, 224–226, 229, 241, 254–255, 266; discourse of, 251; and genre, 124; and the imaginary, 150–151; invaded, 262; narrative of, 241, 254, 273–274, 292–293; and philosophical awareness, 11, 31, 35, 88, 105, 107–108, 111, 119–120, 132, 136, 139, 147, 183, 228, 233–234, 253, 273–274, 297; as reader, 147, 211; and representation, 30, 120, 132, 136, 274; and self-delusion, 151, 202, 233, 270; split, 150–151; and subconscious discourse, 181, 207–210, 218, 241; and the symbolic, 150. *See also* Being; Feeling; Genre specific themes; Subject; Subjectivity

Sensations, xvii, 7–8, 27, 58, 72, 196, 198, 212, 217; movement, 53, 189; pain, 232, 253; pleasure, 173, 201, 266, 289; space, 52; time, 47, 60, 103, 111, 119, 132. *See also* Feelings

Senses, 50, 70, 204, 238; apparatus as, xix; limited by apparatus, 11; producing illusion, 30; multisensory, 76–77, 106, 231, 283, 285. *See also* Perception

Setting as apparatus. *See* Genre specific settings

Sloan, De Villo, 300
Smith, Barbara Herrnstein, 210, 211, 212
Sontag, Susan, 286
Story and genre and discourse, xviii, 85, 91, 118, 126, **137–139**, 148, 154–156, 159, 187, 195–196, 240–242, 250, 284; and narrator, 11, 78–79, 135, 146, 175, 177, 181, 223, 247–256, 263, 271, 299

Strauss, Johann, 241, 242, 243
Subconscious, 23, 55, 58, 115, 147, 166, 181, 184, 212, 219, 235, 272; ego, 236, 281; fetishism, 83, 103, 189, 267. *See also* Genre specific themes: voyeurism; Vision

Subject, 41–42, 157, 291, 293, 294; to the apparatus, 105, 108, 119; its constitution, 160; of desire, 148, 150, 254; of discourse, 160; at discursive intersection, 148, 293; effect, 107; as eye, 44; and genre, 255; genre specific, 139, 147, 160; of illusion, 169; and merging, 282; narrating, 254; as origin of meaning, 113, 235, 282; of perception, 82, 86, 105, 131, 157, 286; position, 107, 114–115, 125, 150, 160, 166, 216, 234–235, 244, 251, 254, 262, 269, 289, 293, 294, 300; and power, 269; as reader, 211; and regression, 252; of representation, 25; self-aware, 136; split,

Subject *(continued)*
151; transcendental, 44, 85–86, 105, 113, 131, 157, 275, 281, 286; and victim, 15. *See also* Being; Genre specific themes; Self

Subjectivity, 7, 20, 28, 35, 41, 43, 45, 50–51, 103, 107, 115, 150, 165, 184, 207, 233, 235, 255, 268, 271, 281, 291; of apparatus, 85–86, 88, 136, 168, 175; of characters, 72, 76, 85, 119, 123, 165, 175, 210; and reader, 85; and regression, 252; of spectator, 55, 57, 118

Tessari, Roberto, 207, 288
Thomas, Dylan, 297
Todorov, Tzvetan, 125, 126, 128, 153, 292
Tomashevski, Boris, 294
Tommaseo, Niccoló, 280
Tropes, 167, 266. *See also* Genre specific themes: irony
  metaphor, xviii, xxi, 7, 9–10, 19, 29, 41, 43, 46, 49, 54, 58–59, 70, 85, 90, 100, 105, 108, 114, 127, 137, 146, 153, 163, 168–170, 174–177, 184, 188, 192–193, 196, 198, 201–202, 211, 216, 221, 222–223, 227, 231, 241–242, 260, 269, 276–277, 280, 290; unmetaphoring, 10, 58, 202, 251, 277–278
  metonymy, 6–7, 9–10, 19, 74, 83–84, 99, 108, 158, 168, 179–180, 265, 276
  personification, 12, 14, 19, 90, 110, 113, 134–135, 141, 165–167, 177, 185–188, 191, 198, 200, 210–211, 249, 251, 262, 267–269, 289, 296
  secondarization, 277
  similitude, 48–49, 79, 120, 151, 157–158, 260–261, 267, 294
  symbol, 9, 28, 72, 196, 218
  synaesthesia, 77–78, 80–81, 88, 101, 117–118, 127–128, 147–148, 152, 286
  synecdoche, 10
Die Truppe, 164
Tyler, Parker, 287, 288

Unmetaphoring. *See* Tropes: metaphor
Unreal. *See* Reality

Viertel, Berthold, 164
Vision. *See also* Apparatus, specific types: optical mediation; Visual representation
  and blindness, 45, 66, 70, 77–78, 80–81, 93, 112, 118, 148–150, 154–156, 160, 215
  camera eye, 3, 5, 10, 20, 26, 65, 85, 151, 171, 175, 179, 184, 276; subjective, 168, 175, 286
  cinematic, 22–23, 27–28, 47, 52, 70, 75–76, 83–84, 95, 100–101, 109, 116–117, 119, 124, 132, 167, 180, 184, 186, 217, 223, 233, 260, 276, 298
  and control, 149, 216, 225
  and education, 45, 87
  human eye: and other anatomical parts, 9, 106, 199; and/as apparatus, 4, 31–32, 44, 50, 65, 127, 158, 171, 177, 195, 228, 283, 287; and dream, 58; and ears, 4, 77–78, 80, 101, 118, 260, 285; and identity, 6, 27, 60, 100, 168, 178, 180, 198, 199, 220, 242, 262; impassive, 12; and insight, 11, 21, 66; and memory, 58, 89; mind's, 89; as subject, 44; and synaesthesia, 47, 80–81, 118; and/as tropes, 167, 198, 211, 217, 231
  instrumental, 184, 218, 270, 271
  light, 46–47, 179, 223; allegorical, 220; and blindness, 203; and color, 82–84; dazzling, 66; and film apparatus, 16, 18, 60, 71, 113, 127, 131, 135, 151, 158, 160, 165, 176, 205, 215, 223, 243, 286, 290; and filters, 71; flicker, 48, 54, 158, 176; history of, 33, 104; and image, 48; of imagination, 49; and painting, 16, 18; reflections, 70; refraction, 116; ripple of, 87, 215; shift of, 82–84; and style, 72, 89
  look, 15–16, 31–32, 48–50, 86, 111, 132, 144, 149–152, 156, 203, 217, 231–232, 236, 238, 251, 263, 294
  and memory, 132, 136
  painter's, 5–6, 16, 86, 267, 296
  point of view, xx, 5, 8, 12, 15, 31–32, 62, 68, 72, 84, 90, 93, 149–152, 157, 167, 175–177, 182, 184, 263, 286, 294
  subjective, 271
  tropes for, 53, 55, 64, 80, 82, 85
  typology of, 46, 49, 51, 59, 66, 77, 85–87, 90, 106, 120, 128, 134, 139, 148, 150, 168, 175, 184, 187, 238, 262, 265, 282
  visualization, 89, 128, 156, 281; of contradiction, 21; images in the mind, 40–41, 77, 87–88, 106, 178, 281; of truth, 205
Visual artists: Giorgio De Chirico, 75–76, 284–285; Dobuzhinski, 45, 87; Juan Gris, 201; Janvier, 196; René Magritte, 284; Michelangelo, 187; Rembrandt, 86; Peter Paul Rubens, 188; John Ruskin, 48; Jean Antoine Watteau, 26
Visual arts, theories of
  expressionism, 72, 88–89, 101, 130, 158
  surrealism, 53, 60, 76, 194, 197, 284

Visual arts, types of
  drawing, 26, 45, 132, 188, 200
  painting, 5–6, 16, 51, 58, 75–76, 83, 86–87, 113, 119, 137, 141, 170, 193, 196, 200, 207, 219, 265, 267, 272, 275, 279, 281, 284, 287, 288, 296; animated, 94–95, 113, 287–288
  photograph, 41, 71, 94, 119, 131, 132, 186, 223, 238, 271, 281; pin-up, 83, 87; poster, 80, 83–84, 91, 129, 160, 195, 293; publicity still, 80; via satellite, 157; slide, 48, 49, 56, 113, 114, 130, 131, 134, 136; snapshot, 41–42, 84; stereoscopy, 40, 130
  photography, xix, 20–21, 36, **40–45**, 50–51, 71, 83–84, 110–111, 121, 129, 131–132, 136, 154, 270, 278, 279, 287, 296; and absence, 29, 281; and autism, 156, 281; and death, 14, 42, 286; and dream, 196; its effect of real, 21, 24; emulsion, 40–41, 43, 48, 131, 158; enframing, 221–222; and identity, 132; and imagination, 40; and memory, 40–42, 48–49, 119, 281; and mental picture, 40, 43; as philosophical topos, 110, 277; and space, 41, 131, 223; and time, 27, 30, 41–42, 130–131, 223, 286
  picture book, 189
  plate, 48
Visual representation, 4, 8, 42, 65, 69–70, 74–77, 79–81, 83–85, 89, 154, 200–201, 216, 267, 284, 286, 296; and apparatus, 219; and boundaries, 49; and displacement, 53; ekphrasis, 128; via film, 43; and individuation, 236; and language, 46, 155; and lighting, 16; and memory, 45, 47, 87; paragone topos, 109; picturesque, 70; and reader, 53, 64; and reality, 51; and repetition, 65; and soundtrack, 47, 74, 140; and synaesthesia, 77, 79, 118, 285, 286; and tropes, 70
Vladimir, not Nabokov, 22. *See also* Estragon

West, Nathanael: *The Day of the Locust*, xviii, xx, 139, 163–164, 174–175, 181, **192-206**, 208, 216–217, 219, 223, 226, 228, 232, 234, 245–246, 251–252, **265-268**, 270
Wilson, Edmund, 174–175, 191
Worley, Joan Yvonne, 297
Wyers-Weber, Frances, 299

Zamora, Lois Parkinson, 297
Zipper, 219, 220

Designer:	U.C. Press Staff
Compositor:	Prestige Typography
Text:	10/12 Times Roman
Display:	Helvetica
Printer & Binder:	Maple-Vail Book Manufacturing Group

OHIO UNIVERSITY LIBRARY
Please return this book as soon as you have finished with it. In order to avoid a fine it must be returned by the latest date stamped below. All books are subject to recall after two weeks or immediately if needed for reserve.

MAY 2 8 1997   JUN 0 9 1997

FEB 0 6 1996